Navigating AI in Academic Libraries:

Implications for Academic Research

Kathleen Sacco
Lake-Sumter State College, USA

Alison Norton
Lake-Sumter State College, USA

Kevin Arms
Lake-Sumter State College, USA

Published in the United States of America by
IGI Global
701 E. Chocolate Avenue
Hershey PA, USA 17033
Tel: 717-533-8845
Fax: 717-533-8661
E-mail: cust@igi-global.com
Web site: https://www.igi-global.com

Library of Congress Cataloging-in-Publication Data

CIP PENDING

ISBN13: 9798369330531
EISBN13: 9798369330548

Vice President of Editorial: Melissa Wagner
Managing Editor of Acquisitions: Mikaela Felty
Managing Editor of Book Development: Jocelynn Hessler
Production Manager: Mike Brehm
Cover Design: Phillip Shickler

British Cataloguing in Publication Data
A Cataloguing in Publication record for this book is available from the British Library.

All work contributed to this book is new, previously-unpublished material.
The views expressed in this book are those of the authors, but not necessarily of the publisher.

Table of Contents

Detailed Table of Contents

Jesubukade Emmanuel Ajakaye, Federal Polytechnic, Ayede, Nigeria

The application of artificial intelligence provides opportunities to help in the curation and management of library collections to serve the user community better. Librarians are saddled with the responsibility of taking care of and maintaining information resources in the library collections. Curating and managing the library collections is an important task in the library system and can be daunting, from selection to ordering, acquiring selected information resources, processing these resources, stocktaking, and weeding. AI tools provide intelligent help in reducing time spent on repetitive functions and aid librarians in making informed decisions. Collection development librarians must understand the impact of AI tools in their section, make meaning from large datasets, devise metadata systems, and lay the proper framework for cataloguing and classifying these information resources. This ensures that the goal of the library is to provide its patrons with appropriate collections that meet the needs of the library's user community within its limited financial and human resources.

Stefka Tzanova, York College, CUNY, USA

This chapter discusses the use of Artificial Intelligence (AI) in scholarly communications and academic research juxtaposing benefits/advantages and constraints of these new technologies in the context of academic librarianship. The latest development in AI impacts both the educational activities and the research process in academic institutions, hence libraries have to adapt in order to provide adequate support to diverse curricula and research projects. Accordingly, we explore various types of AI and how the roles of academic librarians are tuned to support all phases of AI driven research process – from formulation of hypothesis, to the dissemination of the results. In addition, we will look on AI's impact on scholarly communications from the perspective of librarians as experts in knowledge discovery and preservation.

Chapter 3

    Emmanuel Chidiadi Onwubiko, Alex Ekwueme Federal University,
      Nigeria

In this millennium, the world is exploring another product of Information and Communication Technology known as artificial intelligence (AI). Artificial Intelligence which is the simulation of human intelligence processes by machines, especially computer systems has find itself almost in every facet of human activities . In the academic world, the academic libraries more so in developed countries have come to explore this phenomenal technology and some academic researchers have cashed into it seeing as a short cut to academic research while some perceived it as a monster that may consume the worth of academic research. This chapter therefore focuses on the effect of exploring AI in academic libraries on academic research

Chapter 4

    Adebowale Jeremy Adetayo, Adeleke University, Nigeria
    Folashade Munirat Lawal, Afe Babalola University, Nigeria
    Abiodun Olusegun Odunewu, Olabisi Onabanjo University, Nigeria

This article aims to explore the potential threat posed by AI chatbots to librarianship and advocate for a balanced approach to integrating AI while upholding human contributions.The chapter examines the evolving roles of librarians, chatbot capabilities and limitations, impacts from library professionals, and the irreplaceable value of librarians.The chapter suggest that while chatbots offer efficiency in handling routine inquiries, concerns arise regarding their ability to replace librarian expertise. Librarians remain vital for personalized assistance, advocating intellectual freedom and privacy, and inclusive engagement. Libraries should adopt a collaborative model leveraging AI to enhance efficiency while preserving the unique human qualities librarians bring. This chapter contributes to the discourse on AI chatbots in librarianship by advocating for a balanced approach that integrates emerging technologies with human-centered values, allowing libraries to progress responsibly.

Sanchita Ghosh, Brainware University, India
Saptarshi Kumar Sarkar, Brainware University, India
Piyal Roy, Brainware University, India
Bitan Roy, Brainware University, India
Amitava Podder, Brainware University, India

Libraries are vital in promoting digital literacy and information fluency in the digital era. They offer access to digital resources, equipping individuals with skills like computer literacy, critical thinking, and data comprehension. Libraries also empower multi-layer functions like media literacy, fact-checking competency, and accountability. Librarians are respected for their ability to guide users in the ever-changing digital landscape. Collaborative Learning Spaces allow visitors to interact with upper technologies, engage in digital storytelling, and create new ideas. Libraries collaborate with educational institutions and advocate for amplifying digital literacy programs. By adopting future technologies, adapting to customer needs, and encouraging lifelong learning, libraries continue to drive digital skills and information fluency.

Jeremy Norton, Lake-Sumter State College, USA

Artificial Intelligence (AI) stands at the forefront of educational transformation, offering community colleges unprecedented opportunities to enhance learning experiences and administrative efficiency. However, the integration of AI into community college systems brings forth a series of policy challenges that necessitate nuanced governance frameworks within the structured federal system in the United States with different authorities given to the national government, the states, and educational institutions. This chapter explores the intricate policy landscape surrounding AI in community college education. Delving into existing policy frameworks, emerging trends, and evolving regulations will show the multifaceted intersection between AI technology and governance and what should be done to address this new reality.

Chapter 9

Beverly Gibson, Lake-Sumter State College, USA
Courtney Noelle Green, Lake-Sumter State College, USA

This chapter aims to illuminate the innovative intersection between literature, artificial intelligence (AI), and collaborative pedagogy by detailing a partnership between an English instructor and a librarian. As the landscape of education evolves, integrating new technologies like AI into literature classes offers an exciting avenue for engaging students and fostering interdisciplinary connections. This collaboration seeks to bridge the gap between traditional literary studies and emerging technological advancements through the lens of a literature course focused on and informed by AI. The literature course in question revolves around narrative perceptions of AI and the way they inform current perceptions of AI. Through this lens, the course will address writing in the digital age, teaching students how to use AI as a cited tool to enhance their own ideas in coursework. The librarian's expertise plays a pivotal role in curating and navigating the vast array of AI resources in terms of research, evaluation, synthesis, and citing – thus enhancing the overall learning experience.

Chapter 10

Ganiyu Ojo Adigun, Ladoke Akintola University of Technology, Nigeria
Gboyega Adio, Ladoke Akintola University of Technology, Nigeria
Oluwole O. Durodolu, University of South Africa, South Africa

In the dynamic currents of the Fifth Industrial Revolution (5IR), we witness a profound transformation shaping knowledge systems and redefining the roles of both librarians and users. This epoch marks a significant departure propelled by cutting-edge technologies such as AI, IoT, and biotechnology. Fundamental principles guiding this revolution encompass sustainability, interdisciplinary expertise, ethical considerations, and adaptability. In this evolving landscape, libraries have evolved into vibrant centers offering digital resources, expert data management, and tailored services. Consequently, librarians and users alike must acquire crucial skills like digital literacy, data literacy, and information curation. Embracing AI, understanding cybersecurity, and adapting to evolving responsibilities are imperative for both stakeholders. The 5IR heralds an era of democratized access to knowledge, breaking down geographical barriers and positioning libraries as pivotal hubs for data management.

Chapter 11

    Tracy Ann Elliott, Florida Gulf Coast University, USA
    Katelyn Ramirez Velazco, Florida Gulf Coast University, USA
    Precious A. Goodson, Florida Gulf Coast University, USA

During the 2023-24 academic year, Florida Gulf Coast University piloted education start-up Pangea's reading engagement tool, Alethea, which incorporates generative AI (GPT-4). The development partnership with FGCU was a contributing factor in Clarivate's purchase of Pangea. The results of the pilot have been extraordinary. Using FGCU library as a case study, this chapter describes a development partnership with commercial products integrating AI. The case study describes how the product has been utilized, the role of librarians in implementation, findings from multiple studies, including encouraging results of a mixed methods study in which 85% of students reported Alethea helped them understand and recall important themes and main ideas from course reading material. Faculty using Alethea reported student mastery of threshold concepts as described within the ACRL Framework for Information Literacy.

Preface

Artificial Intelligence (AI) has rapidly become a transformative force across various sectors, and academia is no exception. As AI continues to evolve, its influence on academic libraries, research methodologies, and information management is becoming increasingly profound. This edited volume, *Navigating AI in Academic Libraries: Implications for Academic Research*, is an exploration of this transformative impact, offering a comprehensive examination of the challenges, opportunities, and innovations that AI presents to academic institutions.

Our goal in compiling this book is to provide a platform for scholars, librarians, researchers, and practitioners to share their insights and expertise on the intersection of AI and academic research. This volume delves into critical topics such as the use of AI in information literacy classrooms, the impact of AI on traditional library research methods, and the collaboration between faculty and librarians in the era of AI. We also explore significant issues like plagiarism, copyright, and bias in AI tools, offering strategies and solutions to navigate these challenges.

This book brings together contributions from various disciplines, fostering a holistic understanding of AI's role in academia. It addresses the implications of AI on scholarly publishing, open access initiatives, and the curation and management of library collections. Additionally, we examine how AI can enhance information retrieval systems, providing more efficient and effective access to academic resources.

We envision this volume as a valuable resource for a diverse audience, including researchers, academics, policymakers, and students. Whether you are a novice seeking to understand the basics of AI in academia or an expert looking for the latest research and practices, this book offers a comprehensive overview of the current landscape.

As editors, we are grateful to the contributors who have shared their knowledge and perspectives, enriching the discourse on AI in academic libraries. We hope this book serves as a catalyst for further exploration and collaboration, ultimately advancing the understanding and application of AI in the academic world.

ORGANIZATION OF THE BOOK

Chapter 1: Exploring Artificial Intelligence (AI) Tools for Curating and Managing Library Collections

The integration of artificial intelligence into library management is revolutionizing the way collections are curated and maintained, offering librarians tools to enhance efficiency and decision-making. This chapter delves into how AI can assist librarians in managing the complex processes of selection, acquisition, processing, stocktaking, and weeding within library collections. By leveraging AI tools, collection development librarians can effectively analyze large datasets, devise robust metadata systems, and establish frameworks for cataloging and classifying resources. This not only optimizes the use of limited financial and human resources but also ensures that library collections are tailored to meet the evolving needs of their user communities.

Chapter 2: AI in Scholarly Communications and Academic Research

Artificial intelligence is reshaping scholarly communications and academic research, presenting both opportunities and challenges for academic libraries. This chapter examines how AI influences every stage of the research process, from hypothesis formulation to the dissemination of results, and how librarians are adapting to support these AI-driven methodologies. By exploring different AI applications, the chapter highlights the dual role of academic librarians as both facilitators of research and experts in knowledge discovery and preservation. Additionally, it addresses the impact of AI on scholarly communications, emphasizing the need for libraries to evolve in response to these technological advancements.

Chapter 3: Effect of Exploring Artificial Intelligence in Academic Libraries on Academic Research: An Overview

The rapid adoption of artificial intelligence in academic libraries has sparked diverse reactions within the academic community. This chapter provides an overview of the effects of AI on academic research, particularly within academic libraries in developed countries. It discusses the dual perceptions of AI as both a powerful tool that can expedite research and a potential threat that could undermine the value of academic inquiry. By exploring these contrasting views, the chapter sheds light on the transformative role AI plays in academic research and the ongoing debate surrounding its integration into academic libraries.

Chapter 4: Are Artificial Intelligence Chatbots a Threat to Librarianship?

As AI chatbots become increasingly prevalent in libraries, concerns about their impact on the profession of librarianship have emerged. This chapter explores the potential threats posed by AI chatbots and advocates for a balanced approach to their integration. It examines the evolving roles of librarians, the capabilities and limitations of chatbots, and the unique value that human librarians bring to the table. The chapter argues that while chatbots can enhance efficiency in handling routine inquiries, they cannot replace the personalized assistance, intellectual freedom, and privacy advocacy that librarians provide. By proposing a collaborative model that leverages both AI and human expertise, the chapter contributes to the ongoing discourse on the future of librarianship in the age of AI.

Chapter 5: Role of Libraries in Promoting Digital Literacy and Information Fluency

In the digital age, libraries play a crucial role in fostering digital literacy and information fluency. This chapter discusses how libraries provide access to digital resources and equip individuals with essential skills such as computer literacy, critical thinking, and data comprehension. It highlights the importance of media literacy, fact-checking, and accountability, all of which are essential in navigating the ever-changing digital landscape. By creating collaborative learning spaces, libraries enable visitors to engage with cutting-edge technologies, participate in digital storytelling, and generate new ideas. The chapter also emphasizes the importance of libraries in partnering with educational institutions to amplify digital literacy programs and support lifelong learning.

Chapter 6: Navigating the AI Policy Landscape: AI in Community College Education

The integration of artificial intelligence into community college education presents both opportunities and policy challenges. This chapter explores the complex policy landscape surrounding AI in community colleges, focusing on the need for nuanced governance frameworks within the federal system of the United States. By examining existing policy frameworks, emerging trends, and evolving regulations, the chapter provides insights into the intersection between AI technology and governance in the context of community college education. It highlights the importance of addressing these policy challenges to ensure that AI integration enhances learning experiences and administrative efficiency.

Chapter 7: Generative AI Ethical Conundrum: Librarians as Artificial Intelligence Literacy Apostles in the Educational Space

Generative AI is transforming education by offering customized learning experiences, but it also raises ethical concerns about the authenticity of content. This chapter discusses the ethical conundrum posed by generative AI and the critical role librarians play as literacy apostles in advancing information literacy and fostering critical thinking. By integrating digital literacy with ethical considerations, the chapter proposes a theoretical framework that empowers individuals to responsibly engage with technology in the digital age. It introduces the Library-AI Handshake model, which underscores the need for librarians to bridge the AI literacy skills gap and promote the ethical adoption and use of generative AI.

Chapter 8: Optimizing the Use of Artificial Intelligence (AI) in Library Services in the 21st Century

Artificial intelligence is increasingly embedded in daily computing activities, often without users being fully aware of its presence. This chapter explores how AI technologies such as speech recognition, natural language processing, and machine learning are being integrated into library services. By leveraging AI's ability to recognize patterns at scale, libraries can enhance their role as prime sources of information access in society. The chapter highlights the transformative impact of AI on library services, emphasizing the need for libraries to stay ahead of technological advancements to continue meeting the growing demand for information in the 21st century.

Chapter 9: Teaching Literature in the Age of AI: A Collaborative Approach to Engaged Learning

This chapter explores the intersection of literature, artificial intelligence, and collaborative pedagogy through the lens of a partnership between an English instructor and a librarian. By integrating AI into literature classes, this collaboration seeks to bridge the gap between traditional literary studies and emerging technological advancements. The chapter discusses how AI can be used as a tool to enhance students' understanding of narrative perceptions of AI and its impact on current perceptions of technology. The librarian's expertise in curating and navigating AI resources is crucial in enriching the learning experience, ultimately fostering interdisciplinary connections and engaged learning in the digital age.

Chapter 10: Innovation and Skills Needed for Sustainable Knowledge Systems in the Fifth Industrial Revolution: Implications for Libraries and Users

The Fifth Industrial Revolution (5IR) is characterized by the convergence of cutting-edge technologies such as AI, IoT, and biotechnology, leading to a profound transformation of knowledge systems. This chapter examines the implications of 5IR for libraries and their users, emphasizing the need for new skills such as digital literacy, data literacy, and information curation. It discusses how libraries have evolved into vibrant centers of digital resources and expert data management, and how both librarians and users must adapt to the changing landscape. The chapter underscores the importance of embracing AI, understanding cybersecurity, and developing interdisciplinary expertise to thrive in the 5IR era.

Chapter 11: Clarivate's New Generative AI Reading Engagement Platform: A Development Partnership Led by the University Library

This chapter presents a case study of Florida Gulf Coast University's partnership with education start-up Pangea to pilot a generative AI reading engagement tool, Alethea. The partnership contributed to Clarivate's acquisition of Pangea, and the chapter details the implementation and outcomes of the pilot program. The case study highlights the role of librarians in the successful integration of AI into educational tools, with findings showing that 85% of students reported improved understanding and recall of course material. The chapter also discusses how the AI tool aligned with the ACRL Framework for Information Literacy, contributing to enhanced student learning and engagement.

IN CONCLUSION

As we conclude this preface, it is our hope that this edited volume serves as a pivotal resource for those navigating the evolving landscape of artificial intelligence within academic libraries. The chapters presented here offer a diverse array of insights, reflecting the multifaceted nature of AI's impact on academic research, scholarly communication, and the broader mission of libraries. By bringing together the expertise of scholars, practitioners, and librarians, we aim to foster a deeper understanding of AI's transformative potential while addressing the challenges and ethical considerations that accompany its integration.

This book is not merely a collection of research and reflections; it is a call to action for continued collaboration, innovation, and critical thinking in our field. As AI continues to shape the future of education and research, it is imperative that we, as stewards of knowledge, remain adaptable and forward-thinking. We invite our readers to engage with the ideas presented in this volume, to contribute to the ongoing discourse, and to apply these insights within their own institutions. Together, we can navigate the complexities of AI and ensure that academic libraries continue to thrive as centers of learning, innovation, and community in the digital age.

Sincerely,

Kathleen Sacco, Alison Norton, and Kevin Arms

Editors

Chapter 1
Exploring Artificial Intelligence (AI) Tools for Curating and Managing Library Collections

Jesubukade Emmanuel Ajakaye
https://orcid.org/0000-0002-8966-4422
Federal Polytechnic, Ayede, Nigeria

ABSTRACT

The application of artificial intelligence provides opportunities to help in the curation and management of library collections to serve the user community better. Librarians are saddled with the responsibility of taking care of and maintaining information resources in the library collections. Curating and managing the library collections is an important task in the library system and can be daunting, from selection to ordering, acquiring selected information resources, processing these resources, stocktaking, and weeding. AI tools provide intelligent help in reducing time spent on repetitive functions and aid librarians in making informed decisions. Collection development librarians must understand the impact of AI tools in their section, make meaning from large datasets, devise metadata systems, and lay the proper framework for cataloguing and classifying these information resources. This ensures that the goal of the library is to provide its patrons with appropriate collections that meet the needs of the library's user community within its limited financial and human resources.

DOI: 10.4018/979-8-3693-3053-1.ch001

INTRODUCTION

Artificial intelligence (AI) has revolutionized every aspect of library activities. The library goals and objectives are always user-centric hence, library collections must be useful to their patrons. The application of artificial intelligence helps in the curation and management of library collections to serve the user community better. Librarians are saddled with the responsibility of taking care of and maintaining information resources in the library collections. The library collections contain tangible and intangible information resources available to patrons in a library, including books (textbooks, reference books, rare books), and other published documents. The development of emerging media has made these inclusive of "connections" made within the scholarly communication industry. Consortium building with other libraries, subscription to databases, and negotiation of license terms for bundles of eBooks and online journals provided by publishing firms are part of the library collections managed by librarians. "Librarians and library management make selections and recommendations based on criteria such as quality and appropriateness" (Colbjornsen, Brenna, and Edquist, 2022).

The quality of library collections determines the satisfaction of library users and the process of curating and managing the library collections is called "collection development". Collection development involves several activities related to building and managing of variety of information resources to meet the desperate needs of users (Kamau & Elegwa, 2022). The collection development department of the library acquires, manages, develops, preserves, safeguards, interprets, and displays information materials in various ways (Colbjornsen, Brenna, and Edquist, 2022). AI tools can help complement the responsibilities of librarians in the curation and management of library collections which include taking care of these resources, analyzing the needs and wants of patrons to inform selection on information resources, acquiring, maintaining, carrying out periodic weeding on the collections as well as promoting the library collections to the user community.

The application of artificial intelligence to library activities has changed the way patrons' access and use information, largely because their of the ever-dynamic information needs which have also affected the way information resources are being collected and managed. Several operations and information service delivery have been improved due to the implementation of AI tools for these operations, ranging from collection development to answering user reference queries to engagement with patrons. Technology has various impacts on various departments in the library. Each section should thereby chart its roadmap for the effective delivery of its responsibilities in achieving the library's collective goal. The library can train AI tools on the materials consulted by the patrons, thereby curating recommendations of materials that users will need but do not exist in the library. Machine learning

(ML) an aspect of artificial intelligence can provide more metadata necessary for connecting library collections with the users. Libraries are now particularly pushing for machine learning and artificial intelligence tools that can help process predictably incredibly diverse library collections.

User behaviours and preferences can be analysed with AI tools, this will help the collection development librarian curate resources tailored to the recommendations received from the library patrons. Such personalized collection development will ensure that all categories of library user discover and engage with resources that align with their specific interests. A plethora of data is available to libraries nowadays which is termed big data. Big Data are sets of voluminous and sometimes complicated data that traditional data processing applications cannot effectively collect, store, clean, analyse, share or effectively transmit (Oseji and Sani, 2022). Users' massive data through their heatmap of resources consulted in the library, publishing firms and also vendors create metadata of resources available which libraries can acquire to improve their library collections. It becomes a daunting task during the selection process but, AI tools can take input of these datasets, predict and recommend to the library's resources to be acquired for the library collection. Libraries can effectively track information resources in the library collection while making decisions for the selection and acquisition of new additions.

A basic understanding of AI tools will help with the curation of library collections, but a more advanced skill might be needed for the management of these library collections. Data should be taken as the basis for a data-driven approach to make decisions or predictions of what to include in the library collection. Libraries now use collaborative data mining techniques and test analytics to optimize library collection. Machine learning enables the system to discover, that is, it trains to develop appropriate models within data. The training involves the machine exploring input data and learning from patterns. Fine-tuning the parameters and hyperparameters ensures that there is an improvement in the accuracy in the level of predicting the output (Cox and Mazumdar, 2022). Robotics is also employed in the management of library collections, especially in the manual task of sorting used and returned books or even shelf reading. Robots in libraries can retrieve books from the shelves and also ensure proper arrangements of the library collections (Cox and Mazumdar, 2022).

Development of AI tools in Libraries

In the early 1990s, the idea of using AI tools in libraries was suggested. AI functions in libraries cover various tasks such as subject indexing, shelf organization, building collections, technical assistance, answering queries, and information retrieval. The advancement of AI programming has enabled the realization of smart libraries, which is now on the horizon. This assertion is backed by the work of AI experts and scholars who are crafting intelligent systems resembling librarians - known as library robots. AI is poised to greatly benefit library functions and services, elevating the role of libraries in our fast-changing digital society. AI integration into libraries will affect how information resources are utilized, streamline search capabilities, and promptly address inquiries. Although there is a perception that AI distances librarians from users, rather than replacing their tasks, it is expected to enhance libraries' productivity. Additionally, AI will significantly enhance library operations and services, elevating the relevance of libraries in our ever-evolving digital society (Basak et al., 2024).

Numerous studies have explored the development and application of Artificial Intelligence in providing library information resources and services. Balleste (2002) offers an introduction to Artificial Intelligence (AI) in library services. The paper elucidates the concept of AI and its potential benefits for libraries, providing illustrations and recommending vendors for additional insights. Drawing from firsthand experience in AI implementation, the author seeks to debunk the notion that AI is confined to science fiction, presenting it as a pertinent and beneficial technology for libraries in the 21st century. Han (2021) opined the view that AI can assist in data gathering and analysis for making library management decisions and alleviate the workload on library staff. The study suggests that combining AI with human expertise can produce a more efficient and knowledgeable library management system. Additionally, the author discusses the benefits of employing AI in library management, such as reduced working hours and decreased errors, potentially resulting in increased customer satisfaction. To further advance AI development, the paper underscores the importance of collaboration between library directors and academics.

Tian (2021) talked about applying artificial intelligence in vocational college library systems and suggested employing a collaborative approach with multiple intelligent agents, along with content filtering and learning optimization, to offer personalized information services. Through data mining, the library system aligns traditional document retrieval outcomes with the reader's preferences. The writer stresses the importance of intelligent services as a fresh path for library advancement and the necessity of adopting innovative technology to achieve "double first-class" libraries. Moreover, the writer underscores the advantages of AI in libraries, providing ubiquitous, personalized, and efficient services. In the age of significant machine intelligence, libraries encounter both challenges and chances to reshape their services. Third-party firms, known as "data aggregators", frequently offer digital reading promotional services. The piece underscores the growing trend of online reading and the necessity for libraries to adjust their services to match readers' needs. AI technology has the potential to improve library services by recognizing customers' interests and reading patterns, enabling customized recommendations according to user preferences and reading records. This technology empowers libraries to offer personalized suggestions to users, taking into account, factors like reading duration for each book or article (Lin et al., 2023).

Mupaikwa (2024) demonstrated that artificial intelligence and machine learning have been applied in libraries to aid reference services, indexing and abstracting, information retrieval, cataloguing and classification, and collection management, among other functions. Various machine learning techniques such as KNearest neighbour, Bayesian networks, fuzzy logic, support vector machines, clustering, and classification algorithms were also utilized. Key obstacles impeding the adoption of artificial intelligence and machine learning in libraries included insufficient infrastructure, inadequate funding, and limited awareness among librarians. The research suggested librarian training and curriculum updates for library schools. Furthermore, it proposed further exploration of Python-based innovations for libraries.

Tomiuk (2024) noted that the most widely used AI applications currently include natural language processing and virtual reference librarians (chatbots), while the less common ones are robot guides and facial recognition. Although research-oriented institutions in wealthier nations are more inclined to adopt AI due to their resources, libraries worldwide are also experiencing an AI-driven shift. This involves employing IT tools like smart book chutes, intelligent bookshelves, mobile inventory systems, and self-check-in/out machines. AI has the potential to significantly benefit libraries by enhancing virtual services, referencing, cataloguing, collection development, acquisition/technical services, and instruction. While librarians anticipate significant changes to their roles due to AI, they express minimal concern about job displacement. The study further reported that issues faced in the implementation include the immaturity of commercial solutions, security and privacy concerns alignment with library values, funding limitations, and the need for technical expertise.

Modern libraries have transformed from centralized, paper-based computer systems into distributed networks encompassing both digital and non-digital materials. They now offer a blend of innovative and traditional services. Faced with a significant rise in available materials and user demands, libraries must leverage new technology to fulfil their missions despite limited resources. AI holds immense promise for libraries as it can handle routine computer input tasks. Artificial intelligence may also have the ability to reason, plan, learn and collaborate with users or other agents in libraries. Library and information science have also advanced in utilizing intelligent computer systems. The operation and management of libraries entail numerous repetitive, meticulous, laborious, and time-consuming tasks. Many libraries moved towards automation of the majority of their activities to increase efficiency and effectiveness. Artificial intelligence techniques enhance the accuracy of library operations (Chemulwo and Sirorei (2019).

Typical library functions involve repetitive tasks carried out by librarians, including technical duties such as collection development and management. While many libraries have adopted automation through information technology, these systems still necessitate significant human interaction and engagement. For example, when organizing library information resources - such as classification and cataloguing - librarians must manually determine a collection's metadata before entering it into the system. The information landscape changes from time to time and can be enormous for humans to keep up with. The application of artificial intelligence tools presents an opportunity for best practices in applying new knowledge and achieving improved outcomes. Libraries focus more on getting information materials that will be useful to meeting their patron's information needs while saving time. Libraries in developed countries are positioned to take full advantage of AI by implementing several services in addition to available services before.

The infrastructure of a smart library includes components like a data centre, AI-driven robots, large visual screens, and dual identification methods to enhance privacy (Gul & Bano, 2019). There is a growing demand for smart library applications, with popular features including facial recognition, RFID-based applications, indoor navigation, seat reservation, self-service printing/photocopying, and smart lockers (Bi et al., 2022). These libraries utilize innovative technologies such as the Internet of Things, RFID, Wi-Fi, Bluetooth Low Energy (BLE), Natural language processing (NLP), deep learning, recommender systems, and Optical character recognition (OCR), resulting in new services.

Application of Artificial Intelligence in the Curation Cycle and Management of Library Collection

The application of artificial intelligence to library operations is not an attempt to replace humans with machines but to reduce repetitive functions and aid in delivering their jobs to allow for effectiveness and efficiency. The library provides access to a wide range of information resources to all members of their user community irrespective of age, education level, social status, or background. They strive to be holders of all appropriate books needed by their user community. These collections are expected to be current, engaging, inclusive, relevant, and appropriate for all levels of users. Libraries are expected to prioritise quality over quantity when curating and managing their collections. The adoption of AI in libraries is likely to result in the expansion of librarians' skills and the addition of new competencies helping to improve overall service delivery in the library.

AI in libraries is a complex and evolving concept, encompassing multiple technologies such as business analytics, natural language processing, machine learning, computer vision, and robotics. The impact of AI on library activities is diverse, ranging from search engines and library system interfaces to conversational agents, user management, and robotic process automation. Cox and Mazumdar, (2022) noted some use cases in the application of AI in libraries. Their "Use Case I" focused on the application of AI to back-end operations. They posited that AI tools complete clerical and manual tasks. For collection development, AI tools are applied for knowledge discovery about library users. They are able to give insights for understanding techniques relevant to the form of data programming for curating the library collection. The use of Robotic Process Automation (RPA) allows the system to perform repetitive tasks previously performed manually where limited human judgement is needed to work on text or data. This could include retrieving data from sources, processing it and returning the output.

Vijayakumar and Sheshadri (2019) discussed that library patrons play an important role in building library collections and online resources in particular. Various systems have been integrated for the acquisition of library resources. The Monograph Selection Advisor stands out as a pioneering initiative in utilizing this evolving technology, particularly in building library collections. It focuses on modelling the item-by-item decisions made by subject bibliographers when selecting monographs. The essential requirement is that the knowledge base must be sufficiently comprehensive, and the interface must be user-friendly enough for the library to retrieve the desired information from the system. A particular challenge that presents itself is the enhancement of library metadata generation. Libraries obtain thousands of pieces of metadata for both print and digital resources from various vendors as part of the purchasing and acquisition process, which are then made accessible to library users. In instances where an e-book platform lacks metadata, libraries create their own. For the growing number of born-digital resources, machine learning offers a range of potential tools to assist libraries in generating metadata for digital resources. This not only speeds up the metadata generation process but also significantly enhances the comprehensiveness and variety of subject terms used in cataloguing.

Lin et al., 2022 reported that these applications are relevant in all library automation flows from processing input metadata from all forms, migrating these data from one system to another or reconciling inputs from several sources. For the management of the library collections, robots can be used to weed information resources based on set criteria. This use case drives efficiency in the collection development processes as they relieve humans of mundane tasks. The presence of big data in libraries can be used to evaluate their enormous data holding, which gives a better understanding of their patrons, needs, and characteristics and enables them to deliver new and enhanced services, especially in their collection development. Big data can help mine information on the library collection, it is, therefore, possible to track library user's activity. Analysis on this dataset creates user stories and decisions can be made on the library collections and improve overall user experience and user satisfaction. The recommender system can work on big data and does not only recommend to users what information resources they might need that are available in the library, but it can also recommend to librarians what information resources users might need that are not available in the library collection. It helps in setting up and keeping up-to-date collections.

Robots are programmable, multipurpose manipulators that are automatically controlled and can operate in several axes. They can either be stationary or portable and are used in various automation applications. Despite the increasing provision of digital services and resources by libraries, many are still acquiring a significant number of printed documents. This dual pressure to offer both electronic and printed resources has led to significant space constraints for numerous libraries, particularly academic and research libraries. To address this challenge, many libraries have adopted a Comprehensive Approach to Printed Material (CAPM). The goal of CAPM is to develop a personalized robotic scanning system based on a series, allowing users to browse imprints in real-time via a web interface. When a user requests an item through the CAPM system, a robot retrieves it. The item is then passed to another robotic system, which automatically opens and flips through the pages (Vijayakumar and Sheshadri, 2019).

The weeding and audit process is an ongoing process in the curation cycle which ensures that the library collection stays current and reflective of the ever-dynamic information needs of its user community. Various criteria are considered while weeding and they can be transformed into sets of commands for an AI system to follow. The criteria for weeding and auditing information resources in a library collection include:

1. Factually inaccurate materials and obsolete items in the library must be removed. It becomes important to weed when current information resources do not match the current guidelines for selection or are no longer reflective of the collection development policy.
2. Worn-out materials whose physical conditions have deteriorated, including those whose appearance is outdated, dirty, mouldy, beyond repair or not worthy of repair are to be completely weeded from the collection. Those "loved to death" (books worn out from frequent use) must be replaced after being weeded from the library collection.
3. The library is expected to weed previous editions of information material when newer editions are available, or a current information format or resource is available.
4. Information resources that current users do not find engaging or poorly written and presented must be removed from the library collection. The younger generation nowadays expects to find fascinating and engaging materials which

meet their information needs within a short time frame. Information resources especially e-resources could be more appropriate for these categories of users.

5. Materials that no longer serve the interest of the parent body are to be removed. The curation of information resources in the library is done in line with the vision and mission of the parent institution therefore, any material that does not meet the established goals must be removed.

These guidelines can be programmed into AI tools that give recurrent updates on materials that need to be weeded or, the library Robot can be programmed to complete these tasks. Collection development librarians and subject specialists are in the best position to identify which public domain materials could be digitized and made more accessible to institutional scholars and local communities. They are also in the best position to identify AI tools that work perfectly and are suitable for the curation and management of the library collection. Identifying the components of collection development involves assessing user needs, evaluating the existing collection, establishing selection policies, coordinating selections, reassessing, managing collection storage, and strategizing for resource sharing.

Incorporating Rules guiding AI applications in Collection Development Policy

Every library around the world has its collection development policy which are set of rules that guide the collection development activities. Libraries must curate and maintain a sound and robust collection to be able to actively meet the information needs of their patrons. The quality and relevance of the collection affects the extent of use of the collection by the patrons and this is why it is important for the application of AI tools. The collection of library information resources needs careful consideration in preparation and planning which is referred to as collection development. Buraimo et al (2023) posit that collection development is the qualitative and quantitative procedure of building up and improving existing library collections. A collection development policy is a formal written statement of principles guiding the development and management of the library's collection. It includes the definition of the user community, criteria for selection, mode of acquisitions, rules guiding weeding, as well as key factors to consider while evaluating the library's collection.

Collection development policy removes bias, and sorts issues around diversity, equity and inclusion thereby instructions are clearly stated for adopted AI tools to follow. Managing libraries effectively and efficiently requires precise consideration of the composition of their collections and how they will be developed. Collection development policy includes community analysis, selection, acquisition, processing, weeding and evaluation. The collection development policy is a standard for selecting, acquiring, weeding and evaluating the library's collection. Collection development policy is therefore a useful guideline to staff when engaging in collection development activities.

Community Analysis: ML algorithms can be used to classify users into categories or even new clusters may be discovered thereby giving insights into which materials to be considered during the collection development processes for the library. Also, a User-based collaborative filtering algorithm can be used to understand the preferences of users over a given period. The collection development policy must include what kind of data to be collected and ensure that the personal privacy of their users is upheld to avoid breaches of AI use ethics.

Selection: Output at the community analysis becomes the input for the AI tool to be used for the selection of the information resources to be added to the library collection. The understanding gained from the community analysis helps the AI tool to curate information resources based on the user needs identified. Also, there's an input of information resources which could include publishers list and databases, vendors list among others. The AI algorithm identifies and ranks the selected information resources, and the librarian can make final decisions on which to buy viz a viz the available funding available.

Acquisition: Based on the selection decision, guidelines for acquiring the selected information resources can be developed. The AI tools can send automated emails to publishers and vendors whose materials have been selected to forward invoices and also discuss the delivery of information resources. While the human librarian will be more involved in this process, AI tools can carry out supportive roles in the tracking of selected resources and sorting out acquired resources from those not yet acquired.

Processing: At this stage, the AI tool is embedded into the integrated library management system. The system automatically assigns accession numbers to the information materials and is able to extract other useful information at this point. This can be easily imported into CSV format and save librarian a lot of stress, especially in third-world countries that use hardcopies accession registers to complete their task.

Weeding: The guidelines for weeding in the collection development policy will be item-based collaborative filtering. The ML algorithm filters based on metadata of the information material, data like date of publication, date of last use, frequency of user consultation, and content categorization among others will determine the usefulness of the information materials to the ever-dynamic information needs of the users. The guidelines can also develop rules for investigating the output against current user preferences and make intelligent decisions on materials to be weeded out from the library collections.

Evaluating: The usefulness of the information resources in the collection is important hence the need for evaluation. ML algorithms can be used to evaluate each material in the collection. This will be a daunting task for humans to carry out because of the large collection in the library. The collection development policy must contain the guidelines for the evaluation. What criteria will the system evaluate, and a response must be determined.

Proper application of the collection development policy leads to a balanced collection which is able to cater for the information needs of the library's user community to a large extent. The collection development policy ensures the management of the library collection and must be synchronized with the activities of AI tools to achieve optimum results and satisfy the information needs of the library patrons. The collection development policy can also define the extent to which AI tools can be used for its processes. It sets a control and standard with global best practices taking into consideration the peculiarity of the library and its environment.

Artificial Intelligence Combating Problems of Collection Development

The application of AI tools can combat the challenges facing the curation and management of library collections. Giri, Sen, and Mahesh (2015) argued that collection development faces concerns in determining the appropriate number of copies needed for books that are in high demand and require multiple copies in the library. Their study reported that there was no consistency in the approach to deciding the number of copies to be acquired for the library collection. Furthermore, they noted that all the libraries arbitrarily decided on the number of copies to be purchased. ML can actively predict the titles that will need more copies based on usage and demand. Item statistics gives insight during training on an ML model which predicts the information material that will experience heavy usage at a certain period and the library can make decisions toward the acquisition of the materials.

Consequently, while the Library Development Committee (LDC) makes the final decision as to the items to be purchased for the library, it is impossible to meet because of other duties that demand their time while having less time to analyse current needs. An intelligent system can complete these duties based on the collection development policy, and generate items based on needs assessment ranking. The Library Development Committee can make final decisions based on available funds and can attend to other responsibilities they are saddled with. Also, as noted by Olubiyo (2023), problems may arise when a given title is needed by a lot of users at the same time, maximum value should be compared to funding limits. Also, feedback from the circulation department as well as surveys from the users can reveal the need for additional copies of the title to be purchased to meet the demand needs of the patron. A simple ML algorithm can also solve this problem. The algorithm takes input from statistics of usage of every item in the library collection and based on users' preferences, can send prompts about materials in demand.

Smart Libraries as the Future

To conclude, the application of AI has moved libraries past automation to self-sustaining repetitive functions carried out by machines. This is not to say that AI tools will replace humans in the delivery of library services, but they bring seamlessness and cute finesse into the delivery of these library services, thereby improving effectiveness and efficiency. We can agree that curating and managing the library collections is an important task in the library system and can be daunting from selection to ordering, acquiring of selected information resources, processing of these resources, stock taking and weeding are daunting tasks carried out by librarians. Library automation through the integrated library management system has helped to improve the tasks and lessen the burdens of some repetitive functions. Now, AI tools provide intelligent help to identify and create actionable plans relating to the vision and mission statement of the parent institution and the library and can perform some of these processes through a set command programmed by the human librarian thereby saving on time and energy. Collection development librarians must understand the impact of AI tools in their section, how to make meanings from large datasets, devise metadata systems and lay the proper framework for cataloguing and classifying these information resources. This ensures that the goal of the library to provide the library patron with appropriate collections that meet the needs of the library's user community within the limited financial and human resources is met.

REFERENCES

Balleste, R. (2002). The future of artificial intelligence in your virtual libraries. *Computers in Libraries*, 22(9), 10–15.

Basak, R., Paul, P., Kar, S., Molla, I. H., & Chatterjee, P. (2024). The Future of Libraries with AI: Envisioning the Evolving Role of Libraries in the AI Era. In Senthilkumar, K. R. (Ed.), *AI-Assisted Library Reconstruction* (pp. 34–57). IGI Global., DOI: 10.4018/979-8-3693-2782-1.ch003

Buraimo, O., Madukoma, E., Oduwole, A. A., & Olusanya, F. O. (2023). Collection development policy and utilization of academic library resources in Nigeria. *Library and Information Perspectives and Research*, 5(2), 28–40. DOI: 10.47524/lipr.v5i2.29

Chemulwo, M. J., & Sirorei, E. C. (2019). Managing and adapting library information services for future users: Applying artificial intelligence in libraries. In Osuigwe, N. E. (Ed.), *Managing and adapting library information services for future users* (pp. 145–164). IGI Global., DOI: 10.4018/978-1-7998-1116-9.ch009

Colbjornsen, T., Brenna, B., & Edquist, S. (2022). Curating collections in LAMs. In Rasmussen, C. H., Rydbeck, K., & Larsen, H. (Eds.), *Libraries, Archives, and Museums in Transition* (pp. 87–99). Routledge., DOI: 10.4324/9781003188834-9

Cox, A. (2022). How artificial intelligence might change academic library work: Applying the competencies literature and the theory of the professions. *Journal of the Association for Information Science and Technology*, 74(3), 367–380. DOI: 10.1002/asi.24635

Cox, A. M., & Mazumdar, S. (2022). Defining artificial intelligence for librarians. *Journal of Librarianship and Information Science*, 1–11. DOI: 10.1177/09610006221142029

Giri, R., Sen, B. K., & Mahesh, G. (2015). Collection development in Indian academic libraries: An empirical approach to determine the number of copies for acquisition. *DESIDOC Journal of Library and Information Technology*, 35(3), 184–192. DOI: 10.14429/djlit.35.3.7806

Han, K. (2021). Research and exploration of metadata in artificial intelligence digital library. *Journal of Physics: Conference Series*, 1915(2), 022061. DOI: 10.1088/1742-6596/1915/2/022061

Kamau, G. W., & Elegwa, A. L. (2022). Factors influencing collection development process at the University of Nairobi Library. *Library Management*, 43(3/4), 207–217. DOI: 10.1108/LM-09-2020-0127

Lin, C. H., Chiu, D. K., & Lam, K. T. (2022, September). Hong Kong academic librarians' attitudes toward robotic process automation. *Library Hi Tech*, 7. Advance online publication. DOI: 10.1108/LHT-03-2022-0141

Lin, X., Sun, Y., & Zhang, Y., & R, K. M. (2023). Application of AI in Library Digital Reading Promotion Service. *2023 IEEE International Conference on Integrated Circuits and Communication Systems (ICICACS)*, 1–6. DOI: 10.1109/ICICACS57338.2023.10100096

Mupaikwa, E. (2024). The Application of artificial intelligence and machine learning in academic libraries. In Khosrow-Pour, M. (Ed.), *Encyclopedia of Information Science and Technology* (6th ed.). IGI Global., DOI: 10.4018/978-1-6684-7366-5.ch041

Olubiyo, P. O. (2023). Collection development in academic libraries: Challenges and way forward. *International Journal of Library and Information Science Studies*, 9(3), 1–9. DOI: 10.37745/ijliss.15/vol9n319

Oseji, N. A., & Sani, J. O. (2022). Utilizing the potentials of big data in library environments in Nigeria for recommender services. *Library Philosophy and Practice (e-journal)*. 7467. https://digitalcommons.unl.edu/libphilprac/7467

Sani, J. O., & Oseji, N. A. (2022). Utilizing the potentials of big data in library environments in Nigeria for recommender services. *Library Philosophy and Practice (e-journal)*. 7467. https://digitalcommons.unl.edu/libphilprac/7467

Subaveerapandiyan, A., & Gozali, A. A. (2024). AI in Indian libraries: Prospects and perceptions from library professionals. *Open Information Science*, 8(1), 1–13. DOI: 10.1515/opis-2022-0164

Tian, Z. (2021). Application of artificial intelligence system in libraries through data mining and content filtering methods. *Journal of Physics: Conference Series*, 1952(4), 042091. DOI: 10.1088/1742-6596/1952/4/042091

Tomiuk, D., Zuccaro, C., Plaisent, M., Öncel, A. G., Benslimane, Y., & Bernard, P. (2024). Investigating factors affecting artificial intelligence (AI) adoption by libraries at top-rated universities worldwide. In Holland, B., & Sinha, K. (Eds.), *Handbook of Research on Innovative Approaches to Information Technology in Library and Information Science* (pp. 103–125). IGI Global., DOI: 10.4018/979-8-3693-0807-3.ch006

Vijayakumar, S., & Sheshadri, K. N. (2019). Applications of artificial intelligence in academic libraries. *International Journal on Computer Science and Engineering*, 7(18), 136–140. DOI: 10.26438/ijcse/v7si16.136140

ADDITIONAL READING

Affum, M. Q. (2023). The Transformative Impact of Artificial Intelligence on Library Innovation. *Library Philosophy and Practice (e-journal)*. 7999. https://digitalcommons.unl.edu/libphilprac/7999

Cox, A. M., Pinfield, S., & Rutter, S. (2019). The intelligent library: Thought leaders' views on the likely impact of artificial intelligence on academic libraries. *Library Hi Tech*, 37(3), 418–435. DOI: 10.1108/LHT-08-2018-0105

Johnson, P. (2014). *Fundamentals of Collection Development and Management* (3rd ed.). American Library Association.

Manoharan, G., Ashtikar, S., & Nivedha, M. (2024). Integrating Artificial Intelligence in Library Management: An Emerging Trend. In Senthilkumar, K. R. (Ed.), *AI-Assisted Library Reconstruction* (pp. 144–157). IGI Global., DOI: 10.4018/979-8-3693-2782-1.ch008

Pirgova-Morgan, L. (2023). *Looking towards a brighter future: the potentiality of AI and digital transformations to library spaces. Digital Futures research report: Artificial Intelligence (AI) in Libraries Project.* University of Leeds Libraries.

Subaveerapandiyan, A. (2023). Application of Artificial Intelligence (AI) In Libraries and Its Impact on Library Operations Review. *Library Philosophy and Practice (e-journal)*. 7828. https://digitalcommons.unl.edu/libphilprac/7828

KEY TERMS AND DEFINITIONS

Artificial Intelligence: This technology helps machines simulate human intelligence and complete tasks effectively and efficiently.

Collection Development: These are all activities involved in maintaining a balanced collection that meets the needs of the user community, including community analysis, selection, acquisition, and processing, which are all guided by a collection development policy.

Curation: This involves selecting, organizing and maintaining information materials to form a library collection.

Intelligent Library: This library has adopted the use of artificial intelligence in its library processes from collection development to the provision of access to the library collections.

Library Collections: This includes all information resources (physical and electronic) available and accessible to the users in a library.

Library System: This is the entire processes, tools, human resources, information resources in the library design working together to ensure the library achieves its aims and objectives.

Metadata: Metadata are the keywords or data describing and providing information on a particular information resources.

Chapter 2
AI in Scholarly Communications and Academic Research

Stefka Tzanova
York College, CUNY, USA

ABSTRACT

This chapter discusses the use of Artificial Intelligence (AI) in scholarly communications and academic research juxtaposing benefits/advantages and constraints of these new technologies in the context of academic librarianship. The latest development in AI impacts both the educational activities and the research process in academic institutions, hence libraries have to adapt in order to provide adequate support to diverse curricula and research projects. Accordingly, we explore various types of AI and how the roles of academic librarians are tuned to support all phases of AI driven research process – from formulation of hypothesis, to the dissemination of the results. In addition, we will look on AI's impact on scholarly communications from the perspective of librarians as experts in knowledge discovery and preservation.

INTRODUCTION

Artificial Intelligence (AI) is a set of powerful data driven technologies aimed to simulate intelligent behavior by some artificial agent - usually a computer program. The application of AI in scholarly communications, an umbrella term for the "system through which research and other scholarly writings are created, evaluated for quality, disseminated to the scholarly community, and preserved" is not a novelty (ACRL, 2003). For instance, the Meta search engine (formerly Sciencescape Inc.) was born as an intelligent tool aimed to annotate millions of copyrighted papers

DOI: 10.4018/979-8-3693-3053-1.ch002

from BioMed Central, American Medical Association, Elsevier, Taylor and Francis, SAGE, Walters Kluwer, Royal Society and Karger Publishers. Until recently, AI tools were predominantly predictive i.e., based on statistical analysis and machine learning algorithms to identify patterns. The years 2018-2022 marked the development and introduction of another type of AI, generative AI, which can create new content from information it was trained on according to a transformed input or so-called prompt. Arguably, the most popular practical implementation of generative AI is ChatGPT by OpenAI, a chatbot which uses neural networks and combines large language models with natural language processing. Upon its introduction, ChatGPT demonstrated remarkable capabilities to interact with humans in a conversational way, to answer follow-up questions and to challenge incorrectly stated principles. As Borji (2023) points out, such capabilities were a game changer because the system could pass the Turing test (formulated by Alan Turing in the late 1950s) which determines a machine's "intelligent behavior" by looking at whether or not "the system acts like a human". Hence, it was assumed that ChatGPT can write publishable scientific papers (Getahun, 2022).

The generative AI (GAI) tools in research were envisioned to handle data collection, do exploratory data analysis, formulate research questions, conduct explorative data analysis, prepare literature reviews and synthesis, provide coding assistance for data analysis among others. Shortly, many generative AI applications expanded. For instance, DALLE-2 is a generative AI model used to convert text to 3D images, AlphaTensor can create algorithms, Codex can create code from text, and Galactica can convert conversational text to scientific text. The applicability of ChatGPT to scholarly communications and academic research was tested by various experimental studies. The results outline the limitations of technology and prove that ChatGPT itself is not a universal tool that will solve all problems (Bhattacharjee & Liu, 2024). In fact, it revealed new problems related to ethics, bias, manufactured results (so called hallucination), fake data and fabrication of references to list few (Borji, 2023). Consequently, changes in the policies and regulations associated with the use of AI in scholarly communications were introduced by publishers, funding agencies and educational institutions. In this chapter, we will trace the use of AI in scholarly communications and academia juxtaposing the benefits/advantages and constraints of these technologies in the context of academic librarianship. Accordingly, we will explore how the roles of academic librarians are attuned to support all phases of AI driven research process – from formulation of hypothesis, to the dissemination of the results. In addition, we will look on AI's impact on scholarly communications from the perspective of librarians as experts in knowledge discovery and preservation.

Definitions and Types of AI

AI is a term which originates in the late 1950s and in general describes intelligent behavior by a computer program. The formal definitions of AI also known as rationalistic views, focus on the program and symbolic representations itself and disregard comparisons to human intelligence. These classifications originate in a principle formulated by George Boole in 1854, namely that logical behavior can be described with a set of mathematical equations and thus intelligence can be conveyed by an artificial agent. AI is defined by Dobrev (2018) formally as a "program whose IQ is bigger than 0.7", where IQ is stated as the average success of a program in performing tasks in a set of test environments. Obviously, the Turing test cannot be used in above mentioned formal AI definitions because it doesn't consider the concept of rationality as manifestation of intelligence; i.e., it does not test the ability of a formal system/program to perform actions in order to maximize its own performance or to generate useful information. Per this test, the intelligence assessment of the machine is based on the computer's ability to produce responses indistinguishable from the ones generated by a human in a course of human-computer interaction.

The parallel existence of both formal and informal characteristics of AI caused Russel and Norvig (2016) to propose several alternative definitions of AI, each one combining human and machine perceptions. Their first AI designation focused on human perspective and defines AI as a system that "acts like a human" and thus it covers the Turing test. The second description emphasizes programs that "think as a human" and consequently cover formal definitions of AI. The third one focuses on humans, but also incorporates rationality, i.e. it defines a system that can "think rationally" and/or "act rationally". This type of AI, also called human-centered AI (HCAI), seeks to expand the abilities of, or address, specific societal needs of with use of AI while the human retains control of the interaction. HCAI can explore one or more different technologies, each of which aims to simulate different aspects of intelligent behavior.

Furthermore, depending on the AI output there are two types - predictive AI (PAI) and generative AI (GAI). The latter is a set of machine learning models that can generate new data, i.e., the outputs are objects that look like the ones on which the model is trained, while the former formulates predictions over existing data sets. The common feature of all generative AI implementations is that they can generate new data that look similar to the training data sets. ChatGPT is the most popular instance of generative AI. ChatGPT cuts texts in statistically meaningful chunks using probabilities for words and sentences learned in training phases and then the resulting pattern is used to compile a new text. It is important to mention that ChatGPT is not flawless and has its limitations. For instance, generative AI tend to propagate and even multiply the bias in training data sets.

AI in scholarly Communications and Academic Research

- **AI in academic research**

The applicability of particular type of AI in research is determined by several considerations. The most important ones are the accuracy of the artificial intelligence agent and its trustworthiness. The former defines the capabilities of AI-enabled applications to generate output non-distinguishable from the one generated by human-driven research. The latter depends on the quality of both the data and quality of the data training set. For instance, generative AI trustworthiness is related to bias inherited from a training data set. All generative AI applications tend to amplify the inherited bias so the generated output could be completely wrong when the application is trained on a set that doesn't adequately represents the actual problem (the effect is called "artificial hallucination"). More detailed discussion about biases in data driven AI can be found in a survey by Ntoutsi (2020).

A major problem related to AI implementation in research is the lack of transparency "by design" that is common to AI-enabled applications. Both predictive AI and generative AI use machine learning algorithms, but in a different way and to different ends. However, machine learning algorithms (e.g., deep learning) are difficult to trace, because they don't provide intermediate results, nor do they explain the path of inference to communicating with humans. In addition, the quality of generative AI output depends on prompts, so several conversation extrapolations are typically needed in order to get customized response (Rice et al., 2024). Thus, despite the popularity of one or another AI application, the choice of AI (predictive or generative) should take into consideration the data types associated with particular study. For instance, predictive AI is widely used in medical research, because it operates on structured and labeled data. In contrast, generative AI completes unsupervised learning and operates on non-labeled data. That feature may be beneficial in a context of data-driven studies because generative AI application can create utterly new data set and thus can provide different context of the output. Using incompatible types of AI in a study however may compromise the results.

- **AI in scholarly communications**

The Association of College and Research Libraries (ACRL) defines scholarly communications as "the system through which research and other scholarly writings are created, evaluated for quality, disseminated to the scholarly community, and preserved for future use [… it] includes both formal means of communication, such as publication in peer-reviewed journals". In the science context, research papers aim to fulfil particular and clearly identifiable gap in knowledge and understanding.

Research papers rely on extensive literature review, and combine the latter with analysis aiming to outline the common principles, findings and/or theories associated with a particular scientific topic. In order to serve scholarly communications needs, various types of AI have been used in each step of the process - information retrieval, manuscript preparation, reference management, journal selection, plagiarism check, quality assessment and peer review process. The utilized AI tools can be divided in 2 large groups – those based on predictive AI and those based on generative AI.

- **Predictive AI in scholarly communications**

Research papers rely on extensive literature review to contextualize a particular problem or identify gaps in scholarly publications that can help generate a research hypothesis. Most of the AI-enabled search engines are designed to fit a particular type of research. In particular, many of the current implementations originate as research projects from academia. Semantic Scholar was intended to serve neuro-science, computer science, and geoscience (Fricke, 2018) and was developed in collaboration with CiteSeerX by Pennsylvania State University twenty years ago (Wu et al., 2019). Modern AI-assisted systems add natural language processing and large language models. In non-generative information retrieval, the widely used AI technologies are blockchain, natural language processing, and various machine learning algorithms. The latter are used to create "searchable knowledge graphs" which connect visual and textual research results into single depiction of available data to a machine learning assisted depiction of data and hypotheses (Liechti et al., 2017). Elsevier successfully combines the following AI tools: machine learning for taxonomy building and data mining; natural language processing in algorithmic information extraction and semantic technologies; heuristics in relevancy ranking and evaluation of quality (Gabriel, 2019). The overall accuracy can be improved by minimizing gaps in a database by a systematic routine. Such an approach has been applied in LitCOVID - a database for COVID literature (Chen, 2021). The system loops daily over PubMed records using NCBI E-utilities tools. The harvested publications are filtered against "COVID relevancy" criteria by machine learning algorithm and are further curated by geolocation, topic, and chemical extraction (medication). The curated publications are then imported into a database. The search engine associated with the database allows string text searching and Boolean searching or field search-ing when users can search by abstract, countries, authors, medications, journals, and topics (Chen et al., 2021). The citation and bibliographic management tools also rely on predictive AI and especially on machine learning models to identify the quality of citations and their references. In this process, AI is used to check the authenticity of the research hypothesis and to compare the publication with other publications. AI has also been applied during the process of screening for inclusion. Sometimes this step is called the filtering phase since it aims to identify papers to be included or excluded from the literature review. This is a typical classification in fixed pool problem where each element of the pool (research paper) has its own context. The early AI tools implement disagreement-based classification algorithm and achieve poor results because the procedure considers all possible hypotheses and ignores the interdependencies between hypotheses. The attempts to improve screening include implementation of the crowd-based screening SuperMemo algorithm (Krivosheev et al., 2018) or set of machine learning algorithms such as SVM, Logistic Regression, and Random Forest classifiers (Harrison et al., 2020). Nevertheless, as Wagner pointed out, the AI implementations used in inclusive screening prove to result in "inconsistent and potentially erroneous screening decisions" According to Wagner, AI-enabled non-generative algorithms for research hypothesis generation performed fine in well-structured areas such as information systems and computer science but become unreliable where the formulation of hypothesis requires challenge of a set of assumptions (Wagner et al., 2022).

o   **Academic writing, journal selection and plagiarism check**

Historically, AI role in scholarly communications has been viewed as a possible assistant to scientific writing and several AI-enabled tools with different scope and specialization (e.g., business, chemistry) are already available to researchers. Some of the tools are just simple bots, and few are complete writing platforms. The latter uses predictive AI and machine learning algorithms combined with language analysis and tools for syntax, grammar and text management. Typical examples are Grammarly and its co-product AI Writer. Both programs use deep learning algorithms combined with advanced language analysis (Fitria, 2021), with integrated spelling and grammar checker among other editing tools. In addition, some AI-enabled writing tools are specifically designed for academia and support various citation styles (Ecarnot et al., 2015). Newer predictive AI applications add paraphrasing and modifications based on similarities and are usually applied after failing the plagiarism check (Shaikh, 2020). However, with the development of generative AI many of the writing tools based on traditional AI technologies have become obsolete. A typical example is the closure of InterKit, the popular writing app.

Journal selection is yet another component in the information retrieval process which uses rule-based systems. For instance, OA Journal Finder from Crimson.ai follows a search algorithm using a "validated journal index" supported by the Directory of Open Access Journals (DOAJ) to avoid potential predatory journals (Ghosal et al., 2018). Plagiarism checks typically use traditional classification algorithms (k-means) occasionally combined with natural language processing. For example, Ithenticate provides a side-by-side comparison of text content and source materials and presents a "similarity index" as a percentage, indicating the amount of overlapping phrasing (Razack et al., 2021). Predictive AI plagiarism checkers may also use document source comparison, manual search for characteristic phrases or stylometry. The first one compares a given document to a set of other documents and generates score of similarity; the second one uses phrases inside the document which are unique to this document and stylometry applies statistical analysis on literary style on papers written by the same author (Nwohiri et al., 2021).

- **Generative AI in scholarly communications**

The next evolution leap in scholarly communications is marked by the introduction of generative AI to scholarly communications workflow. The advances in neural networks technology combined with multifold increase in computing power have led to the development of large language models. They can create new algorithms that are probability text responders with a goal to replace human writing (Luitse & Denkena, 2021). In terms of scholarly communications, the revolutionizing agent became a chatbot called ChatGPT, which combines neural networks based large language models with natural language interface. The abilities of the system are remarkable, because it has 175B parameters and is extensively trained over the whole Internet. Thus, the expectations were that ChatGPT could easily assist during or even substitute all stages in the scholarly communications process. Huang and Tan argue that ChatGPT could be used to create content which can be subsequently edited by scientists; utilized to handle data; applied to improve writing by identifying gaps in arguments (in addition to auto correction of errors); providing diverse perspectives; formulating research questions and titles, translating into other language(s), etc. (Huang & Tan, 2023). However, as the experimental studies show, despite all of its tremendous potential, the current technology has flaws such as algorithmic limitations, hallucinations, errors and biases due to incoherent training, and possible ethics violations introduced by the system.

o **Information retrieval**

When introduced as a chatbot, generative AI looks like a universal solution to creating quality literature reviews. Unfortunately, as several studies show ChatGPT is not suitable to generate reviews due to multiple problems, three of which we will discuss here. The first one is low accuracy which can vary depending on the academic discipline. The second is low level of trustworthiness and the third is introduced bias(es). In fact, the research hypothesis generation itself is prone to ethical concerns and as such the many already available generative AI-enabled automatic hypothesis generation tools avoid areas with complex ethical landscape such as behavioral sciences or social sciences. For instance, Lo explores seven electronic databases (Academic Search Ultimate, ACM Digital Library, Education Research Complete, ERIC, IEEE Xplore, Scopus, and Web of Science) and shows that the majority of the included articles were written in English by researchers in the USA, UK and Australia (Lo, 2023). In addition, the percentage of peer reviewed papers was only 64% of all publications, raising questions about the quality of the provided information. Furthermore, there was a large variation in the accuracy of ChatGPT generated literature reviews across different disciplines. In STEM disciplines, medicine, and law the performance of ChatGPT was unsatisfactory. That result is in line with the result shown by Haman and Školnik who prompted ChatGPT to generate a list of 10 seminal academic articles with DOI in the medical field. The authors looped the prompt and found out that only eight out of 50 papers were correct publications (Haman & Školník, 2023).

o   **Academic writing**

As shown above, ChatGPT is an example of generative AI with relatively modest success in preparing large and all-encompassing literature reviews across different disciplines. Since the focus of a chatbot is to generate text, it was suggested that the abilities of ChatGPT to generate new text could be the inflex point in writing a full scientific paper. The capabilities of ChatGPT to generate a complete paper was tested by Thunström, and colleagues who generated a demo paper and co-authored it with Gpt Generative Pre-Trained Transformer. Unfortunately, the generated paper has no scientific value (Gpt Generative Pretrained Transformer, 2022). After the initial enthusiasm a growing stream of studies have aimed to evaluate the actual performance of ChatBots in scientific writing (Ahaley et al., 2023; Doyal et al., 2023; Khalifa et al., 2024; Kocoń et al., 2023). Most of them are in the area of medicine and focus on ChatGPT, but all found significant flaws in ChatGPT's capability for academic writing. For instance, Buholayka prompted ChatGPT to generate a case report for Cureus Journal of Medicine and stated that "ChatGPT was found to be inadequate in generating scientifically accurate case reports, as it produced reports with critical flaws such as incorrect diagnoses and fabricated references" (Buholayka et al., 2023). The authors of this study articulated some ethical violations imposed by the software and recommend the "ChatGPT to be closely scrutinized by experts". Similar study in the social sciences was conducted by Lozic and Štular. They used six ChatBots (ChatGPT-4, ChatGPT-3.5, Bing, Bard, Cloud 2 and Aria) and found out that both ChatGPT versions generate approximately 50% correct content, Bing generates approximately 28% correct content, Bard generates mostly incorrect content and Aria and Cloud 2 generate about 10% correct content. The authors measured the ability of chatbots to create original scientific contributions by comparing them to human-generated articles. Authors mention that the "AI chatbots did not reach this (human) level by far" (Lozić & Štular, 2023). In addition, the study of reasoning errors, hallucinations, and biases revealed that none of the six chatbots demonstrate any critical thinking. Furthermore, the hallucinations were most common in fabricated references, but could also occur in the text. From an ethics point of view, the study revealed that all chatbots demonstrated three types of bias: "language bias, neo-colonial bias, and citation bias" (Lozić & Štular, 2023). 92% of all generated references were in English, 88% of them were from western authors, and 75% were for sources dated prior to 2005. The authors conclude that "… AI chatbots are not capable of generating a full scientific article that would make a notable scientific contribution to the humanities or, we suspect, to science in general." (Lozić & Štular, 2023).

Recently Kacena published results of an experiment aimed to test the ability of ChatGPT-3 and ChatGPT-4 to generate review articles. The authors used a multi-stage process in which each section of the paper was generated by a separate query (human generated). The outputs were combined within a loop of four queries each dedicated to generation of a title, document summary, linking documents and condensing the text with preserving the citations. The results show that on one of the topics the errors were much higher, but the key finding was that the AI generated paper has 70% incorrect references (Kacena et al., 2024). Awosanya conducted a similar study for generating a research paper with ChatGPT and found about 40% erroneous citations, which included both incorrect citations and fabricated citations (Awosanya et al., 2024). The consistency of the reported results suggests that the current level of trustworthiness of a scientific paper written by generative AI is about 60%. Considering the current level of ChatGPT technology, the authors of both studies suggested applying a closely monitored human-controlled-AI-assisted approach since it would take intermediate amount of time and it would require fewer corrections compared to using an AI-only generated counterpart.

o **Generative AI and plagiarism**

In professional literature, there are discussions whether generative AI applications such as ChatGPT commit plagiarism or not (Jarrah et al., 2023). There are several strong arguments supporting generative AI created text as an example of broadly defined plagiarism. The first (and non-disputable one) stems from the fact that all generative AI instances operate on statistical likelihood algorithms over huge data set(s) and thus produce information similar to one presented in training set(s) (despite possible variability). As Cotton points out the chatbots are incapable of generating new ideas and conduct original research (Cotton et al., 2024). An additional argument is that all generative AI instances are not explanatory, so their outcome is without any citation of the original work or author attribution. These arguments initiated several distinctive views toward the use of generative AI in scholarly communications.

The first one seeks to establish regulations by requiring humans to take responsibility for the output. A good argument in this case is the publication "Chatbots, Generative AI and Scholarly manuscripts" (May 2023) from World Association of Medical Editors (WAME) (Zielinski, 2023), (WAME, May 2023). In that publication, the WAME asserts that "Only humans can be authors" and "Authors must take public responsibility for their work" (WAME, 2023). The reasoning behind this is that generative AI can generate various texts, but they are de-facto permutations over database holding the work of others. Therefore, because the machine generated outputs do not have an "author" responsible for the content plagiarism is possible. Consequently, WAME requires human authorship for any work and an obligation to disclose any use of AI in manuscript preparation "In the interests of enabling scientific scrutiny, including replication and identifying falsification, the full prompt used to generate the research results, the time and date of query, and the AI tool used and its version, should be provided" (WAME, 2023). As Cheng (Cheng & Wu, 2024) points out "authors are responsible for the work done by chatbots in the manuscript (including the accuracy and non-plagiarism of the presented content) and must acknowledge all sources, including materials generated by chatbots". For the editors, WAME recommends the use of tools to detect content generated or altered by AI and asserts that these tools "must be available regardless of their ability to pay for them" (Zielenski, 2023). In addition, generative AI chatbots cannot be listed as co-author because they "do not fulfil the criteria for a study author because they cannot take responsibility for the content and integrity of scientific paper" (Stokel-Walker, 2023). Similarly, JAMA journals' policies aim to "preclude the inclusion of nonhuman AI tools as authors" (Flanagin et al., 2023).

The second view completely prohibits the use of generative AI in manuscript preparation. For instance, many major publishers including Elsevier, Taylor & Francis and IOP "have barred researchers from uploading manuscripts and sections of text to generate AI platforms to produce peer-review reports" (Lund et al., 2023). It is worth to mention that the ban onto AI-generated texts was also adopted by research agencies such as National Institute of Health (NIH) and Australian Research Council. The use of generative AI is forbidden in grant proposals and in grant reviews. In addition, NIH funds projects aimed to boost detection of AI-generated texts via their CAREER program.

The third approach addresses the educational process. Many Universities recognize the corruptive potential of generative AI and some have moved to prohibit the its use on campus and in academic work (Cassidy, 2023). However, the effectiveness of such a measure is questionable because the generative AI applications are freely available over the Internet and students may use them outside the campus networks. In addition, AI is already "embedded" in many popular applications such as Google mail (Chung & Huang, 2022) or Google Earth Engine (Yang et al, 2022) and thus is beyond user's reach and control.

On the technical side, the main question is if the detection of AI-generated text will be ever feasible. In their study Chakraborty analyzes different options and give definitive answer that "...Specifically, we demonstrate that detecting AI-generated text is nearly always feasible, provided multiple samples are collected" (Chakraborty et al., 2023). In their paper Minder defines eight features of a text which can be used by detecting software to distinguish between AI-generated, AI-rephrased, or human-generated texts (Minder et al., 2023). The features cover semantic criteria for the sentences, document wide criteria, readability criteria, error-based criteria, readability, text vector and AI feedback. The choice of features and algorithm are critical for the applicability of the AI-detection software. For example, the popular anti AI-text classifier called GPTZero relies on patterns, i.e. it implements the assumption that the AI-generated text holds repetitive patterns, while the human text is more diverse. Unfortunately, the decreasing accuracy of this tool (with every new version of ChatGPT) shows the limitations of used algorithms. As another example, OpenAI's own classifier called "New AI classifier for indicating AI written text" was discontinued by the company due to low accuracy rate. More advanced approaches may employ innovative machine learning algorithms (e.g. XBoost) or some combinations of non-generative AI instances such as rule-based systems and/or transformer systems (Mitrovic et al., 2023). Kirchenbauer suggests using watermarks in scientific texts. The "watermark can be embedded with negligible impact on text quality, and can be detected using an efficient open-source algorithm without access to the language model API or parameters" (Kirchenbauer et al., 2023). We have to highlight the fact that AI plagiarism is understood by research communities, so several classifiers are developed entirely in academia. These were typically trained against texts across various scientific disciplines. For instance, the classifier developed by Minder uses XBoost, and is capable of two distinguishing AI-generated or AI-rephrased text from human-written text with accuracy of 98% and has a predictive performance of almost 79% (Minder et al., 2023). As the study by Bhattacharjee and Liu shows, the predictions from ChatGPT detector are highly unreliable. Even trained with human-written texts the ChatGPT fails to recognize human-written text in 95% of the cases (Bhattacharjee & Liu, 2024). At the current level of technology, the problem of recognizing AI-generated or AI-rephrased text is hard to solve and is getting more complex with new updated versions of the software due to discrepancies in the maturity of chatbots technology and detection software (Sankar et al., 2023).

The academic librarian's perspective of generative AI induced plagiarism should cover all three approaches mentioned above. That translates to the requirement to expand the AI-literacy with topics of AI-rooted plagiarism, manuscript preparation, AI-induced pitfalls and their prevention. In other words, within the AI-literacy framework the academic librarians can discuss with patrons the convolutions in scholarship communications caused by generative AI and focus on methods to prevent AI-rooted plagiarism. For instance, librarians can demonstrate to patrons the capabilities of generative AI to create human-like output which is difficult to detect as plagiarized by typical plagiarism checkers such as Turnitin of GPTZero and then advocate for "anti-plagiarism" strategies. When writing a report/essay/overview the requirement of personal opinion(s) could be made mandatory because the latter is/are difficult to be auto-generated by generative AI.

o   **Generative AI as a peer reviewer**

Opinions on the use of generative AI as peer reviewer are divided. On one hand most of the authors recognize the risks of using generative AI as a reviewer due to possible perpetuation of bias and non-neutral language in AI use (e.g., gender, racial, political, or other biases based on individual characteristics (Hosseini & Horbach, 2023). In addition, most authors focus on peer reviewer's responsibilities such as accountability, transparency, and confidentiality and all three can be violated by generative AI applications.

Noticing that ChatGPT capabilities increase with each new version, Saad conducted an empirical comparative study of two consecutive versions of ChatGPT (3.5 and 4.0) as reviewer. Their finding shows a slight improvement of the correlation score in ChatGPT-4 vs. ChatGPT-3.5 when comparing a human-written peer review with an AI-generated peer review. The authors concluded that "… [H]owever, a fully automated AI review process is currently not advisable, and ChatGPT's role should be regarded as highly constrained for the present and in near future." (Saad et al., 2024). Nevertheless, some journals accept reviewers using AI as a supporting tool, but require peer reviewers to disclose and describe their use of generative AI in order to educate researchers for the shortcomings of ChatGPT such as bias and ethical problems. For example, Mehta argues that before incorporating ChatGPT into the review process the reviewers must undergo ethical training and recognize potential limitations and bias of such technology" (Mehta et al., 2024).

As stakeholders in scholarly communications academic librarians should advise their patrons about the limitations of AI-text detectors and point out that the detector may not be accurate for the given text because its training set did not cover enough scientific manuscripts in a particular domain. Academic librarians also have to help patrons understand the applicability of AI technology to plagiarism detection.

Librarians should be aware and should inform patrons about the main negative features of generative AI systems – that they are not explanatory and could cause bias. Consequently, any use of generative AI in manuscript creation may have potential ethical and privacy implications for the authors. Librarians should educate users about common principles of using generative AI in manuscripts - generative AI should be applied as basic tool only, generative AI cannot be used to create or alter or manipulate original research data, generative AI cannot be credited as an author and generative AI use must be disclosed by authors. In addition, librarians should notify faculty who serve as peer reviewers that generative AI must not be used as reviewer and that publicly available generative AI implementations ought not to be used in the peer review process since the generative AI implementations cannot be copyrighted.

AI Literacy

AI literacy denotes the complexity of various skills, knowledge and values aimed to help users to achieve cognitive engagement and develop trust in AI technology in order to ensure effective and secure use of AI applications. Engagement of users with AI technology is defined by Davenport and Ronanki as "cognitive engagement" (Davenport & Ronanki, 2018). AI literacy includes also ethical considerations awareness. Wang defines AI literacy as the "ability to appropriately recognize, utilize, and evaluate AI-based technologies by considering ethical principles" (Wang et al, 2023). Ridley and Pawlick-Potts (2021) define AI literacy as the relation of people to algorithmic thinking where the latter communicates computer and digital literacy. Per this view AI literacy cannot be seen as the direct successor of all preceding literacies such as digital literacy, computational literacy, scientific literacy and data literacy; rather, it is a new type of literacy which has inherited relations to the others. AI is conceptualized by Ng taxonomy (Ng et al., 2021) as merger of understanding, capabilities to use, capabilities to evaluate and awareness of ethics challenges in a context of AI technology. In Ng's definition understanding denotes the existence of preliminary knowledge about AI even before actual engagement; usage denotes skills to use AI; evaluation denotes ability and knowledge to select suitable AI tools and evaluate critically AI decisions and finally judging from the perspective of consequence in using AI. On more philosophical level Celik explores the determinants of AI literacy in a framework of cognitive absorption, digital divide and computational thinking, where cognitive absorption is defined as state of deep involvement with technology, computational thinking is defined as problem-solving process conducted by humans with use of computers, and digital divide defined as unequal access to AI based technologies (Celik, 2023). The study states that higher access to AI technology in day-to-day activities is a predictor for higher computational thinking and consequently to higher cognitive engagement. Librarians should have algorithmic thinking and cognitive engagement with AI technology in order to teach students AI literacy by examples. Vital elements in that process are the critical evaluation of the AI-enabled output, the ability to evaluate the scope and type of errors, and finally possible ethical implications such as lack of fairness, accountability, etc. (Long & Magerko, 2020). Presumably college students have basic AI understanding so librarians can provide them with challenging assignments such as writing literature reviews and discussing the ethical implications of AI-generated list of sources.

The increased impact generative AI has over academia, scholarly communications and research presents new challenges for academic librarians. These should be addressed as expansions of AI-literacy content. In particular, an important issue to discuss is the safe use of generative AI in academic writing. Several studies explore the outcome of generative AI applied to different parts of manuscript preparation - abstract, summary, actual content, etc. For instance, Torp used generative AI for both final exams and final project of his class at George Washington University. He found that generative AI did well on factual answers, but fail on scholarly writing (Thorp, 2023). In similar manner, Blanco-Gonzalez (2023) studied the role of ChatGPT in scientific writing and outlined its advantages and disadvantages in context of drug discovery research (Blanco-Gonzalez et al, 2023). The team reported that even generative AI can help in text generation and in organization of the information, it cannot be used to generate a new content since the generated facts and references "were clearly incorrect". In a similar manner Gao tested the ability of ChatGPT to generate new abstracts based on high-impact journal abstract samples and found that AI-generated abstracts score high on AI output detector programs, but low on plagiarism detectors (Gao et al, 2022). In all cases the generative AI potential to help content creators was noted in terms of quick text generation, organizing of data, and generation of hints of ideas. At the same time, the negative effects including plagiarism were also noted. Therefore, academic librarians should teach the patrons that there is no universal recipe for "safe use" of generative AI. The librarians must convey to public the understanding that generative AI's fitness to academic writing is determined primarily by the ethics considerations i.e. by the level of human-AI complementarity and thus depends on the ability of users to understand generative AI's ethical limitations and dangers and to navigate wisely through the creative process.

Adaptation, Transformation and Revival – how AI Changed Academic Librarians

The speed of technological innovations is fueled by the advances in data driven and algorithm defined technologies. For instance, the first publicly accessible generative AI implementation ChatGPT gained one million users from November 2022 to March 2023 and currently has more than 180 million users worldwide. Academic libraries are users of AI (generative AI and predictive AI), but only 65% of librarians' duties are susceptible for direct automation (Cox, 2023). Consequently, the main changes in academic librarianship are dictated by the application of different AI technologies to the creative component of librarians' work, namely to the knowledge discovery process. On a professional level, the effect of adopting algorithms and AI has the appearance of a "versatile" librarian - a professional whose qualifications as librarian are merged with skills from other professions. Thus, the modern academic librarian is a convolution of librarian, educator, researcher, data curator, archivist, and recently even prompt manager. In terms of job duties, the first and foremost effect of AI is the extension of the role of librarians as educators because the traditional Information Literacy (IL) is enriched and expanded with new AI literacy (AIL) perspective. Second, the knowledge discovery in the age of algorithms is AI driven, which requires familiarity with various AI-enabled products in order to manage library collections that can be interfaced to AI-driven system.

In academia librarians may be expected to evaluate or recommend different AI applications. The latter requires that librarians to have excellent communication skills and the ability to convey their message to IT departments, to understand the potential of particular AI product, along with its limitations and risks. Librarians have to expand their role as educators and add an AI component to IL. They have to understand and educate patrons about bias, plagiarism, transparency and ethical issues caused by AI. The required knowledge and skills include a good grip of AI concepts and technologies plus understanding of various AI types used in one or other application. In addition, librarians need to have skills to manage and customize the AI application when needed. That role tangents to the role of prompt engineer. Indeed, librarians do not have direct access to the code and cannot correct hidden flaws or bias in the algorithm itself, but hey can participate in the development of optimal prompts for generative AI systems and provide valuable feedback about accuracy and bias of given AI application. More importantly prompt skills are vital for optimal use of generative AI so librarians might include such topic in their AI literacy teaching. Lund even makes a case for a new librarian role - prompt engineering librarian (Lund, 2023). In terms of day-to-day activities librarians may use chatbots such as ChatGPT as an alternative to search engines. However, librarians have to inform their patrons about the limitations and bias of such chatbots emphasize on critical thinking and evaluation of the quality of the answers provided by ChatGPT (Cox, 2023).

CONCLUSION

AI has a long presence in scholarly communications and academic research in its capacity of AI-driven tools for all aspects of research and dissemination of results. AI tools followed the development trajectory of AI technology and application of one or other model (generative or predictive) is determined by the specific task, type of data, availability, structure and organization of data and other factors. The common AI technologies for both generative and predictive AI are natural language processing and machine learning. For instance, Elsevier and other publishers tend to improve and tweak the existing search engines by adding natural language processing, semantic analysis, and extended machine learning algorithms to handle their extensive databases. On the other hand, chatbots based on large language models such as ChatGPT and some others have undertaken scientific writing, information retrieval, generating abstracts, suggesting topics, and research questions. Indeed, generative AI has tremendous potential to revolutionize scholarly communications and expand research because it can generate text, correct errors, etc., so it was assumed – an unsubstantiated assumption – that generative AI is ready to write and publish research papers without human intervention. As several studies demonstrate, chatbots, while attractive, are not ready to publish articles since AI-generated text is a form of plagiarism, almost always presenting permutations of materials from its training base – and most importantly, generative AI can introduce various biases, is non-transparent and can ignite problems with privacy and copyright.

From the perspective of academic librarians, the AI expansion may cause loss of some jobs associated with routine activities, but it can also transform the cognitive and creative part of librarianship. In particular, AI in academic research and scholarly communications dictates that librarians' role grows into a versatile librarian – the professional whose strong library background is enriched with skills and principal knowledge from other professions. In the core of the transformation is AI literacy and prompt-engineering literacy taught by librarians as shareholders of SC. The AI-literacy itself is a complex phenomenon which has both social and technical dimensions. It aims to develop AI centric cognitive adoption in academic communities.

REFERENCES

Ahaley, S. S., Pandey, A., Juneja, S. K., Gupta, T. S., & Vijayakumar, S. (2023). ChatGPT in medical writing: A game-changer or a gimmick? *Perspectives in Clinical Research*, ●●●, 10–4103. DOI: 10.4103/picr.picr_167_23

Awosanya, O. D., Harris, A., Creecy, A., Qiao, X., Toepp, A. J., McCune, T., Kacena, M. A., & Ozanne, M. V. (2024). The utility of AI in writing a scientific review article on the impacts of COVID-19 on musculoskeletal health. *Current Osteoporosis Reports*. Advance online publication. DOI: 10.1007/s11914-023-00855-x PMID: 38216806

Bhattacharjee, A., & Liu, H. (2024). Fighting fire with fire: Can ChatGPT detect AI-generated text? *SIGKDD Explorations*, 25(2), 14–21. DOI: 10.1145/3655103.3655106

Blanco-Gonzalez, A., Cabezon, A., Seco-Gonzalez, A., Conde-Torres, D., Antelo-Riveiro, P., Pineiro, A., & Garcia-Fandino, R. (2023). The role of AI in drug discovery: Challenges, opportunities, and strategies. *Pharmaceuticals (Basel, Switzerland)*, 16(6), 891. DOI: 10.3390/ph16060891 PMID: 37375838

Borji, A. (2023). A categorical archive of ChatGPT failures. *arXiv preprint arXiv:2302.03494*. DOI: 10.21203/rs.3.rs-2895792/v1

Buholayka, M., Zouabi, R., & Tadinada, A. (2023). The readiness of ChatGPT to write scientific case reports independently: A comparative evaluation between human and artificial intelligence. *Cureus*, 15(5). PMID: 37378091

Cassidy, C. (2023). Australian universities to return to 'pen and paper' exams after students caught using AI to write essays. *The Guardian, 10.*

Celik, I. (2023). Exploring the determinants of artificial intelligence (AI) literacy: Digital divide, computational thinking, cognitive absorption. *Telematics and Informatics*, 83, 102026. DOI: 10.1016/j.tele.2023.102026

Chakraborty, S., Bedi, A. S., Zhu, S., An, B., Manocha, D., & Huang, F. (2023). On the possibilities of AI-generated text detection. *arXiv preprint arXiv:2304.04736.*

Chen, Q., Allot, A., & Lu, Z. (2021). LitCovid: An open database of COVID-19 literature. *Nucleic Acids Research*, 49(D1), D1534–D1540. DOI: 10.1093/nar/gkaa952 PMID: 33166392

Cheng, K., & Wu, H. (2024). Policy framework for the utilization of generative AI. *Critical Care*, 28(1), 128. DOI: 10.1186/s13054-024-04917-z PMID: 38637898

Chung, C., & Huang, Y. (2022). The innovation of the AI and Big Data Mail Processing System. *Journal of Research & Method in Education*, 12(1), 1–8. DOI: 10.31031/COJEC.2022.02.000536

Communication Committee, T. A. C. R. L. S.ACRL Scholarly Communication Committee. (2003). SCHOLARLY COMMUNICATION: Principles and strategies for the reform of scholarly communication: Issues related to the formal system of scholarly communication. *College & Research Libraries News*, 64(8), 526–547. DOI: 10.5860/crln.64.8.526

Cotton, D. R., Cotton, P. A., & Shipway, J. R. (2024). Chatting and Cheating: Ensuring academic integrity in the era of ChatGPT. *Innovations in Education and Teaching International*, 61(2), 228–239. DOI: 10.1080/14703297.2023.2190148

Cox, A. (2023). How artificial intelligence might change academic library work: Applying the competencies literature and the theory of the professions. *Journal of the Association for Information Science and Technology*, 74(3), 367–380. DOI: 10.1002/asi.24635

Cox, C., & Tzoc, E. (2023). ChatGPT: Implications for academic libraries. *College & Research Libraries News*, 84(3), 99. DOI: 10.5860/crln.84.3.99

Davenport, T. H., & Ronanki, R. (2018). Artificial intelligence for the real world. *Harvard Business Review*, 96(1), 108–116.

Dobrev, D. (2018). The IQ of artificial intelligence. *arXiv preprint arXiv:1806.04915*.

Doyal, A. S., Sender, D., Nanda, M., & Serrano, R. A. (2023). ChatGPT and artificial intelligence in medical writing: Concerns and ethical considerations. *Cureus*, 15(8). PMID: 37692694

Ecarnot, F., Seronde, M. F., Chopard, R., Schiele, F., & Meneveau, N. J. E. G. M. (2015). Writing a scientific article: A step-by-step guide for beginners. *European Geriatric Medicine*, 6(6), 573–579. DOI: 10.1016/j.eurger.2015.08.005

Fitria, T. N. (2021). Grammarly as AI-powered English writing assistant: Students' alternative for writing English. *Metathesis: Journal of English Language, Literature, and Teaching*, 5(1), 65–78. DOI: 10.31002/metathesis.v5i1.3519

Flanagin, A., Kendall-Taylor, J., & Bibbins-Domingo, K. (2023). Guidance for authors, peer reviewers, and editors on use of AI, language models, and chatbots. *Journal of the American Medical Association*, 330(8), 702. DOI: 10.1001/jama.2023.12500 PMID: 37498593

Fricke, S. (2018). Semantic Scholar. *Journal of the Medical Library Association: JMLA*, 106(1), 145. DOI: 10.5195/jmla.2018.280

Gabriel, A. (2019). Artificial intelligence in scholarly communications: An elsevier case study. *Information Services & Use*, 39(4), 319–333. DOI: 10.3233/ISU-190063

Gao, C. A., Howard, F. M., Markov, N. S., Dyer, E. C., Ramesh, S., Luo, Y., & Pearson, A. T. (2022). Comparing scientific abstracts generated by ChatGPT to original abstracts using an artificial intelligence output detector, plagiarism detector, and blinded human reviewers. BioRxiv, *2022-12* DOI: 10.1101/2022.12.23.521610

Getahun, H. (2022). After an AI Bot Wrote a Scientific Paper on Itself, the Researcher behind the Experiment Says She Hopes She Didn't Open a "Pandora's Box". *Business Insider Nederland, 9.*

Ghosal, T., Verma, R., Ekbal, A., Saha, S., & Bhattacharyya, P. (2018). An AI aid to the editors. Exploring the possibility of an AI assisted article classification system. *arXiv preprint arXiv:1802.01403.*

Haman, M., & Školník, M. (2023). Using ChatGPT to conduct a literature review. *Accountability in Research*, •••, 1–3. DOI: 10.1080/08989621.2023.2185514 PMID: 36879536

Harrison, H., Griffin, S. J., Kuhn, I., & Usher-Smith, J. A. (2020). Software tools to support title and abstract screening for systematic reviews in healthcare: An evaluation. *BMC Medical Research Methodology*, 20(1), 1–12. DOI: 10.1186/s12874-020-0897-3 PMID: 31931747

Hosseini, M., & Horbach, S. P. J. M. (2023). Fighting reviewer fatigue or amplifying bias? considerations and recommendations for use of ChatGPT and other large language models in scholarly peer review. *Research Integrity and Peer Review*, 8(1), 4. DOI: 10.1186/s41073-023-00133-5 PMID: 37198671

Huang, J., & Tan, M. (2023). The role of ChatGPT in scientific communication: Writing better scientific review articles. *American Journal of Cancer Research*, 13(4), 1148. PMID: 37168339

Jarrah, A. M., Wardat, Y., & Fidalgo, P. (2023). Using ChatGPT in academic writing is (not) a form of plagiarism: What does the literature say. *Online Journal of Communication and Media Technologies*, 13(4), e202346. DOI: 10.30935/ojcmt/13572

Kacena, M. A., Plotkin, L. I., & Fehrenbacher, J. C. (2024). The use of artificial intelligence in writing scientific review articles. *Current Osteoporosis Reports*, 22(1), 1–7. DOI: 10.1007/s11914-023-00852-0 PMID: 38227177

Khalifa, A. A., & Ibrahim, M. A. (2024). Artificial intelligence (AI) and ChatGPT involvement in scientific and medical writing, a new concern for researchers. A scoping review. *Arab Gulf Journal of Scientific Research*. Advance online publication. DOI: 10.1108/AGJSR-09-2023-0423

Kirchenbauer, J., Geiping, J., Wen, Y., Katz, J., Miers, I., & Goldstein, T. (2023, July). A watermark for large language models. In *International Conference on Machine Learning(pp.* 17061-17084*). PMLR.*

Kocoń, J., Cichecki, I., Kaszyca, O., Kochanek, M., Szydło, D., Baran, J., Bielaniewicz, J., Gruza, M., Janz, A., Kanclerz, K., Kocoń, A., Koptyra, B., Mieleszczenko-Kowszewicz, W., Miłkowski, P., Oleksy, M., Piasecki, M., Radliński, Ł., Wojtasik, K., Woźniak, S., & Kazienko, P. (2023). ChatGPT: Jack of all trades, master of none. *Information Fusion*, 99, 101861. DOI: 10.1016/j.inffus.2023.101861

Krivosheev, E., Casati, F., & Benatallah, B. (2018). Crowd-based multi-predicate screening of papers in literature reviews. In *Proceedings of the 2018 World Wide Web Conference, pp.* 55-64. *2018.* DOI: 10.1145/3178876.3186036

Liechti, R., George, N., Götz, L., El-Gebali, S., Chasapi, A., Crespo, I., Xenarios, I., & Lemberger, T. (2017). SourceData: A semantic platform for curating and searching figures. *Nature Methods*, 14(11), 1021–1022. DOI: 10.1038/nmeth.4471 PMID: 29088127

Lo, C. K. (2023). What is the impact of ChatGPT on education? A rapid review of the literature. *Education Sciences*, 13(4), 410. DOI: 10.3390/educsci13040410

Long, D., & Magerko, B. (2020, April). What is AI literacy? Competencies and design considerations. In *Proceedings of the 2020 CHI Conference on Human Factors in Computing Systems(pp.* 1-16*).* DOI: 10.1145/3313831.3376727

Lozić, E., & Štular, B. (2023). Fluent but not factual: A comparative analysis of ChatGPT and other AI chatbots' proficiency and originality in scientific writing for humanities. *Future Internet*, 15(10), 336. DOI: 10.3390/fi15100336

Luitse, D., & Denkena, W. (2021). The great transformer: Examining the role of large language models in the political economy of AI. *Big Data & Society*, 8(2), 20539517211047734. DOI: 10.1177/20539517211047734

Lund, B. (2023). The prompt engineering librarian. *Library Hi Tech News*, 40(8), 6–8. DOI: 10.1108/LHTN-10-2023-0189

Lund, B. D., Wang, T., Mannuru, N. R., Nie, B., Shimray, S., & Wang, Z. (2023). ChatGPT and a new academic reality: Artificial Intelligence-written research papers and the ethics of the large language models in scholarly publishing. *Journal of the Association for Information Science and Technology*, 74(5), 570–581. DOI: 10.1002/asi.24750

Mehta, V., Mathur, A., Anjali, A. K., & Fiorillo, L. (2024). A. K. Anjali, and Luca Fiorillo. The application of ChatGPT in the peer-reviewing process. *Oral Oncology Reports*, 9, 100227. DOI: 10.1016/j.oor.2024.100227

Mindner, L., Schlippe, T., & Schaaff, K. (2023, June). Classification of human-and ai-generated texts: Investigating features for chatgpt. In *International Conference on Artificial Intelligence in Education Technology(pp.152-170).* Singapore: Springer Nature Singapore. DOI: 10.1007/978-981-99-7947-9_12

Mitrovic, S., Andreoletti, D., & Ayoub, O. (2023). ChatGPT or human? detect and explain. *Explaining Decisions of Machine Learning Model for detecting short ChatGPT Generated Text.*

Ng, D. T. K., Leung, J. K. L., Chu, S. K. W., & Qiao, M. S. (2021). Conceptualizing AI literacy: An exploratory review. *Computers and Education: Artificial Intelligence*, 2, 100041.

Ntoutsi, E., Fafalios, P., Gadiraju, U., Iosifidis, V., Nejdl, W., Vidal, M. E., Ruggieri, S., Turini, F., Papadopoulos, S., Krasanakis, E., Kompatsiaris, I., Kinder-Kurlanda, K., Wagner, C., Karimi, F., Fernandez, M., Alani, H., Berendt, B., Kruegel, T., Heinze, C., & Staab, S. (2020). Bias in data-driven artificial intelligence systems—An introductory survey. *Wiley Interdisciplinary Reviews. Data Mining and Knowledge Discovery*, 10(3), e1356. DOI: 10.1002/widm.1356

Rice, S., Crouse, S. R., Winter, S. R., & Rice, C. (2024). The advantages and limitations of using ChatGPT to enhance technological research. *Technology in Society*, 76, 102426. DOI: 10.1016/j.techsoc.2023.102426

Ridley, M., & Pawlick-Potts, D. (2021). Algorithmic literacy and the role for libraries. *Information Technology and Libraries*, 40(2). Advance online publication. DOI: 10.6017/ital.v40i2.12963

Russell, S. J., & Norvig, P. (2016). *Artificial intelligence: a modern approach.* Pearson.

Saad, A., Jenko, N., Ariyaratne, S., Birch, N., Iyengar, K. P., Davies, A. M., Vaishya, R., & Botchu, R. (2024). Exploring the potential of ChatGPT in the peer review process: An observational study. *Diabetes & Metabolic Syndrome*, 18(2), 102946. DOI: 10.1016/j.dsx.2024.102946 PMID: 38330745

Sankar Sadasivan, V., Kumar, A., Balasubramanian, S., Wang, W., & Feizi, S. (2023). Can AI-Generated Text be Reliably Detected? *arXiv e-prints, arXiv-2303*.

Shaikh, S. A. (2020). Use of AI for Manuscript Writing–A Study Based on Patent Literature. *Allana Management Journal of Research, Pune*, 10, 1–8.

Stokel-Walker, C. (2023). ChatGPT listed as author on research papers: Many scientists disapprove. *Nature*, 613(7945), 620–621. DOI: 10.1038/d41586-023-00107-z PMID: 36653617

Thorp, H. H. (2023). ChatGPT is fun, but not an author. *Science*, 379(6630), 313–313. DOI: 10.1126/science.adg7879 PMID: 36701446

Transformer, G. G. P., Thunström, A. O., & Steingrimsson, S. (2022). Can GPT-3 write an academic paper on itself, with minimal human input? *2022. hal-03701250*

Wagner, G., Lukyanenko, R., & Paré, G. (2022). Artificial intelligence and the conduct of literature reviews. *Journal of Information Technology*, 37(2), 209–226. DOI: 10.1177/02683962211048201

Wang, B., Rau, P. L. P., & Yuan, T. (2023). Measuring user competence in using artificial intelligence: Validity and reliability of artificial intelligence literacy scale. *Behaviour & Information Technology*, 42(9), 1324–1337. DOI: 10.1080/0144929X.2022.2072768

Wardat, Y., Tashtoush, M. A., AlAli, R., & Jarrah, A. M. (2023). ChatGPT: A revolutionary tool for teaching and learning mathematics. *Eurasia Journal of Mathematics, Science and Technology Education*, 19(7), em2286. DOI: 10.29333/ejmste/13272

Wu, J., Kim, K., & Giles, C. L. (2019, May). CiteSeerX: 20 years of service to scholarly big data. In *Proceedings of the Conference on Artificial Intelligence for Data Discovery and Reuse* (pp. 1-4). DOI: 10.1145/3359115.3359119

Yang, L., Driscol, J., Sarigai, S., Wu, Q., Chen, H., & Lippitt, C. D. (2022). Google Earth Engine and artificial intelligence (AI): A comprehensive review. *Remote Sensing (Basel)*, 14(14), 3253. DOI: 10.3390/rs14143253

Zielinski, C.. (2023). *(May 2023) Chatbots, generative AI, and scholarly manuscripts WAME recommendations on chatbots and generative artificial intelligence in relation to scholarly publications*. WAME. DOI: 10.32412/pjohns.v38i1.2135

Zielinski, C., Winker, M., Aggarwal, R., Ferris, L., Heinemann, M., Lapeña, J. F., & Citrome, L. (2023). Chatbots, ChatGPT, and scholarly manuscripts-WAME recommendations on ChatGPT and chatbots in relation to scholarly publications. *Afro-Egyptian Journal of Infectious and Endemic Diseases*, 13(1), 75–79.

KEY TERMS AND DEFINITIONS

Artificial Intelligence: Artificial intelligence (AI) is defined as intelligent performance expressed by artificial body. Typically, AI is associated with some brainy behavior demonstrated by a "system", which is usually a computer program.

Generative AI: A set of Machine Learning models that can generate new data, i.e., the output are objects that look like the ones on which model is trained; ChatGPT is the most popular instance. The technology originated in 1960 chatbots.

Machine Learning: Machine Learning (ML) allows for the programming of the computers by using data instead of explicit instructions. ML is programming by examples - the computer learns to perform a task by examples of that task. Machine learning is a computer algorithm(s) which 'learn' about specific task through statistical modelling of (typically large amounts of) data.

Natural Language Processing: is part of AI and denotes the set of computational methods aimed at analyzing and processing the human (natural) language.

Artificial Intelligence System: A program running on a computer which infers from the input how to generate predictions, content, recommendations or discussions. Systems vary in their level of autonomy.

Artificial Intelligence in Libraries: From libraries' perspective AI is a technological implementation of the synergy between computing and psychology which can be used to increase librarians' productivity by providing techniques to conduct tasks quicker and in better way; to improve quality of library services; to enhance the quality of information yields and to advance the communication with patrons.

AI Literacy: AI literacy cannot be precisely defined and should be explained as a broad convolution of three different quantities: knowledge about AI principles, ability to use AI in tools, services and applications, and ability to critically evaluate AI output.

Chapter 3
Effect of Exploring Artificial Intelligence in Academic Libraries on Academic Research:
An Overview

Emmanuel Chidiadi Onwubiko
https://orcid.org/0000-0001-9386-4972
Alex Ekwueme Federal University, Nigeria

ABSTRACT

In this millennium, the world is exploring another product of Information and Communication Technology known as artificial intelligence (AI). Artificial Intelligence which is the simulation of human intelligence processes by machines, especially computer systems has find itself almost in every facet of human activities . In the academic world, the academic libraries more so in developed countries have come to explore this phenomenal technology and some academic researchers have cashed into it seeing as a short cut to academic research while some perceived it as a monster that may consume the worth of academic research. This chapter therefore focuses on the effect of exploring AI in academic libraries on academic research

INTRODUCTION

The emergence of information and communication technologies (ICTs) have brought an undeniable transformation in library operations and the ways services are provided to users and other stakeholders and the inclusion of ICT facilities in

DOI: 10.4018/979-8-3693-3053-1.ch003

the management of the library has tremendous positive effect in the management of the library (Onwubiko, 2021). The underlying factor is that, it is no longer in the front burner, that the emergence of information and communication technology (ICT) spearheaded by the information super highway the internet did transformed the globe as their activities delved into every facet of the human life. In this millennium, the world is exploring another product of Information and Communication Technology known as artificial intelligence (AI). The obvious is that in past two decades, one may say that the greatest technological invention powered by computer is artificial intelligence (AI). Artificial Intelligence which is the simulation of human intelligence processes by machines, especially computer systems (Laskowski & Tucci, 2024) has taken hold of almost every aspect of human activities even in some cases, doing better what the human cannot do. The belief is that AI has the potential to change how we live, work and play. It has been effectively used in business to automate tasks done by humans, including customer service work, lead generation, fraud detection and quality control. In a number of areas, AI can perform tasks much better than humans. Particularly when it comes to repetitive, detail-oriented tasks, such as analyzing large numbers of legal documents to ensure relevant fields are filled in properly AI tools often complete jobs quickly and with relatively few errors (TechTarget, 2024).

Libraries especially, academic libraries are not left out in the phenomenal transformation. The belief across academic librarians and academic information managers which may not be far from the truth is that the rapid advancements in AI and robotics have brought about transformative changes across various industries and academic libraries should not be in the exception. Academic Libraries serve as information hubs fostering learning, research and community engagement. Integrating AI and robotics into library services therefore has the potential to enhancing user experience and expanding access to information in innovative ways (TechTarget, 2024). The bottom line is that academic libraries which include colleges and university libraries are specifically established to support the tripartite functions of learning, teaching and research in their various parent institutions. One known fact is that a nation cannot develop in isolation of her human resources. Tertiary institutions which by definition are institutions for the advancement and dissemination of knowledge are important agents in the development of human resources of any nation which is achieved through research. This major role in national development, writes Onwubiko (2020), is achieved through their programmes of teaching, learning and research totally backed up by the academic libraries which serve as the information hub and pivot on which all academic activities revolve especially academic researches with which the worth of every institution of higher learning is scaled. As explained by Rosowsky (2022), research on timely and important topics attracts attention, which in turn leads to greater institutional visibility and reputation. As an academic institution becomes known for its research in certain fields, they become magnets for students, faculty, grants, media coverage and even philanthropy. Research so to speak, develops and broadens the mind of the researcher, especially in higher degrees, and the researcher in turn makes available his discovery or new knowledge. Academic research According to Hornsby (2015) is a careful study of subject especially, in order to discover new facts or information about the subject. In this regard, the ultimate aim of any research is to increase knowledge of the subject and to use the results of the research to improve on the existing situation or to seek solutions to problems. It is against this backdrop that Nworgu (2015) posits that research is man's attempt to probe into the unknown aspect of the environment with a view to finding answers to perplexing and unanswered questions. Research results therefore, contribute to the body of existing knowledge and enable researchers to discover new ideas.

Academic libraries to this end, serve as veritable tool for researchers to carry out meaningful academic researches that can stand the test of time in the academia and also prove the worth of the researcher as well as are specifically providing relevant and up to date information to enhancing faculty members researches in an era of .publish or you perish. On the other hand, with the invention of Artificial intelligence and the inclusion in academic libraries as one the means of enhancing services, its function in academic research has obtained relevant attention in recent years. This transformative technology, powered by machine learning algorithms and data analytics, is completely changing the research landscape. As with the aid of AI, researchers can process vast amounts of data, extract meaningful insights, and automate repetitive tasks (Abbadia, 2023). The assertion is that, AI has the potential to fasten the pace of scientific discovery and enhance the quality of research outcomes In fact, AI has brought about notable changes to academia, revolutionizing the way research is conducted, knowledge is generated, and education is delivered.

The integration of AI technologies in academia has also the potential to streamline processes, enhance research outcomes and foster innovation. Against the true state and nature of academic research, Artificial Intelligence (AI) has the potential to revolutionize academic research by automating repetitive tasks, analyzing large data sets, and even generating hypotheses. Machine learning algorithms can sift through voluminous literature, highlight gaps in existing research, and suggest new avenues for inquiry (LinkedIn, 2024). As noted by Bakare-Fatungase, Adejumo and Idowu-Davies (2024) the significant place of AI in contemporary research discourse cannot be neglected as research has shown it to be pushing the frontiers of research, remodeling of methodologies, re-modification of existing processes, raises researchers engagement and accomplishment creating room for a revolutionized academic journey. Britannica (2024) also affirm to the above assertion as it also reveals that Artificial Intelligence (AI) has a significant shift in the technological environment in recent years. Artificial intelligence (AI), which is commonly defined as a machine's capacity to mimic intelligent human behavior, has grown from a science fiction idea to a real, widespread force that affects many facets of our everyday life.

The above scenario no doubt makes a researcher a passerby and not a participant. A critical analysis therefore of the potentials of AI, if left unchecked, will play down the true purpose of academic research and academic researchers may no longer see the actual values of academic libraries. Furtherance, if the effect of the use of AI in academic research is not highlighted regardless of its accrued benefits; it would pose as a danger spice to the true essence of academic research and the optimal utilization of academic libraries for research.

It is against this backdrop, that this chapter is set to discuss effect of exploring AI in academic libraries on academic research as an overview. The chapter will look at academic libraries, AI, and academic research as concepts, the impact of AI on academic research, application of AI in academic research, effect of exploring AI in academic libraries on academic research and ethical challenges of AI driven academic research from which conclusion and recommendations will be drawn.

Artificial Intelligence (AI): What is it?

Artificial intelligence is assumed to be the brain in machine format but has been professionally defines as the simulation of human intelligence in machine that are programmed to think like humans and mimic their actions. It is powered by machine learning which is a sub-set of the AI that provides systems the ability to automatically learn and improve from experience without being explicitly programmed as well as the algorithm – a set of rules or instructions which guide and help the AI system to learn from data (Abbadia, 2023). Britannica (2024) refers to it as a variety of tools and systems intended to provide robots the ability to carry out operations that normally call for human intelligence covering the ability to solve problems, pick up knowledge from experience, comprehend spoken language, and even visualize as humans. Technological developments in machine learning, neural networks, and computing power have propelled the rise of AI, bringing in a world of previously unimaginable possibilities.

AI is also according to Olayinka (2023) the ability of a digital computer or computer-controlled robot to execute tasks often associated with intelligent beings. The phrase is widely given to the endeavor of producing systems with human-like cognitive processes, such as the ability to reason, discover meaning, generalize, or learn from past experience. Since the development of the digital computer in the 1940s, it has been proved that computers can be taught to perform extremely complex jobs with great proficiency, such as discovering proofs for mathematical theorems or playing chess. AI research has mostly focused on the following aspects of intelligence: learning, reasoning, problem solving, to discuss a few.

The Learning Stage: The learning stage is the first stage in the growth process of artificial intelligence, just as it is with humans. There are several types of artificial intelligence learning. The most basic method is trial and error. In the context of artificial intelligence development, the learning process entails memorizing of particular things such as different issue solutions, vocabulary, and foreign languages, among others. Through this learning process, artificial intelligence algorithms can keep track of any activities or moves that resulted in favorable outcomes, allowing the program to harness this knowledge within its data if similar situations emerge in the future.

Reasoning Stage: The second fundamental component of artificial intelligence is reasoning. While the concept of mental thinking has mainly been limited to the human mind for much of recorded history, much of the development of artificial intelligence is based on software programs that can draw conclusions and inferences from a situation without the need for human intervention. Furthermore, these inferences are classified into two types: inductive and deductive reasoning. The most significant difference between these forms of reasoning is that in the deductive case the truth of the premises guarantees the truth of the conclusion, whereas in the inductive case the truth of the premise lends support to the conclusion without giving absolute assurance. It has been quite successful to train computers to make conclusions, particularly deductive inferences. True reasoning includes more than just making assumptions; it entails making assumptions that are pertinent to finding a solution for the specific problem or circumstance.

Problem Solving: The third major component that makes up the development of artificial intelligence programs and systems is problem-solving. Problem solving, particularly in artificial intelligence, can be defined as a methodical search through a set of feasible actions to achieve a stated goal or solution. Problem-solving techniques are classified as either special purpose or general purpose. A special-purpose method is tailored to a specific problem and frequently takes advantage of highly unique elements of the setting in which the problem is embedded. A general-purpose approach, on the other hand, is applicable to a wide range of problems.

As noted, AI is therefore a major advancement in the field of information and communication technology especially in terms of its capacity to produce fresh, original information and depends on pre-established rules as well as uses sophisticated algorithms to produce information materials on its own (Davenport & Mittal, 2022) This involves explains Lawton, (2023) creating realistic text and graphics that can imitate the creative processes of humans. Prominently in the areas of linguistic models such as GPT-3 (Generative Pre-trained Transformer 3) and picture generators like DALL-E, which have the ability to generate extraordinarily creative and cohesive outputs Lawton added.

Academic Research

The maxim is; 'publish or you perish' which implies that your relevance as an academia in any university in Nigeria is based on the number of publications credited to you. Furthermore, the ranking of any university nationally, intercontinental and globally depends on the research contributions made by her academic staff. This scenario shows the importance attached to academic by both the academics and university management and by implications the global nations as results from academic researches contribute a lot in national and global development.

Generally, research is the systematic investigation into and study of materials and sources in order to establish facts and reach new conclusions. It is therefore a creative and systematic work undertaken to increase the stock of knowledge. It involves the collection, organization, and analysis of evidence to increase understanding of a topic, characterized by a particular attentiveness to controlling sources of bias and error (Fleetwood.2023) According to the American sociologist Babbie (1998), research is a systematic inquiry to describe, explain, predict, and control the observed phenomenon. It involves inductive and deductive methods.

As explained by Sheridan library (2023), academic research involves a thorough investigation into what is known about a given topic in which in most cases, one will be required to examine and analyze scholarly sources when completing a particular research. Scholarly sources which an academic researcher may obtain from the academic library will assist him or her to add depth to his or her understanding; strengthen the argument and reduce bias and misconceptions.

Academic Library

As libraries situated within tertiary institutions, academic libraries are by obligation to provide effective information services that would enhance teaching, learning, and research within the university community. Research plays an important role in universities and other higher institutions of learning. Though teaching and learning are important aspects of the tertiary education system, more emphasis is on research. Research, in particular, is crucial to the survival of tertiary institutions being the fundamental process of knowledge acquisition. For members of faculty to impart knowledge, they must engage in research to deepen their understanding of concepts, and for students to learn, there is also the need to conduct research, with the view of seeking and identifying solutions to problems. Research is essential within the academic environment as it remains the only way to solve the problems in education and society

The academic libraries to this end are at the forefront in the provision of relevant information resource materials to the academic community which comprises of the students, lecturers, staff, researchers and the entire personnel in the academic environment, in other to support teaching, learning and research needs. Academic libraries therefore play the role of collaborators when they provide services such as research data management, open scholarships, bibliometric and systematic reviews to their research work.

The Use of AI in Academic Research

Artificial intelligence (AI) has found numerous applications in academic research across various disciplines that the impact has drawn significant attention in recent years. This transformative technology, powered by machine learning algorithms and data analytics, is revolutionizing the academic research landscape along the following:

By enabling researchers to process vast amounts of data, extract meaningful insights, and automate repetitive tasks, AI has the potential to accelerate the pace of scientific discovery and enhance the quality of research outcomes. It pertinent to know that AI algorithms extract valuable insights from large datasets, revolutionizing research across disciplines;

By enhancing data analysis and pattern recognition as AI algorithms can analyze large datasets and identify patterns, correlations, and trends that may not be easily recognizable by humans alone. This is particularly useful in fields such as genomics, climate science, and social sciences;

By natural language processing (NLP) as this NLP techniques enable computers to understand and generate human language. In fact, researchers utilize NLP to analyze large volume of textual data, extract information, summarize documents, and detect sentiment. It has applications in fields like literature, linguistics, and social sciences;

Through the use of Computer vision. The AI-based computer vision systems can process and interpret visual data, such as images and videos. The importance is that researchers utilize computer vision to analyze medical images, satellite imagery, and surveillance footage, among others. It has applications in fields like biology, astronomy, and environmental sciences;

The usage of AI in academic research has also been notable in drug discovery and development as AI is being used to accelerate the process of drug discovery by predicting the properties and interactions of potential drug compounds.

Machine learning models can analyze vast amounts of chemical and biological data to identify potential drug targets and design novel molecules;

Another area is in robotics and automation in that AI-powered robots and automated systems are increasingly being used in academic research to perform tasks such as lab experiments, data collection, and sample processing. These robots can work 24/7, reducing human error and increasing efficiency in research workflows;

AI also has these Recommendation systems in which AI algorithms can provide personalized recommendations based on user preferences and behaviors. In academia, these systems can suggest relevant research papers, conferences, or collaborations based on a researcher's interests and previous work;

As a transformative technology, powered by machine learning algorithms and data analytics, it is fashioned in a way that it can be used for simulation and modeling. AI techniques, such as machine learning and neural networks, can be used to create complex models and simulations. Researchers can use these models to study and predict phenomena in fields like physics, economics, and social sciences;

It is also being used for knowledge discovery and synthesis. As regards to this, AI can assist researchers in discovering and synthesizing information from vast amounts of existing research papers, patents, and other academic sources and with this, can help identify research gaps, find relevant literature, and generate new insights;

AI can also be used in academic research by researchers to enhance their scientific discovery. This made possible as AI can assists researchers in hypothesis generation, experiment design, and data analysis, accelerating the research process;

Furthermore, AI-enabled automation streamlines research workflows, automating tasks like data collection and analysis, improving efficiency (Abbadia, 2023).

Exploring AI in Academic Libraries: Impact on academic research

Stating the obvious, the emergence AI has brought about remarkable transformation to academic world as it has gone ahead revolutionizing the way research is conducted, knowledge is generated, and education is delivered. The inclusion of AI technologies in academia has the propensity to streamlining processes, enhancing research outcomes, and fostering innovation. Looking at the various ways AI is impacting academic research holistically; it pertinent to state AI has tremendously brought about transformation in academic research and some of these transformations write Abbadia (2023) are as follows:

In the first instance, AI has impacted on the way data is being analyzed. As a result of the emergence of AI researchers now leverage AI algorithms to analyze vast amounts of data quickly and efficiently. The use of this AI tool enables researchers to identify patterns, correlations, and trends that may not be easily discernible through traditional methods.

Furthermore, AI is transforming the research process itself. As it can assist researchers in literature review and knowledge synthesis by automatically scanning and extracting relevant information from a wide range of scientific papers. This not only saves time but also helps researchers stay up-to-date with the latest advancements in their field.

AI also has the potential to augment human capabilities in academia. It can automate repetitive tasks, freeing up researchers' time to focus on higher-level cognitive activities. This includes automating data collection, analysis, and even manuscript writing. By streamlining these processes, researchers can devote more time to critical thinking, hypothesis generation, and exploring new research avenues.

Challenges in AI-driven Academic research

While AI-driven academic research offers significant benefits, in exploring AI in academic libraries there are also several challenges and ethical considerations that researchers need to address. Here are some of the key challenges and ethical considerations associated with AI in academic research:

Data bias and fairness: AI systems are trained on data, and if the training data is biased or reflects societal prejudices, the AI models can perpetuate those biases. Researchers need to carefully curate and preprocess data to ensure fairness and mitigate bias in AI models (Greenstein, 2022).

Privacy and data protection: AI research often involves handling large amounts of data, including personal and sensitive information. Researchers must ensure that data collection, storage, and analysis adhere to relevant privacy regulations and obtain informed consent from participants (Gupta, 2018)

Transparency and interpretability: Some AI algorithms, such as deep learning models, can be considered black boxes, making it difficult to understand and interpret their decision making processes. In academic research, it is important to strive for transparency and develop methods to explain the reasoning behind AI-driven results (Zoldi, 2024).

Reproducibility and robustness: Researchers should aim for reproducibility by providing clear documentation of their AI models, algorithms, and datasets. It is crucial to ensure that AI models are robust and can generalize well to unseen data, avoiding over fitting or biased results. (Nah, Zheng, Cai, Siau, & Chen, 2023).

Intellectual property and ownership: AI research often involves collaboration and the use of pre-existing datasets and models. Clear guidelines need to be established regarding intellectual property rights, data ownership, and the sharing of AI models and code among researchers (Tad, 2023).

Accountability and liability: As AI becomes more autonomous, questions of accountability and liability arise. Researchers must consider the ethical implications of their AI systems and be aware of the potential risks and consequences associated with their deployment (Nah, Zheng, Cai, Siau, & Chen, 2023).

Social impact and job displacement: AI technologies have the potential to disrupt industries and automate certain job roles. Researchers should be mindful of the social impact of their AI-driven research and work towards ensuring a just transition, job creation, and minimizing negative consequences (Johnson, 2020).

Dual-use and misuse: AI technologies developed for academic research can have both positive and negative applications. Researchers should be mindful of potential dual-use scenarios and consider the ethical implications of their work to prevent misuse or unintended harm (Egelhofer and Lecheler, 2019).

Adverse Effect of AI on Academic Research

The survey revealed that many students believe AI negatively impacts their understanding of concepts, research skills, creativity, and critical thinking. Interestingly, despite these challenges, some students also highlighted the potential benefits of AI in improving academic performance if used correctly. Inasmuch as scientists are constantly exploring new tools to advance their research which include the use of artificial intelligence (AI). As noted, AI can be very helpful as it has the power of improving communication, accelerating discovery and enhancing education. But it can also cause some problems if one is ignorance of its potential negative effects which include inter-alia:

The data that AI uses might be biased and not fair to everyone. As Paullada, Raji, Bender, Denton & Hanna, (2021) explained large volumes of data are used to train AI models and in a situation the training set contains biased information, there is the likelihood that the AI will reinforce and magnify such biases in its outputs which may lead to unjust or discriminatory results, particularly in delicate fields like criminal justice, lending, hiring or in respects to people's race and culture most especially against Africa or indigenous identities.

People might start relying too much on AI and forget to think for themselves. As posited by Egelhofer and Lecheler (2019) the capacity of AI to disseminate false information, trick and mislead people, and erode confidence in institutions and the media poses a serious threat to the stability of society while Dwivedi, Kshetri, Hughes, L., et al., (2023) noted that the spread of content created by AI threatens the legitimacy of human creativity in addition to undermining confidence in digital media. AI-generated content challenges conventional ideas of authorship and intellectual property rights as it becomes more and more similar to authentic human creations

AI might make mistakes when it tries to understand data. In this regard, Li & Chang (2023) reveal how research has demonstrated the negative impact of inaccurate information on the general public's perception, decision-making process, and society's stability in that false information has become a threat to our society, In this vein Altay, Berriche, Heuer, Farkas and Rathje (2023) opine that difficulty increases when highly persuasive fake narratives are created by AI, making it harder to distinguish between fact and fiction.

Using AI states Patron (2023) might be unfair to some people and raises ethical concerns. Expressing their views on this issue, Dwivedi, Kshetri, Hughes, et al. (2023) asserted that the creation of realistic material may put users' privacy at risk and buttressed that deep-fake technology can be used to produce convincing films of people saying or doing things they never did, violating people's privacy and possibly damaging their reputations which is an act of defamation of character. Large-scale datasets are frequently analyzed by AI systems in order to identify and reproduce patterns, raising questions about the privacy of the training data.

Furtherance, when AI uses data that is not fair or inaccurate, the responses to scientist questions will be biased or inaccurate as well. This can cause problems and have a negative impact on new discoveries. As explained, AI might not be able to recognize some people's faces if the training data for facial recognition technology was only limited to images of white individuals. This can have serious consequences because it might cause the wrongful arrest of certain populations (SITNFlash, 2020)

Another concern is that researchers might start to think that AI knows everything and can replace human researchers. While AI can assist researchers in understanding large amounts of data, it cannot replace creativity, intuition, and critical thinking skills that are essential in scientific research. Relying too much on AI can lead to a lack of diversity in research perspectives and limit our own scientific discoveries. The argument is that AI algorithms can analyze vast amounts of chemical data to identify potential drug candidates, but only human intuition and creativity can look at other important factors, like unforeseen side effects that cannot be predicted by the algorithm (Heaven, 2023).

There is also the problem of Misinterpretation of data. Sometimes AI might make a mistake when it tries to understand scientific data. As explained by Zoldi (2024) many AI systems group facts together probabilistically, going back to the way AI has learned to associate data elements with one another. However, these details are not in most cases revealed when using applications like ChatGPT. Consequently, data trustworthiness is called into question. This is because AI is not as smart as people are. It may not understand the context and nuances of scientific language, leading to inaccurate responses. AI might not be able to understand the difference between two things that look very similar but are actually different. This can cause a problem if scientists use AI to make important decisions based on wrong information.

Evidence has shown that AI algorithms are used to analyze large amounts of genetic data to identify patterns and associations that may be difficult for humans to detect. However, these algorithms may not take into consideration the biological function of the gene, making it difficult to determine whether the genetic variant is actually causally related to the disease or whether it is simply a bystander. This can lead to potentially harmful interventions (Dias &Torkamani, 2019).

Using AI in research raises ethical concerns around data privacy, data security, transparency and ownership. AI algorithms require large amounts of data to function, and it is important to ensure that the information that scientists use is obtained ethically and with the proper consent of the individuals involved. Additionally, the use of AI in research may lead to the commodification of data, where individuals' personal information is bought and sold without their knowledge or consent.

As illustrated, a researcher may collect personal data from individuals without their informed consent, or they may use data that has been obtained unethically, such through hacking or unauthorized access. This can result in harm to individuals, such as identity theft or financial fraud (Raimundo & Rosário, 2021).

CONCLUSION AND RECOMMENDATIONS

There are now two schools of thought in the academia in respect of the place of AI in academic research as some do appreciate its impact while the other are considering it as a python that is being fed with milk that may eventually consume the owner. Emphatically, researchers and lecturers are more excited about how AI is improving productivity. The most interesting thing about this phenomenon is that it is changing the paradigms of qualitative research especially in the study of population and analysis of data. With AI, it is now practicable to conduct a qualitative study of even a thousand subjects and manage the unstructured nature of data gathering during such studies. The obvious is that many have not even begun to fathom the tremendous changes AI is bringing to the world.

The other school of thought is of the view that AI does possess an independent mind in the way humans do, it is essential to recognize that AI systems can still surpass their creators' capabilities more so, when it comes to processing vast amounts of data (data mining) and performing complex tasks at speeds above human match. In addition, AI systems can continuously learn and improve their performance, potentially leading to advancement beyond human comprehension. To this end, one critical aspect to consider is the potential for untended consequences or misuse of AI technology. If not properly controlled or guided, AI systems could indeed pose risks including the possibility of swallowing their creators metaphorically by outspacing human control or understanding. This scenario no doubt, underscores the importance of ethical considerations, regulations and responsible development of AI technologies. Academia and artificial intelligence (AI) are becoming increasingly intertwined, and as AI continues to advance, it is likely that academics will continue to either embrace its potential or voice concerns about its risks. Be that as it may, it is natural for one to really bother about the vice that may be accruable from the use of AI in academic research from its use by unscrupulous users but one thing is sure, because of man's ability to adapt to situations fast, man is also disposed to use the same AI to counter those vices.

To mitigate therefore the potential negative impact of AI on academic research and to maximize the gains of exploring AI in academic libraries on academic research, the following recommendations are made:

> As AI continues to evolve, it is essential for researchers to adapt and embrace this powerful tool while also being mindful of its limitations and ethical implications. This they have to do by striking a balance between AI-driven automation and human ingenuity, researchers can unlock new possibilities, advance scientific knowledge, and contribute to the transformative potential of AI in the realm of academic research.

Academic Researchers as professionals who worth their onus must address bias, transparency, privacy, and accountability as to ensuring ethical and responsible utilization AI tools for research.

University librarians and heads of faculties should ensure that the data used to train AI algorithms is diverse, unbiased, and obtained ethically;

Academic researcher should use AI as a tool to complement human researchers, rather than as a replacement. This means, that researchers should see the application of AI tools in research as a means and not an end as not to miss the ethos behind academic research;

Academic researcher should on regular bases, implement bias checks on AI algorithms to ensure they are not perpetuating bias;

Academic researchers should also as a matter of need validate results obtained through AI analysis using independent methods;

Academic libraries' management should as a matter of policy, establish clear guidelines and protocols for the ethical use of AI in research, including data privacy and ownership.

As posted on X (formerly Twitter) by Mushtaq bilal, a postdoctoral researcher at the University of Southern Denmark, The future of academia is likely to be transformed by AI language models such as ChatGPT - a computer program that simulates and processes human conversation (either written or spoken), allowing humans to interact with digital devices as if they were communicating with a real person as it will redefine the future of academic research but the challenge is that most academics do not know how to use it intelligently. The deduction in this context, is that academic researcher should true training acquire the intelligence needed to utilize AI tools like the ChatGPT.

Finally, it is important for academic researchers to approach the use of AI with caution and thoughtfulness noting that while AI can certainly enhance academic research, we must ensure that it is not used to replace human researchers or perpetuate bias and discrimination. We must also be mindful of the ethical implications of using AI in research and take steps to protect the privacy and ownership of data. The underscored fact is that while AI has the potential to enhance academic research, academic researchers should proceed with caution and consider its potential negative impact. By being mindful of these concerns and taking steps to mitigate them, we can ensure that AI is used in a responsible and ethical manner that benefits scientific research and society as a whole.

REFERENCES

Abbadia, J. (2023) Exploring the role of AI in academic research. Retrieved from https://mindthegraph.com/blog/ai-in-academic-research/

Altay, S., Berriche, M., Heuer, H., Farkas, J., & Rathje, S. (2023). A survey of expert views on misinformation: Definitions, determinants, solutions, and future of the field. *Harvard Kennedy School (HKS). Misinformation Review*, 4(4). Advance online publication. DOI: 10.37016/mr-2020-119

Babbie, E. R. 91998). The practice of social research (8th ed). Belmont: Wadsworth Publishing Co., Bakare-Fatungase, O. D., Adejuwon, F. E & Idowu-Davies, T. O. (2024). Integrating artificial intelligence in education for sustainable development. In *Using Traditional Design Methods to Enhance AI-Driven Decision Making* (pp. 231-245). IGI Global.

Britannica (2024). Definition and meaning of artificial intelligence. Available at https://www.britannica.com/technology/artificial-intelligence

Chukwu, S. A. J., Emezie, N., Nwaohiri, N. M., Haco-Obasi, F. C., Obiano, D. C., & Bernard, I. I. (2021). Information Literacy: Academic Librarians as Stakeholders in the Learning Process: with Focus on Federal University of Technology, Owerri". *Library Philosophy and Practice (e-journal)*. Available at https://digitalcommons .unl.edu/cgi/viewcontent.cgi?article=11762&context=libphilprac

Davenport, T. H., & Mittal, N. (2022). "How generative AI is changing creative work". *Harvard Business Review. Available at* https://hbr.org/2022/11/how-generative -ai-is-changing-creative-work

Dias, R., & Torkamani, A. (2019). Artificial intelligence in clinical and genomic diagnostics. *Genome Medicine*, 11(1), 70. Advance online publication. DOI: 10.1186/ s13073-019-0689-8 PMID: 31744524

Dwivedi, Y. K., Kshetri, N., Hughes, L., Slade, E. L., Jeyaraj, A., Kar, A. K., Baabdullah, A. M., Koohang, A., Raghavan, V., Ahuja, M., Albanna, H., Albashrawi, M. A., Al-Busaidi, A. S., Balakrishnan, J., Barlette, Y., Basu, S., Bose, I., Brooks, L., Buhalis, D., & Wright, R. (2023). Opinion Paper: So what if ChatGPT wrote it? Multidisciplinary perspectives on opportunities, challenges and implications of generative conversational AI for research, practice and policy. *International Journal of Information Management*, 71, 102642. Advance online publication. DOI: 10.1016/j.ijinfomgt.2023.102642

Egelhofer, J. L., & Lecheler, S. (2019). Fake news as a two-dimensional phenomenon: A Frame work and research agenda. *Annals of the International Communication Association*, 43(2), 97–116. DOI: 10.1080/23808985.2019.1602782

Fleetwood, D. (2023). What is Research? Definition, methods, types & examples. Retrieved From https://www.questionpro.com/blog/what-is-research/

Greenstein, B. (2022, April, 20) AiThority: Interview with Bret Greenstein, Partner, Cloud & Digital – Analytics Insights at PwC. Available at https://aithority.com/technology/analytics/aithority-interview-with-bret-greenstein-partner-cloud-digital-analytics-insights-at-pwc/#

Gupta, A. (2018). The Evolution of Fraud: Ethical Implications in the Age of Large-Scale Data Breaches and Widespread Artificial Intelligence Solutions Deployment. Available at from https://www.researchgate.net/publication/323857997_The_Evolution_of_Fraud_Ethical_Implications_in_the_Age_of_Large-Scale_Data_Breaches_and_Widespread_Artificial_Intelligence_Solutions_Deployment

Haleem, A., Javaid, M., Quadi, M. A., & Suman, R. (2022). Understanding the role of digital technologies in education: A Review. Science Direct, 3, 275 – 285. Available at https://www.sciencedirect.com/science/article/pii/S2666412722000137

Heaven, W. D. (2023, March 9). AI is dreaming up drugs that no one has ever seen. Now we've got to see if they work. MIT Technology Review. Retrieved from https://www.technologyreview.com/2023/02/15/1067904/ai-automation-drug-development/

Hornsby, A. S. (2015). Research. Oxford Advanced Learner's Dictionary of Current English, Oxford University Press Johnson, B. (2020). Automation and its implications for social inequality. *Journal of Technology and Society*, 22(2), 59–63.

Laskowski, N., & Tucci, L. (2024). What is artificial intelligence (AI)? Retrieved from http://www.techtarget.com/what-is-artificial intelligence/

Lawton, G. (2023).What is Generative AI? Everything you need to know. Tech Accelerator, available at https://www.techtarget.com/searchenterpriseai/definition/generative-AI

Li, J., & Chang, X. (2023). Combating Misinformation by Sharing the Truth: A Study on the Spread of Fact-Checks on Social Media. *Information Systems Frontiers*, 25(4), 1479–1493. DOI: 10.1007/s10796-022-10296-z PMID: 35729965

Liu, M., Ren, Y., Nyagoga, L. M., Stonier, F., Wu, Z., & Yu, L. (2023). Future of education in the era of generative artificial intelligence: Consensus among Chinese scholars on applications of ChatGPT in schools. *Future in Educational Research*, 1(1), 72–101. DOI: 10.1002/fer3.10

Nah, F. F.-H., Zheng, R., Cai, J., Siau, K., & Chen, L. (2023). Generative AI and ChatGPT: Applications, challenges and AI-human collaboration. *Journal of Information Technology Case and Application Research*, 25(3), 277–304. DOI: 10.1080/15228053.2023.2233814

Nworgu, B. C. (2015). Educational Research Basic Issues and Methodology. Nsukka: University Trust Publishers Olayinka, I.A. (2023). Application and use of artificial intelligence (AI) for library services delivery in academic libraries in Kwara State, Nigeria. Library Philosophy and Practice (e-journal)-7998. https://digitalcommons.unl.edu/libphilprac/7998

Onwubiko, E. C. (2020). *Library Plus*. Lambert Academic Publishing.

Onwubiko, E. C. (2021). *Modern Approaches in Librarianship*. Lambert Academic Publishing.

Onwubiko, E. C. (2023). Analysis of serials citations in postgraduate theses in library and information science in public universities in Southeast, Nigeria. An unpublished PhD Dissertation of Nnamdi Azikiwe University, Awka, Nigeria

Patron, M. (2023). Bias in the training data. Retrieved from https://www.mariecuriealumni.eu/newsletters/35th-mcaa-newsletter/special-issue-proceed-caution-potential-negative-impact-ai

Paullada, A., Raji, I. D., Bender, E. M., Denton, E., & Hanna, A. (2021). Data and its (dis)contents: A survey of dataset development and use in machine learning research. *Patterns (New York, N.Y.)*, 2(11), 100336. https://www.sciencedirect.com/science/article/pii/S2666389921001847. DOI: 10.1016/j.patter.2021.100336 PMID: 34820643

Raimundo, R., & Rosário, A. T. (2021). The Impact of Artificial Intelligence on Data System Security: A Literature Review. *Sensors (Basel)*, 21(21), 7029. DOI: 10.3390/s21217029 PMID: 34770336

Rosowsky, D. (2022). The role of research at universities: Why it matters – Forbes. Retrieved from https://www.forbes.com-davidrosowsky

Sheridan Library. (2023). What is Academic Research? Retrieved from https://sheridancollege.libguides.com/academic-research

SITNFlash. (2020, October 26). Racial discrimination in face recognition technology –science in the News. Science in the News. Retrieved from https://sitn.hms.harvard.edu/flash/2020/racial-discrimination-in-face-recognition-technology/

Tech Target. (2024). How does AI works? Retrieved from https://www.techtarget.com/serachenterpriseai/definition/ai

Zoldi, S. (2024, May 9). Navigating the wild AI with Dr. Scott Zoldi. Available at https://www.fico.com>blogs>navigating-wild-ai-dr-scott-zoldi/

KEY TERMS AND DEFINITIONS

Academic Libraries: Are libraries situated within tertiary institutions such as the university, college of education and polytechnics with the mandate and obligation to provide effective information services towards the realization of the tripartite functions of the parent institution which are teaching, learning and research.

Academic Research: Involves a holistic investigation into an identified problem in which the academic researcher is expected to adopt specific research methodology in line with objective(s) that the research is aimed to achieve with which data are collected, analyzed and conclusion drawn.

Academic Researcher: Is one who is a specialist in a particular subject area mostly associated with academic institutions and undertake to study and analyse a subject which is eventually published as a paper, an article in a journal or as a book.

Artificial Intelligence: As the name denotes is a replication of human intelligence planted in machines as the brain and programmed to think and act as human but powered by computer. This is so noticed in robots.

Human Intelligence: Is God endowed intellectual capability of man with which he recognizes challenges and solves problems with high levels of motivation and self awareness and with it also conceptualizes ideas, comprehends things around him, learn as well as apply logic and reasoning.

Information and Communication Technology (ICT): Is a combination of computers and other related technologies used in information creation, processing, storage, sharing and transmission made popular by the famous information super-highway, the internet. Ultimately, it is the integration of computers and telecommunications technologies with the purpose of enabling and enhancing information accessibility, storage, dissemination, understanding and manipulation by users.

Research: Is a step-by-step examination of a situation or an enquiry made with a view to providing an answer or a solution to an identified problem through the study of materials and sources in order to establish facts and reach new conclusions. In the academics, it is an avenue of increasing the stock of knowledge.

Chapter 4
Are Artificial Intelligence Chatbots a Threat to Librarianship?

Adebowale Jeremy Adetayo
https://orcid.org/0000-0001-7869-5613
Adeleke University, Nigeria

Folashade Munirat Lawal
https://orcid.org/0000-0002-7620-9156
Afe Babalola University, Nigeria

Abiodun Olusegun Odunewu
Olabisi Onabanjo University, Nigeria

ABSTRACT

This article aims to explore the potential threat posed by AI chatbots to librarianship and advocate for a balanced approach to integrating AI while upholding human contributions. The chapter examines the evolving roles of librarians, chatbot capabilities and limitations, impacts from library professionals, and the irreplaceable value of librarians. The chapter suggest that while chatbots offer efficiency in handling routine inquiries, concerns arise regarding their ability to replace librarian expertise. Librarians remain vital for personalized assistance, advocating intellectual freedom and privacy, and inclusive engagement. Libraries should adopt a collaborative model leveraging AI to enhance efficiency while preserving the unique human qualities librarians bring. This chapter contributes to the discourse on AI chatbots in librarianship by advocating for a balanced approach that integrates emerging technologies with human-centered values, allowing libraries to progress responsibly.

DOI: 10.4018/979-8-3693-3053-1.ch004

I. INTRODUCTION

The rapid advancement of artificial intelligence (AI) has ushered in a new era of automated communication, with AI chatbots becoming increasingly prevalent across various industries. These sophisticated systems, powered by cutting-edge natural language processing and machine learning algorithms, have demonstrated remarkable proficiency in simulating human-like conversations (Adetayo, 2023b). Prominent examples such as OpenAI's ChatGPT, Anthropic's Claude, Google's Gemini, and Microsoft's Copilot showcase the impressive capabilities of modern AI in understanding context, personalizing interactions, and providing efficient responses to user inquiries.

The widespread adoption of AI chatbots, driven by their potential to enhance customer service while reducing operational costs, has ignited a passionate debate within the library community. At the heart of this discourse lies a fundamental question: How will these technological marvels impact the traditional role of librarians? (Paulson, 2024). Historically, the role of librarians has demonstrated remarkable adaptability, evolving in tandem with societal needs and technological advancements. The current AI revolution presents both opportunities and challenges for the profession. Proponents argue that AI chatbots could revolutionize library services by handling routine tasks, thereby freeing human librarians to focus on higher-value activities such as specialized instruction, community engagement, and strategic planning. Conversely, skeptics express concern that an overreliance on AI could potentially erode the expertise, empathy, and human connection that have long been hallmarks of quality library services (AIstraight, 2023; Choice 360, 2023).

Recent developments in AI technology have brought about profound changes in library operations, extending far beyond simple chatbot interactions. AI-driven data analytics are now being leveraged to optimize library management, facilitating more informed decision-making in critical areas such as collection development, resource allocation, and budget planning. Furthermore, AI-powered platforms are fostering knowledge sharing and interdisciplinary collaboration, connecting researchers and patrons with shared interests across diverse fields of study.

Despite these technological advancements, a growing body of evidence suggests that the absence of the "human touch" in AI interactions represents a significant limitation. The unique value proposition of human librarians lies in their capacity for nuanced judgment, cultural sensitivity, and personalized assistance – qualities that even the most advanced AI systems struggle to replicate convincingly.

As libraries continue to evolve in the digital age, there is a compelling opportunity to develop an integrated model that harnesses the strengths of both AI chatbots and human librarians. By leveraging AI to handle repetitive queries and streamline routine processes, librarians can redirect their focus towards delivering high-touch, personalized services that prioritize ethical considerations and community impact (Adetayo, 2023a; Ask.com, 2023; Gecko, 2023). The integration of AI into library services has also catalyzed important discussions regarding AI literacy among library professionals. As AI tools become increasingly central to modern library operations, the ability to effectively use, critically evaluate, and responsibly manage these technologies is rapidly becoming an essential competency for librarians. This shift presents both challenges and opportunities: while AI has the potential to significantly enhance library services, it also necessitates a proactive approach to professional development, ensuring that librarians acquire the skills needed to navigate this new technological landscape without compromising the core humanistic values of librarianship.

This chapter aims to:

1. Conduct a thorough investigation into whether AI chatbots pose a genuine threat to the field of librarianship, examining both the potential risks and opportunities presented by this technology.
2. Provide a comprehensive comparative analysis of the capabilities of emerging AI technologies and human librarians within the context of contemporary library environments.
3. Advocate for a balanced, forward-thinking strategy that leverages the strengths of AI while preserving and enhancing the essential human contributions to patron services, ensuring that libraries remain vibrant, relevant, and user-centered institutions in the digital age.

II. EVOLVING ROLE OF LIBRARIANS IN A DIGITAL LANDSCAPE

A. Historical Overview of Core Functions

Librarians have served as stewards of knowledge throughout history, facilitating access to information while adapting their roles to suit evolving societal needs and technologies. In ancient civilizations, librarians preserved written works in repositories like the Library of Alexandria (El-Abbadi, n.d.). During the Middle Ages, monastic librarians safeguarded religious and cultural heritage texts (Nebbiai, 2020).

The modern concept of librarianship emerged during the Renaissance, as librarians organized collections, catalogued materials, and provided reference services to newly public libraries, fostering intellectual inquiry through increased access to knowledge enabled by the printing press (Cesnik, 2001).

Librarianship transformed again in the 20th century with new organization systems and computerized catalogs, allowing librarians to uphold equitable access to information. The digital revolution brought perhaps the most profound shift as information became digitized online, requiring librarians to provide digital literacy training, IT support, and electronic resources (American Libraries Magazine, 2011; Wenborn, 2018). Librarians also engaged in digital outreach as social media created new virtual communities (Adetayo & Gbotoso, 2023).

B. Expansion Into Digital Literacy, Data Services, Makerspaces

Librarians have expanded beyond traditional information retrieval roles to meet emerging community needs in the digital age by providing:

Digital Literacy Training: With growing reliance on technology for communication and information access, librarians now serve as digital literacy educators (Kenton & Blummer, 2010; Merga, 2020). They offer workshops on skills from online navigation to privacy protection, aiming to empower diverse patrons with equitable access to digital resources (Rempel & McMillen, 2008).

Data Services: To support advanced data-driven research, librarians assist patrons in locating datasets, accessing repositories, conducting analysis with software tools, and implementing best practices for organization and preservation (Dudden & Protzko, 2011; Horwood et al., 2004). They also collaborate with researchers on open access data publication (Rahaman, 2023).

Makerspaces: Librarians have established creative hands-on learning spaces featuring 3D printers, electronics, and more for experimentation and innovation (Aiyeblehin et al., 2018). Through facilitating workshops and enabling project prototyping, librarians cultivate knowledge-sharing while providing access to entrepreneurial skill-building (Burnette, 2017; Hoppenfeld & Malaf, 2015; Kirkwood & Evans, 2012).

C. Human relationships at the Heart of Inclusive Library Impact

While libraries have rapidly expanded their technological offerings, human connections remain at the heart of librarians' ability to create inclusive community impact. Librarians provide:

Personalized Assistance: By building rapport with patrons, librarians can offer guidance tailored to individuals' unique needs, backgrounds, and learning styles. This human touch bridges divides, ensuring all feel valued in pursuing knowledge.

Community Engagement: Librarians bring people together through organizing book clubs, cultural events and more, fostering belonging and social cohesion (Veros, 2019). These activities promote cross-cultural empathy and understanding.

Empathetic Support: Whether assisting struggling students, unemployed residents, or lending an ear, librarians demonstrate compassion that establishes trust between patrons and institutions (Bodaghi et al., 2016; Wojciechowska, 2020). This makes libraries welcoming havens.

Advocacy and Representation: Through inclusive collections and programming, librarians elevate diverse voices to reflect the entire community (Figueroa & Shawgo, 2022; Winston & Li, 2000). Representing marginalized groups promotes social equity and justice by validating patron identities.

Libraries as Communal Spaces: Most vitally, libraries functionally serve as communal hubs centered around the shared physical spaces that bring together patrons across ages and demographics to read, reflect, relate, and brainstorm (Adetayo et al., 2023). Whether collaborating on projects, attending author talks, or simply greeting familiar faces while browsing the stacks, the dedicated physical infrastructure of libraries fosters social bonds and knowledge sharing. Through vast reading rooms, movable furnishings enabling reconfiguration for evolving needs, secluded carrels for intense focus, and adjacent cafes nurturing contemplation, libraries empower communities by designing spaces purpose-built to fuel learning, creativity, and relationships. Unlike the isolation of solitary virtual environments, the embodied experience offered by library spaces cultivates civic participation, innovation, and the serendipitous discoveries emerging from shared human experiences represented via multi-sensory environments (Bieraugel & Neill, 2017). This infrastructure intentionally engineered to catalyze face-to-face community flourishing remains impossible for technologies to replace.

III. CAPABILITIES AND LIMITATIONS OF AI CHATBOTS

AI chatbots offer significant capabilities in streamlining library information retrieval and processing. Leveraging natural language processing and machine learning, chatbots swiftly analyze patron queries and provide relevant real-time responses, enhancing accessibility and convenience (X. Chen, 2023).

A major asset is their ability to handle high volumes of inquiries simultaneously without performance declines. Unlike human librarians who experience fatigue or bandwidth limitations, chatbots can address concurrent patron needs promptly (Adetayo, 2023a). AI chatbots offer significant capabilities in streamlining library information retrieval and processing, enhancing accessibility and convenience. However, their limitations become apparent when faced with complex or ambiguous language lacking clear intent or context. Unlike human librarians who can provide nuanced assistance tailored to individual needs and contexts, chatbots may struggle in such scenarios. As they rely on algorithms rather than qualitative assessment, chatbots may struggle with queries requiring critical thinking or subject matter expertise, like literary critiques or specialized research (Critical Thinking Sectets, 2024).

The principal benefits chatbots offer are 24/7 availability and scalable assistance. Unlike the fixed schedules of human staff, chatbots enable patrons round-the-clock access to basic library services from any location, accommodating diverse needs and schedules. Since chatbots have automated and digital infrastructure without human constraints, they readily adapt to fluctuations in demand without performance declines (Fokina, 2024). By handling repetitive inquiries, chatbots also reduce staff workloads so librarians can focus on advanced tasks.

Observed Impact

Dr. Almuth Gastinger, a Senior Academic Librarian at the Norwegian University of Science and Technology (NTNU), provided insights into the discussions surrounding AI tools like ChatGPT among Norwegian librarians. Despite not having personal experience with ChatGPT, Dr. Gastinger highlighted that approximately 35% of her colleagues have integrated such tools into their practices. However, an incident arose where students attempted to borrow non-existent books based on ChatGPT's recommendations. This underscores the importance of verifying information and has sparked ongoing discussions regarding integrating AI into academics (IFLA, 2023).

Similarly, Rajen Munoo, Head of Learning Services & Research Librarian at the Li Ka Shing Library in Singapore, acknowledged widespread conversations about ChatGPT in both the university and professional circles. However, specific insights into its effectiveness, limitations, and impacts on duties remain unclear - suggesting an area for further evaluation to understand its implications (IFLA, 2023).

Meanwhile, Christopher Cox, Dean of Libraries and Elias Tzoc, associate dean for teaching and learning and research at Clemson University discussed ChatGPT's rapid emergence and capabilities in generating content. While some praise its potential as a digital assistant, concerns about misuse have led to bans in some settings. Cox highlighted potential impacts on tasks like metadata creation and reference questions, envisioning a future where ChatGPT complements or replaces search methods. However, careful consideration of ethical issues is warranted (Cox & Tzoc, 2023).

Adding to the discourse, Dr. Leo S. Lo, Dean at the University of New Mexico, sees opportunities for ChatGPT to streamline processes like cataloging and re-search queries. However, he emphasizes the need for AI literacy to navigate ethical considerations. Similarly, Dr. Ray Pun sees potential as a learning tool but stresses addressing privacy and integrity concerns amidst adoption. These perspectives highlight both promises and challenges of integrating AI into libraries, calling for thoughtful dialogue (IFLA, 2023).

Collectively, these insights showcase ongoing discussions surrounding emerging AI tools in diverse library settings globally. While routine tasks may increasingly be managed by AI, qualitatively assessing information credibility and establishing ethical frameworks appear vital before wider adoption unfolds.

While AI chatbots promise efficient, scalable services, they can inadvertently perpetuate harmful biases and lack transparency - posing risks from an ethical perspective . As algorithmic systems built by analyzing patterns in training data, chatbots reflect embedded societal biases around race, gender, culture and more (Xue et al., 2023). Without proactive bias detection testing and human oversight of data inputs and decision-making processes, AI chatbots used in library services could provide discriminatory book suggestions, reinforce stereotypes in answering patron queries, or exclude marginalized groups. For example, initial trials of library chatbots demonstrated higher error rates for non-native English speakers (Han et al., 2023), which recent AI chatbots has improved on. The proprietary nature of commercial chatbot software also precludes transparency about how algorithms are trained and how responses are generated based on patron questions (Blackman & Ammanath, 2022). This lack of explainability means biases may persist undetected. As public institutions serving diverse communities, libraries must implement rigorous algorithm audits, staff training in ML ethics, push vendors for transparent AI practices, and continuously monitor chatbot performance across user groups to uphold equitable, inclusive and ethical services as core values. With human librarians overseeing operations guided by social conscience rather than just computational metrics, libraries can thoughtfully navigate risks in pursuing AI advancements.

IV. IRREPLACEABLE VALUE OF HUMAN LIBRARIAN EXPERTISE

A. Research, Evaluation, Quality Control of Information

Human librarians provide unparalleled expertise in the intertwined domains of research, evaluation, and quality control of information:

1. Research Methodology: As trained professionals, librarians leverage in-depth knowledge of specialized databases, search strategies, and multidisciplinary information resources. When assisting patrons with inquiries, librarians apply critical thinking to locate authoritative, relevant sources using advanced techniques. They further empower patrons by advising on research design, citation, literature review, and more (Dudden & Protzko, 2011).

2. Information Evaluation: Librarians evaluate source credibility, reliability, bias and relevance by applying subjective human judgment rather than just algorithms. Their domain expertise in recognizing misinformation, logical fallacies and partisan skewing helps patrons navigate information overload to make discerning decisions, especially amidst today's saturation of fake news (Batchelor, 2017; De Paor & Heravi, 2020; Neely-Sardon & Tignor, 2018).

3. Quality Control: Through careful selection, acquisition and cataloging guided by accuracy, authority and currency benchmarks, librarians curate trustworthy collections. Furthermore, by continuously reviewing resources and removing outdated or inaccurate materials, librarians uphold libraries' reputations as reliable information authorities that communities can depend on (Ashikuzzaman, 2020; Stanford, 2023).

B. Understanding Diversity for Personalized Recommendations

1. Cultural Competence from Community Engagement:
   i. Diversity/Inclusion Experience: Through direct community engagement, librarians gain competencies in navigating differences and promoting representation in collections/services (Goulding, 2009). They partner with cultural groups to develop inclusive programs celebrating heritage and identity (Moran, 2021).
   ii. Adaptive Communication: Librarians bridge cultural and linguistic divides by adapting communication styles to connect with each patron respectfully (IFLA, 2020, 2022). Whether accommodating learning preferences, language barriers or norms, librarians focus on fostering belonging.
   iii. Ongoing Training: Librarians actively hone cultural competencies through continual formal and informal training opportunities attuned to the evolving needs of the communities they serve (Mestre, 2010). They seek out the latest best practices in diversity training, antiracism education, and multicultural awareness from credible programs and experts. This sustained enrichment ensures skills, mindsets and practices stay relevant.
2. Personalized Recommendations: Skilled in active listening and dialogue, librarians engage patrons to identify distinctive interests, preferences and requirements (Brophy, 2007; Smith & Fitt, 1982). Whether suggesting books, articles or multimedia, librarians draw on their deep knowledge of collections and advisory expertise to curate customized recommendations fulfilling each individual's needs and goals. As no two patrons are identical, this personal touch remains out of reach for AI.

C. Upholding intellectual freedom and patron privacy

Human librarians serve as vital stewards upholding patron rights to intellectual freedom and privacy:

Intellectual Freedom Advocacy: Librarians champion patron access to information without censorship across perspectives as essential for critical thinking, democracy and discovery (Fallis, 2007; Oltmann, 2016). Resisting infringements on controversial materials that spark discussion, librarians promote free civil discourse and inquiry in the face of political or social opposition.

Privacy Protection: Enshrined in codes of ethics, librarians respect patron confidentiality regarding borrowing records, research and personal data which remains protected from unauthorized access (Garoogian, 1991). Unlike AI chatbots that collect user data for analytics, librarians prioritize security through encryption, anonymity and data retention limits (ALA, 2019; T. Y. Chen et al., 2021). This culture of trust supports inclusion where patrons can safely explore sensitive topics free of judgment or surveillance.

However, adopting AI systems presents new challenges in upholding patron rights. Granting chatbots access to confidential records and personal data raises unprecedented privacy vulnerabilities that libraries must mitigate to prevent exploitation. Algorithms must also be continually audited to ensure impartial recommendations - preventing marginalized perspectives from being automatically filtered out. Through governance upholding transparency and fairness, librarians can lead conscientious AI adoption respecting patron dignity while centering on truth and intellectual freedom.

V. RESHAPING LIBRARIAN ROLES IN AN AI-ASSISTED FUTURE

As AI integration transforms library tasks, human librarians face some job automation but limited full displacement due to irreplaceable expertise:

1. Task Automation: AI assists librarians by handling routine factual inquiries such as library hours, printer locations, and directional questions. This frees up valuable librarian time to focus on more complex patron requests – from in-depth research consultations to tailored reading recommendations. Additionally, AI facilitates metadata creation, reducing the burden of cataloging new collections. It also enables enhanced discovery tools like book recommendation algorithms to connect patrons with relevant materials. Most importantly, automation handles common inquiries so that librarians can prioritize judgment-intensive tasks that rely on human expertise – such as evaluating patron needs, providing guidance

on specialized research topics, and developing community outreach programs. Essentially, AI automation provides the bandwidth for librarians to focus on the complex questions and custom services at the heart of the profession, while more straightforward informational requests are efficiently handled through technology.

2. Limited Job Displacement: While excellent at information retrieval, AI chatbots cannot replicate librarians' skills in research consultancy, instruction, community building, ethical oversight, privacy protection and inclusion advocacy - tasks requiring critical thinking, nuanced communication and human values (Cox & Tzoc, 2023; Paulson, 2024). With empathy, contextual understanding and complex qualitative analysis remaining core service components out of AI abilities, human librarians continue serving irreplicable roles.

3. Specialized Services: Librarians can provide enhanced research consultations like systematic reviews, specialized instructional sessions on using academic databases, and tailored collection development around campus research areas. By collaborating deeply with stakeholders from faculty to biotech professionals, librarians can facilitate ambitious projects advancing learning and knowledge creation.

4. Community Engagement: As central community pillars, librarians can organize literacy drives, cultural heritage events, author talks and more to spur lifelong civic participation. Partnerships with local groups also enable impactful programming addressing pressing social issues. For example, collaborating with public health networks empowers librarians to provide programming countering health misinformation or bringing health screening services on-site.

5. Professional Development: With bandwidth opened up by AI assistance, librarians can actively advance their skills and credentials through advanced degrees, cutting-edge certifications, conferences sharing best practices, and research publishing. Staying abreast of emerging technologies and methodologies allows deeper community contributions.

6. Information Literacy: Librarians must educate users on AI through workshops, tutorials, and embeddable course content - including capabilities, limitations, biases and privacy implications. By promoting critical thinking, librarians empower communities to evaluate AI information and protect their rights.

7. Role Evolution: As curators, stewards and architects in knowledge and information systems, librarians adopt elevated roles guiding ethical use of data and digital artifacts. However, translating principles into practice remains an ongoing challenge. Librarians can help address responsible AI application through pragmatic collaboration and innovation leadership – driving positive impacts.

CONCLUSION

The debate over AI chatbots posing a threat to librarianship is nuanced. While chatbots offer efficiency in handling routine inquiries, they cannot replace the irreplaceable - the skills, expertise and human connection by librarians. Librarians have historically adapted to suit changing needs and technologies, as they continue doing so today. From expanding into digital literacy and data services to fostering inclusive engagement, librarians play a vital role in promoting access to information, critical thinking, and advocating for intellectual freedom. While chatbots excel in scalable assistance, they face limitations with complex queries and may perpetuate biases if not carefully monitored. Moreover, integrating AI systems presents new challenges in upholding patron privacy rights - which librarians must thoughtfully navigate. In an AI-assisted future, librarians will continue providing personalized help, curating trustworthy collections, advocating for diversity, and fostering community bonds - roles that cannot be replicated by AI. While some tasks may be automated, the unique values librarians bring cannot be replaced. Moving forward, libraries must adopt a balanced approach - leveraging AI for efficiency while maintaining the human touch core to librarianship. With ongoing training in AI literacy and ethical considerations, librarians can collaborate to responsibly integrate chatbots - enhancing certain functions but not compromising on their duty to patrons. The future of library services lies in harmonizing emerging technologies with human-centered values. With ethical frameworks guiding its implementation, AI can facilitate knowledge access immensely while librarians continue serving as the heart of libraries.

REFERENCES

Adetayo, A. J. (2023a). ChatGPT and Librarians for Reference Consultations. *Internet Reference Services Quarterly*, 27(3), 131–147. Advance online publication. DOI: 10.1080/10875301.2023.2203681

Adetayo, A. J. (2023b). Conversational assistants in academic libraries: Enhancing reference services through Bing Chat. *Library Hi Tech News*. Advance online publication. DOI: 10.1108/LHTN-08-2023-0142

Adetayo, A. J., Adekunmisi, S. R., Otonekwu, F. O., & Adesina, O. F. (2023). The role of academic libraries in facilitating friendships among students. *IFLA Journal*, 49(4), 694–703. Advance online publication. DOI: 10.1177/03400352231191540

Adetayo, A. J., & Gbotoso, A. O. (2023). Outreach Programs Revitalizing the Patronage of Public Libraries in Nigeria. *Portal (Baltimore, Md.)*, 23(2), 231–247. DOI: 10.1353/pla.2023.0017

AIstraight. (2023, June 20). *Will AI Replace Librarians? Uncovering the Positive Impacts of AI*. https://aistraight.com/ai-replace-librarians/

Aiyeblehin, J. A., Onyam, I. D., & Akpom, C. C. (2018). Creating Makerspaces in Nigerian Public Libraries as a Strategy for Attaining National Integration and Development. *International Journal of Knowledge Content Development & Technology*, 8(4), 19–31. DOI: 10.5865/IJKCT.2018.8.4.019

ALA. (2019). *Privacy and Confidentiality Q&A*. https://www.ala.org/advocacy/intfreedom/privacyconfidentialityqa

American Libraries Magazine. (2011, May 25). *The Digital Revolution and the Transformation of Libraries*. https://americanlibrariesmagazine.org/2011/05/25/the-digital-revolution-and-the-transformation-of-libraries/

Ashikuzzaman. (2020, September 22). *Library Collection Development Process*. https://www.lisedunetwork.com/collection-development-process/

Ask.com. (2023, October 17). *Chatbot vs Human Interaction: The Pros and Cons of AI-Powered Conversations*. https://www.ask.com/news/chatbot-vs-human-interaction-pros-cons-ai-powered-conversations

Batchelor, O. (2017). Getting out the truth: The role of libraries in the fight against fake news. *RSR. Reference Services Review*, 45(2), 143–148. DOI: 10.1108/RSR-03-2017-0006

Bieraugel, M., & Neill, S. (2017). Ascending Bloom's Pyramid: Fostering Student Creativity and Innovation in Academic Library Spaces. *College & Research Libraries*, 78(1), 35–52. DOI: 10.5860/crl.78.1.35

Blackman, R., & Ammanath, B. (2022, June 20). *Building Transparency into AI Projects*. https://hbr.org/2022/06/building-transparency-into-ai-projects

Bodaghi, N. B., Cheong, L. S., & Zainab, A. N. (2016). Librarians Empathy: Visually Impaired Students' Experiences Towards Inclusion and Sense of Belonging in an Academic Library. *Journal of Academic Librarianship*, 42(1), 87–96. DOI: 10.1016/j.acalib.2015.11.003

Brophy, P. (2007). Communicating the library: Librarians and faculty in dialogue. *Library Management*, 28(8–9), 515–523. DOI: 10.1108/01435120710837792

Burnette, M. (2017). Tacit knowledge sharing among library colleagues: A pilot study. *RSR. Reference Services Review*, 45(3), 382–397. DOI: 10.1108/RSR-11-2016-0082

Cesnik, B. (2001). Digital Libraries. *Yearbook of Medical Informatics*, 10(01), 147–150. DOI: 10.1055/s-0038-1638099 PMID: 27701600

Chen, T. Y., Chiu, Y. C., Bi, N., & Tsai, R. T. H. (2021). Multi-Modal Chatbot in Intelligent Manufacturing. *IEEE Access : Practical Innovations, Open Solutions*, 9, 82118–82129. DOI: 10.1109/ACCESS.2021.3083518

Chen, X. (2023). ChatGPT and Its Possible Impact on Library Reference Services. *Internet Reference Services Quarterly*, 27(2), 121–129. Advance online publication. DOI: 10.1080/10875301.2023.2181262

Choice 360. (2023, May 15). *"Do We Need Librarians Now that We Have ChatGPT?"*. https://www.choice360.org/libtech-insight/do-we-need-librarians-now-that-we-have-chatgpt/

Cox, C., & Tzoc, E. (2023). ChatGPT: Implications for academic libraries. *College & Research Libraries News*, 84(3), 99. DOI: 10.5860/crln.84.3.99

Critical Thinking Sectets. (2024). *Critical Thinking and Artificial Intelligence*. https://criticalthinkingsecrets.com/critical-thinking-and-artificial-intelligence/

De Paor, S., & Heravi, B. (2020). Information literacy and fake news: How the field of librarianship can help combat the epidemic of fake news. *Journal of Academic Librarianship*, 46(5), 102218. DOI: 10.1016/j.acalib.2020.102218

Dudden, R. F., & Protzko, S. L. (2011). The Systematic Review Team: Contributions of the Health Sciences Librarian. *Medical Reference Services Quarterly*, 30(3), 301–315. DOI: 10.1080/02763869.2011.590425 PMID: 21800987

El-Abbadi, M. (n.d.). *Library of Alexandria*. Retrieved February 10, 2024, from https://www.britannica.com/topic/Library-of-Alexandria

Fallis, D. (2007). Information ethics for twenty-first century library professionals. *Library Hi Tech*, 25(1), 23–36. DOI: 10.1108/07378830710735830

Figueroa, M., & Shawgo, K. (2022). "You can't read your way out of racism": Creating anti-racist action out of education in an academic library. *RSR. Reference Services Review*, 50(1), 25–39. DOI: 10.1108/RSR-06-2021-0025

Fokina, M. (2024, January 23). The Future of Chatbots: 80+ Chatbot. *Stat*, 2024, •••. https://www.tidio.com/blog/chatbot-statistics/

Garoogian, R. (1991). Librarian/patron confidentiality: An ethical challenge. *Library Trends*, 4(2), 216–233. https://www.ideals.illinois.edu/bitstream/handle/2142/7774/librarytrendsv40i2d_opt.pdf?sequ

Gecko. (2023). *Human versus Chatbot - what works best?* https://www.geckoengage.com/articles/human-versus-chatbot-what-works-best/

Goulding, A. (2009). Engaging with community engagement: Public libraries and citizen involvement. *New Library World*, 110(1–2), 37–51. DOI: 10.1108/03074800910928577

Han, S., Liu, M., Pan, Z., Cai, Y., & Shao, P. (2023). Making FAQ Chatbots More Inclusive: An Examination of Non-Native English Users' Interactions with New Technology in Massive Open Online Courses. *International Journal of Artificial Intelligence in Education*, 33(3), 752–780. DOI: 10.1007/s40593-022-00311-4

Hoppenfeld, J., & Malaf, E. (2015). Engaging with entrepreneurs in academic and public libraries. *RSR. Reference Services Review*, 43(3), 379–399. DOI: 10.1108/RSR-02-2015-0011

Horwood, L., Sullivan, S., Young, E., & Garner, J. (2004). OAI compliant institutional repositories and the role of library staff. *Library Management*, 25(4/5), 170–176. DOI: 10.1108/01435120410533756

IFLA. (2020, May 20). *Gateways to Cultural Diversity: Libraries as multicultural hubs*. https://blogs.ifla.org/lpa/2020/05/20/gateways-to-cultural-diversity-libraries-as-multicultural-hubs/

IFLA. (2022, January 7). *Libraries as Cultural Rights Defenders: Looking ahead to Culture, Heritage, and Development in 2022*. https://www.ifla.org/news/libraries-as-cultural-rights-defenders-looking-ahead-to-culture-heritage-and-development-in-2022/

IFLA. (2023, May 14). *ChatGPT in Libraries? A Discussion*. https://blogs.ifla.org/cpdwl/2023/05/14/chatgpt-in-libraries-a-discussion/

Kenton, J., & Blummer, B. (2010). Promoting Digital Literacy Skills: Examples from the Literature and Implications for Academic Librarians. *Community & Junior College Libraries*, 16(2), 84–99. DOI: 10.1080/02763911003688737

Kirkwood, H., & Evans, K. (2012). Embedded Librarianship and Virtual Environments in Entrepreneurship Information Literacy: A Case Study. *Journal of Business & Finance Librarianship*, 17(1), 106–116. DOI: 10.1080/08963568.2011.630583

Merga, M. K. (2020). School Librarians as Literacy Educators Within a Complex Role. *Journal of Library Administration*, 60(8), 889–908. DOI: 10.1080/01930826.2020.1820278

Mestre, L. S. (2010). Librarians working with diverse populations: What impact does cultural competency training have on their efforts? *Journal of Academic Librarianship*, 36(6), 479–488. DOI: 10.1016/j.acalib.2010.08.003

Moran, M. (2021). Public librarians and community engagement: The way forward. *Advances in Librarianship*, 48, 139–146. DOI: 10.1108/S0065-283020210000048015

Nebbiai, D. (2020). Scriptoria and Libraries: An overview. In *The Oxford Handbook of Latin Palaeography* (pp. 737–768). Oxford University Press. DOI: 10.1093/oxfordhb/9780195336948.013.99

Neely-Sardon, A., & Tignor, M. (2018). Focus on the facts: A news and information literacy instructional program. *The Reference Librarian*, 59(3), 108–121. DOI: 10.1080/02763877.2018.1468849

Oltmann, S. M. (2016). Public Librarians' Views on Collection Development and Censorship. *Collection Management*, 41(1), 23–44. DOI: 10.1080/01462679.2015.1117998

Paulson, O. (2024). *Is There A Risk ChatBots And AI Will Steal My Librarian Job?* https://aiwhim.com/is-there-a-risk-chatbots-and-ai-will-steal-my-librarian-job/

Rahaman, T. (2023). Open Data and the 2023 NIH Data Management and Sharing Policy. *Medical Reference Services Quarterly*, 42(1), 71–78. DOI: 10.1080/02763869.2023.2168103 PMID: 36862609

Rempel, H. G., & McMillen, P. S. (2008). Using Courseware Discussion Boards to Engage Graduate Students in Online Library Workshops. *Internet Reference Services Quarterly*, 13(4), 363–380. DOI: 10.1080/10875300802326350

Smith, N. M., & Fitt, S. D. (1982). *Active Listening at the Reference Desk. 21*(3), 247–249. https://www.jstor.org/stable/25826744

Stanford. (2023, February 28). *Collecting in support of Stanford's teaching and research.* https://news.stanford.edu/report/2023/02/28/building-stanfords-collections/

Veros, V. (2019). Metatextual Conversations: The Exclusion/Inclusion of Genre Fiction in Public Libraries and Social Media Book Groups. *Journal of the Australian Library and Information Association*, 68(3), 254–267. DOI: 10.1080/24750158.2019.1654741

Wenborn, C. (2018, April 11). *How Technology Is Changing the Future of Libraries.* https://www.wiley.com/en-us/network/research-libraries/libraries-archives-databases/library-impact/how-technology-is-changing-the-future-of-libraries

Winston, M. D., & Li, H. (2000). Managing Diversity in Liberal Arts College Libraries. *College & Research Libraries*, 61(3), 205–215. DOI: 10.5860/crl.61.3.205

Wojciechowska, M. (2020). Social capital, trust and social activity among librarians: Results of research conducted in 20 countries across the world. *Library & Information Science Research*, 42(4), 101049. DOI: 10.1016/j.lisr.2020.101049

Xue, J., Wang, Y.-C., Wei, C., Liu, X., Woo, J., & Kuo, C.-C. J. (2023). Bias and Fairness in Chatbots: An Overview. *ArXiv*. https://arxiv.org/abs/2309.08836v2

ADDITIONAL READING

Ahmadi, A. (2023). ChatGPT: Exploring the threats and opportunities of artificial intelligence in the age of chatbots. *Asian Journal of Computer Science and Technology*, 12(1), 25–30. DOI: 10.51983/ajcst-2023.12.1.3567

Cox, A. (2023). How artificial intelligence might change academic library work: Applying the competencies literature and the theory of the professions. *Journal of the Association for Information Science and Technology*, 74(3), 367–380. DOI: 10.1002/asi.24635

Harisanty, D., Anna, N. E. V., Putri, T. E., Firdaus, A. A., & Noor Azizi, N. A. (2023). Is adopting artificial intelligence in libraries urgency or a buzzword? A systematic literature review. *Journal of Information Science*, •••, 01655515221141034. DOI: 10.1177/01655515221141034

Verma, V. K., & Gupta, S. (2022). Artificial Intelligence and the Future Libraries. *World Digital Libraries-. International Journal (Toronto, Ont.)*, 15(2), 151–166.

KEY TERMS AND DEFINITIONS

Artificial Intelligence: Artificial Intelligence refers to the development of computer systems and software capable of performing tasks that typically require human intelligence, such as learning, problem-solving, decision-making, and natural language processing. AI systems can use techniques like machine learning, deep learning, and natural language processing to automate tasks and make decisions.

AI Chatbots: AI chatbots are conversational agents powered by artificial intelligence. They are designed to engage in natural language dialogs, answer questions, and assist users with various tasks. AI chatbots leverage natural language processing and machine learning to understand user inputs and generate contextual responses.

Librarianship: Librarianship is the professional field focused on managing and curating information resources, providing reference and research assistance, and facilitating access to knowledge and information. Librarians are information professionals who work in a variety of settings, including public libraries, academic libraries, school libraries, and special libraries.

Human Librarians: Human librarians are information professionals who have specialized training and expertise in library science. They are responsible for tasks such as cataloging and organizing library materials, assisting patrons with research and information queries, developing library collections, and designing programs and services to meet the information needs of their communities.

Chapter 5
Role of Libraries in Promoting Digital Literacy and Information Fluency

Sanchita Ghosh
Brainware University, India

Saptarshi Kumar Sarkar
Brainware University, India

Piyal Roy
Brainware University, India

Bitan Roy
Brainware University, India

Amitava Podder
https://orcid.org/0009-0004-9268-3781
Brainware University, India

ABSTRACT

Libraries are vital in promoting digital literacy and information fluency in the digital era. They offer access to digital resources, equipping individuals with skills like computer literacy, critical thinking, and data comprehension. Libraries also empower multi-layer functions like media literacy, fact-checking competency, and accountability. Librarians are respected for their ability to guide users in the ever-changing digital landscape. Collaborative Learning Spaces allow visitors to interact with upper technologies, engage in digital storytelling, and create new ideas. Libraries collaborate with educational institutions and advocate for amplifying

DOI: 10.4018/979-8-3693-3053-1.ch005

digital literacy programs. By adopting future technologies, adapting to customer needs, and encouraging lifelong learning, libraries continue to drive digital skills and information fluency.

1. INTRODUCTION

The use of special education technology is any form of device or software that is used to assist students with special educational needs or disabilities in meeting their learning targets. (Peterson et al. 2015) These include resources that promote accessibility and a variety of learning styles through assistive technology and adaptive learning environments. AI has been a disruptive factor in many areas, including education, in the last few years. Artificial intelligence (AI) is defined as technologies that can duplicate human intellects in terms of reasoning, learning and problem solving (Russell & Norvig, 2022). AI algorithms' improvements along with the large amount of data and computer power have led to the novel developments in education notably in special education. The possibilities of improving the educational experiences and the achievement of the kids with disabilities are immense when the AI and special education technologies are combined. AI-based learning tools as compared to traditional teaching methodologies are capable of customizing programs to the requirements of individual learners ((Pullen et al. 2019) et al. 2019). AI in education would allow teachers to meet the different needs of students with disabilities more appropriately and make their classrooms more inclusive. The objective of this chapter is to examine how artificial intelligence (AI) will change the special education technology. We will examine the state of the art of the special education technology today, describe its main uses in this field, cover ethical problems that might occur, and demonstrate the difficulties and opportunities for the years to come.

2. HISTORICAL PERSPECTIVE

The first decade of the 20th century' gave birth to special education gadgets as educators placed resources for you willing to help kids with disabilities. Frank Haven Hall's invention of the Braille typewriter in 1892 greatly changed written communication for those who are blind or visually impaired. Technology-based innovations such as custom designed software for instruction, communication support, and hearing aids advanced education accessibility and learner potentials for a student with impairment. Personal computers and early educational software design that worked toward the new direction of being customized and adaptive became available in the late seventies and the eighties. These developments heightened the application of special education technology. The special education technology was first invented in the 1950s and the AI has played a very significant role in it. The machine learning algorithms, methods of the natural language processing, and the intelligent tutoring systems are the major accomplishment steps in the development of artificial intellect. AI's potential in health care appeared for the first time in 1974 when MYCIN system was developed, and later detected its diagnostic abilities which were as professional as those of a human specialist. Thus, the development of such systems was started to be called for further educational purposes, for instance, adaptive technology for children with impairments and personalized learning systems AI has been used in special education to design adaptable learning ecosystems and intelligent tutoring systems in a way which suits the user. The Cognitive Tutor marked the entry of AI algorithms into the education field in arithmetic practice using individualized training which emerged in the 1980's. This is an example of how AI can be utilized to customize education depending on the student's performance and learning styles. Both the technologies for synthetic voices and natural language processing has been a boon in assisting the students with language and speech problems, enhancing their team work and interactions by removing that barrier. The trail for the coming deployments of various AI applications in the special education appears to be already laid by the case studies of the use of AI in special education.

3.CURRENT LANDSCAPE OF SPECIAL EDUCATION TECHNOLOGY

A range of tools and resources are included in special education technology, which is intended to accommodate the requirements of children with disabilities or special needs. These technologies may be divided into a number of categories, such as instructional software, assistive technology, adaptive learning systems, and augmentative and alternative communication (AAC) devices. But even with all of the technological progress, instructors and students still have difficulties when putting these tools to use. The lack of resources and access, especially in impoverished places, might make it difficult to get the instruments that are required. Due to the lack of adequate accessibility features in many digital resources and educational software packages, accessibility and usability concerns still exist. In special education settings, educators frequently lack the professional development opportunities and training necessary to use technology successfully. Technical proficiency should be included in training programs, along with tactics for fostering inclusive learning environments and making use of technology to

3.1 Opportunities for Improvement Through AI Integration

Artificial intelligence (AI) offers promising potential to address the challenges faced by teachers and students in special education settings.

- **Personalized Learning:** AI-powered adaptive learning systems that evaluate student data may be used to provide personalized instruction and interventions tailored to each student's particular learning needs and preferences (Pullen et al. 2019)
- **Data-driven Decision Making:** Artificial intelligence (AI) algorithms can analyze large datasets to identify patterns and trends in student performance, assisting educators in making well-informed decisions about instructional strategies, modifications, and interventions (Pullen et al. 2019)
- **Natural Language Processing (NLP):** Wolf and Burleson (2017) state that NLP technology can help language-challenged pupils by enabling them to synthesis and identify speech, hence enhancing their communication abilities.

4. APPLICATIONS OF AI IN SPECIAL EDUCATION TECHNOLOGY

Natural language processing (NLP), adaptive learning systems, tailored learning experiences, assistive technologies for students with impairments, and AI-driven assessment and progress tracking tools are just a few of the ways that artificial intelligence (AI) technology has transformed education. With the help of AI algorithms, personalized learning systems evaluate student data and modify training to match each student's needs. This results in focused interventions, fast feedback, and specially created content. By using AI algorithms to dynamically modify the speed, subject matter, and degree of difficulty of education in response to student performance and advancement, adaptive learning systems foster student autonomy, engagement, and mastery of learning objectives. AI-driven assistive technologies improve accessibility and support for students with impairments. Examples of these include computer vision and object recognition, speech recognition and synthesis, prosthetics, and mobility aids. Students that struggle with communication can benefit from artificial intelligence (AI) systems' ability to comprehend, interpret, and produce human language thanks to natural language processing (NLP) technology. AI-driven solutions for tracking progress and assessments evaluate student performance data, spot patterns in learning outcomes, and tailor instruction to a varied student population using machine learning algorithms.

4.1 Personalized Learning Experiences

AI is able to assess student data and adjust instruction to meet the needs and preferences of individual students, enabling personalized learning experiences (Pullen et al. 2019) Personalized learning systems assess students' learning preferences, areas of strength, and areas of weakness using AI algorithms so that teachers may modify their approach. To assist students in achieving their learning objectives, AI-driven tutoring tools, for example, can provide targeted interventions, immediate feedback, and customized material (VanLehn et al. 2011).

4.2 Adaptive Learning Systems

Adaptive learning systems use AI algorithms to dynamically adjust the pace, content, and difficulty level of instruction based on students' performance and progress (Pullen et al. 2019) These systems analyze data from student interactions to identify areas of competency and those that require further support in order to deliver customized learning routes. Adaptive learning technologies promote student autonomy, engagement, and mastery of learning objectives by providing tailored scaffolding and challenges (((Anderson et al. 1995) et al. 1995) ; al., 1995).

4.3 Assistive Technologies for Students with Disabilities

AI-driven assistive technology increases accessibility and offers additional support in several domains to students with disabilities. For example, because to developments in computer vision and object recognition technologies, visually impaired pupils may now independently explore their environment (Miesenberger et al., 2018). Voice recognition and synthesis technology facilitate effective communication and self-expression for those with speech and language impairments (Iuculano et al. 2015). Artificial intelligence-driven prosthesis and mobility aids increase independence and mobility for students with physical constraints (Borg et al. 2012).

4.4 Natural Language Processing for Communication Support

Natural language processing (NLP) technology enables artificial intelligence (AI) systems to understand, interpret, and generate human language, which can be beneficial for students who have communication difficulties (Iuculano et al. 2015). Several NLP technologies, such as sentiment analysis, language translation, and speech recognition, can assist students in a range of communication tasks. For example, predictive text algorithms can assist language-challenged individuals in writing messages or participating in online discussions (Mayer et al. 2013)

4.5 AI-Driven Assessment and Progress Tracking Tools

Artificial intelligence (AI)-based assessment systems use machine learning algorithms to analyze student performance data and identify trends in learning outcomes and development. Through the provision of adaptive assessments, monitoring of student involvement, and provision of data for instructional decision-making, they enhance accessibility and optimize learning outcomes for a diverse student body.

5. CASE STUDIES AND EXAMPLES

Artificial intelligence (AI), particularly in intelligent tutoring systems, has to be included into special education to support students with learning disabilities. Social contact and communication are enhanced by NLP-capable social robots and Carnegie Learning's Cognitive Tutor software, which enhances instruction and learning chances. The integration of AI in special education has positively impacted the social skills and engagement of children with impairments. A University of Washington study found that while utilizing VR-based therapy, teenagers with autism were able to interact and communicate more socially. Mindspark is a program developed by Educational Initiatives in India that uses artificial intelligence (AI) algorithms to provide tailored arithmetic teaching to students with a range of learning challenges. In a randomized controlled trial, students who received personalized AI-based instruction outperformed those in traditional classrooms in terms of learning gains. These success stories show how artificial intelligence (AI) may enhance learning outcomes and student engagement for kids with disabilities.

5.1 Impact of AI on Student Outcomes and Engagement

AI has a significant impact on student outcomes and engagement in special education programs. It can provide personalized learning, increase engagement, and improve academic achievement by tailoring the learning experience to each student's needs and pace. This can be achieved by adjusting difficulty levels, providing targeted instruction, and catering to different learning styles. This personalization leads to a more engaging learning experience, fostering a sense of accomplishment and motivation meta-analysis of multiple research projects found that AI-based systems lead to increased academic achievement due to effective practice, immediate feedback, and increased focus and time on task. AI-driven assistive technologies, such as text-to-speech and speech-to-text tools, can help students with reading difficulties access information, improve their writing and dyslexia, and enable deaf or hard of hearing students to participate fully in classroom activities. AI-powered assistive technology fosters independence and self-reliance in students with disabilities by removing barriers to learning and communication. However, the effectiveness of AI depends on how it is implemented and integrated with a comprehensive special education program. Overall, AI offers a promising approach to enhance student outcomes and engagement in special education, but its effectiveness depends on how it is implemented and integrated with the program.

5.2 Enhancing Communication: AI in Augmentative and Alternative Communication (AAC)

AAC (alternative and augmentative communication) devices are instruments made to help people who have severe speech or language impairments. These gadgets vary in complexity from straightforward, low-tech solutions like picture boards to sophisticated, high-tech systems with speech-generating devices (SGDs). AAC devices are primarily intended to improve communication for people with impairments, allowing them to express themselves, engage in social interactions, and take part more fully in educational and professional environments (Beukelman et al. 2020).

AAC devices can be categorized into three main types:

- **No-Tech and Low-Tech AAC:** These gadgets, which include picture exchange systems, books, and communication boards, run off electricity and don't require batteries.
- **Mid-Tech AAC:** These are low-featured electronic gadgets, such basic SGDs that play recorded messages.
- **High-Tech AAC:** These are high-tech electronic gadgets that can produce synthesized speech and frequently have features like voice recognition and predictive text. Examples of these gadgets are tablets, computers, and advanced SGDs.

Artificial Intelligence (AI) has great promise for improving AAC devices' usability and efficacy. These gadgets can provide more individualized, effective, and organic communication experiences by incorporating AI. The following are some significant ways AI is changing AAC technology:

i. **Predictive Text and Word Prediction**: By analyzing a user's past inputs, artificial intelligence (AI) systems can anticipate the word or phrase the user will type next. This feature facilitates faster communication and lessens the work involved in crafting communication. For instance, machine learning models are used by predictive text solutions, such as those created by SwiftKey (now a part of Microsoft), to deliver precise word predictions, improving typing productivity for AAC users (Elsahar et al. 2019).

ii. **Natural Language Processing (NLP)**: NLP makes it possible for AAC devices to produce and comprehend human language in a way that is appropriate for the setting. This facilitates the conversion of user input into speech that sounds more realistic. By using NLP approaches, AAC devices may decipher unclear inputs and offer pertinent recommendations, improving user satisfaction and streamlining communication (Beukelman et al. 2020). The study of how computers and human language interact is the subject of the artificial intelligence discipline known as natural language processing, or NLP. It makes it possible for machines to comprehend, decipher, and react to human language in a way that is both practical and meaningful. NLP has revolutionized the way that assistive and alternative communication (AAC) technologies facilitate communication for students with disabilities. This section examines how NLP is used in AAC devices, providing practical examples and their effects.

Case Study: An program called SwiftKey predicts text and has been modified for usage with AAC devices. It offers extremely precise word predictions by learning from the user's writing style, which speeds up and eases the burden of communication for people with physical limitations that restrict their typing pace (Elsahar et al. 2019).

5.3 NLP Applications to Help Students with Disabilities Communicate

NLP technology allows for more natural, fluid, and productive conversations, which helps close the communication gap for children with impairments when using AAC devices. The following are some important applications:

iii. **Speech Recognition and Synthesis:** Users with restricted mobility can operate their AAC devices by speaking commands into advanced speech recognition software. Furthermore, voice synthesis enabled by AI generates more customized and natural-sounding speech outputs. To give realistic and customized voice options, businesses like Google and Amazon have created advanced voice synthesis technologies that can be included into AAC devices (Wang et al. 2017).

Case Study: Dysarthria and Speech Recognition: An NLP-based speech recognition system specifically designed for people with motor speech disorders, such as dysarthria, was created at the University of Sheffield through a project. After the system was trained on the distinct speech patterns of dysarthric speakers, recognition accuracy increased dramatically, strengthening the speakers' capacity for communication (Christensen et al. 2012).

iv. **Image and Object Recognition:** By identifying objects or images that users point to or gaze at and producing corresponding spoken words or phrases, AI-driven image and object recognition can support users with severe physical limitations in communicating. For example, Microsoft's Seeing AI app, which can be modified for AAC, uses machine vision to describe people, objects, and text in the environment (Miesenberger et al., 2018).

v. **Context-Aware Messaging**: AAC devices can provide more pertinent and well-thought-out responses when they are able to comprehend the context of discussions thanks to NLP. This is especially helpful in social interactions that are dynamic and subject to sudden changes in circumstance.

Case Study: Collaborative Writing Initiative: An NLP-driven AAC system that helps kids with learning difficulties write better by offering context-aware recommendations and corrections in real-time was developed as part of the CoWriter project, a cooperation between the University of Geneva and EPFL (Huang et al. 2024).

5.4 Impact on Communication and Quality of Life

AI has the capacity to gain knowledge from user interactions over time and modify itself to suit each user's unique requirements. By personalizing these gadgets, AAC devices become more responsive and intuitive. Adaptive learning algorithms improve the usability and efficiency of AAC devices by customizing their vocabulary and interface (King, 2011). The communication skills of people with disabilities are greatly improved by the incorporation of AI into AAC devices. Increased independence, better social contact, and an overall superior quality of life are the results of these developments. AI helps close the communication gap between users and AAC devices, enabling them to express themselves more fully and engage in community activities. Artificial Intelligence (AI) is transforming the AAC space by enhancing the efficiency, personalization, and naturalness of device communication. These upgrades not only improve the gadgets' functionalities but also greatly raise the standard of living for people who struggle with communication. AI has the ability to significantly change AAC and other assistive technology as it develops, providing new avenues for inclusivity and

6. ETHICAL CONSIDERATION

Since special education technology powered by artificial intelligence (AI) gathers and uses personal student data, privacy concerns are raised. AI systems may violate students' right to privacy since they rely on vast volumes of data to draw judgments. Concerns of student confidentiality, authorization, and data security are brought up by this data collecting. To allay these worries, educators and legislators must establish precise guidelines for the gathering, storing, and application of data in AI-driven special education programs. These include getting consent with full knowledge, protecting personal data from unwanted access, and putting strong cybersecurity measures in place to prevent data exploitation.

6.1 Bias and Fairness in AI Algorithms for Special Education

Artificial intelligence (AI) algorithms employed in special education technology have the potential to accentuate or perpetuate biases and disadvantages, particularly those related to gender, racism, socioeconomic status, and disability. This might lead to biased outcomes for underrepresented student populations. To lessen bias and enhance justice, developers should prioritize transparency, responsibility, and diversity when creating and deploying algorithms. This means ensuring that training datasets include a range of representations, conducting extensive testing and validation procedures, and frequently assessing AI systems for equity and justice.

6.2 Ensuring Inclusivity and Accessibility in AI-Driven Technologies

AI-driven solutions must be inclusive and accessible for special education. Developers should adopt a universal design approach that considers a variety of needs and ability levels. This includes integrated accessibility features, customizable user interfaces, support for multiple sensory modalities, and alternative input methods. Engaging in communication with end users can help guarantee that particular accessibility requirements are met.

6.3 AI Chatbots and Virtual Assistants for Real-Time Support

NLP-powered AI chatbots and virtual assistants empower students with impairments in real-time, improving their communication skills and helping with a range of activities.

- **AI Chatbots**: AI chatbots employ natural language processing (NLP) to communicate with users in natural language, answering their questions and holding discussions. These chatbots can provide instant conversational support by being embedded into AAC devices.

Case Study: Alternative for Emotional Assistance: People with autism have used Replika, an AI chatbot created for emotional assistance, to practice social interactions and communicate their emotions. Users can enhance their communication skills in a secure and encouraging setting by using the chatbot's comprehension and responsiveness to a broad spectrum of emotional emotions (Burke et al., 2021).

- **Virtual Assistants**: NLP is used by virtual assistants such as Siri, Google Assistant, and Alexa to interpret and carry out voice orders, complete tasks, and deliver information. With the integration of these aides into AAC devices, users can carry out daily tasks with greater independence.

Case Study: Violet, a business that specializes in non-standard speech recognition technology, has linked its system with Amazon Alexa. This enables voice commands to be used by people with speech difficulties to operate smart home appliances, retrieve information, and improve communication. The integration serves as an example of how NLP can improve technology's usability and accessibility for individuals with impairments (Voiceitt, 2021).

NLP applications in AAC devices significantly enhance communication for students with disabilities by providing more natural, intuitive, and efficient interactions. From predictive text to context-aware messaging and AI chatbots, these technologies are making a profound impact on the lives of individuals with communication challenges. By continuing to integrate and refine NLP capabilities, AAC devices can become even more powerful tools for fostering independence, inclusion, and social participation.

7. FUTURE DIRECTIONS AND CHALLENGES

Special education technology is going toward the intersection of AI and tailored learning, and many recent advancements are changing the landscape in this area:

- **Augmented Reality (AR) and Virtual Reality (VR)**: It is possible to create immersive learning environments that satisfy the different needs of students with disabilities by utilizing AR and VR technologies. (Mukhtarkyzy et al. 2022) (2013) asserts that these technologies can provide chances for experiential learning, virtual field trips, and interactive simulations that enhance student comprehension and engagement.

- **Emotion Recognition and Affective Computing**: Artificial intelligence (AI)-driven systems with the ability to recognize and respond to their students' emotions may help and personalize social-emotional learning. By analyzing physiological data, facial expressions, and vocal intonations, these systems can provide adaptive feedback and therapies to promote resilience and well-being (Picard et al. 2000).

- **Blockchain for Secure Data Management** Blockchain technology allows for the safe management of sensitive student data on a transparent, decentralized network. By leveraging blockchain technology, special education technology providers may increase data privacy, integrity, and interoperability while granting students control over their personal data (Tapscott et al. 2016).

7.1 Potential Barriers to Widespread Adoption

Although artificial intelligence (AI) has much to offer special education technology, there are a few barriers that might keep it from being used widely:

- **Cost and Resource Constraints**: Deploying AI-driven technologies often requires significant infrastructure support, specialist knowledge, and financial investment. It's probable that many educational establishments lack the resources and know-how required to properly integrate and sustain these technologies, particularly those located in low-income areas (Bateman et al. 2019)

- **Lack of Training and Professional Development**: Educators and special education professionals can find it challenging to acquire the knowledge and skills required to properly integrate AI into their lesson plans. Teachers need to have access to extensive training and professional development programs in order to employ AI-driven technology to serve different learners in an effective manner. In 2015. Peterson et al.

- **Ethical and Legal Concerns**: Ethical worries concerning AI systems' fairness, bias, and data privacy significantly impede adoption. Educators, policymakers, and tech developers must navigate complex legal and ethical frameworks to ensure that AI-driven technologies protect students' rights, enhance justice, and minimize potential hazards (Noble, 2018).

7.2 Research Gaps and Areas for Further Exploration

The topic of artificial intelligence (AI) for special education technology has a number of research gaps and areas that require more investigation.

- **Long-Term Effects on Learning Outcomes**: More research is needed to assess the long-term impacts of AI-driven treatments on kids' academic achievement, social-emotional development, and post-school outcomes. Longitudinal studies can provide valuable information on the efficacy and long-term sustainability of AI-driven special education technology, claim VanDerHeyden et al. (2020).
- **Inclusive Design and User Experience**: To ensure that AI-driven solutions are accessible and useful for all students, including those with disabilities, inclusive design concepts and user-cantered methodologies should be prioritized in future research. By including stakeholders in the design and development process, learning environments may be made more egalitarian and inclusive (Rose et al. 2002).
- **Cross-Cultural and Multilingual Perspectives**: Studying the environmental, linguistic, and cultural factors influencing the effectiveness of AI-driven special education programs is necessary to advance global diversity and inclusion. Cross-cultural research can have an impact on the development of culturally aware AI systems and instructional techniques that meet the diverse needs of students from different backgrounds (Wozniak et al.2015).

8. SUPPORTING COGNITIVE AND BEHAVIOURAL INTERVENTIONS

Particularly for kids with exceptional needs, artificial intelligence (AI) holds great promise for revolutionizing the monitoring and evaluation of student behaviour in educational environments. Teachers and doctors can obtain profound insights into student behaviour patterns by utilizing AI, which makes it possible to provide more successful interventions and assistance.

- **Tracking and Analysing Student Behaviour:** Tracking and Analysing Student Behaviour Real-time tracking and analysis of student behaviour is becoming more and more common with the usage of AI technologies like computer vision and machine learning. In order to spot patterns and trends in behaviour, these systems are able to record and analyze data from a variety of sources, such as interaction logs, wearable sensors, and video feeds.

- **Classroom Management Systems Enhanced by AI:** Machine learning algorithms are used by AI-based classroom management systems, such as ClassDojo, to monitor student conduct. According to Lam et al. (2018), these systems evaluate participation, attentiveness, and social interaction data from classroom interactions to give teachers timely feedback and useful insights. These tools aid instructors in comprehending the root causes of behavioural problems and developing customized solutions by highlighting patterns.
- **Automated Intervention Strategies Based on Behavioural Data:** The creation and application of automated intervention techniques is another application for AI. AI systems are able to suggest individualized solutions that are catered to the unique requirements of every learner through the analysis of behavioural data. IBM Watson for Education uses artificial intelligence (AI) to deliver behavioural interventions and customized learning experiences. Watson can provide focused treatments, such more practice exercises or social-emotional learning activities, to address particular needs by evaluating student data, including academic performance and behavioural trends (Chen et al. 2016). This methodology guarantees that interventions are grounded in facts and evidence, hence augmenting their efficacy.

8.1 Cognitive Skill Development

By creative methods like gamification and cognitive training programs, AI-driven tools are also being utilized to improve cognitive abilities like memory and attention.AI technology can be used to develop customized cognitive training curricula that adjust to the unique requirements of every learner. These programs pinpoint areas of cognitive impairment and offer focused exercises to strengthen these abilities using data-driven insights.

- **Case Study: Lumosity**: Personalized brain training activities to improve memory, focus, and problem-solving abilities are provided by Lumosity, an AI-driven cognitive training platform. The platform ensures a personalized training experience that changes with the user's development by using machine learning algorithms to adjust the exercises' difficulty and type based on the user's performance (Hardy et al. 2011).

8.2 Gamification and AI for Cognitive Training

An additional effective strategy for developing cognitive skills is gamification, which is the use of game design principles outside of gaming environments. Gamification in conjunction with AI can produce interesting and successful cognitive training scenarios.

- **Case Study: CogniFit**: CogniFit creates cognitive training games that focus on particular cognitive skills by combining AI and gamification. After evaluating the user's cognitive strengths and limitations using AI, the platform suggests tailored games that target cognitive skills including memory, attention, and executive function. CogniFit encourages users to persist with their training regimens and produce greater results by making cognitive training enjoyable and interesting (Ballesteros et al. 2014).

AI has the ability to significantly improve behavioral and cognitive therapies for students with exceptional needs. Teachers are able to use data-driven, tailored interventions and obtain important insights by using AI to monitor and evaluate student behavior. Furthermore, cutting-edge methods for improving cognitive abilities are provided by gamification techniques and AI-driven technologies, which improve the efficacy and appeal of training. These technologies will probably have a greater influence on special education as they develop further, opening up new avenues for meeting the varied requirements of kids.

9. DATA-DRIVEN DECISION MAKING

Because it helps with data gathering and analysis, artificial intelligence (AI) is essential to special education. Digital learning platforms and wearable technology are only two of the sources from which AI-powered applications collect and evaluate many kinds of educational data, including behavior, performance, and engagement. AI systems examine this data in order to find patterns and insights that can direct intervention and instructional tactics.Real-time feedback and monitoring systems driven by AI offer instant insights into student behavior and performance, facilitating timely correction. Classcraft is one example of a tool that gamifies classroom management by tracking student behavior in real time. In special education, predictive analytics is especially helpful in identifying kids who may struggle academically and in creating interventions to assist them prevent or decrease such challenges. Predictive analytics employs artificial intelligence (AI) to estimate future educational outcomes.

9.1 Data Collection and Analysis

Particularly in special education, artificial intelligence (AI) is vital to the gathering and processing of educational data. AI helps educators make better decisions, customize interventions, and enhance educational outcomes for students with special needs by processing enormous volumes of data in real-time. AI-powered tools are skilled at gathering a wide range of educational data, such as behaviour, performance, and engagement from students. Numerous sources, including wearable technology, digital learning platforms, and classroom interactions, can provide these data points. This data is analyzed by AI algorithms to find trends and insights that might guide intervention and teaching tactics.

- **Case Study: Learning Analytics and AI**: AI-enhanced learning analytics solutions gather information on how students engage with course material and how they perform on tests. Systems such as BrightBytes, for example, employ artificial intelligence (AI) to evaluate data from several sources, giving teachers thorough assessments on their students' progress and pinpointing areas that need improvement (West et al. 2012). Teachers can better understand each student's individual learning needs and adjust their education by using a data-driven approach.

9.2 Real-Time Monitoring and Feedback Systems

AI-powered real-time monitoring and feedback systems give educators instant insights into the performance and conduct of their students, enabling prompt remediation. These systems can monitor a range of parameters, including assignment completion, participation rates, and engagement levels. They can also give teachers and students immediate feedback.

- **Case Study: Classcraft**: Classcraft is an AI-powered tool that tracks student behavior in real time and gamifies classroom management. The platform gathers information about student interactions and gives prompt feedback to promote positive behavior and involvement. Instructors can utilize the information to pinpoint students who might want more help and to carry out focused interventions (Abramovich et al. 2013).

9.3 Predictive Analytics

Using artificial intelligence (AI) to forecast future educational outcomes from historical and present data is known as predictive analytics. Predictive models are very helpful in special education when it comes to identifying pupils who may struggle academically and developing interventions to help them avoid or lessen such issues. Large datasets can be analyzed by AI algorithms to forecast a variety of educational outcomes, including academic achievement, graduation rates, and the chance of developing learning disabilities. Artificial Intelligence (AI) has the potential to offer educators valuable insights for creating customized learning plans and interventions by spotting patterns and trends.

- **Case Study:** Early Intervention Programs Using Predictive Analytics: AI is used by initiatives like Early Warning Systems (EWS) to identify pupils who may be at risk of falling behind. These programs look at information about conduct, grades, and attendance to find students who can benefit from extra help. For instance, the Chicago Public Schools' EWS employs predictive analytics to identify children who may be at risk of dropping out, enabling teachers to take early action and offer focused assistance (Heppen et al. 2008).

9.4 Early Identification of Learning Disabilities Through Predictive Models

Learning difficulties can also be early detected with predictive models. Artificial Intelligence is able to identify indicators of learning problems and suggest more testing and assistance by examining data from examinations, student performance, and behavioral observations.

- **Case Study:** Using AI to Identify Dyslexia Eye tracking technologies and machine learning algorithms are used by AI-driven products such as Lexplore to detect dyslexia in pupils. The technology examines pupils' eye movements while they read to identify dyslexia symptoms with a high degree of accuracy. For students with dyslexia, early diagnosis improves results by enabling educators to offer tailored treatments and support (Rello et al. 2015).

For special education, the use of AI in data gathering, analysis, and predictive analytics has a lot to offer. AI supports educators in making data-driven decisions that improve educational tactics and interventions by offering real-time monitoring and feedback. Early detection of learning problems and customization of interventions to each student's specific requirements are made possible by predictive analytics.

The potential for AI technologies to revolutionize special education through data-driven decision-making will only increase as they develop further.

10. ENHANCING PERSONALIZED LEARNING

Personalized learning experiences are made possible by AI-powered adaptive learning systems, which are made to dynamically change course content based on each student's performance and learning requirements. By analyzing student data and tailoring course materials to individual needs, these systems employ algorithms to pinpoint problem areas and offer targeted solutions. Through assignments, tests, and participation in activities, they gather data about how students interact with the course material. Based on this analysis, they can change the teaching approach, add more resources, or increase the level of difficulty. Newton, DreamBox Learning, and Smart Sparrow are a few special education examples of adaptive learning platforms. These platforms offer strategies and customized data to better learning outcomes, with advantages like customized learning trajectories, prompt feedback and assistance, increased engagement, and focused interventions. For kids with impairments, individualized education plans, or IEPs, are essential in the field of special education. AI greatly enhances the efficacy and efficiency of the IEP preparation and administration processes. AI solutions streamline the creation and management of IEPs by automating procedures and providing data-driven insights. In order to assist instructors in creating comprehensive IEPs, AI may examine student data, including behavioral reports, testing results, and progress tracking. Additionally, AI systems have the ability to continuously track students' progress and modify IEPs as necessary. Numerous IEP process processes can be automated by AI, improving process efficiency and reducing teachers' administrative workload. It can gather and evaluate data from multiple sources on its own, guaranteeing that IEPs are founded on accurate and comprehensive data. AI can assist teachers in creating personalized, practical learning objectives and suggest the optimal learning tactics depending on each student's needs and developmental stage.

11. ADAPTIVE LEARNING SYSTEMS

AI-powered adaptive learning systems dynamically modify course material in response to each student's performance and learning requirements. Personalized learning experiences are provided by these systems, which address the various requirements of students—special education pupils in particular. Algorithms are used by AI-driven adaptive learning systems to evaluate student data and customize course materials to each student's needs. In order to offer individualized learning paths, these systems continuously evaluate the performance, preferences, and learning styles of their students. They assist in identifying problem areas for kids and provide focused interventions as a result. These systems collect information about how students engage with course material through assignments, quizzes, and activity participation. To ascertain the student's comprehension and areas of difficulty, the AI examines this data. The analysis is used by the system to modify the instructional strategy, add more resources, or raise the difficulty level.

Examples of Adaptive Learning Platforms in Special Education

A number of platforms for adaptive learning are made expressly to help kids with unique needs. These platforms provide methods and tailored information to improve learning results.

- **Knewton**: Knewton's AI-powered adaptive learning platform analyzes student data to tailor instruction. It provides students with learning difficulties with tailored support by modifying the speed and difficulty of lessons in real-time (Knewton, n.d.).
- **DreamBox Learning**: DreamBox Learning offers an adaptive math program that continuously assesses student performance and provides personalized instruction. It supports diverse learners, including those with special educational needs, by adjusting content to match their unique learning profiles (DreamBox Learning, n.d.).
- **Smart Sparrow**: This program gives individualized training and is a continuous student performance assessor for math. By customizing information to fit each learner's own learning profile, it accommodates a varied range of learners, including those with special educational needs (DreamBox Learning, n.d.).

11.1 Benefits for Students with Diverse Learning Needs

For students with a range of learning demands, AI-driven adaptive learning systems provide the following advantages:

- **Personalized Learning Paths**: These programs adapt course material to each student specifically, making sure that every student gets instruction according to their level and speed.

- **Immediate Feedback and Support**: Students can comprehend their errors and pick up new skills right away with the aid of adaptive learning systems, which offer real-time feedback.
- **Enhanced Engagement**: Adaptive learning systems boost students' motivation and engagement by providing content that aligns with their interests and skill levels.
- **Targeted Interventions**: By identifying problem areas and offering tailored interventions, these systems make sure that students' learning gaps are quickly filled.

11.2 Individualized Education Plans (IEPs)

Personalized learning goals and tactics for students with disabilities are outlined in Individualized Education Plans (IEPs), which are crucial in the field of special education. AI significantly contributes to the creation and administration of IEPs, improving process effectiveness and efficiency.AI technologies automate a number of processes and offer data-driven insights, which simplify the construction and administration of IEPs

- **Development of IEPs**: AI can examine student data, such as behavioral reports, assessment results, and progress monitoring, to assist teachers in creating thorough IEPs. This analysis guarantees that the plans are grounded in current, reliable data regarding the requirements and abilities of the students.
- **Management and Monitoring**: AI programs are able to keep an eye on students' development in real time and adjust IEPs as needed. This continuous observation ensures that the learning objectives and tactics are still applicable and successful.

11.3Automation and Optimization of Personalized Learning Goals and Strategies

Numerous IEP process steps can be automated by AI, increasing process efficiency and lessening the administrative load on teachers.

- **Automated Data Collection**: AI systems are capable of autonomously collecting and analyzing data from a variety of sources, including behavioral observations, attendance records, and classroom assessments. IEPs are based on complete and reliable data thanks to this automatic data collecting.
- **Optimization of Learning Strategies**: AI is able to recommend the best learning approaches based on the demands and development of the student.

For instance, the AI may suggest that a student concentrate on learning new abilities or move on to more difficult material if they demonstrate improvement in a particular area.

- **Personalized Goal Setting**: AI can help teachers create individualized, realistic learning objectives for each student. AI assists in ensuring that objectives are reachable and in line with current circumstances by evaluating past data and forecasting future performance.

AI-driven adaptive learning systems and AI's role in managing IEPs significantly enhance personalized learning in special education. Adaptive learning platforms provide customized learning experiences, while AI streamlines the development and management of IEPs, ensuring that educational strategies are tailored to the unique needs of each student. The integration of AI in special education holds promise for improving learning outcomes and creating more inclusive and effective educational environments.

12. RECOMMENDATIONS FOR PRACTITIONERS AND POLICYMAKERS

Lawmakers and practitioners may successfully integrate artificial intelligence (AI) into special education curricula by putting these suggestions into practice:

I. **Professional Development**: Provide educators with opportunities for professional development and in-depth training so they may become more skilled at using AI-driven technologies. Training should cover both technical skills and pedagogical approaches in order to successfully incorporate AI into educational methods (Peterson et al. 2015).

II. **Universal Design for Learning (UDL)**: Embracing the UDL principles will ensure that all students, irrespective of ability or chosen learning style, may make inclusive and accessible use of AI-driven technology. Develop curricula that offer many platforms for representation, expression, and engagement in order to satisfy the needs of a diverse student body (Rose et al. 2002).

III. **Data Literacy and Privacy Awareness**: Educate practitioners about the ethical implications of artificial intelligence and data privacy issues. Provide educators with the knowledge and skills necessary to make decisions about data collection, usage, and protection that adhere to all relevant laws and rules (Mayer et al. 2013)

12.1 Policy Recommendations for Ethical AI Implementation

Legislators may contribute to ensuring that AI is applied responsibly in special education by putting these legislative ideas into practice:

I. **Data Governance Frameworks**: Establish clear guidelines and protocols governing the collection, storage, and utilization of student data in special education technologies driven by artificial intelligence. In data governance frameworks, make sure that student privacy, consent, and data security are prioritized along with accountability and transparency (Mayer et al. 2013)

II. **Equity and Inclusion Mandates**: Policy frameworks should integrate standards for equality and inclusiveness in order to address concerns about bias and fairness in AI algorithms. Require developers and suppliers to conduct bias assessments, audits, and transparency reports in order to identify and mitigate algorithmic biases that might perpetuate inequality (Buolamwini et al. 2018).

III. **Accessibility Standards**: Implement accessibility standards and guidelines to ensure that AI-driven technology is usable and accessible for students with disabilities. To promote equal access to educational opportunities, enforce conformity to accessibility requirements, such as the Americans with Disabilities Act (ADA) and the Web Content Accessibility requirements (WCAG) (Rose et al. 2002).

12.2 Collaboration Between Stakeholders to Maximize Benefits and Mitigate Risks

Cooperation between stakeholders is essential to optimizing the benefits and lowering the risks of AI in special education:

I. **Interdisciplinary Collaboration**: Policymakers, academics, technologists, educators, and other stakeholders should be encouraged to co-design and co-implement AI-driven special education initiatives. According to VanDerHeyden et al. (2020), interdisciplinary teams must to be encouraged to make use of their distinct perspectives and specialties in order to come up with original solutions that address the complex issues facing the industry.

II. **Community Engagement**: Involve parents, kids, advocacy groups, and community organizations in the decision-making process to ensure that AI-driven special education initiatives take into account their needs, preferences, and worldviews. Encourage open communication, honesty, and participative techniques in order to foster consensus and trust among stakeholders. In 2015. Peterson et al.

III. **Continuous Evaluation and Feedback**: Establish mechanisms for ongoing evaluation, monitoring, and commenting in order to analyze the effectiveness, equity, and ethical implications of AI-driven special education resources. To identify areas that require improvement and make the necessary adjustments to implementation plans, get feedback from stakeholders and end users (Pullen et al. 2019)

13. IMPROVING ACCESSIBILITY

The way non-verbal and speech-impaired students communicate is being revolutionized by AI-driven speech and language processing technologies, which also improves their accessibility and educational prospects. Key areas in which AI-based tools are assisting students with speech difficulties are speech recognition and synthesis. While text-to-speech (TTS) technology converts written text into spoken words, Google's Speech-to-Text and Apple's Siri rely on sophisticated algorithms to accurately transcribe spoken words. AI-driven translation and interpretation services facilitate better communication and learning for nonverbal pupils. Through the use of augmentative and alternative communication (AAC) technology, nonverbal children can communicate by having their thoughts translated into spoken language. In multilingual learning environments, non-verbal students can engage more completely thanks to real-time translation systems like Google Translate. AI-powered assistive technology, including smart glasses and screen readers, offers students with impairments a fresh approach to learning. Students with visual impairments can freely access digital content with the use of screen readers like JAWS and NVDA. Real-time audio descriptions of their surroundings are provided by smart glasses such as Google Glass and OrCam MyEye, which enhances users' interaction with their surroundings. AI-powered robotic aides give students with limited mobility a sense of independence by assisting them in navigating their physical surroundings. Physical accessibility in educational environments is further enhanced by automated accessibility elements including voice-activated workstations, elevators, and doors.

13.1 Speech and Language Processing Tools

Artificial intelligence (AI)-driven speech and language processing technologies are transforming the way non-verbal and speech-impaired students communicate, improving their educational opportunities and accessibility in general. AI-based tools are helping students with speech impairments a lot, especially in the areas of speech recognition and synthesis.

- **Speech Recognition**: Text is generated from spoken words using AI-powered speech recognition technologies. With the help of these technologies, students who struggle with speech can communicate in other ways. To assist students, participate in class conversations and complete tasks orally, Google's Speech-to-Text and Apple's Siri employ sophisticated algorithms to reliably transcribe spoken words (Google Cloud, n.d.; Apple, n.d.).
- **Speech Synthesis**: Text-to-speech (TTS) technology, often known as AI speech synthesis, transforms written text into spoken words. With the help of this technology, students who struggle with speech can input their ideas and have the system read them aloud. Among the notable instances are the natural-sounding voice outputs provided by Microsoft's Azure Cognitive Services and Amazon's Polly (Amazon Web Services, n.d.; Microsoft Azure, n.d.).

13.2 Translation and Interpretation Services for Non-Verbal Students

AI-powered translation and interpretation services help nonverbal students communicate and study more effectively by offering crucial support.

- **Augmentative and Alternative Communication (AAC) Devices**: AI-enhanced AAC devices convert nonverbal pupils' thoughts into spoken language, facilitating communication. Students can communicate themselves more easily thanks to these technologies, which can translate written text, motions, and symbols into speech. In this regard, products such as Tobii Dynavox and Proloquo2Go are frequently utilized (AssistiveWare, n.d.; Tobii Dynavox, n.d.).
- **Real-Time Translation**: Non-verbal kids can benefit from real-time translation services by using AI translation technologies such as Google Translate to communicate with peers and teachers in many languages. According to Google Translate (n.d.), these tools facilitate both text and voice translation, allowing nonverbal students to participate more completely in multilingual learning contexts.

13.3 Assistive Technologies

Education is becoming more inclusive as a result of AI-driven assistive devices that improve both physical and digital accessibility for students with disabilities. Students with a range of disabilities are having a completely new educational experience thanks to assistive devices driven by AI.

- **Screen Readers**: By using AI to translate text on a screen into voice or Braille, screen readers like JAWS (Job Access With voice) and NVDA (NonVisual Desktop Access) allow visually impaired students to access digital content on their own (Freedom Scientific, n.d.; NV Access, n.d.).
- **Smart Glasses**: Artificial intelligence-enabled smart glasses, such as Google Glass and OrCam MyEye, help students who are visually impaired by giving them audio explanations of their surroundings in real time. These gadgets improve the user's interaction with their environment by reading text, recognizing faces, and identifying objects (OrCam, n.d.; Google Glass, n.d.).

13.4 Improvements in Physical Accessibility Using Automation and Robots

Significant progress is being made in enhancing physical accessibility for students with impairments through robotics and automation driven by artificial intelligence.

- **Robotic Assistants**: Students with mobility disabilities can navigate their physical environment with the assistance of AI-driven robotic assistants. For example, Kinova Robotics' JACO robotic arm can help with everyday chores and give students with restricted mobility more independence (Kinova Robotics, n.d.).
- **Automated Accessibility Features**: Additionally, automated elements that improve physical accessibility in educational settings are being developed using AI. In order to make classrooms more accessible to students with physical disabilities, examples include automated doors, elevators, and adjustable desks that respond to voice commands or other inputs (Smith, 2018).

AI-driven assistive technology and speech and language processing tools are greatly improving accessibility in education for students with disabilities. AI is enhancing inclusiveness and assistance for all learners in school by offering cutting-edge assistive devices, translation services, voice synthesis, and enhanced speech recognition. By enhancing physical accessibility and facilitating communication and engagement, these technologies enable students with disabilities to fully participate in educational settings and reach their potential.

14. CONCLUSION

This research investigates the relationship between artificial intelligence (AI) and special education technology, emphasizing the historical evolution and current condition of the technology. Among the applications of AI in special education that are discussed are personalized learning, adaptive learning systems, assistive technology, natural language processing, and AI-driven evaluation tools. The research also addresses privacy, racism, and inclusion as ethical concerns. It offers guidelines for the moral application of AI, standards for integrating AI into curricula, and collaboration amongst stakeholders as recommendations for lawmakers and educators. The study concludes that artificial intelligence (AI) has great promise for transforming special education while simultaneously enhancing equity, inclusivity, and academic achievement. It promotes continued research and innovation, including longitudinal studies, looking at novel uses of AI, and collaborating across academic boundaries, in order to build inclusive, moral, and practical AI-driven technology.

REFERENCES

Abramovich, S., Schunn, C., & Higashi, R. M. (2013). Are badges useful in education?: It depends upon the type of badge and expertise of learner. *Educational Technology Research and Development*, 61(2), 217–232. DOI: 10.1007/s11423-013-9289-2

Anderson, J. R., Corbett, A. T., Koedinger, K. R., & Pelletier, R. (1997). K. R., & Pelletier, R. (1995). Cognitive tutors: Lessons learned. *Journal of the Learning Sciences*, 4(2), 167–207. DOI: 10.1207/s15327809jls0402_2

Baker, R. S., D'Mello, S. K., Rodrigo, M. M. T., & Graesser, A. C. (2010). Better to be frustrated than bored: The incidence, persistence, and impact of learners' cognitive–affective states during interactions with three different computer-based learning environments. *International Journal of Human-Computer Studies*, 68(4), 223–241. DOI: 10.1016/j.ijhcs.2009.12.003

Ballesteros, S., Prieto, A., Mayas, J., Toril, P., Pita, C., Ponce de Leon, L., & Waterworth, J. (2014). Brain training with non-action video games enhances aspects of cognition in older adults: A randomized controlled trial. *Frontiers in Aging Neuroscience*, 6, 277. DOI: 10.3389/fnagi.2014.00277 PMID: 25352805

Bateman, D., & Cline, J. (2019). *Special Education Leadership*. Routledge. DOI: 10.4324/9781351201353

Beukelman, D., & Light, J. (2020). Augmentative and alternative communication: Supporting children and adults with complex communication needs.

Beukelman, D., & Light, J. (2020). Augmentative and alternative communication: Supporting children and adults with complex communication needs.

Borg, J., Larsson, S., Östergren, P. O., Rahman, A. A., Bari, N., & Khan, A. N. (2012). Assistive technology use and human rights enjoyment: A cross-sectional study in Bangladesh. *BMC International Health and Human Rights*, 12(1), 1–11. DOI: 10.1186/1472-698X-12-18 PMID: 22992413

Buolamwini, J., & Gebru, T. (2018, January). Gender shades: Intersectional accuracy disparities in commercial gender classification. In Conference on fairness, accountability and transparency (pp. 77-91). PMLR. Noble, S. U. (2018). Algorithms of oppression: How search engines reinforce racism. NYU Press.

Chen, G., Davis, D., Hauff, C., & Houben, G. J. (2016, April). Learning transfer: Does it take place in MOOCs? An investigation into the uptake of functional programming in practice. In *Proceedings of the Third(2016) ACM Conference on Learning@ Scale* (pp. 409-418).

Christensen, H., Cunningham, S. P., Fox, C., Green, P. D., & Hain, T. (2012, September). A comparative study of adaptive, automatic recognition of disordered speech. In *Interspeech* (pp. 1776-1779). DOI: 10.21437/Interspeech.2012-484

Elsahar, Y., Hu, S., Bouazza-Marouf, K., Kerr, D., & Mansor, A. (2019). Augmentative and Alternative Communication (AAC) Advances: A Review of Configurations for Speech Disabled Individuals.

Hardy, J. L., Drescher, D., Sarkar, K., Kellett, G., & Scanlon, M. (2011). Enhancing visual attention and working memory with a web-based cognitive training program. *Mensa Research Journal*, 42(2), 13–20.

. Heppen, J. B., & Therriault, S. B. (2008). Developing Early Warning Systems to Identify Potential High School Dropouts. Issue Brief. *National High School Center*.

Huang, W., Billinghurst, M., Alem, L., Xiao, C., & Rasmussen, T. (2024). *Computer-Supported Collaboration: Theory and Practice*. John Wiley & Sons. DOI: 10.1002/9781119719830

Iuculano, T., Rosenberg-Lee, M., Richardson, J., Tenison, C., Fuchs, L., Supekar, K., & Menon, V. (2015). Cognitive tutoring induces widespread neuroplasticity and remediates brain function in children with mathematical learning disabilities. *Nature Communications*, 6(1), 8453. DOI: 10.1038/ncomms9453 PMID: 26419418

Koedinger, K. R., Anderson, J. R., Hadley, W. H., & Mark, M. A. (1997). Intelligent tutoring goes to school in the big city. *International Journal of Artificial Intelligence in Education*, 8, 30–43.

Mayer-Schönberger, V., & Cukier, K. (2013). *Big data: A revolution that will transform how we live, work, and think*. Houghton Mifflin Harcourt.

Miesenberger, K., & Kouroupetroglou, G. (Eds.). (2018). Computers Helping People with Special Needs: *16th International Conference, ICCHP 2018,* Linz, Austria, July 11-13, 2018, *Proceedings, Part I* (Vol. 10896). Springer.

Miesenberger, K., Kouroupetroglou, G., Mavrou, K., Manduchi, R., Rodriguez, M. C., & Penáz, P. (Eds.). (2022). Computers Helping People with Special Needs: 18th International Conference, ICCHP-AAATE 2022, Lecco, Italy, July 11–15, 2022, Proceedings, Part I (Vol. 13341). Springer Nature.

Mukhtarkyzy, K., Abildinova, G., & Sayakov, O. (2022). The use of augmented reality for teaching Kazakhstani students physics lessons. [iJET]. *International Journal of Emerging Technologies in Learning*, 17(12), 215–235. DOI: 10.3991/ijet.v17i12.29501

Parsons, S., & Mitchell, P. (2002). The potential of virtual reality in social skills training for people with autistic spectrum disorders. *Journal of Intellectual Disability Research*, 46(5), 430–443. DOI: 10.1046/j.1365-2788.2002.00425.x PMID: 12031025

Peterson-Karlan, G. R. (2015). Assistive technology instruction within a continuously evolving technology environment. *Quarterly Review of Distance Education*, 16(2), 61.

Picard, R. W. (2000). *Affective computing*. MIT press. DOI: 10.7551/mitpress/1140.003.0008

Pullen, P. C., & Kennedy, M. J. (Eds.). (2019). *Handbook of response to intervention and multi-tiered systems of support*. Routledge.

Pullen, P. C., & Kennedy, M. J. (Eds.). (2019). *Handbook of response to intervention and multi-tiered systems of support*. Routledge.

Rello, L., & Ballesteros, M. (2015, May). Detecting readers with dyslexia using machine learning with eye tracking measures. In *Proceedings of the 12th international web for all conference* (pp. 1-8). DOI: 10.1145/2745555.2746644

Rose, D. H., & Meyer, A. (2002). Teaching every student in the digital age: Universal design for learning. Association for Supervision and Curriculum Development, 1703 N. Beauregard St., Alexandria, VA 22311-1714 (Product no. 101042: $22.95 ASCD members; $26.95 nonmembers).

Scassellati, B., Admoni, H., & Matarić, M. (2012). Robots for use in autism research. *Annual Review of Biomedical Engineering*, 14(1), 275–294. DOI: 10.1146/annurev-bioeng-071811-150036 PMID: 22577778

Shortliffe, E. H., & Buchanan, B. G. (1975). A model of inexact reasoning in medicine. *Mathematical Biosciences*, 23(3-4), 351–379. DOI: 10.1016/0025-5564(75)90047-4

Tapscott, D., & Tapscott, A. (2016). *Blockchain revolution: how the technology behind bitcoin is changing money, business, and the world*. Penguin.

VanLehn, K. (2011). The relative effectiveness of human tutoring, intelligent tutoring systems, and other tutoring systems. *Educational Psychologist*, 46(4), 197–221. DOI: 10.1080/00461520.2011.611369

Wang, Y., Skerry-Ryan, R. J., Stanton, D., Wu, Y., Weiss, R. J., Jaitly, N., . . . Saurous, R. A. (2017). Tacotron: Towards end-to-end speech synthesis. *arXiv preprint arXiv:1703.10135*. DOI: 10.21437/Interspeech.2017-1452

. West, D. M. (2012). Big data for education: Data mining, data analytics, and web dashboards. *Governance studies at Brookings, 4*(1), 1-10.

Wozniak, M., Krishnaswamy, D., Callegari, C., Takagi, H., Prasad, N. R., Que, X., & Sandhu, R. (2015). *Advances in Computing, Communications and Informatics*. ICACCI.

KEY TERMS AND DEFINITIONS

Artificial Intelligence (AI): A branch of computer science focused on creating systems capable of performing tasks that normally require human intelligence, such as learning, reasoning, and problem-solving. In special education, AI is used to develop tools that adapt to the individual needs of students.

Personalized Learning: An educational approach that uses AI to tailor instruction to the individual needs, skills, and interests of each student. Personalized learning is particularly beneficial in special education for addressing diverse learning needs.

Adaptive Learning Systems: AI-driven systems that dynamically adjust instructional content and strategies based on real-time analysis of a student's performance. These systems are used in special education to create customized learning experiences.

Assistive Technology: Devices or software designed to aid individuals with disabilities in performing tasks that might otherwise be difficult or impossible. AI enhances assistive technology by improving accessibility and user interaction.

Natural Language Processing (NLP): A field of AI that focuses on the interaction between computers and human language. NLP tools are used in special education to assist students with language impairments by improving communication and comprehension.

Gamification: The application of game-design elements in non-game contexts, such as education, to engage and motivate students. In special education, AI-driven gamification strategies are used to enhance cognitive skill development.

Individualized Education Plan (IEP): A legally required document in the U.S. that outlines personalized learning goals and services for students with disabilities. AI assists in the creation and management of IEPs by providing data-driven insights.

Data-Driven Decision Making: The process of making educational decisions based on the analysis of data collected from various sources. In special education, AI facilitates data-driven decision-making by providing real-time insights into student performance.

Speech Recognition: A technology that converts spoken language into text using AI. It is used in special education to assist students with speech impairments in communicating more effectively.

Augmentative and Alternative Communication (AAC): Tools and strategies used to support individuals with communication difficulties. AI enhances AAC devices by translating non-verbal communication into spoken language, improving accessibility for non-verbal students.

Chapter 6
Navigating the AI Policy Landscape:
AI in Community College Education

Jeremy Norton
Lake-Sumter State College, USA

ABSTRACT

Artificial Intelligence (AI) stands at the forefront of educational transformation, offering community colleges unprecedented opportunities to enhance learning experiences and administrative efficiency. However, the integration of AI into community college systems brings forth a series of policy challenges that necessitate nuanced governance frameworks within the structured federal system in the United States with different authorities given to the national government, the states, and educational institutions. This chapter explores the intricate policy landscape surrounding AI in community college education. Delving into existing policy frameworks, emerging trends, and evolving regulations will show the multifaceted intersection between AI technology and governance and what should be done to address this new reality.

INTRODUCTION

The unveiling of ChatGPT to the public on November 24, 2022, sent shockwaves through the world (Murray & Meyer, 2022). The launch of ChatGPT marked a significant milestone in the field of artificial intelligence and natural language processing. While the concept of Artificial Intelligence had been discussed for decades, this was the first easy to use tool presented to the public. News outlets around the world covered the event, highlighting the capabilities of ChatGPT in

DOI: 10.4018/979-8-3693-3053-1.ch006

generating coherent and contextually relevant responses to user queries. Articles often emphasized the groundbreaking nature of ChatGPT's underlying technology, showcasing its ability to engage in human-like conversations across a wide range of topics – highlighting its "brilliance and weirdness" (Roose, 2022). The launch garnered attention not only from tech enthusiasts but also from professionals in a variety of industries, who recognized the potential of ChatGPT in applications such as customer service, education, and content generation. In addition, there was also a discussion of the dark side of this sort of readily available technology. What did this mean for existing content creators? Students and teachers? Future careers? What sort of government action would be needed, if any? The more technology has been used, the more questions and issues arise.

Large language models such as ChatGPT are highly sophisticated AI systems renowned for their ability to comprehend and generate human-like text in ways that have not been possible before. Through extensive training on diverse datasets sourced from the internet, books, and articles, these models acquire a deep understanding of language structures, including grammar, semantics, and context (Brown et al., 2020). What distinguishes models like ChatGPT is their capability to generate coherent and contextually relevant responses across a wide range of prompts. By leveraging mechanisms like attention, these models can discern the importance of different words within sentences, facilitating the production of text that aligns seamlessly with human language patterns (Bahdanau et al., 2014). Additionally, their adaptability through fine-tuning on specific datasets or tasks enhances their performance in specialized domains or applications (Yang et al., 2019). However, despite their remarkable capabilities, ethical and societal concerns regarding large language models persist. Issues such as biases embedded in training data, the potential for misinformation dissemination, and responsible usage of generated content are paramount (Bender et al., 2021). Therefore, while large language models represent a significant technological advancement, their ethical deployment and responsible integration into various domains require careful consideration and proactive measures.

While it is not the only AI language generator, there are now dozens, the launch of ChatGPT was a turning point in terms of how the public, and students, interact with the vast content available in cyberspace. This was the first time that content could be easily generated by the public using simple prompts and questions. While copy and pasting techniques were used in the past using web content, this was different in scope and applicability. This new technology would require a different approach by educators and institutions to ensure legal, ethical, and fair use of information and the required guidance and policy to ensure the integrity of education in general. The academic world was certainly not ready for what was just launched.

This chapter will cover this policy challenge for education and community colleges in general. First, the basics about policy and law will be discussed and concerning information generally as well as what has been done to this point in time. Next, it will highlight various pitfalls and opportunities concerning AI guidance in college policy. Finally, some suggestions will be offered with an emphasis on what must continue to be done as the issue evolves both legally and technologically.

Policy and Law

Policy and law play crucial roles in shaping the landscape of copyright, fair use, and academic dishonesty. As a legal and policy issue, issues such as this are under the jurisdiction of both state and federal law. Copyright, privacy, and intellectual property are under the purview of the United States government while education policy is the responsibility of the individual states and, when it comes to the administration of rules, the college institutions themselves. The federal and state governments have struggled to address the civil, and potentially criminal, laws that are necessary to handle this new technology.

In the realm of copyright, laws provide the legal framework governing the protection of original works of authorship. The Copyright Act of 1976 in the United States, for instance, establishes the rights of creators and the limitations on those rights. It offers statutory protection for original works fixed in a tangible medium of expression, such as literature, music, and art. However, policy interventions, such as the Digital Millennium Copyright Act (DMCA), complement these laws by addressing emerging challenges in the digital age. The DMCA, enacted in 1998, introduces provisions to protect copyrighted materials in the digital realm, emphasizing the roles of internet service providers and online platforms in enforcing copyright laws (U.S. Copyright Office, 1998). While laws provide the backbone of copyright protection, policies like the DMCA refine and adapt legal principles to contemporary technological contexts.

Fair use represents a critical exception to copyright law, permitting the use of copyrighted material without permission from or payment to the copyright holder under certain circumstances – this allowance is used by educational institutions quite broadly. Defined in Section 107 of the U.S. Copyright Act, fair use encompasses purposes such as criticism, comment, news reporting, teaching, scholarship, and research (Fair Use Index, 2023). While the law delineates the four factors to consider in determining fair use—namely, the purpose and character of the use, the nature of the copyrighted work, the amount and substantiality of the portion used, and the effect of the use upon the potential market—the application of fair use principles still often involves a range of interpretations. Educational institutions and other organizations often develop internal policies to guide fair use practices, offering practical guidelines for navigating complex copyright issues within specific contexts. These policies serve to supplement legal provisions, providing clarity and guidance for users seeking to employ fair use exemptions effectively. Often, within community colleges these guidance documents and resources can be found within library or writing center resources for students as well as in instructor syllabus policies.

In academia, policies and laws converge to address issues of academic integrity and dishonesty. While laws typically do not directly regulate academic misconduct, institutions establish codes of conduct and honor systems to uphold academic integrity standards. These policies outline expectations for students and faculty regarding originality, attribution, and ethical research practices. These policies are usually found in student handbooks issued by the college. Additionally, laws related to fraud, plagiarism, and intellectual property infringement may intersect with academic integrity policies, offering legal recourse in cases of severe misconduct. For example, the Family Educational Rights and Privacy Act (FERPA) in the United States safeguards student privacy rights and confidentiality of educational records, reinforcing the importance of ethical conduct in academic environments for everyone involved including college staff (U.S. Department of Education, 2022). Through a combination of legal frameworks and institutional policies, colleges seek to maintain integrity and uphold the values of scholarship and knowledge dissemination while protecting rights.

The differences between law, policy, and guidance relating to these issues is charted below.

Table 1. Law, policy, and guidance

	Law	Policy	Guidance
Copyright	Encompasses legal statutes such as the Copyright Act of 1976 in the United States, providing the legal framework for protecting original works of authorship.	Policies may include institutional guidelines on copyright compliance, licensing agreements, and digital rights management protocols for vendors.	Guidance may include best practices for creators, such as maintaining documentation of ownership, understanding copyright duration, and utilizing Creative Commons licenses for sharing content.
Fair Use	Defined in legal statutes such as Section 107 of the U.S. Copyright Act, allowing limited use of copyrighted material without permission for purposes such as criticism, comment, news reporting, teaching, scholarship, and research.	Institutional policies may establish criteria for determining fair use within educational contexts, offering guidelines for faculty and students on permissible uses of copyrighted material.	Guidance may include fair use checklists, case studies, and examples to assist users in evaluating whether their use of copyrighted material qualifies as fair use under applicable law and policies.

continued on following page

Table 1. Continued

	Law	Policy	Guidance
Copyright	**Encompasses legal statutes such as the Copyright Act of 1976 in the United States, providing the legal framework for protecting original works of authorship.**	**Policies may include institutional guidelines on copyright compliance, licensing agreements, and digital rights management protocols for vendors.**	**Guidance may include best practices for creators, such as maintaining documentation of ownership, understanding copyright duration, and utilizing Creative Commons licenses for sharing content.**
Emerging AI Issues	Laws may encompass regulations related to data privacy, intellectual property rights, and liability for AI-generated content, such as the Digital Millennium Copyright Act (DMCA) in the United States. There is very little law enacted in this emerging area.	Institutional policies may address ethical considerations in the use of AI technologies, including data protection, algorithmic bias, and responsible AI development practices.	Guidance may include AI ethics frameworks, risk assessment tools, and principles for transparent and accountable AI decision-making, facilitating ethical AI implementation in academic and research settings.

In response to the growing use of AI in education, policymakers worldwide are developing ethical and other guidelines to govern its responsible use. The Biden administration's approach to AI guidance emphasizes both the promotion of innovation and the protection of individuals' rights and well-being through an executive order based on a previously empaneled task force (*The Biden administration*, 2021; Biden, 2023). According to their website, key points of their guidance for federal executive agencies include:

1. **Investment in Research and Development**: The administration has committed to investing in AI research and development to maintain U.S. leadership in technology and innovation.
2. **Ethical AI**: There's a focus on developing and deploying AI systems that are ethical and accountable. This involves ensuring fairness, transparency, and accountability in AI applications, particularly in sensitive areas like healthcare, criminal justice, and finance.
3. **Workforce Development**: Recognizing the impact of AI on the job market, efforts are made to reskill and upskill workers to adapt to changing technologies and to ensure that the benefits of AI are broadly shared across society.
4. **International Collaboration**: The administration advocates for international collaboration on AI standards, ethics, and norms to ensure that AI development aligns with democratic values and human rights.
5. **Privacy and Security**: Prioritizing the protection of privacy and security in AI systems, including measures to safeguard sensitive data and prevent misuse of AI technologies.
6. **Diversity and Inclusion**: Promoting diversity and inclusion in the AI workforce to ensure that the development and deployment of AI technologies represent a wide range of perspectives and experiences.

The Biden administration's AI guidance reflects a potential comprehensive approach to balancing the potential benefits and challenges of AI technologies. Recognizing AI's transformative power, the administration seeks to harness its potential while simultaneously addressing the ethical, legal, and social implications that arise from its widespread adoption. Central to this goal is the commitment to ensure that the benefits of AI are equitably distributed across society, thereby mitigating potential disparities in access and outcomes. In order to achieve this balance, the administration's guidance touches upon various aspects of AI regulation, including issues involving interstate commerce and civil rights. For instance, intellectual property concerns regarding AI-generated content and inventions necessitate a careful examination of existing copyright and patent laws, as well as potential legislative reforms to accommodate the unique nature of AI technologies. Similarly, AI's impact on privacy rights and data protection raises questions about the adequacy of current laws and the need for updated regulations to safeguard personal information in the age of AI.

Despite the administration's focus on AI policy, it is important to note that these initiatives have not yet translated into concrete legal changes. The responsibility for enacting new laws and amending existing ones lies with the US Congress, which must work collaboratively with the administration and other stakeholders to develop a comprehensive legal framework for AI. That process is complicated. Each chamber, the House of Representatives and the Senate, must work within their committee structures to balance practical and political concerns from those stakeholders to structure new bills in order for this to happen, similar to other legislation. Once compromises have been made, both chambers must agree on the same bill language and successfully vote on the package after all procedural steps have been completed. Then, the President has the option to sign or veto the legislation. None of these steps have even been initiated on this issue.

While Congress has not passed any additional laws yet, guidance has been given by their internal research organ. A Congressional Research Service report recommends congressional action to expand copyright laws to include generative AI programs (Congressional Research Service, 2023). It is made clear that current statutes are not sufficient to cover this new technology and the issues large language models create for content producers. In order for an update to occur, Congress and the President must coordinate and agree upon language that will affect businesses, colleges, and the public while protecting the rights of content creators. Such an agreement does not currently exist. The guidance is a good first step, but these changes would not directly affect educational institutions as those are regulated at the state level. Instead, additional, more focused ideas have been given through the specialized cabinet level department, the U.S. Department of Education.

In order to assist from the national perspective, the U.S. Departments of Education compiled general guidance on the use of AI for education. The key recommendations are provided for educators, policymakers, and administrators on the "AI in Education" webpage by the U.S. Department of Education's Office of Educational Technology include the following summarized below (U.S. Department of Education, Office of Educational Technology, 2024):

1. Emphasize Humans in the Loop

Rejecting the notion of AI as replacing teachers. Teachers and other people must be "in the loop" whenever AI is applied in order to notice patterns and automate educational processes.

2. Align AI Models to a Shared Vision for Education

Calling upon content-makers, researchers, and evaluators to determine the quality of an educational technology based not only on outcomes, but also based on the degree to which the models at the heart of the AI tools and systems align to a shared vision for teaching and learning.

3. Design Using Modern Learning Principles

Emphasis on creating AI systems that are culturally responsive and culturally sustaining, leveraging the growth of published techniques for doing so. Further, most early AI systems had few specific supports for students with disabilities and English learners and we must ensure that AI-enabled learning resources are intentionally inclusive of these students.

4. Prioritize Strengthening Trust

Calling for a focus on building trust and establishing criteria for trustworthiness of emerging educational technologies within the associations, convenings, and professional organizations that bring educators, innovators, researchers, and policymakers together.

5. Inform and Involve Educators

Respecting and valuing educators by informing and involving them in every step of the process of designing, developing, testing, improving, adopting, and managing AI-enabled educational technology.

6. Focus R&D on Addressing Context and Enhancing Trust and Safety

Prioritizing investigations of how AI can address the long tail of learning variability and to seek advances in how AI can incorporate contextual considerations when detecting patterns and recommending options to students and teachers.

7. Develop Education-Specific Guidelines and Guardrails

Calling for involvement of all perspectives in the ecosystem to define a set of guidelines and guardrails so that we can achieve safe and effective AI for education.

These recommendations are not enforceable but are structured to serve as guiding principles for educators, administrators, and policymakers seeking to harness the potential of AI technologies to enhance teaching and learning while upholding ethical standards and student privacy. Making many of these suggestions into laws and enforceable rules is largely up to the states due to education being a state power.

In the United States, the relationship between state and federal law is defined by the principle of federalism. While state law cannot supersede national law, the reserved powers of the states grant them the authority to apply educational policy within their borders. State legislatures are responsible for crafting these laws, and rule-making is carried out by state departments of education (Gannon, 2024). As a result, educational policies undergo a multi-step process before they are ultimately implemented at the college level and applied by individual instructors.

Given the relatively recent emergence of artificial intelligence (AI) technologies, few state laws have progressed to the application stage. In response to this new reality, colleges have relied on existing guidance to create trainings, develop syllabus statements, and consider ethical implications when formulating instructor AI policies (Gannon, 2024). The approach taken by colleges regarding students and their education significantly impacts how AI is integrated into the classroom.

Furthermore, local codes of conduct are also being revised to accommodate the use of AI. The Council on State Governments reports that seventeen states have enacted bills in the past few years addressing AI more broadly (Wright, R., 2023). In the realm of education policy, some states have introduced legislation aimed at incorporating AI into K-12 and higher education environments. According to the National Conference of State Legislatures, over 25 states have introduced legislation concerning the responsible use and guardrails for AI (Summary, 2024). These legislative efforts primarily focus on increasing access to AI education and training programs, promoting workforce development in AI-related fields, and integrating AI technologies into curricula to prepare students for future careers. In 2023, California and Oregon became the first two states in the US to provide official guidance to school districts on the use of AI in classrooms, according to a national scan by the

Center on Reinventing Public Education (Dusseault, 2023). However, issues such as academic dishonesty have not been widely adopted in legislative initiatives and the responses by states have been fragmentary.

When and if these laws are created, it will be incumbent upon state agencies and colleges to establish rules and administrative procedures. By actively engaging with AI policy at the state level, community colleges can contribute to shaping the future of AI in education and ensuring that its integration benefits students and educators alike. As AI continues to evolve and permeate various sectors, proactive legislative and educational efforts will be crucial in preparing the workforce and fostering responsible AI adoption.

Rule-making for AI use in the classroom at the state government level involves a multifaceted approach to regulate the integration of artificial intelligence technologies into educational settings while ensuring ethical, equitable, and effective implementation. While specific regulations will vary by state, the general process typically follows established procedures for education policy development, with a focus on addressing the unique challenges and opportunities presented by AI in the classroom.

A notable instance of state-level rule-making for AI use in education can be observed in the case of California. In response to the growing integration of AI technologies in educational settings, the California Department of Education took the initiative to develop a comprehensive set of guidelines for the ethical use of AI in schools. The "Ethical Use of Artificial Intelligence in Education" guidance document was initially released in 2020, with the aim of providing schools and districts with recommendations on the responsible deployment of AI technologies while prioritizing student privacy and promoting equity (California Department of Education, 2020).

To ensure that the guidelines encapsulated a wide range of perspectives and concerns, the rule-making process involved extensive engagement with various stakeholders, including educators, researchers, technology experts, and advocacy groups. Such broad participation allowed the guidelines to reflect a consensus on best practices for AI use in educational settings, thereby fostering a more inclusive and responsible approach to AI integration.

Furthermore, the draft guidelines underwent a public comment period, allowing the wider community to provide valuable feedback before the guidelines were finalized and officially adopted by the state education agency. This commitment to transparency and collaboration demonstrates the importance of incorporating diverse viewpoints when establishing policies and regulations for the ethical use of AI in education.

By implementing clear guidelines for AI use in education, California's rule-making process serves as an exemplary model for other states looking to navigate the complex task of integrating AI technologies into classrooms while simultaneously protecting student rights and promoting equitable access to educational opportunities. As AI continues to evolve and permeate various sectors of society, the need for proactive legislative and educational efforts will only grow, making California's approach a valuable resource for other states seeking to develop their own AI policies and guidelines.

Community Colleges

In examining the issue of academic dishonesty and its relationship to the understanding of AI and its use, distinct dynamics are present in community colleges compared to universities and K-12 institutions.

At universities, where specialization and depth of knowledge are typically emphasized, there may be a higher expectation for students to engage in original research and critical analysis. However, with the ever-increasing availability and sophistication of AI tools, there is also a growing concern about the potential for academic dishonesty in these institutions. Students may be enticed to use AI-generated content or automated writing tools to produce papers or assignments, circumventing the process of independent research and critical thinking. As such, it is vital for universities to address these concerns and enforce strict academic integrity policies to uphold the quality of research and scholarship.

On the other hand, at community colleges, where the focus often lies on practical skills, workforce readiness, and the wide breadth of general education, the role and implications of AI tools must be addressed differently. With the transformative nature of AI in many industries and fields, there is an increasing need for community college students to develop a basic understanding of AI concepts and applications. Community colleges have an essential role in preparing students to navigate the rapidly changing technological landscape of their chosen careers.

Incorporating discussions on the ethical implications of AI use in academia into course curricula can help students develop a deeper understanding of responsible research practices and the importance of academic honesty. This may involve implementing plagiarism detection software to identify instances of AI-generated content, providing clear guidelines on acceptable sources and citation practices, and fostering a culture of academic integrity through education and awareness initiatives.

Community colleges play a pivotal role in addressing the challenges and opportunities presented by AI in education. By offering workshops and training sessions on effectively and responsibly using AI tools, these institutions can foster a comprehensive understanding of AI and its potential impact on academic integrity.

This approach equips students with the necessary skills and knowledge to excel in a world that is becoming increasingly influenced by AI technologies.

Moreover, the responsibility of addressing AI use in community colleges is largely shared by individual instructors. Instructors are at the forefront of integrating AI technologies into their teaching practices and fostering an environment that promotes ethical AI use among students.

Community colleges must support instructors in this endeavor by offering professional development opportunities and resources that enhance their understanding of AI and its applications in the classroom. Instructors should also be encouraged to develop syllabus policies that clarify expectations around AI use, such as acceptable sources for research and guidelines for citing AI-generated content. This transparency helps ensure that students are aware of their responsibilities regarding academic honesty and ethical AI use.

In addition, community colleges can incorporate AI-related topics into relevant courses and programs, enabling students to explore the principles, ethical considerations, and responsible use practices of AI technologies. By incorporating AI education into the curriculum, students become better prepared to navigate the ethical challenges associated with AI in both academic and professional contexts.

As AI continues to evolve, community colleges must keep up with the latest developments by implementing policies and procedures that are aligned with federal and state guidelines. These efforts are essential in promoting responsible AI use in education and safeguarding academic integrity. While it is still early in the process, the proactive engagement of community colleges in this endeavor is crucial to meet the challenges and opportunities presented by AI technologies.

Creative policies implemented in college syllabi concerning the use of AI for students completing coursework can encompass various approaches to promote ethical AI use, academic integrity, and critical thinking skills. Here are some examples to consider:

1. AI Usage Guidelines: Include clear guidelines in the syllabus regarding the use of AI tools and resources for completing coursework. Specify acceptable and unacceptable uses of AI, such as prohibiting the use of AI-generated content for assignments or exams without proper citation or acknowledgment.

2. AI Ethics Discussions: Incorporate discussions on the ethical implications of AI use in academia into course content. Encourage students to critically examine the ethical considerations surrounding AI technologies, including issues related to bias, privacy, transparency, and accountability.

3. AI Awareness Assignments: Assign readings, case studies, or projects that explore real-world examples of AI applications and their impact on society, education, and the workforce. Prompt students to reflect on the ethical dilem-

mas and challenges associated with AI use and develop strategies for ethical decision-making.

4. AI Integrity Pledges: Introduce an AI integrity pledge at the beginning of the semester, where students commit to using AI tools responsibly, ethically, and in accordance with academic integrity standards. This pledge can serve as a reminder of students' responsibility to uphold ethical principles in their academic work.

5. AI Research Projects: Incorporate AI-related research projects into the coursework, where students explore topics related to AI ethics, bias mitigation, algorithm transparency, or AI applications in their field of study. Encourage students to critically evaluate existing AI technologies and propose solutions to ethical challenges.

6. AI Impact Assessments: Require students to conduct impact assessments of AI technologies on various stakeholders, including students, educators, communities, and society at large. Prompt students to consider the potential benefits, risks, and ethical implications of deploying AI technologies in different contexts.

7. AI Evaluation Criteria: Provide students with evaluation criteria for assessing the credibility, reliability, and ethical considerations of AI-generated content or sources. Teach students how to critically evaluate AI tools and algorithms for accuracy, bias, fairness, and transparency.

8. AI Lab Sessions: Offer lab sessions or workshops where students can gain hands-on experience with AI tools and technologies under the guidance of instructors or AI experts. Provide opportunities for students to experiment with AI tools in a controlled environment and discuss ethical considerations in real-time.

By incorporating creative policies and activities into college syllabi, instructors can empower students to engage with AI technologies responsibly, ethically, and critically, while also fostering a deeper understanding of the societal implications of AI use, both now and the future.

Policy Frameworks

Community colleges employ various policy frameworks to address academic dishonesty, aiming to uphold integrity and maintain academic standards. These frameworks typically include codes of conduct outlining prohibited behaviors such as plagiarism, cheating on exams, and falsifying data relating to state and federal law while implementing academic policy (Miller & Salinas, 2019). Additionally, institutions often establish procedures for reporting suspected violations, conducting investigations, and imposing sanctions when necessary. Policies may also incorporate educational components, such as workshops on citation practices and academic ethics, to promote awareness and prevent misconduct. By implementing clear and consistent guidelines, colleges seek to foster a culture of academic honesty and accountability among students and faculty alike.

The Integration of AI policy into existing academic dishonesty frameworks can enhance detection, prevention, and response mechanisms using these same policy frameworks. While laws have not been updated fully, these initial steps assist with navigating these complex issues. Institutions can develop policies that address the ethical use of AI tools for academic purposes, ensuring transparency and accountability in their deployment. Guidelines may delineate acceptable applications of AI, such as text similarity detection software for plagiarism detection, while also establishing safeguards to protect student privacy and confidentiality. Many colleges have already created statements concerning AI use in the classroom (*Artificial Intelligence Draft Policies*, 2023; *Student Code of Conduct*, 2023). Moreover, institutions have incorporated AI ethics training into academic integrity programs, equipping students and faculty with the knowledge and skills to navigate the ethical implications of AI technologies in research and learning environments. While it is still early, but the urgency of the topic in regards to training has been emphasized by the larger academic community at many levels (Langreo & Frajtova, 2024; *Vanderbilt*, 2024). Educational institutions should leverage their strengths even in an incomplete policy environment – teach the tools and larger academic expectations while enforcing adjusted codes of conduct using available tools.

Existing Issues and Challenges

While the policies and laws are being developed, the existing issues posed by AI are being handled in a few ways. The quest is on to create and implement tools to detect those students that violate college policy in AI use. Turnitin, a widely used plagiarism detection software, has been actively working to combat the misuse of AI in academic dishonesty. In addition to its existing role as a tool to detect copy and paste type plagiarism from a variety of sources and the reuse of student submissions, Turnitin seeks to also detect language generating modes such as ChatGPT (Turnitin, 2023, January). With the proliferation of AI-generated content and sophisticated plagiarism techniques, Turnitin has attempted to enhance its algorithms and detection capabilities to identify and deter AI-generated plagiarism. The results have been mixed as the technology continually changes. However, using available mechanisms, Turnitin has attempted to understand the scope of the problem. According to an internal report by the company, AI tools have been used substantially by students already (more than 80% of content) in 3.3 percent of total submissions to their system with over 10% having 20 percent AI generated content (Turnitin, 2023, July). Based on these staggering reports and experiences in the classroom, educators have reacted by enforcing the policies on academic dishonesty that already exist. The issue is that professors know that these tools are being used, but AI detection is also in its infancy. That has not stopped some from trying and the results have been problematic in practice.

In spring 2023, a professor at Texas A&M University-Commerce implemented such a policy in his business class. Using data given to him by loading student work into ChatGPT itself, he was informed that many submissions were AI. With this AI generated evidence, he proceeded to fail a large proportion of his students due to academic dishonesty policy (Klee, 2023). This led to students being denied diplomas, a furor amongst those students who claimed they were not cheating, and a further investigation by the university on how this action should take place (Ankel, 2023). It has been shown that errors are routinely made by large language models such as ChatGPT as they are language algorithms and simply piece together words to create answers based on vast knowledge bases. Many AI chatbots contain warnings that information could be faulty. One specific issue of note is the application of hallucinations by the tool. AI language generators will simply invent text, sources, or other "facts" with the same confidence as any other information (Lacy, 2024). When an answer is immediately unclear to the model, it will make up an answer. Hallucinations are often seen in AI image generators when extra fingers are given to people. Words work the same way. The fact is, at this point, ChatGPT cannot determine if something is AI generated.

Another case involves, a senior student at the University of California Davis, who was falsely accused of cheating by a new AI detection tool integrated into Turnitin's plagiarism-checking software, GPTZero (Jiminez, 2023). The tool, which UC Davis had secured early access to, flagged Stivers' paper as AI-generated content, leading to a cheating accusation from her professor. However, she was able to appeal the accusation by providing evidence such as the Google document history of her writing, which demonstrated that she did not use AI in the instance cited. This case demonstrates the fallibility of these tools, even a cutting-edge one like GPTZero, for conducting these tasks for professors. The results of AI or other detection tools present are not definitive, and many educational institutions have pulled back when it comes to enforcement of academic dishonesty policies in practice. It is simply difficult to prove that an AI tool was used in isolation of other factors. The real-world consequences for the students, administration, and instructors demonstrate the precarious position community colleges and other institutions find themselves in. There are currently no tools that give definitive, ultimately enforceable AI detection for use by instructors on student submissions when enforcing academic dishonesty policy.

These cases highlight the complexities of academic dishonesty cases involving AI, as traditional notions of plagiarism and citation may not always be sufficient to address the unique challenges posed by AI-generated content. Moreover, it underscores the importance of establishing clear guidelines and policies regarding the use of AI in academic settings, as well as the need for students to understand and adhere to these rules to maintain academic integrity.

What to do now

Colleges can take proactive measures to ensure an equitable and legal response to fair use and academic dishonesty concerns related to the use of AI by students in their work. Firstly, institutions can develop clear policies and guidelines that address the ethical use of AI tools in academic settings. These policies should outline expectations for students regarding the proper attribution of sources, the prohibition of AI-generated content without proper citation, and the consequences of violating academic integrity standards. By establishing transparent guidelines, colleges provide clarity to students and educators alike, fostering a culture of ethical conduct and accountability.

Secondly, colleges can invest in educational initiatives to raise awareness about the ethical implications of AI use in academic work. Educators can integrate discussions on AI ethics into curriculum across disciplines (each potentially being unique), helping students understand the importance of responsible AI use and the potential consequences of unethical behavior (D'Agostino, 2023). Workshops, seminars, and online resources can further supplement these efforts, providing students with practical guidance on navigating fair use principles and avoiding plagiarism when utilizing AI tools. Utilizing existing resources such as libraries and learning centers in these efforts would prevent duplicated effort. As the legal frameworks change, those specialized community college faculty and staff will have to update internal guidelines to reflect new realities. By empowering students with the knowledge and skills to navigate ethical challenges related to AI, colleges promote a culture of integrity and academic honesty as they have always done.

Additionally, colleges can leverage technology to enhance academic integrity efforts in the age of AI. This includes implementing plagiarism detection software that is capable of identifying AI-generated content and distinguishing it from original work. For this goal, the technology itself must improve to a point that legal and ethical benchmarks can be met in relation to academic dishonesty procedures and codes of conduct. Moreover, institutions can explore the development of AI-driven tools that assist educators in detecting and addressing academic dishonesty more effectively as they come online. By harnessing technology in this way, colleges can stay ahead of emerging challenges posed by AI use while upholding legal and ethical standards in academic work. Ultimately, a multifaceted approach that combines clear policies, educational initiatives, and technological solutions is essential for ensuring an equitable and legal response to fair use and academic dishonesty concerns related to the use of AI by students.

When it comes to individual instructors, syllabus policies should be adjusted to meet the guidance being created within college level procedures. Ensuring fairness and clarity for both the student and the instructor are paramount. Here are some recommendations for syllabus policies that should be considered:

1. **Define appropriate use**: Develop clear guidelines for students on the appropriate use of AI in completing coursework, including how AI can be used as a learning aid but not as a substitute for original work.

2. **Provide resources**: Offer training sessions and educational materials to students and faculty about responsible AI use and the potential consequences of academic dishonesty involving AI.

3. **Establish detection methods**: Invest in and implement technology and tools that can identify AI-generated content, so that educators can determine when students have used AI inappropriately with caveats built in and students being made aware of their use.

4. **Establish consequences**: Create and communicate clear consequences for violating academic honesty policies involving AI, including potential disciplinary actions.

5. **Support faculty development**: Provide professional development opportunities for educators on how to recognize and address academic dishonesty involving AI in their classrooms.

6. **Encourage open dialogue**: Foster an environment where students feel comfortable discussing AI-related academic challenges and seeking guidance on proper use.

7. **Establish ethical guidelines**: Incorporate ethical considerations surrounding AI use into the college's broader academic integrity policies, highlighting the importance of honesty, transparency, and fairness.

8. **Promote responsible AI use**: Encourage and highlight positive examples of AI use in the classroom, so that students and faculty can learn from those who are using the technology effectively and ethically.

These policies should be reviewed and updated regularly as AI technology continues to evolve, ensuring that community colleges remain at the forefront of addressing academic dishonesty and promoting the ethical use of AI when students are at the beginning of their higher education careers.

CONCLUSION

In recent years, the rapid advancements in artificial intelligence (AI) have significantly transformed the landscape of community college education, presenting both remarkable opportunities and complex challenges. As AI technologies continue to evolve, policymakers are tasked with the responsibility of navigating this ever-changing policy environment at local, national, and global levels.

To effectively integrate AI into community college education, it is imperative that policymakers prioritize essential aspects such as data privacy, algorithmic transparency, equity, and accountability. This can be achieved through the development of tailored policy frameworks and collaborative initiatives that seek to maximize the benefits of AI while minimizing potential risks and drawbacks. A strong emphasis on data privacy is crucial to ensure that the sensitive information of students and staff remains protected and secure. By implementing robust data protection measures, community colleges can foster trust and confidence in AI-powered systems.

Algorithmic transparency is another critical component, as it allows stakeholders to understand the decision-making processes and logic behind AI technologies. This helps to prevent biases and unfair outcomes, promoting a more equitable educational experience for all students.

Equity in AI usage is vital to address the digital divide and ensure that students from diverse backgrounds have equal access to technology-driven learning opportunities. By bridging the gap, community colleges can enable students to develop the skills necessary for success in an increasingly digital world.

Accountability is also a key element of an effective AI policy framework, establishing clear roles and responsibilities for all stakeholders involved in AI implementation. This helps to create a culture of responsible AI adoption and promotes continuous improvement of AI-driven initiatives. Through ongoing dialogue and adaptive governance, community colleges can harness the transformative power of AI while upholding ethical principles and safeguarding the interests of all stakeholders.

The integration of AI in education has brought about significant changes in teaching and learning methodologies. However, the rapid advancements in AI technologies have outpaced the development of relevant legal frameworks, creating challenges for community colleges as they navigate an unclear legal landscape. Despite the growing use of AI in education, many state legislatures and state education departments have not yet enacted specific laws or policies to guide its application in colleges and universities. The lack of clear legislative guidance on AI use in education leaves community colleges in a precarious position. These institutions must strike a delicate balance between promoting innovation and upholding academic integrity while contending with potential legal and ethical issues that arise from AI implementation.

In the absence of specific AI policies for students and instructors, community colleges must rely on existing state and federal laws governing technology use, privacy, and intellectual property. However, these laws may not fully address the unique challenges posed by AI technologies, such as the potential for plagiarism or bias in AI-generated content. Furthermore, community colleges may also need to navigate discrepancies between state and federal regulations related to AI in education. For instance, while some states have begun exploring legislation to regulate AI technologies, others have not yet taken significant steps in this direction. This patchwork of regulations can create uncertainty for community colleges operating in multiple states or for those attempting to align their policies with evolving legal standards.

The absence of clear legal guidelines also places a greater burden on individual community colleges to develop their own policies and procedures related to AI use. This can result in inconsistent approaches among institutions, making it difficult for students and instructors to understand their rights and responsibilities when engaging with AI technologies.

Given the uncertainty surrounding the legal landscape, community colleges must remain proactive in monitoring developments in AI-related legislation and adapting their policies accordingly. This includes fostering open dialogue with stakeholders, collaborating with legal experts, and staying abreast of best practices in AI policy development. By taking a forward-looking approach to AI regulation, community colleges can help ensure a responsible and equitable future for AI in education.

For any future policy to be successful, it will require proactive engagement with administrators, educators, students, and policymakers to share best practices, address emerging challenges, and identify innovative solutions.

REFERENCES

Ankel, S. (2023, May 17). *Professor fails half his class after ChatGPT falsely said it wrote their papers*. Business Insider. https://www.businessinsider.com/professor -fails-students-after-chatgpt-falsely-said-it-wrote-papers-2023-5

Artificial intelligence draft policies (2023). Institutional Effectiveness and Grant Development. Austin Community College. https://offices.austincc.edu/institutional -effectiveness-and-grant-development/master-syllabi/artificial-intelligence-draft -policies/

Bahdanau, D., Cho, K., & Bengio, Y. (2014). Neural machine translation by jointly learning to align and translate. *arXiv preprint arXiv:1409.0473*.

Bender, E. M., Gebru, T., McMillan-Major, A., & Shmitchell, S. (2021, March). On the dangers of stochastic parrots: Can language models be too big? In *Proceedings of the 2021 ACM Conference on Fairness, Accountability, and Transparency* (pp. 610-623). DOI: 10.1145/3442188.3445922

Biden, J. (2023, October 30). *Executive order on the safe, secure, and trustworthy development and use of artificial intelligence*. The White House. https://www .whitehouse.gov/ briefing-room/presidential-actions/2023/10/30/executive-order- on-the-safe-secure-and-trustworthy-development-and-use-of-artificial-intelligence/

Brown, T., Mann, B., Ryder, N., Subbiah, M., Kaplan, J. D., Dhariwal, P., & Amodei, D. (2020). Language models are few-shot learners. *Advances in Neural Information Processing Systems*, 33, 1877–1901.

Congressional Research Service. (2023, September 29). Generative artificial intel- ligence and copyright law. *CRS Reports*. https://crsreports.congress.gov/product/ pdf/LSB/ LSB10922

D'Agostino, S. (2023, March 21). GPT-4 is here. But most faculty lack AI policies. *Inside Higher Ed*.https://www.insidehighered.com/news/2023/03/22/gpt-4-here -most-faculty-lack-ai-policies

Dusseault, B. (2024, March). *New state AI policies released: Signs point to in- consistency and fragmentation – Center on Reinventing Public Education*. Center on Reinventing Public Education. https://crpe.org/new-state-ai-policies-released -inconsistency-and-fragmentation/

Fair Use Index. (2023, November). *U.S. Copyright Office*. https://www.copyright .gov/fair-use/

Gannon, K. (2024). *Guidance for syllabus statements on the sse of AI tools*. Chicago Center for Teaching and Learning. https://teaching.uchicago.edu/sites/default/files/2023-09/CCTL_AI%20Syllabus%20Statements.pdf

Jimenez, K. (2023, April 12). How AI detection tool spawned a false cheating case at UC Davis. *USA Today.*https://www.usatoday.com/story/news/education/2023/04/12/how-ai-detection-tool-spawned-false-cheating-case-uc-davis/11600777002/

Klee, M. (2023, May 17). Texas A&M professor wrongly accuses class of cheating with ChatGPT. *Rolling Stone.*https://www.rollingstone.com/culture/culture-features/texas-am-chatgpt-ai-professor-flunks-students-false-claims-1234736601/

Lacy, L. (2024, April 1). *Hallucinations: why ai makes stuff up, and what's being done about it.* CNET. https://www.cnet.com/tech/hallucinations-why-ai-makes-stuff-up-and-whats-being-done-about-it/

Landy, K. (2024, February 28). The next step in higher ed's approach to AI (opinion). *Inside Higher Ed.*https://www.insidehighered.com/opinion/views/2024/02/28/next-step-higher-eds-approach-ai-opinion

Langreo, L., & Frajtova, A. (2024, March 25). Teachers desperately need AI training. How many are getting it? *Education Week.*https://www.edweek.org/leadership/teachers-desperately-need-ai-training-how-many-are-getting-it/2024/03

Miller, A., & Salinas, C.Jr. (2019). A document analysis of student conduct in Florida's community colleges. *Community College Journal of Research and Practice*, 43(10-11), 796–802. DOI: 10.1080/10668926.2019.1600606

Murray, A., & Meyer, D. (2022, December 12). The advent of OpenAI's ChatGPT may be the most important news event of 2022. *Fortune.*https://fortune.com/2022/12/12/openai-chatgpt-biggest-news-event-of-2022/

Roose, K. (2022, December 5). The brilliance and weirdness of ChatGPT. *The New York Times.* https://www.nytimes.com/2022/12/05/technology/chatgpt-ai-twitter.html

Student Code of Conduct. (2023, May 2). Macomb Community College. https://www.macomb.edu/about-macomb/college-policies/administrative/student-code-of-conduct.html

Summary artificial intelligence 2023 legislation. (2024, January 12). National Conference of State Legislatures. https://www.ncsl.org/technology-and-communication/artificial-intelligence-2023-legislation

The Biden administration launches the National Artificial Intelligence Research Resource Task Force. (2021, June 10). The White House. https://www.whitehouse.gov/ostp/news-updates/2021/06/10/the-biden-administration-launches-the-national-artificial-intelligence-research-resource-task-force/

Turnitin. (2023, January 13). *Sneak preview of Turnitin's AI writing and ChatGPT detection capability.* Turnitin. https://www.turnitin.com/blog/sneak-preview-of-turnitins-ai-writing-and-chatgpt-detection-capability

Turnitin. (2023, July 25). *Turnitin AI detection feature reviews more than 65 million papers.* Turnitin. https://www.turnitin.com/press/turnitin-ai-detection-feature-reviews-more-than-65-million-papers

U.S. Copyright Office. (1998, December). *The Digital Millennium Copyright Act of 1998.* U.S. Copyright Office. https://www.copyright.gov/legislation/dmca.pdf

U.S. Department of Education. (2021, August 25). *Family Educational Rights and Privacy Act (FERPA).* https://www2.ed.gov/policy/gen/guid/fpco/ferpa/index.html

U.S. Department of Education, Office of Educational Technology. (2024). *AI in Education.* https://tech.ed.gov/ai/

Vanderbilt to host first AI Training Day on March 5. (2024, February 28). Vanderbilt University. https://news.vanderbilt.edu/2024/02/28/vanderbilt-to-host-first-ai-training-day-on-march-5/

Wright, R. (2023, December 6). *Artificial intelligence in the states: emerging legislation.* The Council of State Governments. https://www.csg.org/2023/12/06/artificial-intelligence-in-the-states-emerging-legislation/

Yang, Z., Dai, Z., Yang, Y., Carbonell, J., Salakhutdinov, R. R., & Le, Q. V. (2019). Xlnet: Generalized autoregressive pretraining for language understanding. *Advances in Neural Information Processing Systems*, ●●●, 32.

KEY TERMS AND DEFINITIONS

· **Fair Use:** Fair use is a provision in U.S. copyright law allowing limited use of copyrighted material without permission for purposes like criticism, teaching, and research. Section 107 outlines factors to determine fair use, including the purpose of use and the effect on the market value of the work.

· **Large Language Models (LLMs):** LLMs are AI systems like ChatGPT that generate human-like text by processing vast amounts of data. They use advanced mechanisms to produce coherent and contextually relevant responses across diverse prompts.

· **Federalism:** Federalism is a system where power is divided between a central authority and individual states or regions. In the U.S., it allows both federal and state governments to legislate and govern over specific areas, balancing national and local needs.

· **Intellectual Property:** Intellectual property (IP) refers to creations of the mind, such as inventions and artistic works, protected by law from unauthorized use. Key types include copyrights, patents, trademarks, and trade secrets.

· **Rule-Making:** Rule-making is the process by which government agencies establish regulations to implement and enforce laws. It involves creating detailed guidelines and procedures to apply laws effectively in specific contexts.

· **Ethical AI:** Ethical AI involves principles ensuring that AI technologies are used responsibly, with respect for privacy, fairness, and transparency. It addresses issues like algorithmic bias and the equitable use of AI.

· **Academic Integrity:** Academic integrity involves maintaining honesty and responsibility in educational settings, avoiding plagiarism and cheating, and ensuring original work is properly cited.

· **Plagiarism Detection Software:** Plagiarism detection software identifies copied or closely paraphrased content by comparing documents against extensive databases of sources. It helps ensure originality and academic integrity, including detecting AI-generated text.

Chapter 7
Generative AI Ethical Conundrum:
Librarians as Artificial Intelligence Literacy Apostle in the Educational Space

Basirat Olubukola Diyaolu
https://orcid.org/0000-0002-2049-674X
Federal University of Agriculture, Abeokuta, Nigeria

Oluwabunmi Dorcas Bakare-Fatungase
https://orcid.org/0000-0002-4665-3969
Lead City University, Nigeria

Khadijat D. Ajayi
https://orcid.org/0000-0003-4730-3829
Crescent University, Abeokuta, Nigeria

ABSTRACT

Generative-AI is revolutionizing education by transforming paradigms and creating customized learning experiences. However, ethical issues arise due to the blurring of lines between authentic and generated content which creates an ethical conundrum. Librarians play a crucial role in being literacy apostle by advancing information literacy and fostering critical thinking in the educational space. The fusion of digital literacy and ethics creates a theoretical framework that empowers individuals to thrive in the digital age while fostering responsible engagement with technology. The Library-AI Handshake model showed the need for Librarians to fill the AI literacy skill set gap that is a bane to the ethical adoption and use of generative-AI.

DOI: 10.4018/979-8-3693-3053-1.ch007

INTRODUCTION

The emergence and advancement of Generative Artificial Intelligence (Generative AI) has brought about a new era of innovation, altering how data is created, generated, engaged, analyzed, and used. These technologies are making a significant impact in virtually all human fields of which the educational landscape is core knowing fully well that this space forms the bedrock of every sustainable society. Pertinent within this space are Librarians who are custodians of human knowledge, the heartbeat of educational institutions are saddled with the responsibilities of ensuring that there is orderliness within the information-disordered ecosystem by instilling the requisite Information Literacy (IL) skills in both students and educators alike. This is expected to guide against the bane of misinformation and disinformation that has plagued every technological epoch of which the ethical conundrum weaved around the discourse of generative AI is generating heated global concern.

The significant place of generative AI in contemporary educational discourse cannot be neglected as research has shown it to be pushing the frontiers of education, remodeling teaching methodologies, re-modification existing educational processes, raises student engagement and accomplishment which creates room for a revolutionalized academic journey (Bakare-Fatungase et al., 2024). With the use of sophisticated algorithms that are frequently trained on enormous datasets, generative AI allows machines to create material autonomously that mimics the creative processes of humans thus making academic methods seamless. These technological capabilities have created a lot of enthusiasm and optimism, but they also bring up moral questions that need to be carefully thought through by stakeholders in the educational sector. Also, as these capabilities grow rapidly, an ethical challenge which is a difficult problem emerges, raising serious concerns about the appropriate application, social consequences, and honorable and noble usage of these new technologies to guide against lack of academic integrity in the educational space. Similarly, Bakare-Fatungase et al. (2024) affirmed AI's enormous potential within the educational sphere, but also raises ethical and other fundamental issues that are crucial to the traditional pedagogical domain.

Significant obstacles to the ethical application of generative AI include problems like bias in training datasets that result in discriminating outputs, potential abuse for malevolent intent, and indistinct boundaries between generated and real information. This poses a challenge to educators as their jobs are changing in an era marked by significant breakthroughs in digital technology and AI to suit the changing requirements of students who see the latter as the savior of academic rigor. Within this paradigm is a chasm that needs to be filled to ensure that educators and students are ethically salvaged from falling prey to the misuse and the disorientation of the Utopian information false belief. In this respect, Librarians are expected to bring to bear their professional competencies as AI literacy apostles and ethical advocates by situating themselves as the go-between among students, generative AI, and educators. These information experts are trained to help students and educators navigate the complexity of the generative-AI domain by acting as information stewards, fact pointers, and knowledge pools and encouraging latent critical thinking capabilities, ethical and netiquette considerations, stimulating generative-AI student-lecturer bond and providing a deeper comprehension of the digital world.

The generative AI ethical intricacies experienced by students and educators call for urgent global attention. It is on this premise that this chapter will explore the ethical dimensions of generative AI with a specific focus on the critical role that librarians play as AI literacy apostles in guiding students and educators through this convoluted terrain. By providing a comprehensive understanding of the ethical conundrums surrounding generative AI, this chapter seeks to equip educators, librarians, and students with the knowledge and tools necessary to navigate these challenges within the educational space. As a result, it can be said that in the rapidly evolving landscape of AI, the rise of generative AI presents unparalleled opportunities and ethical challenges that are calling out for Librarians globally to fulfill this role.

EMERGENCE OF ARTIFICIAL INTELLIGENCE AND GENERATIVE-AI

Artificial Intelligence (AI) has caused a significant shift in the technological environment in recent years. Artificial intelligence (AI), which is commonly defined as a machine's capacity to mimic intelligent human behavior, has grown from a science fiction idea to a real, widespread force that affects many facets of our everyday lives. In its widest definition, AI refers to a variety of tools and systems intended to provide robots the ability to carry out operations that normally call for human intelligence (Britannica, 2024). This covers the ability to solve problems, pick up knowledge from experience, comprehend spoken language, and even visualize as humans. Technological developments in machine learning, neural networks, and computing power have propelled the rise of AI, bringing in a world of previously unimaginable possibilities.

On the other hand, Generative-AI is a major advancement in the field of AI, especially in terms of its capacity to produce fresh and original information (Davenport & Mittal, 2022). In contrast to conventional AI models that depend on pre-determined rules, generative AI uses sophisticated algorithms to produce information materials on its own. This involves creating realistic text, graphics, and even music that can imitate the creative processes of humans. Prominent instances comprise linguistic models such as GPT-3 (Generative Pre-trained Transformer 3) and picture generators like DALL-E, which have exhibited the ability to generate extraordinarily creative and cohesive outputs (Lawton, 2023).

GENERATIVE-AI IN CONTEMPORARY EDUCATION SPACE

Generative-artificial intelligence (Generative-AI) in contemporary education space is transforming the whole process of how educational institution runs their academic routines of teaching and learning. Bakare et al. (2023:170) averred this as situating educators and learners in the sphere of "learning, unlearning, re-learning, and up-skilling be able to navigate this technological space seamlessly".Thus revolutionizing how educators teach as well as how students learn and assimilate. Haleem et al. (2022) opined that this innovative technology fosters creativity, customization, and efficiency rather than only serving as an addition to conventional schooling. Generative AI has several ways of influencing the educational setting. Liu et al., (2023) identified the multifaceted roles of generative AI and its' potential to shape the future of education to include customized educational opportunities, AI-powered tutoring programs, content production and enhancement, as well as automating tasks in administration and prospects for the future.

Customized Educational Opportunities

Generative AI has aided teachers to customize lessons to meet the needs of each unique student. Artificial intelligence (AI) algorithms are used by adaptive learning platforms to evaluate students' performance data, pinpoint strengths and shortcomings, and modify content delivery in real-time. This individualized approach improves the understanding, engagement, and general academic performance of students. Furthermore, Technologies like generative adversarial networks (GANs), recurrent neural networks (RNNs), and transformer models such as Open-AI's GPT (Generative Pre-trained Transformer) series are all included in the category of generative artificial intelligence. With the aid of these technologies, machines may now produce content on their own, imitating the originality and adaptability of humans.

In addition, through the analysis of individual learning styles, preferences, and performance data, generative AI enables individualized learning experiences (Bakare-Fatungase et al., 2024). As a result, the systems can create customized instructional materials such as exercises, tutorials, and quizzes to meet the varying needs of learners. Das et al. (2023) research shows how personalized learning models driven by generative AI can improve students' engagement and academic results. It enhances adaptive assessment systems, which dynamically modify material and difficulty levels based on real-time student answers. Therefore, by utilizing machine learning algorithms, these systems create personalized tests and quizzes that provide the right amount of challenge and comprehension. Munna & Kalam (2021) demonstrate how adaptive evaluation systems help students learn more deeply and become proficient in their skills. In the same vein, educators can harness generative AI in the development of curriculum and instructional content that speaks to the contemporary intellectual needs of students.

Multimedia content creation, textbook writing, and even code generation are facilitated by tools such as GPT-3. It increases the potential of AI-generated content to improve learning resources and encourage innovation in teaching methods. Even outside of typical classroom settings, learners can receive individualized instruction and support from virtual tutors and mentors powered by generative AI. These platforms facilitate engaging discussions, give clarifications, and give assignment feedback to students seamlessly. Research by Shahzad et al. (2023) shows how well AI tutors support self-directed learning and augment traditional classroom education.

AI-Powered Tutoring Programmes

Generative-AI-powered tutoring programs are giving students individualized and flexible help. Depending on each user's unique learning preferences and styles, these systems can produce interactive content, tests, and simulations. Students consequently receive focused support, promoting a more successful and efficient learning environment. Personalized learning paths are generated by AI-powered tutoring systems through the analysis of student performance data through algorithms. Based on the learner's strengths, limitations, and learning style, these systems adaptively modify the curriculum and training (Walkington, 2013). For example, learning platforms such as Duolingo & Khan Academy provide tailored language and math learning experiences, respectively, meeting the demands of a wide range of learners.

In addition, AI-powered tutoring programs encompass cognitive tutoring systems that use artificial intelligence (AI) algorithms to mimic one-on-one tutoring engagements and provide learners with instant feedback and scaffolding support. Bakare-Fatungase, et al. (2024) affirmed this as improved personalized learning which is having a significant impact on students' output. These systems combine pedagogical techniques with cognitive science ideas to improve learning results (Guo et al., 2021). Notable instances are the conversational agent Auto-tutor from Carnegie Learning and the math Cognitive Tutor from Carnegie Learning. Also, Natural Language Processing (NLP) is frequently used in AI-powered tutoring programs to enable communication between the system and the student. These computers can comprehend and provide human-like replies thanks to NLP, which promotes interesting learning environments (Dia & Ke, 2022).

Natural Language Processing (NLP) techniques are used by Chabots such as Woebot and IBM Watson Tutor to offer mental health support and individualized tutoring, respectively. Bakare & Omeiza (2023:213) revealed: "Chatbots have the potential to create, foster and mastermind a dynamic and interesting learning environment that can keep students motivated and interested thanks to their capacity to deliver immediate feedback, individualized responses, and a conversational interface". Large volumes of data on student interactions are gathered by AI-powered tutoring programs, and this data can be examined to guide pedagogical decision-making and instructional design. Using learning analytic approaches on this data, teachers may spot trends, forecast student performance, and make wise interventions to help students learn.

Content Production and Enhancement

The generation of educational content is being revolutionized by generative AI. Teachers can create learning materials, exams, and instructional content with the use of language models like GPT-3, which can produce writing that, will be coherent and pertinent to the situation. Furthermore, AI-powered technologies are improving the production of multimedia content, including interactive simulations and movies, which improve the educational experience. By automating tasks that were previously completed by instructional designers and instructors, generative AI speeds up the creation of material. For example, tests, worksheets, and lecture notes can be created by AI-driven systems based on the preferences and particular learning goals of the students. Furthermore, by tailoring content to each learner's unique learning preferences and skill level, generative AI makes it possible to create personalized learning experiences. Not only can generative AI make content development easier, but it also improves already existing instructional resources (Lim et.al., 2023).

Artificial Intelligence (AI) algorithms can add interactive features, multimedia information, and real-world examples to textbooks, lectures, and online courses through methods like natural language generation (NLG) and picture synthesis. Furthermore, by translating materials into other languages and cultural contexts, generative AI can help with the localization of instructional content. The creation of adaptive learning environments where instructional material dynamically adapts based on student's progress and feedback is facilitated by generative AI. Gao et al. (2024) opined AI systems can maximize learning outcomes by generating tailored learning pathways, recommending supplemental resources, and providing targeted feedback by assessing students' performance data and learning patterns.

Automating Tasks in Administration

Modern schooling must prioritize administrative efficiency, and generative AI has the capability of simplifying a lot of administrative work. Artificial Intelligence (AI) is freeing up educators to concentrate more on teaching and less on administrative tasks by automating grading and assessment procedures, managing timetables, and allocating resources. Generative AI simplifies the student enrollment process in educational sectors by automating processes like course registration, document verification, and application processing. AI-driven systems can evaluate student data, spot enrollment patterns, and make tailored course recommendations based on factors like hobbies, job objectives, and academic standing.

Additionally, generative AI makes it easier to integrate student information systems (SIS) smoothly, ensuring data quality and legal compliance. Through the analysis of institutional data, such as teacher availability, classroom utilization, and course demand, generative AI can be used to optimize scheduling and resource allocation. Timetables, teaching assignments, and facility allocation can all be efficiently generated by AI algorithms, reducing conflict and optimizing resource use. Furthermore, predictive analytic is made possible by generative AI to foresee future resource requirements and make proactive plans to satisfy changing demands in education. Also, generative AI improves communication and support services for staff, teachers, and students through Chabot, virtual assistants, and automated help-desk systems.

AI-driven Chabot may answer questions instantly, assist users with administrative tasks, and give 24/7 individualized support. Bakare (2024) opined Chatbots play a significant role in ensuring that students and educators alike have access to inhibited responses to their queries in the actualization of their varied tasks. Furthermore, natural language understanding (NLU) powered by generative AI can accurately read user queries and refer difficult problems to human administrators when necessary. By automating data entry, report generating, and document creation processes, generative AI streamlines administrative procedures. An AI-embedded system is capable of producing reports, memorandum, and presentations on their own. They can also evaluate unstructured material and extract pertinent information. Additionally, by integrating with current software systems, generative AI makes workflow automation easier, decreasing manual error and improving operational efficiency.

Prospects for the Future

Generative AI has the potential to significantly transform education in the future. Its incorporation in education sectors may completely transform educational administration through the provision of personalized services, adaptive decision-making, and predictive analytic. Global student learning could become more immersive, customized, inclusive, and in the long run sustainable. In addition, to maximize administrative results, future research projects might concentrate on improving AI algorithms for natural language comprehension, creating moral guidelines for AI administration, and encouraging cooperation between AI systems and human administrators.

GENERATIVE- AI ETHICAL CONUNDRUM

With its unparalleled potential for content production, language generation, and problem-solving, the Generative Artificial Intelligence (Generative-AI) has accelerated innovation in many areas. But great power also comes with great responsibility and the use of generative AI presents several moral issues that need to be carefully thought out thoroughly to guide against any iota of confusion (Humphreys et al., 2024). As a result, it is important to explore and understand the complex ethical dilemma associated with generative AI. Humphreys et al. (2024) stated that given its creative capabilities, generative AI presents several complex ethical dilemmas that call into question responsible development, use, and application with several important things to think about such as unintentional discrimination and bias, false information and manipulation, privacy issues, absence of responsibility, unlawful use, risks to security, loss of employment, informed consent, dual-use predicament, and regulatory obstacles.

Unintentional Discrimination and Bias

Large volumes of data are used to train generative AI models, and if the training set contains biased information, the AI may reinforce and magnify such biases in its outputs. This may lead to unjust or discriminatory results, particularly in delicate fields like criminal justice, lending, and hiring, or concerning people's race and culture most especially against African or Indigenous identities. Multiple interrelated aspects might be identified as the origins of bias in generative AI. Firstly, using skewed datasets for training is detrimental to human existence. These databases frequently represent historical injustices and stereotypes, mirroring societal pre-conceptions(Paullada et al., 2021).

Furthermore, even while the algorithms are meant to avoid bias, their structure and optimization procedures may unintentionally reinforce it. Additionally, there may be blind spots in recognizing and reducing prejudice as a result of the under representation of varied perspectives among AI researchers and developers. In generative AI, bias can take many different forms in various modalities. For example, in text creation, language models may generate outputs that display discrimination related to race, gender, or culture, which could perpetuate stereotypes and marginalize particular groups. Similarly, Giffen et al. (2022) stated that algorithms may produce images throughout the image-generation process that support and reflect preexisting visual stereotypes, hence escalating societal prejudices. Furthermore, bias can affect how AI systems make decisions, which can result in unfair outcomes that are detrimental to human co-existence.

Inadvertent prejudice and discrimination in generative AI have far-reaching and complex consequences. These prejudices according to Ferrara (2024) can worsen already-existing disparities, support discrimination, and thwart initiatives for social justice and equity from a societal perspective. Furthermore, prejudiced AI systems have the potential to reduce technological trust, escalating tensions between underprivileged communities and technological progress. Furthermore, the use of jaundiced AI systems in vital fields like law enforcement and healthcare might have negative effects on people, treating them unfairly and escalating inequality. Intentional bias and discrimination in generative AI must be addressed with a multi-modal strategy that takes legal, ethical, and technological aspects into account. Algorithmic bias can be reduced with the use of technological interventions like transparent datasets curation, different datasets discovery techniques, and transparency measures.

False Information and Manipulation

Errors or fabrications presented as facts are called false information, frequently used interchangeably with disinformation. False information spreads quickly through the use of social media platforms and digital communication channels. Research has demonstrated the negative impact of inaccurate information on the general public's perception, decision-making process, and society's stability (Li & Chang, 2023). False information has been a threat to our society, Altay et al. (2023) opined that difficulty increases when highly persuasive fake narratives are created by generative AI, making it harder to distinguish between fact and fiction.

Deep-fake audio, text, and video content, among other types of fake content, may be produced with great convincing by generative AI. This gives rise to worries regarding the dissemination of false information, fake news, and the capacity to sway public opinion or trick people which is an act of misinformation. In generative AI, misleading information spreads through a variety of channels. The ease with which AI-generated content can imitate human-created content and obfuscate the boundaries between the two is a major source of concern that can be blurred by Librarians.

In generative AI, manipulation techniques entail the purposeful creation of content to influence perceptions, actions, or beliefs. According to Lenca (2023) these strategies include emotional manipulation, cognitive bias exploitation, and persuasion approaches. Generative AI models are capable of producing customized stories intended to elicit particular reactions from the viewer, insinuating subtle kinds of control (Feuerriegel et al,, 2024). Also, generative AI's automated nature makes it possible to produce and distribute altered information quickly and widely, which increases its influence on society. Furthermore, bad actors can use generative AI to produce propaganda, false information, and fake news that is incredibly lifelike. This undermines confidence in trustworthy sources of information and helps propagate false narratives. Moreover, the difficulty in preventing the spread of incorrect information is made worse by the speed at which AI-generated content is shared on social media sites, where it may swiftly reach large audiences with no control.

Privacy Issues

The creation of realistic material may put users' privacy at risk. For instance, deep-fake technology can be used to produce convincing films of people saying or doing things they never did, violating people's privacy and possibly damaging their reputations which is an act of defamation of character. Large-scale datasets are frequently analyzed by generative AI systems to identify and reproduce patterns, raising questions about the privacy of the training data (Dwivedi et al., 2023). When these databases include private or sensitive data, privacy issues increase. Text generation models trained on social media posts, for example, can unintentionally reveal personal information or private discussions, raising concerns about permission and data ownership.

The laws governing privacy and generative AI are still developing, and the policies that are in place frequently are not designed to handle the particular problems that these technologies present. According to Hoofnagle et al. (2019) while some protections are provided by privacy laws like the California Consumer Privacy Act (CCPA) in the US and the General Data Protection Regulation (GDPR) in Europe, it is unclear whether these rules apply to content generated by artificial intelligence. In addition, tracking out the sources of synthetic media and holding people liable for its production and distribution makes it more difficult to enforce privacy regulations in the context of generative AI. Legislative reforms and regulatory frameworks that are specific to generative AI's unique qualities and privacy consequences are therefore urgently needed.

Absence of Responsibility

One of the most significant challenges in the ethical discourse surrounding generative AI is the lack of clear lines of responsibility. AI systems are devoid of agency, intentional, and moral reasoning, in contrast to human creators. It can be difficult to assign blame for the results of generative AI. It can be unclear who should be held responsible for damaging or immoral information produced by an AI system developer, users, or both. Therefore, boundaries should be set so that culprits of the misuse of the generative AI system can be held culpable.

Although generative AI's lack of accountability presents serious moral conundrums, it also has far-reaching effects on creativity and innovation(Nah et al., 2023). AI systems have the potential to provide a more transparent and innovative creative atmosphere by relieving human creators of some of their responsibilities (De Cremer et al., 2023). But this flexibility also carries a risk: unbridled AI creation could unintentionally reinforce prejudices, disseminate false information, or create offensive stuff.

Unlawful Use

The same technologies that have positive applications might also be abused for negative ends. Generative artificial intelligence (AI) has the potential to generate realistic phishing emails and mimic people for fraudulent purposes. The ability of generative AI to create extremely realistic deep-fakes, forged papers, and even fake news presents serious ethical questions. Egelhofer & Lecheler (2019) opined that the capacity of generative AI to disseminate false information, trick and mislead people and erode confidence in institutions and the media poses a serious threat to the stability of society. Furthermore, these hazards are increased by the accessibility of access to such technology, which allows malevolent actors to use it with little technical know-how for malicious ends.

Taking legal and regulatory action against the illicit use of generative AI presents substantial obstacles. Modern rules and regulations frequently fall behind the rapid evolution of technology, leaving emergent concerns unaddressed (Shumakova et al., 2023). Furthermore, because criminals operate across borders and jurisdictional boundaries are blurred, the global character of the internet makes enforcement activities more difficult. It is essential to strive toward creating strong legal frameworks that strike a balance between innovation and accountability to reduce the risks related to the exploitation of generative AI.

The spread of content created by generative AI threatens the legitimacy of human creativity in addition to undermining confidence in digital media. AI-generated content challenges conventional ideas of authorship and intellectual property rights as it becomes more and more similar to authentic human creations (Dwivedi et al., 2023). Furthermore, a wider decline in confidence in human interactions and societal institutions may result from the normalization of lying made possible by generative AI.

Risks to Security

With the increasing sophistication of Generative-AI, there is a chance that it will be utilized to produce increasingly complex cyber threats, such as plausible social engineering schemes or harder-to-detect malware. Moreno (2024) stated that the possibility of malevolent usage of generative AI is one of the main issues surrounding it. The possibility of creating convincing but completely fabricated information increases the risk of deep-fakes, in which people are shown saying or acting in ways they never would have. Such disinformation tactics erode confidence and foment dissension, posing a serious threat to individuals, groups, and even entire nations. Furthermore, by using its capacity to create highly tailored messages or graphics to trick unwary individuals, generative AI can be used as a weapon to create complex phishing attacks.

Traditional cybersecurity procedures might not be able to identify and mitigate these threats when these techniques improve. As a result, Labuz (2023) asserted that it is necessary to create strong protections to prevent these technologies from being abused. This entails putting strict restrictions into place, encouraging truthfulness in information created by AI, and developing detection techniques to counter new risks.

However, Labuz (2023) further affirmed that there is a narrow line that must be drawn between maintaining security and generative AI's capacity for innovation. Strict regulatory policies run the potential of inhibiting innovation and research, which would impede the creation of useful applications in industries like entertainment, healthcare, and the arts. Finding the ideal balance necessitates both proactive steps to mitigate the risks without unreasonably slowing down development and a sophisticated awareness of the hazards involved.

Loss of Employment

In some industries, generative AI's automation potential may result in job displacement. This presents moral dilemmas regarding the effects of mass job loss on society and the duty of legislators and innovators to deal with these effects. More reason, there is the need for job skilling, and up-skilling so that the generative AI is seen as an enabler for one's job and not a dis-placer. The system will only displace redundant or complacent workers who are not ready to be on board the technological innovations brought to bear by these emerging technologies. There are several complex ethical conundrums when generative AI systems replace human labor.

On the one hand, proponents contend that automation can improve human welfare by reducing monotony, fostering creativity, and increasing efficiency. Critics, especially those in vulnerable communities, voice worries about the loss of livelihoods, economic inequity, and job displacement (Johnson, 2020).

The application of generative AI will have significant negative effects on society and the economy in the form of widespread unemployment. Johnson (2020) indicated that income disparity may worsen as displaced workers find it difficult to adjust to changing labor marketplaces. Furthermore, it is important to recognize that losing a job has a psychological toll that affects people's well-being and social cohesiveness.

Resolving the moral dilemma associated with job loss requires strong policy frameworks and regulatory actions (Acemoglu & Restrepo, 2017). To mitigate unfavorable outcomes, governments, industry stakeholders, and academia must work together to create policies like reskilling programs, tests with universal basic income, and ethical criteria for AI deployment.

Informed Consent

Informed consent is a concern when using generative AI in different applications like Chat-bots or virtual assistants. Users cannot always recognize when they are speaking with an AI system instead of a human, raising questions regarding openness and confidence. Appropriate AI literacy education would have imbued in users the strategies of knowing whether they are interacting with a machine or a human.

Dual-Use Predicament

Technologies utilizing generative artificial intelligence can be used both constructively and destructively. A major ethical concern is finding a balance between encouraging innovation and limiting malevolent use. The principle of Netiquette which emphasizes the ethical ways of interacting in cyberspace and the usage of emerging technologies will broaden the horizon of users on the moral basis of using the generative AI system.

Regulatory Obstacles

The creation of thorough laws has lagged behind the generative AI field's explosive growth. Legal frameworks and ethical standards are required to guarantee the proper development and use of these technologies. From all indications, it is important to note that collaboration between researchers, developers, librarians, legislators, and ethics is necessary to address these ethical issues, providers, and benchmarks for responsible generative AI usage

LIBRARIANS AND THE EDUCATIONAL SPACE: AN INFORMATION LITERACY (IL) DISCOURSE

The way education is changing in the digital age has elevated information literacy to a prominent position in scholarly discussions. As information literacy champions in this setting, librarians assist students, educators, and the general public in navigating the immense ocean of the information ecosystem glut. Chukwu et al. (2021) examined how important it is for librarians to promote information literacy in classroom settings through the following listed strategies such as dynamics of information overload and the need for guidance; teaching information literacy skills; adapting to technological changes and emerging trends; fostering a culture of lifelong learning for the sustainability of the educational landscape, information literacy in the age of misinformation, mal-information, and disinformation, and collaborative partnerships with educator and stakeholders.

Dynamics of Information Overload and the Need for Guidance

The way we acquire and use information has changed dramatically as a result of the widespread use of digital technologies. But there are drawbacks to this unheard-of level of access. Studies reveal that the human brain has limited cognitive capacity. When people are overloaded with information, they suffer from cognitive overload, which impairs their ability to make decisions, reduces their capacity for critical thought, and raises their stress levels (Belabbes et al., 2023). Information overload and generative AI together increase the hazards of the spread of synthetic content and produce ethical quandaries. With people having to navigate a more complicated information terrain, the actuality of content generated by artificial intelligence makes it more delicate to distinguish between fact and fabrication. Likewise, there are serious societal hazards associated with the quick spread of false information made possible by generative AI, similar to polarization, trust corrosion, and public opinion manipulation.

There is an urgent need for direction to help people successfully traverse this digital maze when faced with information overload. There are several ways to provide guidance, such as teaching information literacy, developing critical thinking abilities, and providing cognitive tools for organizing and prioritizing information. Furthermore, Luo et al. (2021) averred that individualized advice based on a person's preferences and cognitive capacities can lessen the negative impacts of information overload and enable people to make wise decisions in the face of a sea of data. The success of guidance mechanisms, however, depends on their capacity to adjust to the changing digital environment and deal with new issues including the spread of false information and disinformation campaigns.

In a time where knowledge is abundant, librarians play an ever more important and indispensable role. Librarians act as guides, and information torch-bearers in assisting people in the dynamics of separating reliable sources from false information, as lecturers and students frequently struggle with an abundance of information. Based on their proficiency in information retrieval and evaluation, librarians are well-suited and professionally trained to assist the duo of students and educators in navigating the intricacies of the digital information environment.

Teaching Information Literacy Skills

The rise of information sources made possible by technological developments gave rise to the idea of information literacy (Onuoha & Obiano, 2019). In the early days of librarianship, they were in charge of instructing students in standard research techniques including using databases and catalogue. However, the definition of information literacy grew to include critical analysis, moral application, and effective information communication as data became more digital and accessible.

The pivotal role of librarians as information literacy experts cannot be overemphasized as they are saddled with the responsibilities of the advancement of information literacy abilities of their clientele. Librarians actively participate in teaching students how to identify bias, critically analyze sources, and synthesize knowledge beyond the scope of their traditional roles. Through tutorials, workshops, and group projects, librarians equip students with the knowledge and abilities needed to be astute information producers and responsible consumers.

Adapting to Technological Changes and Emerging Trends

Rapid technical breakthroughs brought about by the digital age have changed how information is accessed, shared, and used. Digital literacy is sacrosanct for librarians, who are deemed techy-info-leaders showing the way in adjusting to these developments. Librarians assist people in acquiring the requisite digital skills necessary for success in the classroom, from using online databases to comprehending copyright concerns in the digital sphere and being responsible users in cyberspace The appropriate information literacy advocacy hinged on emerging trends will translate to ensuring that knowledge garnered in the classroom can be leverage on solving different societal issues which at the long run makes students and lecturers contribute significantly to the society.

Numerous emerging trends are shaping the landscape of information literacy education in educational spaces. An example of such a trend is the growing emphasis on media literacy, which encompasses the ability to critically evaluate and analyze various forms of media content. Kryloval–Greg (2020) opined that with the proliferation of fake news and misinformation, librarians are the number one play as they play a crucial role in equipping students with the skills to discern credible sources from unreliable ones.

Fostering a Culture of Lifelong Learning for the Sustainability of the Educational Landscape

Within educational institutions, librarians help foster a culture of lifelong learning. Librarians encourage educators and students to view learning as a lifetime endeavor by highlighting the value of ongoing research and intellectual curiosity. This goes a long way in ensuring the sustainability of the educational ecosystem and promoting an informed society. The library develops into a vibrant information hub for groundbreaking research, promoting an inquisitive attitude that transcends formal schooling.

Otoide & Idahosa (2018) asserted librarians are no longer just information stewards but active educators who work with instructors to incorporate information literacy into the curriculum. This brought about the change of acknowledgment for librarians as agents of lifelong learners with critical thinking abilities.

Information Literacy in the Age of Misinformation, Mal-information, and Disinformation

Librarians are at the forefront of the fight against misleading information in a time when misinformation, mal-information, and disinformation abound in the information ecosystem thus creating a bane to the credibility of information products and services. They instruct users in critical thinking, dependable sources, and fact-checking techniques which are indispensable skills needed in the knowledge economy. Librarians enable people to be astute information consumers by providing them with the tools and proficiency necessary to successfully negotiate a challenging information environment.

Collaborative Partnerships with Educator and Stakeholders

To smoothly incorporate information literacy into the curriculum, librarians work collaboratively with educators and stakeholders. By working together, educators and librarians may create assignments that highlight essential information literacy competencies, guaranteeing graduates can successfully traverse, assess, and contribute to the information ecosystem and the knowledge economy.

THEORETICAL DISCOURSE (FUSION OF THEORIES ON DIGITAL LITERACY AND DIGITAL ETHICS)

A fascinating theoretical framework that aims to comprehend, negotiate, and influence the changing terrain of the digital society is presented by the fusion of digital ethics and digital literacy (Dalsgaard & Ryberg, 2023). Despite being separate ideas, they are intrinsically linked and affect how people in the digital age engage with information, technology, and one another. The duo investigated the intersection of digital ethics and digital literacy. Therefore, looking at the opportunities for convergence between these philosophies could be best explained by defining digital literacy, understanding digital ethics, and the synergy of digital literacy and digital ethics. Others are critical thinking in the digital age, navigating information ecosystems, empowering digital citizens, and educational implications.

Defining Digital Literacy

This is the ability to navigate, assess, and use digital information and communication technologies successfully which are all included in the concept of digital literacy. It entails a collection of sociolect-emotional, technological, and cognitive abilities that enable people to actively engage and interact seamlessly in the digital environment. Beyond technological competence, digital literacy includes media literacy, information fluency, and critical thinking in a digital environment without being stuck.

Understanding Digital Ethics

Conversely, digital ethics tackles the moral and ethical issues that come with using digital technologies. It entails a careful analysis of how technology affects people individually, in groups, and throughout society. Privacy, data security, digital rights, algorithmic fairness, and the larger effects of technology on social justice and equity are important ethical issues. This is a ravaging issue in cyberspace as most people navigating this clime lack the appropriate ethical culture to create a sane digital space.

The Synergy of Digital Literacy and Digital Ethics

A symbiotic and intricate relationship arises when digital ethics and digital literacy come together. Digital ethics offers the moral foundation for responsible and conscientious interaction in the digital sphere, while digital literacy gives people the technological and emotional abilities to navigate around it. Collectively, they serve as the cornerstone for making morally sound decisions in the intricately linked world of digital technology.

Critical Thinking in the Digital Age

The fusion of these theories places a strong emphasis on critical thinking in the digital age. Digital literacy encourages individuals to question, analyze, and synthesize digital information effectively and constructively. Digital ethics guides individuals to critically embrace netiquette in assessing the ethical implications of their digital actions, promoting responsible and conscientious use of technology without hampering the feelings or self-esteem of others.

Navigating Information Ecosystems

When digital ethics and literacy are combined, people are better able to traverse the complex information ecosystem seamlessly. As they gain an awareness of the ethical issues surrounding online collaboration, digital communication, and information sharing, they develop into astute consumers and producers of digital content that promotes the sustainability of the human race.

Empowering Digital Citizens

In the context of digital citizenship, the confluence of these ideologies is especially pertinent. People become responsible digital citizens who make valuable contributions to the digital community when they are equipped with appropriate digital literacy skills and are directed by digital ethics principles. This empowerment goes beyond one's actions and includes support for digital rights, privacy, and the advancement of moral technology.

Educational Implications

The integration of digital ethics with digital literacy has significant consequences for educational settings. It needs a comprehensive strategy for digital education that combines the development of skills with moral introspection. Librarians are essential in helping students and educators become ethically aware and technologically literate, enabling them to appropriately navigate the digital world.

TRAJECTORY OF LIBRARIANS IN HUMAN TECHNOLOGICAL INNOVATION

In the dynamic journey of human technological innovation, librarians play a crucial role by being adaptable, visionary, and dedicated to making knowledge accessible despite rapidly changing technological landscapes (Shahzad & Khan, 2023). The librarians' journey from conventional caretakers of tangible collections to creative digital stewards emphasized their crucial role in reshaping the information domain. This involves evolution from custodians to facilitators of digital information products and services; harnessing digital resources; information literacy advocates; integration of emerging technologies; digital access and preservation; community engagement in the digital realm; advocacy for open access and digital inclusion; as well as integrator of technology and futurists.

Evolution from Custodians to Facilitators of Digital Information Products and Services

The digital age has redefined the roles and responsibilities of Librarians to suit contemporary trends. These information professionals have evolved beyond their historical position as keepers of tangible collections to take on the role of facilitators of varied digital information products and services. Their ability to adjust to new technology and digital climes is demonstrated by the transition from overseeing physical collections or products to navigating enormous digital resources in different formats for the provision of library and information services.

Harnessing Digital Resources

Librarians welcome the digitization of resources as well as library automation which are the veritable opportunities of being able to harness digital resources in meeting clientele's information needs without any inhibition.. They developed skills in the acquisition, processing, organizing, and maintaining digital collections, making enormous repositories of human knowledge available to a global audience at the click of a button. Librarian's ability to use and navigate digital resources has become a must as the dictates of contemporary digital space require a topnotch technologically savvy mindset and disposition to be relevant in meeting users' needs who are mostly netizen.

Information Literacy Advocates

Information literacy becomes increasingly important with the advent of the digital era as the space is laced with lots of intricacies and complexities which if not handled with care is gradually becoming a bane overshadowing its positive impacts on human interactions. In this wise, Librarians have become leaders in the field of information literacy and digital user education by helping users to critically assess sources, navigate the complexity of online information, and use digital tools responsibly and efficiently. They are becoming trainers passing down knowledge that is essential for navigating the data-rich digital environment.

Integration of Emerging Technologies

Emerging technologies are being actively incorporated into library services by librarians for the sustainability of human knowledge. Librarians have benefited from technological advancements by using online catalogs and virtual reference services like Chabots to improve user experiences and promote clientele satisfaction. To improve information retrieval and optimize library operations, they embraced library automation, AI, augmented reality, social media technologies, block-chain technologies, gamification, data visualization, and data analytic.

Digital Access and Preservation

To protect priceless digital materials for future generations without constraints, librarians have taken on the task of digital conservation and preservation. They have created solutions to deal with data security, integrity, storage, and format obsolescence, which is extending the life of digital knowledge repositories.

Community Engagement in the Digital Realm

Librarians embraced the digital sphere as part of their community participation. To promote information access outside of the actual library walls and to develop a feeling of community, online forums, virtual events, and digital outreach activities were essential. Librarians in the virtual world become community connectors in bringing people of like minds together to discuss societal problems to proffer solutions.

Advocacy for Open Access and Digital Inclusion

In advocating for digital inclusion and free access to knowledge, librarians play an essential role. They support programs aimed at closing the digital gap and guaranteeing that everyone in society has fair access to digital resources and the advantages of cutting-edge technology.

Integrators of Technology and Futurists

With the ability to foresee technology trends and proactively incorporate innovations into library services, librarians have developed into futurists. They worked with computer engineers, took part in the building of the digital infrastructure, and helped shape how information will be distributed in the future.

Challenges and Ethical Considerations

Librarians faced difficulties and moral dilemmas as technology developed, including privacy issues, digital rights, and the moral use of new technologies. Librarians have evolved into defenders of moral information practices and advocates for the proper use of technology.

LIBRARIANS AS GENERATIVE-AI LITERACY ADVOCATOR IN THE EDUCATIONAL SPACE

Librarians are important advocates and mentors in the modern educational setting when it comes to assisting students in navigating the complexities of generative AI literacy. The work of librarians is becoming multifaceted and redefined as technology develops due to the transition that pervades this technological space. Semeler et al. (2024) asserted that librarians are becoming advocates or apostles of generative-AI literacy, committed to promoting comprehension, critical thinking, and responsible use of these revolutionary technologies through bridging the knowledge gap; curating resources for generative-AI education; workshops and training programs; integration into information literacy programs; ethical considerations and responsible use; encouraging multidisciplinary education; community engagement and public discourse as well as adapting to emerging trends.

Bridging the Knowledge Gap

Librarians are in a good position to close the knowledge gap in generative AI literacy because they are information specialists. They actively work to fathom the nuances of generative AI and use their knowledge to equip educators and students with the skills necessary to understand and manage this rapidly changing technological environment.

Curating Resources for Generative-AI Education

Books, articles, and internet resources that promote generative AI literacy are selected by librarians. They make sure that people have access to trustworthy and current material about generative AI by creating curated reading lists, hosting workshops, and curating digital repositories that are suited to the needs of the educational community.

Workshops and Training Programs

Workshops and training sessions are led by librarians to help deconstruct the principles of generative AI. They offer practical insights into the workings of these technologies, their applications, and their possible implications through interactive seminars. Librarians assist participants in gaining the fundamental knowledge and abilities needed to comprehend, analyze, and critically assess AI system outputs.

Integration into Information Literacy Programs

Generative AI literacy becomes an integral component of broader information literacy programs led by librarians. These programs emphasize the importance of discerning between human-generated and AI-generated content, understanding bias in algorithms, and cultivating ethical considerations in the use of generative AI technologies.

Encouraging Multidisciplinary Education

Librarians support multidisciplinary initiatives in academic disciplines because they understand the interdisciplinary nature of technological trends such as generative AI. They establish forums for discussion across computer science, ethics, the humanities, and other disciplines, promoting a comprehensive view of generative AI that extends beyond its technological components.

Community Engagement and Public Discourse

Librarians actively participate in the community and encourage discussion on the moral ramifications and societal effects of generative artificial intelligence. They plan community gatherings, panel discussions, and expert lectures to raise awareness and promote enlightened public conversation about the proper application of AI technologies. When discussing AI in public, ethical issues like accountability, privacy, and bias are frequently brought up. As information specialists, librarians may add to this conversation by selecting materials that address AI ethics and encourage wise choices (Saeidnia, 2023). Libraries act as catalysts for discussion on the ethical implications of AI technologies by giving people access to a range of viewpoints.

Adapting to Emerging Trends

To keep up with technological breakthroughs, librarians must constantly refresh their knowledge through constant unlearning, relearning, re-skilling, and re-skilling, and be flexible in response to developing trends in generative AI. This guarantees their ability to proficiently lead the academic community through the dynamic terrain of generative AI as the apostle for solving the ethical conundrum.

Ethical Considerations and Responsible Use

Librarians support the appropriate usage of generative AI and ethical considerations. They assist students in resolving moral conundrums involving prejudice, privacy issues, and possible abuse. Librarians promote a culture of responsible and contemplative interaction by encouraging conversations about the implications of generative AI on society.

The Library-AI Handshake Model by Bakare-Fatungase (2024) further speaks to the significant roles of librarians within the generative AI discourse as an apostle in bringing orderliness to the chaos surrounding the ethical adoption and use of these technologies in the educational ecosystem.

Figure 1. Library AI handshake model (Bakare-Fatungase, 2024)

This model is divided into 4 Library-AI Handshake Levels that provide hands-on training sessions librarians as ethical moderators can take both students and educators through to promote the successful integration of these technologies into the nitty-gritty of the educational landscape. The model levels are Fortify, De-marginalize, Perspective, and Foresight. Fortify connotes improving educators' and students' AI information literacy skills. It is at this level that librarians will train students and educators on the netiquette principles T-H-I-N-K that can solve the ethical conundrum. With the required AI information literacy skills, students and educators alike will be able to ask pertinent questions as to the Truthfulness, Healthiness, Inspiring, Necessity, and Kindness of the generative AI content. This knowledge will fortify them in the ethical adoption and use of these technologies.

De-marginalize indicates working with developers to avoid prejudice and not negate the African indigenous knowledge system. It is at this level that librarians will train students and educators on ways of identifying bias, misinformation, disinformation, or malformation of the generative AI information content. Perspective affirms that educators should be trained to be positively disposed to adopt the technology and guide students appropriately. Foresight signifies that with the requisite AI-Literacy skills, both educators and students will positively shape their field of study (educational landscape) when the technology is ethically used, and sustainability refers to the iteration of all the Library-AI Handshake principles without compromising the future generations of lifelong learners and the African indigenous knowledge system.

The novel Library-AI Handshake model shows the pivotal roles of librarians within the generative AI discourse. This model is timely considering the ongoing argument around the ethical adoption of generative AI in African education. This research is expected to be an eye-opener to librarians in bracing up as generative AI torch bearers for its ethical adoption in African education. Also, the model creates an inclusive educational space for all as everyone deserves to be fortified with the needed AI literacy skills to be ardent in the ethical use of these technologies. It also provides an avenue that showcases the library as the bedrock to the successful ethical integration and use of generative AI into the educational domain seamlessly.

SUMMARY

Generative-AI is revolutionizing data creation, analysis, and interaction, but it also raises ethical concerns like bias in training data and potential abuse. This presents a challenge for educators, who must adapt their roles to meet students' changing needs but at the same time promote the academic integrity of the educational landscape to ensure its sustainability. Based on this premise, the pivotal roles of Librarians as crucial in promoting AI literacy, acting as information stewards and promoting critical thinking is emphasized and reinstated in contemporary times. Also, the intersection of digital ethics and digital literacy provides the basis to understand and influence the changing landscape of our digital society, with librarians becoming advocates for comprehension, critical thinking, and responsible use of these technologies. The Library-AI Handshake model showed the need for Librarians to fill the AI literacy skill set gap that is a bane to the ethical adoption and use of generative-AI. There is a prospect for a success story if librarians harness their professional competencies to situate themselves as ethical apostles in solving the ethical conundrum surrounding the adoption and integration of generative-AI into the educational landscape.

CONCLUSION

Generative-AI is revolutionizing education by creating personalized learning environments. However, ethical concerns arise due to its ability to mimic human-authored content. Librarians play a crucial role in promoting information literacy and fostering critical thinking. The blurring of boundaries between created and legitimate content raises moral concerns about responsibility, transparency, and public confidence in information sources. The novel Library-AI Handshake model demonstrates the roles librarians played in the discourse of generative AI. As the model was designed to timely consider the ongoing argument around the ethical adoption of generative AI in African education. This development is an eye-opener for librarians to brace up as generative AI torch bearers for its ethical adoption in African education. In addition, the model has been able to incorporate inclusive for all in educational space. Conclusively, a theoretical framework combining digital ethics and digital literacy encourages responsible use of technology, enabling people to thrive in the digital age. This discussion will guide future studies, instructional strategies, and policy creation.

RECOMMENDATION

Generative-AI systems can generate biased or disinformation-promoting content, so librarians must teach students how to assess and cross-check data. They should also educate students on privacy, risks, and protecting personal information. They should also raise ethical considerations and encourage questioning about AI algorithms. To effectively use Generative-AI, digital literacy is essential, and librarians should provide resources, workshops, and guidance to users.

IMPACT OF THE STUDY

Librarians play a crucial role in promoting AI-literacy in education, helping students and educators develop digital literacy, ethical consciousness, and critical thinking skills to navigate the rapidly changing AI technology ecosystem. Libraries can adopt the Library-AI Handshake Model as the basis for training students and educators on the ethical adoption and use of generative-AI.

REFERENCES

Acemoglu, D., & Restrepo, P. (2017). Robots and jobs: Evidence from U.S. labour markets. *The American Economic Review*, 107(5), 1608–1638. https://www.nber.org/system/files/working_papers/w23285/w23285.pdf

Altay, S., Berriche, M., Heuer, H., Farkas, J., & Rathje, S. (2023). A survey of expert views on misinformation: Definitions, determinants, solutions, and future of the field. *Harvard Kennedy School (HKS). Misinformation Review*, 4(4). Advance online publication. DOI: 10.37016/mr-2020-119

Bakare, O. D., Oladokun, T., Quadri, G. O., & Idowu-Davies, T. O. (2023). ChatGPT and other generative artificial intelligence (AI) tools in teaching and learning as integrative pathways to contemporary university education. In *Creative AI Tools and Ethical Implications in Teaching and Learning* (pp. 168–180). IGI Global. DOI: 10.4018/979-8-3693-0205-7.ch009

Bakare-Fatungase, O. D. (2024). Staying ahead of the digital curve: librarians as panacea of the g-ai conundrum [Powerpoint Slides]. Institute of African Studies, Carleton University, https://carleton.ca/qes/2024/presentation-by-dr-oluwabunmi-bakare-fatungase-at-royal-military-college-kingston/

Bakare-Fatungase, O. D., Adejuwon, F. E., & Idowu-Davies, T. O. (2024). Integrating artificial intelligence in education for sustainable development. In *Using Traditional Design Methods to Enhance AI-Driven Decision Making* (pp. 231–245). IGI Global. DOI: 10.4018/979-8-3693-0639-0.ch010

Belabbes, M. A., Ruthven, I., Moshfeghi, Y., & Rasmussen Pennington, D. (2023). Information overload: A concept analysis. *The Journal of Documentation*, 79(1), 144–159. DOI: 10.1108/JD-06-2021-0118

Britannica (2024). "Definition and meaning of artificial intelligence". https://www.britannica.com/technology/artificial-intelligence

Chukwu, S. A. J., Emezie, N., Nwaohiri, N. M., Haco-Obasi, F. C., Obiano, D. C., & Bernard, I. I. (2021). "Information literacy: Academic librarians as Stakeholders in the learning process: with focus on federal university of technology, owerri". *Library Philosophy and Practice*https://digitalcommons.unl.edu/cgi/viewcontent.cgi?article=11762&context=libphilprac

Dalsgaard, C., & Ryberg, T. (2023). A theoretical framework for digital learning spaces: Learning in individual spaces, working groups, communities of interest, and open connections. *Research in Learning Technology*, 31, ●●●. https://www .researchgate.net/publication/374396037_A_theoretical_framework_for_digital _learning_spaces_learning_in_individual_spaces_working_groups_communities _of_interest_and_open_connections. DOI: 10.25304/rlt.v31.3084

Das, A., Malayiya, S., & Singh, M. (2023). The impact of ai-driven personalization on learners' performance. *International Journal on Computer Science and Engineering*, 11(08), 15–22. https://www.researchgate.net/publication/373424876_The _Impact_of_AI-Driven_Personalization_on_Learners'_Performance

Davenport, T. H., & Mittal, N. (2022). "How generative AI is changing creative work". *Harvard Business Review.* https://hbr.org/2022/11/how-generative-ai-is -changing-creative-work

De Cremer, D., Morini Bianzino, N., & Falk, B. (2023). How generative AI could disrupt creative work. *Harvard Business Review*. https://hbr.org/2023/04/how -generative-ai-could-disrupt-creative-work

Dia, C. P., & Ke, F. (2022). "Educational applications of artificial intelligence in simulation-based learning: A systematic mapping review". *Computer and Education: Artificial Intelligence*, 3:100087.https://www.sciencedirect.com/science/article/pii/ S2666920X2200042X?via%3Dihub

Dwivedi, Y. K., Kshetri, N., Hughes, L., Slade, E. L., Jeyaraj, A., Kar, A. K., Baab-dullah, A. M., Koohang, A., Raghavan, V., Ahuja, M., Albanna, H., Albashrawi, M. A., Al-Busaidi, A. S., Balakrishnan, J., Barlette, Y., Basu, S., Bose, I., Brooks, L., Buhalis, D., & Wright, R. (2023). Opinion paper: "so what if chatgpt wrote it?" multidisciplinary perspectives on opportunities, challenges and implications of generative conversational AI for research, practice and policy. *International Journal of Information Management*, 71, 1–63. DOI: 10.1016/j.ijinfomgt.2023.102642

Egelhofer, J. L., & Lecheler, S. (2019). Fake news as a two-dimensional phenome-non: A framework and research agenda. *Annals of the International Communication Association*, 43(2), 97–116. DOI: 10.1080/23808985.2019.1602782

Ferrara, E. (2024). Fairness and bias in artificial intelligence: A brief survey of sources, impacts, and mitigation strategies. *Sci*, 6(1), 3. DOI: 10.3390/sci6010003

Feuerriegel, S., Hartmann, J., Janiesch, C., & Zschech, P. (2024). Generative ai. *Business & Information Systems Engineering*, 66(1), 111–126. DOI: 10.1007/ s12599-023-00834-7

Gao, Z., Cheah, J. H., Lim, X. J., & Luo, X. (2024). Enhancing academic performance of business students using generative AI: An interactive-constructive-active-passive self-determination perspective. *International Journal of Management Education*, 22(2), 100958. https://www.sciencedirect.com/science/article/abs/pii/S1472811724000296. DOI: 10.1016/j.ijme.2024.100958

Giffen, B. V., Herhausen, D., & Fahse, T. (2022). Overcoming the pitfalls and perils of algorithms: A classification of machine learning biases and mitigation methods. *Journal of Business Research*, 144, 93–106. DOI: 10.1016/j.jbusres.2022.01.076

Guo, L., Wang, D., Gu, F., Li, Y., Wang, Y., & Zhou, R. (2021). Evolution and trends in intelligent tutoring systems research: A multidisciplinary and scientometric view. *Asia Pacific Education Review*, 22(3), 441–461. DOI: 10.1007/s12564-021-09697-7

Haleem, A., Javaid, M., Quadi, M. A., & Suman, R. (2022). "Understanding the role of digital technologies in education: A review". *Science Direct*, 3, 275 – 285. https://www.sciencedirect.com/science/article/pii/S2666412722000137

Hoofnagle, C. J., Sloot, B. V., & Borgesius, F. Z. (2019). The European union general data protection regulation: What it is and what it means. *Information & Communications Technology Law*, 28(1), 1–34. DOI: 10.1080/13600834.2019.1573501

Humphreys, D., Koay, A., Desmond, D., & Mealy, E. (2024). AI hype as a cyber security risk: The moral responsibility of implementing generative ai in business. *AI and Ethics*, 4(3), 791–804. Advance online publication. DOI: 10.1007/s43681-024-00443-4

Johnson, A. (2020). The role of automation in society: Implications for the future. *Journal of Automation Studies*, 5(2), 23–30.

Johnson, B. (2020). Automation and Its Implications for Social Inequality. *Journal of Technology and Society*, 22(2), 59–63.

Kamalov, F., Santandreu Calonge, D., & Gurrib, I. (2023). New era of artificial intelligence in education: Towards a sustainable multifaceted revolution. *Sustainability (Basel)*, 15(16), 12451. DOI: 10.3390/su151612451

Kryloval-Greg, Y. (2020). Advanced information technology tools for media and information literacy training. *The State University of Telecommunications, Solomenska Street.* https://ceur-ws.org/Vol-2393/paper_234.pdf

Labuz, M. (2023). "Regulating deep fakes in the artificial intelligence act." applied cybersecurity and internet governance. https://www.acigjournal.com/Regulating-Deep-Fakes-in-the-ArtificialIntelligence-Act,184302,0,2.html

Lawton, G. (2023). What is generative AI? Everything you need to know. *Tech Accelerator,* https://www.techtarget.com/searchenterpriseai/definition/generative-AI

Lenca, M. (2023). On artificial intelligence and manipulation. *Topoi*, 42(3), 833–842. DOI: 10.1007/s11245-023-09940-3

Li, J., & Chang, X. (2023). Combating misinformation by sharing the truth: A study on the spread of fact-checks on social media. *Information Systems Frontiers*, 25(4), 1479–1493. DOI: 10.1007/s10796-022-10296-z PMID: 35729965

Lim, W. M., Gunasekara, A., Pallant, J. L., Pallant, J. I., & Pechenkina, E. (2023). Generative ai and the future of education: Ragnarök or reformation? a paradoxical perspective from management educators. *International Journal of Management Education*, 21(2), 100790. https://www.sciencedirect.com/science/article/pii/S1472811723000289. DOI: 10.1016/j.ijme.2023.100790

Liu, M., Ren, Y., Nyagoga, L. M., Stonier, F., Wu, Z., & Yu, L. (2023). Future of education in the era of generative artificial intelligence: Consensus among chinese scholars on applications of chatgpt in schools. *Future in Educational Research*, 1(1), 72–101. DOI: 10.1002/fer3.10

Luo, H., Cai, M., & Cui, Y. (2021, December 16). **Cai**, M., & Cui, Y. (2021). Spread of misinformation in social networks: Analysis based on weibo tweets. *Security and Communication Networks*, 2021, 1–23. Advance online publication. DOI: 10.1155/2021/7999760

Moreno, F. R. (2024). Generative ai and deepfakes: A human rights approach to tackling harmful content. *International Review of Law Computers & Technology*, 1–30. Advance online publication. DOI: 10.1080/13600869.2024.2324540

Munna, A. S., & Kalam, M. A. (2021). "Impact of active learning strategy on the student engagement". An Open Access Article Distributed Under the Creative Commons Attribution License. Available at https://creativecommons.org/licenses/by-nc/4.0/

Nah, F. F. H., Zheng, R., Cai, J., Siau, K., & Chen, L. (2023). Generative ai and chatgpt: Applications, challenges, and ai-human collaboration. *Journal of Information Technology Case and Application Research*, 25(3), 277–304. DOI: 10.1080/15228053.2023.2233814

Onuoha, J., & Obiano, D. C. (2019). The impact of information technology on modern librarianship: A reflective study. *Information and Knowledge Management*, 5(11), 52–58.

Otoide, G. P., & Idahosa, M. E. (2018). Faculty-librarian collaborations and improved information literacy: A model for academic achievement and curriculum development. [CJLIS]. *Covenant Journal of Library and Information Science*, 1(1), 63–73.

Paullada, A., Raji, I. D., Bender, E. M., Denton, E., & Hanna, A. (2021). Data and its (dis)contents: A survey of dataset development and use in machine learning research. *Patterns (New York, N.Y.)*, 2(11), 100336. https://www.sciencedirect.com/science/article/pii/S2666389921001847. DOI: 10.1016/j.patter.2021.100336 PMID: 34820643

Saeidnia, H. R. (2023). Ethical artificial intelligence (AI): Confronting bias and discrimination in the library and information industry. *Library Hi Tech News*. Advance online publication. DOI: 10.1108/LHTN-10-2023-0182

Semeler, A. R., Pinto, A. L., Koltay, T., & Rozados, H. (2024). "Algorithmic literacy: Generative artificial intelligence technologies for data librarians". https://www.researchgate.net/publication/377336874_ALGORITHMIC_LITERACY_Generative_Artificial_Intelligence_Technologies_for_Data_Librarians/citations

Shahzad, K., & Khan, S. A. (2023). Effects of e-learning technologies on university librarians and libraries: A systematic literature review. *The Electronic Library*, 41(4), 528–554. DOI: 10.1108/EL-04-2023-0076

Shumakova, N., Lloyd, J. J., & Titova, E. V. (2023). Towards legal regulations of generative ai in the creative industry. *Journal of Digital Technologies and Law*, 1(4), 880–908. DOI: 10.21202/jdtl.2023.38

Walkington, C. A. (2013). Using adaptive learning technologies to personalize instruction to student interests: The impact of relevant contexts on performance and learning outcomes. *Journal of Educational Psychology*, 105(4), 932–945. DOI: 10.1037/a0031882

KEY TERMS AND DEFINITIONS

GENERATIVE ARTIFICIAL INTELLIGENCE: which is also referred to as Generative-AI in this chapter, is a new innovation that evolve as a resort of advancement in technology. Generative-AI is all about how we can create data, analyse data and interact with data.

AI ETHICAL CONUNDRUM: this is an overview of the law governing the privacy that needed to be protected when using artificial intelligence. There should be set of boundaries to guide the misuse of generative-AI system.

THEORETICAL DISCOURSE: this emphasizes critical thinking in relation to digital age. It encompasses all that are involve in enhancing ethical awareness and technology literacy to successfully navigate the digital world.

LIBRARIANS AND THE EDUCATIONAL SPACE: this denote that librarians serve as a midwifery between information and the information seekers in higher institution of learning. They ensure ease of information access and use by both students, lecturers and other community members within an educational space.

TRAJECTORY OF LIBRARIANS: this is an overview of how librarians need to serve as the steward of information acquisition, information organizer, provider and how information can be successfully disseminated among the library users. Its emphasize the crucial role of librarians towards reshaping the information domain.

LIBRARIANS AS GENERATIVE-AI LITERACY ADVOCATOR: this implies that librarians are expected to always be at the forefront of understating packages of information in whatever format. They should possess the skills of better understanding of information to teach and provide information to information seekers.

LIBRARY-AI HANDSHAKE MODEL: this described how librarians can provide hands-on training sessions and act as ethical moderators who have the skills required to take both students and educators through the successful integration of the new technologies into the nitty-gritty of the educational landscape.

Chapter 8
Optimizing the Use of Artificial Intelligence (AI) in Library Services in the 21st Century

Peter Olubunmi Olubiyo

Adeyemi Federal University of Education, Ondo, Nigeria

ABSTRACT

Artificial intelligence already touches many of our daily computing activities, most of the computer systems and mobile phones being developed today have artificial intelligence features and we have probably used them not knowing that they are intelligent machines. Examples of Artificial intelligence in computers are speech recognition, natural language processing, self-driving or autonomous cars, machine learning, deep leaning and robotics. Artificial intelligence works based on perceptual recognition unlike human beings that operate on deep cognition. The power and advantage of Artificial intelligence lies in the fact that computers can recognize patterns efficiently at a scale and speed that human beings cannot. The development of societies in recent times have been facilitated by the growing demand of access to information, and libraries are the prime source in providing this access.

INTRODUCTION

The rapid development of advanced technologies in recent decades is affecting industries in ways we are just now beginning to witness. These innovative technologies are not only changing our everyday experiences, but they are also impacting global-scale processes and trends for entire sectors around the world. Traditional

DOI: 10.4018/979-8-3693-3053-1.ch008

roles are changing, with new skill requirements, new opportunities, and new challenges. In the world of academic and research libraries (ARL), this transformation is impacting librarians, library services, and the very role of the library as we know it. From the digitalization of information to the Internet of Things (IoT), Big Data analysis and intelligent machine learning, technological trends like these are reshaping the way we consume, access and distribute information, as well as our ability to process it, derive meaning out of it and, ultimately, make decisions based on it. In the eye of this storm of changes in habits and experiences stands the library, the traditional provider of high-quality collections of information (Mondal, 2021). Simon, (1995) in Mondal, (2021) pointed that Artificial Intelligence (AI) is related to building software that exhibits intelligence using processes similar to those used by humans for the same activities. Artificial Intelligence mainly focuses on understanding and performing intelligent tasks such as reasoning, learning new skills and adopting to new situations and problems (Mondal, 2021). It is explained in the Merriam Webster (2019) in Mondal, (2021) that, artificial intelligence is "a part of computer science that deals with giving ability to the machines to look like they have natural human intelligence."

Artificial intelligence (AI) has made it possible to provide solutions to pressing challenges facing libraries, such as shelving of books and other library materials, cataloguing and acquisition of library materials, among others. Consequently, library services can be done in more effective and efficient ways for improved user satisfaction (Yusuf, Adebayo, Bello and Kayode, 2022). Therefore, library users can access timely and accurate information quickly and promptly. Fernandez (2016) in Yusuf, Adebayo, Bello and Kayode, (2022) noted that using AI in academic libraries will help to analyze big data, create metadata, and improve search translation. This means that using AI in academic libraries will make library materials more accessible and available, and allow the staff to answer users' queries on AI use. Tella (2020) stressed in Yusuf, Adebayo, Bello and Kayode, (2022) that the need for academic libraries to re-position themselves to take relative advantage of artificial intelligence's potentials by refining the quality of library services in this era of the information age. Talley (2016) also emphasized in Yusuf, Adebayo, Bello and Kayode, (2022) the need for university librarians to embrace AI technologies to provide better services to researchers and other library users. Grant and Camp (2018) as cited in Yusuf, Adebayo, Bello and Kayode, (2022) observed that many academic libraries particularly in developed countries have adopted AI for various library operations, such as circulation and reference services. Sagarjit et al. (2001) in Yusuf, Adebayo, Bello and Kayode, (2022) maintained that the adoption and use of AI have improved user engagement in many developed countries in the world. Access to timely information can only occur in a situation where AI is being used to guide and support, and at the same time user friendly, particularly in information search. For instance, a friendly AI technology will help users search for information with ease, help retrieve information across various collections, and help with users' queries. There are different AI applications in library system such as: descriptive cataloguing, technical services, and collection development; subject indexing, reference services, database searching, and document delivery. Some papers deal with the underlying design issues of knowledge representation and natural language processing. Many authors have previously provided in-depth overviews of AI technologies (Yusuf, Adebayo, Bello and Kayode, 2022).

In brief, Artificial intelligence technologies have become globally recognized as indispensable tools for improving organizational efficiency and productivity. Suffice therefore to say that AI technologies have strongly influenced the world of work in the 21st century library. In the library setting, the adoption of AI can improve library services and provides access to accurate information that can drive growth and development in this information age. Artificial intelligence technologies are now being used in libraries to achieve the organic integration of readers and libraries. With this, readers interact on the same platform, track and acquire the personalized needs and information of users so that users can access accurate, all rounds, and humanized services, at a reduced cost to rationally utilize library resources (Abayomi, Adenekan, Adeleke, Ajayi & Aderonke, 2021).

Concept of Artificial Intelligence

The term artificial intelligence, according to Irizarry-Nones, Palepu & Wallace, (2017) in Omame and Alex-Nmecha, (2020) often conjures images of robots or computers that talk. Artificial intelligence is an aspect of computer science that focuses on how computers learn (Machine Learning), interpret information, vision: character recognition, picture analysis, 3D perception, and modelling of the function of the eye; furthermore, it encapsulates speech recognition, speech production, understanding and use of natural language (Natural Language Processing), and Expert System which continues to gain more attention. Furthermore, artificial intelligence is the programming and development of computers to perform human required-intelligence task, such as speech recognition, decision-making, visual perception, language translation, talking and emotional feelings.

Artificial intelligence already touches many of our daily computing activities, most of the computer systems and mobile phones being developed today have artificial intelligence features and we have probably used them not knowing that they are intelligent machines. Examples of Artificial intelligence in computers are speech recognition, natural language processing, self-driving or autonomous cars, machine learning, deep leaning and robotics. Artificial intelligence works based on perceptual recognition unlike human beings that operate on deep cognition. The power and advantage of Artificial intelligence lies in the fact that computers can recognize patterns efficiently at a scale and speed that human beings cannot. The development of societies in recent times have been facilitated by the growing demand of access to information, and libraries are the prime source in providing this access. The paradigm shift in the format and dynamics of information and knowledge as a result of the rapid advancement in computer technology and software applications especially artificial intelligence, have shifted libraries to a demand of the commensurate supply of the same technologies. Unless libraries begin to exploit the new technologies and innovate their information and services delivery, they may face obsolescence in this era (Omame and Alex-Nmecha, 2020).

History of Artificial Intelligence in Libraries

Wang, (2018) in Yusuf, Adebayo, Bello and Kayode, (2022) declared that the origin of Artificial Intelligence (AI) can be traced to John McCarthy's research in 1955, with the assumption that every aspect of learning and other forms of intelligence can be stimulated through the use of a machine. However, the history of AI usage in academic libraries can be traced to Balleste, in law libraries in the USA in 1998. AI was introduced in libraries because of the various benefits that technology could bring to library operations, which include the opportunity to extend library opening hours, using AI to answer simple questions, providing library guide to library users on the use of the catalogue, assisting distance education, and streamlining cataloguing and circulation library operations, the essence which is to enhance library services (Abayomi, Adenekan, Adeleke, Ajayi & Aderonke, 2021). Artificial intelligence (AI) technologies have become globally recognized as indispensable tools for improving organizational efficiency and productivity. Suffice therefore to say that AI technologies have strongly influenced the world of work in the 21st century. In the library setting, the adoption of AI can improve library services and provides access to accurate information that can drive growth and development in this information age. Artificial intelligence technologies are now being used in libraries to achieve the organic integration of readers and libraries. With this, readers interact on the same platform, track and acquire the personalized needs and information of users so that users can access information accurately, and humanized services, at a reduced cost to rationally utilize library resources (Yusuf, Adebayo, Bello and Kayode, 2022). In the library also, AI can be used to develop programs for effective reference services, good scanning of textbooks, and the identification of appropriate subject categories. Furthermore, AI technologies can assist library users on how they can locate library materials through intelligent tutoring system and automated library services. Therefore, AI adoption and use in libraries will allow for better information processing, and at the same time, better information search that will excite both library personnel and users since there will be easier and faster access to information. Presently, University of Lagos is the only institution in Nigeria that has introduced the use of AI to some of the library services and operations. The level of awareness among library professional on the use of AI for library services and operations is low, therefore the study tends to look at the adoption of AI for effective library services delivery in academic libraries in Nigeria (Yusuf, Adebayo, Bello and Kayode, 2022).

Applications of Artificial Intelligence in Academic Libraries

ALA, (2019) in Omame and Alex-Nmecha, (2020) Artificial Intelligence matters to libraries because it be used for organizing and making available large collections of information. According to Sridevi and Shanmugam (2017) in Omame and Alex-Nmecha, (2020) artificial intelligence is the modern technology which is used to manage the digital library. The ultimate promise of artificial intelligence is to develop computer systems or machines that think, behave and in fact rival human intelligence, and this clearly has major implications on librarianship. Artificial intelligence is not just an intelligent system or software program, it is a biologically motivated technology used to replicate human ways of perceiving and processing information. Intelligent library automation systems rely on artificial intelligence technologies to provide knowledge-based services to library clientele and staff. Artificial intelligence in libraries should not be misconstrued with library automation. While the later implies the degree of mechanization to routine library operations, the former goes beyond just automating library activities, and create intelligent rational systems that behave and act like librarians and requires little or no human intervention. Artificial intelligent systems can replicate and thus replace a human being in the library, although Li, Huang, Kurniawan and Ho (2015) in Omame and Alex-Nmecha, (2020) believed that this invention will never replace librarians, but will center on menial and time-consuming library operations such as shelf reading and leave the librarians to engage with the patrons. University of Lagos, (2020) in Oyetola, Oladokun, Maxwell and Akor (n.d) asserted that Platform Capital's funding in June 2020 allowed the University of Lagos to become the first organisation in Nigeria to employ artificial intelligence. The robots, which are "cloud-based intelligent humanoid robots," have the following features, according to the information provided by Roboscholar: face recognition, surveillance technology, Open API, data management, advert & promotion, book shelf management, research, customizable, and entry validation. Integrating cutting-edge novel technology into standard library operations is the most practical approach to accomplish new aims and objectives in today's wireless and connected environment. To stay up with the trend in the digital age, libraries and librarians are making every effort. It's interesting to note that the bulk of AI features are already widely utilised in word processing or web and mobile application search (such as auto-suggest, relevance ranking, auto-recommendation, bookmarking, and personalization) (autocomplete, spell-checking, translation, voice recognition). Many characteristics can be added to library services to make them more interactive and user-friendly. The application of AI in libraries guarantees that information is available quickly and in inventive ways. Using voice commands to perform informational searches is one illustration of this (Oyetola, Oladokun, Maxwell and Akor n.d).

Sridevi and Shanmugam, (2017) in Omame and Alex-Nmecha, (2020) expressed that some fields of artificial intelligence that are used in library management system include: Natural Language Processing (NLP), Expert Systems (ES), Pattern Recognition, Robotics etc. Succinctly, Natural Language Processing (NLP) is the analysis and generation of natural language text by computers. The goal is to enable natural languages such as French, English, or Chinese, to serve either as the medium through which users interact with computer systems or as the object that a system processes. In libraries, NLP can be used to design intelligent expert reference system or information retrieval system, where users can interact directly with the system using natural languages. McGraw-Hill Encyclopedia of Science and Technology, (2007) in Omame and Alex-Nmecha, (2020) the computer takes in the natural language as input, analyses and processes it, then responds accordingly with the needed information. NLP has been used as medium of interaction in database management systems and as object/input for processing in automatic text translation or text summarization.

Liqin and Feng, (2015) in Yu, Gong, Sun and Jiang (2019), asserted that Artificial intelligence covers almost all of the business activities of the Smart Library. Through the case analysis and systematic review of a large number of domestic and foreign literature and practical applications, the three application areas are summarized as: Intelligent resource system, intelligent management (smart warehouse management and intelligent security management), intelligent services (smart application services, intelligent consulting services, intelligent knowledge services).

• Intelligent resource system with the development of big data and artificial

intelligence technology, the intelligent resource procurement system can automatically collect and integrate all users' personalized demand information and various types of document resource information through deep learning mechanism. Therefore, it is possible to construct an intelligent document resource procurement decision system. Intelligent procurement system construction needs to pay attention to two key points: (1) It is necessary to scientifically and reasonably determine the influencing factors. The library can establish a scientific and objective decision-making model by combining the comprehensive factors such as user group characteristics (such as gender, age, educational background, occupation, etc.), user personalized information (such as in colleges and universities, the number of teachers and students of various majors, subject setting, subject status ranking, school key construction disciplines, teachers and students hobbies, school opening Course name), recommendation and purchase of books (related to professional degree, popularity or utilization of books, book prices, etc.), expert advice (discipline construction, book utilization rate, book reproduction rate, etc.) and annual budget, so as to complete the book ordering plan and optimize the allocation of book purchasing funds. (2) To comprehensively collect and analyze open resources. Through intelligent collection and analysis of open resources, the intelligent procurement system can provide reference for procurement librarians to make decision.

- Intelligent management: Intelligent warehousing management has several

distinct characteristics: (1) realize the self-service management of the book library with the goal of automatic book circulation and paper document management; (2) the books can be stored randomly on the bookshelf, no need for the book number, reducing the multifarious bookshelf arrangement; (3) Introduce a robot system to realize the management of automatic and unmanned counting, checking and sorting of book storage. There are many successful cases in the library intelligent warehouse management system. The ultrahigh-frequency RFID technology intelligent book inventory robot of Nanjing University Library in China mainly uses the automatic identification technology and RF phase technology in RFID technology, as well as machine automation technology to realize the automatic library book counting function.

And the library book inventory can be realized accurately and quickly, so that the library administrator can find and manage the book conveniently and quickly, which greatly reduces the reader's time to find books. Kuilin, Bo, Lijun et.al. (2016) and Jie, (2017) as cited in Yu, Gong, Sun and Jiang (2019) expressed that BookBot, the Hunter Library of North Carolina State University, is a robotic book delivery system that uses high-density automated shelf technology to store up to 2 million items and deliver any item within five minutes of clicking on the online catalog. Kushins (2018) in Yu, Gong, Sun and Jiang (2019) BookBot only accounts for one-ninth of the space of traditional bookshelves, transforming the library from a storage facility into a rich learning and collaborative space environment. Books and other items are bar coded, sorted by size, and stored in more than 18,000 boxes, and each book and item is scanned as it is borrowed or returned from the system, allowing the library's online catalog to track all data at any time.

Choudhury, Lorie, Fitzpatrick et.al (2019) in Yu, Gong Sun and Jiang (2019) observed that the unique Work Robotics Project (CAPM) at the Johns Hopkins University Library in the United States automatically retrieves books on the shelves and carries them to a scanning station outside the bookshelf. CAPM has real-time enhanced browsing and search capabilities, using a combination of robotics, automated systems, and software technologies to find books on shelves through the web. The user enters the requirements into the CAPM system, which starts a robot to find the appropriate book. The user can view or print the required page and choose to return or borrow the book. Once the text is scanned, the user can also use CAPM to perform automatic text analysis options. In addition, LIB-100B, the book loss prevention intelligent terminal of the Library of Southwest University of China, the Automatic Access Center (ARC) of the Villard Merlot Library, and the AVG of the Humboldt University Library in Germany, are bold innovations of intelligent warehouse management of libraries, and also the future development direction of intelligent warehouse management of libraries. 2) Intelligent Security Management. Ping, (2018) in Yu, Gong, Sun and Jiang (2019) added that The library's daily services include seat management, lending management and identity management and other security management, while face recognition, fingerprint recognition and other artificial intelligence technology can further solve the library's security management. For example, face recognition technology specially designed by artificial intelligence technology is used to collect students' face information and bind it with students' information. After binding, students no longer need to carry student identification information, but can directly enter and exit the library through face brushing.

Peirong, Jie, Xu, and Shanshan (2018) in Yu, Gong, Sun, and Jiang (2019) expressed that the identity authentication module uses face recognition technology as a technical support. Previous face recognition technologies are mostly traditional statistical methods such as Adaboost and PCA (Principal Component Analysis). After the deep development of artificial intelligence, deep learning algorithms such as CNN (Convolutional Neural Networks) and RCNN (Region CNN) have emerged. Such algorithms have been qualitatively improved in recognition accuracy and speed. With the improvement of these core algorithms, the application of face recognition technology has algorithm support in the construction of smart libraries. Face recognition technology is mainly composed of four parts: face image acquisition and detection, face image preprocessing, face image feature extraction, matching and recognition.

In summary, according to Mondal (2021), application of AI in Library are extended to:

Reference service is the foremost activity of any library and the expert system will serve as a substitute for reference librarians. REFSEARCH, POINTER, Online Reference Assistance (ORA), AMSWERMAN, PLEXUS all of these systems are advisory systems for locating reference resources and factual data.

Cataloguing: Cataloguing is one of the oldest library techniques. Recent attempts to automate cataloguing through expert systems have focused on descriptive cataloguing because it is rule-based (AACR2). There are two ways to apply artificial intelligence techniques in cataloguing: (a) Human-machine interfaces, where intellectual work is divides between the intermediary and the support system. (b) An expert system with full cataloguing capabilities associated with electronic publishing systems. Since the cataloguing text is generates online, it can be passed through a knowledge-based system, and the intermediary does the cataloguing process without any intellectual input.

Classification: Classification is the basic activity of a knowledge organization. Therefore, it is prominent in all systems that organize knowledge in libraries and information centres. The application of expert systems in the field of library classification includes Coal SORT, EP-X, and BIOSIS.

Acquisition: The users of the library have a significant role to play in building library collection and online resources in particular. Several systems have been incorporating for the acquisition of these resources. Monograph Selection Advisor, a pioneering effort in applying this emerging technology is another area of building library collection. Specifically, the task modelled is the item-by-item decision that a subject bibliographer makes in selecting monographic. The prerequisite is that the knowledge base has to be broad enough and the interfacing aspect must be easy enough for the library to get the desired information from the machine.

Natural Language Processing in Library Services: When we think of the term NLP, the first thing that comes to mind is the ability to speak or write a complete sentence and have a machine process of requesting and speaking. NLP can apply to many disciplines, including libraries. When apply to the field of library and information science, more specifically, to search databases such as the Online Public Access Catalogue (OPAC), indexing is the basis of document retrieval. The purpose of the index is to improve the precision of retrieving parts of the relevant documents; and to reduce the proportion of recalls and related files retrieved.

Machine learning in Library Services: One specific challenge that is ripe is the improvement of library metadata generation. Libraries, through various vendors as part of the purchasing and acquisitions process, acquire thousands of pieces of metadata for print and digital resources made available to their library users. In cases where an e-book platform does not include metadata, libraries they generate their own. For the increasing majority of borndigital resources, machine learning provides an array of possible tools to help libraries generate metadata for digital resources, allowing cataloguing to not only increase the speed of metadata generation but also vastly improve the depth and breadth of subject terms.

Robotics in the Library Services: The robot is "A reprogrammable, multipurpose manipulator, automatically controlled, programmable in three or more axes, which can be fixed on the location or portable for use in automation applications". Libraries providing an increased variety of services and resources for digital libraries, they are still acquiring a great number of printed documents. This combined pressure to provide electronic and printed resources and services has caused serious space constraints for many libraries, especially academic libraries and research. The objective of CAPM (comprehensive approach to printed material) is to build a personalized robotic scanning system based on a series, which allows the browsing of imprints in real time via the web interface. The user includes a CAPM system that, in turn, starts a robot that recovers the item requested. This item is delivered to another robotic system, which opens the item and rotates pages automatically.

Knowledge Acquisition, Representation, and Maintenance: Ideally, there would be two primary ways of creating and updating knowledge bases in intelligent systems: (1) intelligent Library systems would distill new knowledge from full-text and other electronic information sources; and (2) human experts would add their unique insights to this knowledge base by unrestricted natural language dialogues with intelligent systems.

Benefits of Artificial Intelligence in Academic Libraries

Omame and Alex-Nmecha, (2020) expressed that artificial intelligence is the current technology that has evolved with huge prospects and promising applications in libraries. Hence, the need to also explore this tech, its pros and cons, in order to adequately maximize its rich benefits for innovative and optimal services delivery in libraries, as Corke (2013) in Omame and Alex-Nmecha, (2020) asserted that artificial intelligent systems (robots) will be an important technology in this century. In a nutshell, the crux for applying artificial intelligent systems in libraries is the fact that they are less prone to errors unlike human beings; they can work for 24 hours/7 days without getting tired thereby freeing the librarians to do other jobs. Ultimately, since computers can operate efficiently at a scale and speed beyond human abilities, it will maximize speed, efficiency and effectiveness in processing library materials and enhance library services delivery at all levels. Artificial intelligence covers almost all of the business activities of the Smart Library. Through the case analysis and systematic review of a large number of domestic and foreign literature and practical applications, the three application areas are summarized: Intelligent resource system, intelligent management (smart warehouse management and intelligent security management), intelligent services (smart application services, intelligent consulting services, intelligent knowledge services) (Yu, Gong Sun and Jiang, 2019)

- Intelligent services 1) Intelligent application service at present, the technology of

library self-service application service is relatively mature, and the forms and contents of services are also rich and diverse. The main representatives are: Self-service seat management system, self-service library ATM, self-service print copy management, lecture training appointment management system, etc. Self-service applications have the following advantages over traditional application services: (1) Break through the space-time boundary with artificial intelligence to realize instant service in no-show; (2) Extend the service form of library services and expand the scope of service targets, thereby reducing the logistics and labor costs of library services; (3) Enhance the user's willingness to participate and protect the service application privacy of reader users; (4) Promote the rational allocation of service resources and reduce the probability of service errors caused by manual services. The above intelligent application services are visible in the general smart library.

- Intelligent consulting service Consulting services are an important part of library

services. Traditional consulting services are inevitably insufficient, such as the limited number of consulting librarians, the low efficiency of manual consultation, and the time limit for consulting work, etc. The emergence of intelligent consulting services can effectively meet the needs of users' consulting services, make up for the above shortcomings, and realize the library's independent, instant, convenient and all-weather intelligent consulting services.

Qingpu and Mang (2016) in Yu, Gong Sun and Jiang (2019)Intelligent knowledge service or simply put, Knowledge service is the core of library service, and intelligent knowledge service is the new positioning of library service innovation, with strong vitality and broad prospects. The rapid development of artificial intelligence technologies such as cross-media awareness, big data management, deep autonomous learning, virtual bionic functions and simulation language interaction provides convenient conditions for the intelligentization and specialization of knowledge services. The patterns and deep knowledge mining processes of intelligent knowledge service are mainly embodied in intelligent analysis of user behavior, intelligent management of information data and intelligent operation of service business, etc., which are realized through knowledge analysis tools, knowledge presentation methods, research conceptual models and analytical research methods Specific as follows:

a) Intelligent analysis of user behavior. From the perspective of the user, Lixin, Yang &Chenglong (2015) in Yu, Gong Sun and Jiang (2019) the user's application behavior is analyzed through artificial intelligence, and the required knowledge is actively recommended to meet the individualized needs of the user and improve the utilization of knowledge resources; b) Intelligent management of information data. Use literature, patents, science, and personal data to conduct intelligent analysis and forecasting, establish knowledge-related networks, and provide reference for knowledge services; c) The intelligent operation of the service business. From the service business and management process, to enhance the core competitiveness of knowledge services, On the one hand, optimizing knowledge service process can improve service efficiency. On the other hand, it can also provide decision-making and strategic planning for knowledge service. The SoLoMo-based smart service of Huazhong Normal University and the knowledge search engine of Wuhan University have begun to boldly try different forms of intelligent knowledge services

CHALLENGES OF USE OF ARTIFICIAL INTELLIGENCE IN ACADEMIC LIBRARIES

Way Forward

Despite all AI potentials in libraries, academic libraries in Nigeria are yet to adopt and implement AI. Perhaps, this might be due to low level of awareness and adoption of AI's relevance in libraries, as research connecting artificial intelligence (AI) to librarianship remains relatively low. While the use of AI has been increasing exponentially in other fields, this has not been the case in library and information science. The challenges, faced by libraries today, pose a tangible risk to the traditional role of libraries. Libraries are now struggling with operational inefficiency, technological disadvantage, difficulty in maintaining current audiences and engaging new ones, and an inability to demonstrate value and benefits to all stakeholders. Korinek and Stiglitz (2017) as cited in Yusuf, Adebayo, Bello and Kayode, (2022) maintained that advances in AI technologies could bring about job losses or job polarization. AI adoption has the potential for a high rise in inequality due to automation. World Bank (2016) in Yusuf, Adebayo, Bello and Kayode, (2022) maintained that developing countries may be more hinted at the adoption of AI because it will lead to a high job loss rate. The report further states that 69% of job loss will be experienced in India through AI adoption; 72% in Thailand; 77% in China and 85% in Ethiopia. All these studies indicate that AI can lead to job losses and the potential for gross job destruction. International Labor Organization (2018) as stated in Yusuf, Adebayo, Bello and Kayode, (2022) also stressed that with the current trend in technological change based on the adoption of artificial intelligence in different organizations that include libraries, AI adoption has created widespread fear of job losses and a high rise in inequality. Other challenges posed by the adoption of AI in academic libraries include: 1. Financial uncertainty: Tella, (2020) in Yusuf, Adebayo, Bello and Kayode, (2022) When government funds are shrinking and political or economic changes are underway, cultural institutions are often the first to suffer cuts. In many ways, the struggle for institutional or government funding is much like the chicken and egg problem. Libraries are expected to show value for money and demonstrate cost effective practices, but they can't do that without integrating new technologies to upgrade their physical spaces, offer new services, and improve the user experience for today's patrons – all of which requires additional funding. Thus, today's libraries often find themselves in a financial limbo - unable to show value without additional funding. 9 2. Emerging skill gaps: The digitalization of information has impacted both library operations and systems. Today, the digital realm is just as important as the physical one, making it essential for libraries to develop new skills not only to stay competent, but to better serve patrons in the digital age. These services require new competencies, such as: higher levels of digital fluency, the ability to provide the most relevant resources at a much faster pace, and supporting hands-on creative activities to maximize a patron's learning experiences. 3. Competing with today's alternative sources of information: According to a 2017 Horizon report in Yusuf, Adebayo, Bello and Kayode, (2022) a survey found that 68% of college students start their research with Google and Wikipedia. These free providers of information, along with the emerging open access trend in scholarly publication methods, are daring libraries to rethink their distribution of high-quality information in to the context of maintaining a vital presence in the new information landscape. 4. Attracting new and more diverse audiences: For libraries to appeal to their existing audiences and engage new ones, they need to offer services that meet the expectations of the new generation of hyper-connected patrons. This includes rethinking the library's traditional physical space, moving from a quiet place filled with bookshelves for reflective reading and writing to something entirely different. For the library to remain relevant, it needs to become a vibrant space for collaboration and innovative activities, alongside a quiet space for reflective studying. Several of the challenges associated with adopting AI in libraries have been highlighted by CILIP (2021) in Oyetola, Oladokun, Maxwell and Akor (n.d) and other organisations. These include, but are not limited to, copyright and intellectual property rights (IPR), the General Data Protection Regulation (GDPR), the cost of working at scale, the reintegration of project data into systems, a lack of management / executive support, insufficient budget and funding, an inability to keep up with the increasing trend in new technologies, and the challenge of implementing new technologies

CONCLUSION AND RECOMMENDATIONS

Oyetola, Oladokun, Maxwell and Akor (n.d) asserted that advances in digital technology have fundamentally altered how traditional library work is done throughout time. Academic and research libraries all around the world are wired for technology and have incorporated it into all of their internal operations and activities; developing countries like Nigeria are not lagging behind in this race. In Nigeria, the incorporation of technology into library services is not new. Throughout the past twenty years or so, Nigerian libraries have not fallen behind in the adoption and implementation of technological developments to enhance library operations and services. Examples of these technologies include computers, scanning and printing devices, electronic resources, CCTV cameras, social media, and most recently, RFID technology. Innovative technology, like artificial intelligence, is still not widely used.

Some of the recommendations suggested by Yusuf, Adebayo, Bello and Kayode, (2022) include:

1. Government and library management must come together to proffer the way forward for academic libraries in terms of meeting up with the latest standard of the use of AI in libraries
2. Library staff should be exposed to training and retraining in the use of artificial intelligence in delivering of libraries' services in order to achieve improved operational efficiency in libraries where the technology is to be adopted or already adopted.
3. There must be proper policy formulation and implementation prior to, during and after the adoption of AI in African academic libraries.
4. Higher institutions libraries should intensify efforts in adopting artificial intelligence in the delivery of libraries' services for libraries users to gain very high level satisfaction.
5. Government and concerned agencies should provide adequate artificial intelligent hardware and software to aid in the delivery of libraries' services to users.

REFERENCES

Abayomi, O. W., Adenekan, F. N., Abayomi, A. O., Ajayi, T. A., & Aderonke, A. O. (2021). *Awareness and Perception of the Artificial Intelligence in the Management of University Libraries in Nigeria. Journal of Interlibrary Loan.* Document Delivery & Electronic Reserve., DOI: 10.1080/1072303X.2021.19186

Mondal, H. (2021). Application of Artificial Intelligence in library of 21st century. *Library and Information Science Modern Scenario.* Available at: https://www.researchgate.net/publication/353211129

Omame, I. M., & Alex-Nmecha, J. C. **(2020).** Artificial Intelligence in Libraries. Available at: https://www.researchgate.net/publication/338337072

Oyetola, S. O., Oladokun, B. D., Maxwell, C. E., & Akor, S. O. (n.d). Artificial intelligence in the library: Potential implications to library and information services in the 21st Century Nigeria. Available at: https://ssrn.com/abstract=4396138

Yu, K., & Gong, R. Sun, L. & Jiang, C (2019). The Application of Artificial Intelligence in Smart Library. *Advances in Economics, Business and Management Research*, 100, pp. 708-712. Available at: https://creativecommons.org/licenses/by-nc/4.0/

Yusuf, T. I., Adebayo, O. A., Bello, O. A., & Kayode, J. O. (2022). Adoption of artificial intelligence for effective library service delivery in academic libraries in Nigeria. *Library philosophy and practice (e-journal).* Available at:https://digitalcommons.unl.edu/libphilprac/6804

KEY TERMS AND DEFINITIONS

Artificial Intelligence (AI): It is the theory and development of computer systems able to perform tasks normally requiring human intelligence, such as visual perception, speech recognition, decision-making, and translation between languages.

Library and Information Services Delivery (LISD): It is the provision of library information resources and services to patrons.

Chapter 9
Teaching Literature in the Age of AI:
A Collaborative Approach to Engaged Learning

Beverly Gibson
https://orcid.org/0009-0007-5519-0699
Lake-Sumter State College, USA

Courtney Noelle Green
Lake-Sumter State College, USA

ABSTRACT

This chapter aims to illuminate the innovative intersection between literature, artificial intelligence (AI), and collaborative pedagogy by detailing a partnership between an English instructor and a librarian. As the landscape of education evolves, integrating new technologies like AI into literature classes offers an exciting avenue for engaging students and fostering interdisciplinary connections. This collaboration seeks to bridge the gap between traditional literary studies and emerging technological advancements through the lens of a literature course focused on and informed by AI. The literature course in question revolves around narrative perceptions of AI and the way they inform current perceptions of AI. Through this lens, the course will address writing in the digital age, teaching students how to use AI as a cited tool to enhance their own ideas in coursework. The librarian's expertise plays a pivotal role in curating and navigating the vast array of AI resources in terms of research, evaluation, synthesis, and citing – thus enhancing the overall learning experience.

DOI: 10.4018/979-8-3693-3053-1.ch009

INTRODUCTION

In the ever-evolving landscape of academia, the integration of technology has become an indispensable facet of pedagogical innovation. Nowhere is this more apparent than in the realm of literature classes, where the traditional methods of textual analysis and literary criticism are undergoing a transformative shift propelled by the advent of generative Artificial Intelligence (AI). This chapter delves into the implications of AI in academic research within the context of literature courses, exploring the evolving role of technology, the rationale for integrating AI, and the crucial role of interdisciplinary collaboration between instructors and librarians in fostering information fluency.

Depictions of computers, robots, and other AI entities in film, fiction, and art since antiquity have influenced our collective cultural perception of AI. As noted by Cave et al. (2018) in their report for the Royal Society: at best, AI narratives can inspire future development and open productive debate; at worst, they can negatively impact public confidence in developing technologies. If we are to think critically about our hopes and fears for AI as it moves out of the realm of science fiction into reality, we must first confront the narratives that have informed our perceptions to this point.

The traditional approach to literature classes often centers on close reading, critical analysis, and historical contextualization. While these methods remain invaluable, the incorporation of technology has expanded the horizons of literary studies, offering new avenues for exploration and interpretation. From digital archives and text mining to natural language processing and machine learning algorithms, AI technologies provide scholars with powerful tools to navigate the vast corpus of literary texts, uncover patterns, and generate novel insights.

At the heart of integrating AI into literature courses lies a compelling rationale rooted in both pedagogical enrichment and scholarly advancement. By harnessing AI, instructors can engage students in dynamic exercises that foster critical thinking, computational literacy, and interdisciplinary inquiry. Moreover, AI-driven approaches enable scholars to tackle complex research questions with unprecedented efficiency and depth, transcending the limitations of traditional methodologies. Though the foundational skills of critical thinking and expressive writing remain paramount for students, the integration of AI offers the potential to enhance their ability to refine and articulate their ideas. By leveraging AI tools to streamline the process of expressing concepts, students can allocate more time to delve deeper into their analysis of literary topics, thus enriching their scholarly engagement and exploration.

In the AI Literature course, students will examine the way AI has been portrayed in narratives, explore real-world applications and developments in AI, and construct a personal vision for the future of AI. However, the effective integration of AI into literature courses requires more than technological prowess—it necessitates a collaborative effort between instructors and librarians to cultivate information fluency among students. Librarians, with their expertise in information retrieval, database management, and scholarly communication, play a pivotal role in guiding students through the vast landscape of digital resources and AI tools. By collaborating with librarians, instructors can design curriculum modules that seamlessly integrate AI technologies while instilling in students the essential skills of critically evaluating, synthesizing, and ethically utilizing information.

Furthermore, interdisciplinary collaboration between literature instructors and librarians not only enriches the learning experience but also fosters a culture of innovation and adaptability within academia. By bridging the gap between humanities and information science, such partnerships exemplify the transformative potential of interdisciplinary dialogue in navigating the complexities of the digital age.

This chapter explores the practical applications of integrating AI into literature courses. Pedagogical strategies will be discussed, along with the instructional philosophies, observations, and reflections that motivated the creation of the course. In addition, this chapter would not be complete without addressing the fears associated with student use of AI in literature and other writing-based courses. By embracing the relationship between technology and literary studies as symbiotic rather than antagonistic, scholars can chart a course toward a more vibrant, inclusive, and intellectually rigorous academic landscape with a bright outlook for the future.

Literature and Artificial Intelligence: A Theoretical Framework

Technology and the Written Word

The primary objective of any educator is to prepare students for the future. As such, pedagogy is inextricably linked with technology. The study of literature and the written word has weathered numerous technological advances, most of which made the written word more portable and accessible. Akin to the advent of the Internet, the sudden arrival of generative AI has had an immediate impact on how humans interact with the written word. Chatbots such as ChatGPT, Copilot, Claude, and Gemini connect with users via a conversational interface and can respond to questions, ideate, outline, and develop lengthy texts all while maintaining context in the flow of conversation. These chatbots are increasingly being utilized for a broad spectrum of writing tasks, from emails to academic papers (Grammarly, 2024; Nam, 2023).

AI users have quickly determined that getting the best and most accurate results from generative AI requires detailed prompting as part of an iterative process of trial and error. Unlike the highly logical and mathematical coding languages used for most advanced computing, prompting a chatbot requires natural language, or more simply, the written word. Consequently, practitioners who study literature and writing have found that rhetorical skills previously thought irrelevant have suddenly become quite valuable. Chatbots can be directed to use rhetorical appeals to enhance the effectiveness of marketing content or change the tone of a text (Cummings, 2024). The evident overlap of concepts in acronyms and mnemonics developed by educators to instruct both rhetorical analysis and prompting (see Table 1) suggests that proficiency in generative AI usage necessitates an understanding of rhetoric. In fact, one could argue that prompt engineering fundamentally represents a form of reverse-engineered rhetorical analysis.

Table 1. Comparison of acronyms used to teach rhetorical analysis and prompt engineering (own emphasis)

Rhetorical Analysis	Prompting
Speaker *Occasion* *Audience* *Purpose* *Subject* **Tone** (College Board, 2004)	*Context* *Intent* *Style* Commands Outcome (Fozrok, 2023)
Speaker *Purpose* *Audience* *Context* Exigence Choices *Appeals* *Tone* (Newbold, 2021)	*Context* *Role* *Examples* *Audience* *Task* Evaluate (Yang, 2024)

Emerging trends indicate that AI is rapidly becoming a permanent fixture in the workplace. A report by Grammarly (2024) indicates that 89% of business leaders used generative AI in 2023, and 77% of all workers using AI reported that it enhances their job performance. Regardless of major, college students will require, at a minimum, an introduction to AI to prepare them for the future. Consequently, it is logical to integrate AI into the general education curriculum. The clear parallels between prompt engineering and rhetoric make English courses the perfect choice. Although not categorized as a general education course, the course outlined in this chapter is tailored to fulfill the requirements of LIT2000, an approved option for Humanities credit within the State Core Curriculum. In addition, the ideas outlined here could be replicated or condensed in similar first- and second-year English courses (like ENC1101 or ENC1102) to provide students with the necessary introduction to AI required to both future-proof their education and careers. The outcomes of this initiative will demonstrate that English courses can serve as an effective conduit for introducing all college students to generative AI.

Generative AI and Information Literacy

The use of generative AI raises concerns related to academic integrity, copyright infringement, bias, hallucinations, misinformation, disinformation, and the potential outsourcing of critical thinking to machines, and skilled prompting alone is not the solution. The risks of bias and misinformation are inherent in any interaction with AI, regardless of the skill or experience of the user. The only way to mitigate these risks is to critically evaluate the output of any interaction with AI. This is accomplished through one of three lenses: subject area expertise, lateral reading, and source evaluation.

As defined by the Association of College and Research Libraries (ACRL, 2016), information literacy is "the set of integrated abilities encompassing the reflective discovery of information, the understanding of how information is produced and valued, and the use of information in creating new knowledge and participating ethically in communities of learning." Generative AI is at once a tool for information discovery and production, both domains clearly encompassed in the ACRL's definition of information literacy. It is clear then, that information literacy must be a critical component of any course addressing generative AI.

While information literacy skills can and should be taught by all faculty, these skills are predominantly considered the domain of librarians. Lateral reading and source evaluation are information literacy skills addressed explicitly through library instruction and intervention models. Many institutions incorporate library instruction into first-year experience or composition courses, as students will need to employ these critical skills throughout their academic careers. The inclusion of librarians in first-year English classes offers a nearly seamless opportunity for integrating generative AI into these courses.

To effectively prepare students to write with AI, English instructors and librarians must collaborate to establish connections between rhetoric, information literacy, and generative AI.

Language Models & Literary Studies

Just as literature has long been regarded as a mirror reflecting the complexities of human experience, language models, including AI technologies, can also serve as mirrors reflecting the intricacies of contemporary society (Christian, 2020). Literature, through its narratives, characters, and themes, offers insights into human behavior, societal norms, and cultural values. Similarly, language models, by analyzing vast amounts of textual data, reflect the linguistic patterns, biases, and discourses prevalent in society.

Furthermore, literature has the power to influence and shape societal perceptions, attitudes, and aspirations. Literary works can inspire social change, challenge prevailing ideologies, and provoke critical reflection on ethical and moral issues. Similarly, language models, through their generation and dissemination of text, wield influence over public discourse, shaping opinions, and informing decision-making processes.

Language models, as mirrors reflecting the linguistic landscape of society, provide valuable data for analyzing language use, discourse patterns, and semantic structures. By employing large language model usage alongside literary study, scholars can uncover underlying biases, power dynamics, and ethical considerations inherent in AI technologies. Furthermore, language models can serve as tools for generating narratives, facilitating dialogue, and fostering innovation in the interdisciplinary study of AI narratives, usage, and ethics.

AI in Literature

The proposed AI literature course outlined in this chapter seeks to be among the first of its kind to not only address literature concerning intelligent machines, but to also incorporate generative AI in the literary classroom and to encourage generative AI use in student submissions. No doubt, this is a tall order, especially when considering that assignments teaching students AI prompt engineering, response evaluation, and ethical citation practices would fall under several pedagogical categories, primarily within the domains of computer science education, ethics education, and critical thinking.

Therefore, it is critical to acknowledge that the interdisciplinary study of Artificial Intelligence (AI) narratives, usage, and ethics is a multifaceted endeavor transcending traditional disciplinary boundaries. At its core, this framework seeks to understand the complex interplay between human culture, technological innovation, and ethical considerations surrounding AI. By integrating insights from diverse fields such as literature, computer science, philosophy, sociology, and ethics, scholars can unravel the nuanced dynamics shaping our understanding and deployment of AI technologies. This theoretical framework provides a roadmap for navigating the complex terrain of teaching AI narratives, usage, and ethics, illuminating key themes, methodologies, and areas of inquiry in the emerging field of AI pedagogy.

Central to this framework is the analysis of narratives surrounding AI, which encompasses fictional representations in literature, film, and art, as well as real-world discourses in media, politics, and popular culture. By examining how AI is portrayed and conceptualized across different cultural contexts, scholars can discern recurring themes, tropes, and ideological underpinnings. Drawing upon literary theory and cultural studies, this aspect of the framework elucidates how AI narratives both reflect and shape societal attitudes, fears, and aspirations regarding technology and human existence.

The interdisciplinary exploration of AI narratives, utilization, and ethical implications provides a comprehensive framework for comprehending the multifaceted nature of AI technologies in modern society. Through the integration of perspectives from literature, computer science, philosophy, sociology, and ethics, scholars can uncover the cultural, technological, and ethical facets of AI. This theoretical approach offers a holistic method for addressing the complexities inherent in AI, fostering critical discourse, ethical contemplation, and innovative solutions. As AI continues to exert its influence on our global landscape, interdisciplinary collaboration and ethical scrutiny are imperative for effectively navigating the challenges and opportunities it presents.

Pedagogical Approaches

A constructivist approach emphasizes active learning, knowledge construction, and meaning-making, which encourages students to interpret the presented course content within the framework of their previous knowledge and experiences. In the AI-based literature course, students are encouraged to construct their own understanding of AI's role in literature and society through experiential learning and collaborative inquiry. By engaging with AI tools, analyzing narratives, and participating in reflective discussions, students actively shape their knowledge and perspectives on AI technology. This constructivist framework empowers students to take ownership of their learning, develop adaptive skills, and navigate the complex technological landscape of the 21st century. Ultimately, such a pedagogical approach prepares students to become informed, responsible, and empathetic participants in shaping the future of AI and its impact on human culture and consciousness.

In designing an AI-based literature course that integrates AI into assignments while exploring narratives surrounding AI themes, pedagogical strategies must be carefully crafted to engage students in meaningful learning experiences. This section discusses the constructivist pedagogical approaches behind such a course, emphasizing collaborative project-based learning, reflective writing, and Socratic discussions.

Collaborative Project-Based Learning

Collaborative project-based learning fosters active engagement, teamwork, and problem-solving skills. In the AI-based literature course, students will collaborate on projects that involve analyzing AI-related literature, creating multimedia presentations, or developing their own AI-infused narratives. Through collaboration, students leverage diverse perspectives, share expertise, and collectively construct knowledge about AI's implications in literature and society. To support this learning activity, students have the option of using an AI tool of their choice to complete many of the projects in the course, so long as the student employs one of the prompting frameworks presented in the course, assesses the AI-generated response, supplements the AI-generated response with their own thoughts, integrates outside research, and cites the chatbot with a link to the transcript.

Reflective Writing

Reflective writing encourages metacognition and critical reflection. While students will learn how to use generative AI ethically in their coursework, the expectation is not that students will use AI for every assignment. Students will engage in reflective writing exercises that prompt them to analyze their experiences, beliefs, and insights regarding AI technology and its portrayal in literature. By articulating their thoughts through writing, students deepen their understanding, clarify misconceptions, and develop a nuanced perspective on AI's role in shaping human culture and consciousness. As AI can neither reflect nor critically think, all major writing assignments requiring student-generated writing in the course will come in the form of reflective writing focusing on critical thinking. AI will not be permitted in reflective writing assignments.

Socratic Discussions

Socratic discussions promote inquiry, dialogue, and active listening. In the AI-based literature course, Socratic discussions can center around key AI-related themes and ethical dilemmas presented in literary texts. Through open-ended questioning and reasoned debate, students explore complex issues such as AI ethics, consciousness, and the nature of humanity. Socratic discussions encourage intellectual curiosity, critical thinking, and empathy, enabling students to grapple with the moral and existential implications of AI technology. Each class session, one to two students will lead class discussion by presenting their close reading of the text being covered that day, deepening their understanding of the subject matter by actively participating in the creation and dissemination of knowledge. Engagement in Socratic discussion during class and on weekly online discussion boards will be graded. Generative AI may be consulted to summarize or clarify an aspect of the discussion a student finds confusing. Generative AI may be used by the instructor and students to generate questions or examples to expound on discussions, effectively including generative AI as a participant in the Socratic discussions.

Course Learning Objectives

In the AI literature course, the learning objectives are carefully crafted to align with the course's thematic focus on exploring the intersection of artificial intelligence and literature, in addition to traditional learning objectives for a second-year literature course. These objectives encompass a range of cognitive skills, critical perspectives, and ethical considerations that students will develop throughout the course. Below are the specific learning objectives outlined for the course:

- Students will learn to analyze literary works, focusing particularly on themes related to Artificial Intelligence (AI).
- Students will learn to write, discuss, and report on literary works, including those exploring AI themes, at the college level.
- Students will learn to evaluate critical articles and other media related to literary works, with a specific focus on AI themes.
- Students will learn to engineer appropriate prompts to elicit AI-generated responses according to prompting and writing frameworks.
- Students will learn to evaluate AI-generated responses for bias, correctness, and ethical considerations.
- Students will successfully apply a citation system when referencing outside works including AI-generated responses, while adhering to academic standards for attribution and citation.

These learning objectives are designed to guide students in developing a multifaceted understanding of AI's role in literature and society, while also honing their critical thinking, research, and ethical reasoning skills. By achieving these objectives, students will be well-equipped to engage thoughtfully and responsibly with AI technology both inside and outside the academic context.

Course Outline

Below is an outline of the AI literature course as planned for the Fall 2024 iteration. Students are expected to complete all readings and film viewings outside of class before the class meets to discuss the reading or film. All class meetings will open with a 10–15-minute lecture that introduces the literary period and author and any necessary context surrounding the reading or film. Following the brief lecture, presenting students will deliver their close reading of a particular aspect of the text; generally, 1-2 students present per class session, though this can be adjusted to accommodate larger or smaller class sizes or hybrid versus fully seated modalities. On the three planned librarian intervention days, the embedded librarian will provide students with supplemental instruction and library resources, followed by student presentations. Students will complete weekly reading responses and reflection papers outside of class.

The thematic structure of the course allows instructors to modify, adapt, or otherwise supplement the suggested readings at their own discretion. As Cave et al. (2019) note, many AI narratives touch on multiple hopes and fears. For example, it is possible to use Disney Pixar's *WALL-E* to teach themes of Ease & Automation as well as Gratification, but also Alienation when one considers the isolation humans exist in upon the Axiom. This outline is designed only to provide general guidance on what readings might be chosen to teach certain concepts; the themes provided are what overall guide the course. Readings may therefore be swapped out in favor of another that illustrates the theme better or perhaps in a more grade-level appropriate manner for those interested in adapting this course to a K-12 setting.

Week 1 Course Introductions

Students will meet their instructor and become acquainted with the syllabus. In terms of assignments, they will complete a syllabus quiz and an introductory discussion board. Finally, students will view *The Terminator* (1984) and write a film response in which they analyze the portrayal of artificial intelligence in the film and reflect on their current understanding and feelings regarding AI. It is important to note that *The Terminator* (1984) is a rated R film and may not be suitable for all grade levels. A suggested alterative film that is suitable for all ages may be Disney's *Big Hero 6* (2014). In terms of sourcing, the film can be viewed in class during the first week if time allows; otherwise, links to rent the movie from streaming platforms will be provided in the learning management system's modules. Students will sign up for presentation dates spread evenly throughout the term.

Week 2 History & Myths of Intelligent Machines

Students are introduced to a brief history of artificial intelligence and ancient imaginings of intelligent machines. Students will read excerpts of *Argonautica*, the myth of Pandora, the Jewish tradition of the golem, and more. In addition, students will read Genesis 2:4-2:25 Adam and Eve. Presenting students will lead in-class discussions on several topics ranging from comparisons of Talos and the Terminator to the role of creators in myths and various faiths regarding constructed lifeforms. Students will be introduced to AI prompt writing and citing AI-generated responses. Students will complete an assignment that asks them to craft a prompt asking AI to compare creation myths of man versus creation myths of intelligent machines. Students will choose either the CREATE or CISCO frameworks to engineer the prompt. Students will use the prompt to generate a response, then evaluate the response based on their knowledge of the reading, and finally cite the response. Students will only be graded on the quality and thoroughness of the prompt, their analysis of the response, and the citation, not the AI-generated response itself.

Week 3 Ethics of AI Use

The embedded librarian will join the class this week to provide supplemental instruction on AI prompting and response evaluation using CISCO or CREATE. Students will read "The Nine-Billion Names of God" by Arthur C. Clarke. Presenting students will lead in-class discussions on ethical concerns and moral dilemmas raised in the story. In-class lectures will introduce some of the many ethical concerns surrounding the existence and use of AI, focusing specifically on the ethical use of AI in academia. Students will also read "How to Read a Privacy Policy" from the Office of the Attorney General, California Department of Justice. Students will complete a short response applying their learning through an analysis of a privacy policy or terms of service from an AI tool of their choosing (Caines, n.d.). Many ethical concerns and philosophical questions posed in this week will carry forward, building throughout the remainder of the semester with the introduction of further literature from various literary periods.

Week 4 Immortality

Students will read "The Truth of Fact, the Truth of Feeling" by Ted Chiang. Presenting students will lead in-class discussions on several AI themes presented in the text, focusing chiefly on the concept of digital immortality, bias and reliability of written records and technology, as well as the ways in which technology shapes our understanding of the past, present, and future. Students will complete a critical analysis paper on the theme of immortality as it relates to memory preservation and the impact of technology on personal identity. In their paper, students must also consider the implications of these explorations for our understanding of human existence and consciousness and provide an analysis of at least one character's relationship with memory, technology, and truth.

Week 5 Inhumanity

Students will read "The Gentle Seduction" by Marc Stiegler. Presenting students will lead in-class discussions on several AI themes the texts presented including but not limited to: immortality achieved via technological advancements, the loss or redefinition of humanity, ethical implications of achieving immortality, ethical implications of reliance on banned or illegal technology, the nature of human connection in a technologically advanced society, and the parallels between the fictional world of "The Gentle Seduction" and our own relationship with technology. Using the short story as a vehicle to fuel their thinking, students will complete a short response reflection paper that asks them to make predictions of technological advancements (not limited to AI) they expect to see in their lifetimes.

Week 6 Ease & Automation

Students will view Disney Pixar's *WALL-E* (2008). Presenting students will lead in-class discussions on several AI themes the film presents, focusing specifically on dependence on technology, the environmental consequences of machine automation, the impact of automation on employment, and the seductive appeal of a life of only comfort and convenience facilitated by automation at the costly price of human autonomy and skill-degradation. The embedded librarian will return for a brief support session on researching, a refresher on library database access, and citing AI. For their weekly response, students will complete a film response comparing AI themes in *WALL-E* and *Terminator*, specifically focusing on the portrayal of intelligent machines, intended usage of intelligent machines, and human hopes and fears towards a future filled with intelligent machines. Critical sources will be supplied to students to support their responses, though they will have the option to locate additional sources from the library's literary databases should they choose. Students also have the option of using AI tools to generate their responses but must integrate their own thoughts and research and provide MLA in-text and Works Cited citations with links to the chatbot conversation.

Week 7 Obsolescence

Students will read "The Veldt" by Ray Bradbury. Presenting students will lead in-class discussions on technological dependency and human obsolescence themes, character analysis, and symbolism. Students will complete a short critical analysis paper focusing on the theme of AI obsolescence in "The Veldt" and discuss its implications for contemporary society. In the analysis, students will identify the AI technologies at play, analyze how the theme of obsolescence is presented, and consider how the family's reliance on automation leads to their emotional detachment and ultimate downfall.

Week 8 Gratification

Students will read "Introduction" and "Robbie" from Isaac Asimov's *I, Robot*. Presenting students will lead in-class discussions on technology fulfilling the role of a perfect (and preferred) companion, the implications of treating AI as companions or even family members, AI's impact on traditional family structures, AI autonomy and identity. Students will create a slideshow presentation exploring real-world digital companionship and technological dependencies they may have or may identify society as possessing. Students will, of course, automatically think of their smartphones but will be encouraged to think outside of the box. Virtual pets and Roomba vacuum cleaners, for example, make for great topics and demonstrate perfectly how machines already provide a sense of companionship even before intelligence is added. Students will not present their slideshow in class but will instead post to an online discussion board where they will be required to reply to at least three other classmates.

Week 9 Alienation

Students will read "The Sandman" by E.T.A. Hoffman. Presenting students will lead in-class discussions on alienation, ethical implications of not only creating sentient beings but also engaging in romantic relationships with artificial constructs, the uncanny and fear of technology, and finally autonomy and personhood. Students will craft a comparative analysis paper that examines the portrayal of AI themes in Hoffman's "The Sandman" and Asimov's "Robbie," focusing specifically on human gratification and alienation. Students must consider how the characters in each story interact with intelligent machines, and how these interactions shape their understanding of themselves and their world. Students must also identify the role of technology in fulfilling human desires, as well as the potential for technology to isolate individuals from authentic human experiences in both short stories.

Week 10 Dominance

Students will read "Runaround" and "Little Lost Robot" from Isaac Asimov's *I, Robot*. Presenting students will lead in-class discussions on the themes of power, control, and autonomy present in the stories, focusing specifically on human anxiety of maintaining control over intelligent machines. Students will complete their second and final prompting assignment, which asks them to engineer a prompt asking a chatbot of their choice (ChatGPT and Copilot preferred) to analyze at least one human character from "Runaround" and "Little Lost Robot" and how that human character approaches controlling intelligent machines in the narrative. Students will choose either the CREATE or CISCO frameworks to engineer the prompt. Students will use the prompt to generate a response, then evaluate the response based on their knowledge of the reading, and finally cite the response. Students will be graded on the quality and thoroughness of the prompt, their analysis of the response, and the citation.

Week 11 Uprising

Students will read "I Have No Mouth and I Must Scream" by Harlan Ellison. Presenting students will lead in-class discussions on themes of power and control, tyranny and oppression, ethical responsibilities of creators towards their creations, identity, existence, personhood, AI as a mirror reflecting human understanding, and hubris and consequences. Students will complete and submit a slideshow presentation with biographical and literary information on a selected author covered at any point throughout the course, identifying the author's background, influences, and literary period. Students will also identify or interpret the author's viewpoint on technology, artificial intelligence, and the future based on the student's close reading of the work(s) by that author covered in the course.

Week 12 Post-Human, Transhuman, Cyborgs

Students will read a selection of essays and articles by cyborg authors and about cyborgs. Presenting students will lead in-class discussions on post-humanism, transhumanism, cyborgs, cyborg law, and the varying degrees by which singularity may be achieved or may already have occurred. Students will complete a short response reflection that asks them to consider the degree to which they believe singularity has been achieved based on the week's readings and their own outside knowledge of human augmentation and technological integration.

Week 13 Hopes, Fears, Inheritance

Students will read Isaac Asimov's "The Last Question" and "There Will Come Soft Rains" by Ray Bradbury. Presenting students will lead in-class discussions tying the themes of the final two readings to previous readings, as well as analyzing the role intelligent machines may have in a future where humanity is extinct. Following the conclusion of presentations, students will be introduced to the final unit of the course in which students will collaborate on projects that involve analyzing AI-related literature, creating multimedia presentations, or developing their own AI-infused narratives. In Week 13, students will choose the type of deliverable they will submit for their final assignment. Deliverable options include: a creative writing piece about AI centered on at least one of the major themes and/or concepts explored; a slideshow presentation on an AI narrative not covered in the course readings; an AI-generated image based on one of the texts read in class with a supporting explication of how the image depicts the reading or viewing; a critical essay on any of the texts covered in the course, except the narratives for which a critical essay was the weekly writing assignment; a response to a scholarly article, news report, or case study on a recent (no older than 6 months) AI-related issue or topic such as rising ethical questions, use/misuse, automation, job loss and/or job creation, etc. The use of an AI tool is optional but encouraged. Students utilizing an AI tool must provide MLA in-text and Works Cited citations with links to the chatbot conversation.

Week 14 Drafting the Final Project

The embedded librarian returns for their final intervention day, where students will be instructed on the PARSE framework (described below) and how they may use it when approaching their final project. In addition, students will be reminded of various library resources pertaining to AI. Students will complete a rough draft of their final project and submit to a peer review discussion board in the learning management system.

Week 15 Peer Reviewing the Final Project

Students will peer review and provide feedback via discussion board to at least three classmates to receive full credit by Wednesday. Students will submit their final draft by the final Sunday before Finals Week. In addition to their final project, students will complete a final reflection discussing the challenges and benefits of collaborative writing with AI; identify in what ways their worldview has changed since Week 1; and finally, provide their final prediction on how AI will impact their lives, scholarship, careers, and society.

Collaborative Design: Course Development

In line with the thematic focus, this course was born out of fear and hope. In August 2023, the librarian and instructor sat next to each other as the institution hosted a guest speaker discussing artificial intelligence in higher education. The librarian saw an opportunity: generative AI makes information literacy more critical than it has ever been before. This need presents librarians with a chance to elevate information literacy to the forefront of academic discourse. Conversely, the instructor saw a crisis: students might exploit this technology to cheat and avoid critical thinking, finding shortcuts that deprive them of essential skills. During a discussion, the librarian attempted to alleviate the instructor's fears. Still, the positive implications of AI remained elusive to the instructor until later in the day, following exposure to further dialogue and concrete examples of AI in higher education. In that reflective space, following several professional development opportunities, the instructor began to comprehend the potential AI offers and the importance of teaching students information literacy in the era of artificial intelligence.

This final epiphany – what will we need to teach students about AI use? – led to the inception of the AI literature course. As many instructors know, if students have access to a tool that helps them complete an assignment or task faster, inevitably some students will elect to use the tool. A survey conducted in March 2023, less than six months after OpenAI's release of ChatGPT, revealed that 22% of students admitted to using AI tools to help complete schoolwork (Welding, 2023). At the time of the survey, 51% of respondents believed that such use was cheating or plagiarism, even though only 31% said their schools or instructors had prohibited such tools (Welding, 2023). In a subsequent survey released eight months later, the number of students using AI for schoolwork had risen by 34% (Nam, 2023). In addition, 58% of students reported having assignments that required the use of AI tools, and 80% reported that at least one instructor had discussed "the use and ethics of AI in the classroom" (Nam, 2023). It seems that in less than a year, many institutions and instructors arrived at a similar conclusion: students are going to use AI, so it is in everyone's best interest to teach them how to use it effectively and ethically. AI expert Ethan Mollick came to the same conclusion about AI use in the workforce. Mollick (2023) points out that while workers are finding ways to make themselves more effective and efficient, "the inventors aren't telling their companies about their discoveries" (para. 4). The reason, Mollick (2023) suggests, is that "people don't want to get in trouble" (para. 5). This disconnect between practice and policy hinders innovation. Bringing AI into the classroom empowers instructors to educate students on the appropriate and ethical use of such tools within the course and empowers students to share their insights, thereby opening pathways to innovation and collaborative learning.

Having reached a consensus on the importance of information literacy in AI use, the discussion shifted to how to meaningfully present these skills in a literature class. Of course, AI tools could be incorporated into any English class. Instead, the instructor wanted to make the entire class about artificial intelligence, pulling examples from literature that discussed intelligent machines long before they became a reality. At first, the plan was a chronological walkthrough of portrayals of artificial intelligence in literature. That changed when the research of Dr. Stephen

Cave and his team was discovered. Cave et al. (2018) conducted research for the Royal Society about the degree to which narratives of emerging technologies impact public perception. One only needs to consider how often the movie *Terminator* and its AI "Skynet" are invoked in discussions of artificial intelligence to see evidence of how popular culture influences the public. Cave et. al (2018) assert that "exaggerated expectations and fears about AI, together with an over-emphasis on humanoid representations, can affect public confidence and perceptions" (p.4). How then, do we mitigate this exaggerated influence? One solution is to engage directly with it. Thus, was born the idea of guiding students through a variety of popular portrayals of artificial intelligence, allowing them to compare fiction with reality and come to their own conclusions. This new concept for the course was bolstered by another work of Dr. Cave's, in which four dichotomous themes of AI literature were described (Cave & Dihal, 2019). It was these themes and dichotomies that would become the framework for the course.

And so, with the intention of leading students through a thematic analysis of artificial intelligence and providing explicit instruction in the effective and ethical use of AI tools, the work began in earnest. At this stage, the instructor's focus turned to developing course modules and organizing literature and learning activities into the thematic structure while the librarian began investigating pedagogical methods for teaching AI-assisted writing. Interdisciplinary research and discussion about writing instruction and prompting eventually led to the creation of an integrated prompting and writing framework, described below.

Prompting and Writing Frameworks: Interweaving Rhetoric and Information Literacy

Conceptualizing an approach to teaching writing with generative AI requires an intermixing of two recursive, iterative processes. Just as prompting is intrinsically linked to rhetorical analysis, the process of writing with AI closely mirrors its rhetorical equivalent. However, given the potential risks of hallucinations, bias, and misinformation, it is imperative to integrate critical evaluation into the writing process itself. The AI-assisted writing process can be described as *Prompting*, *Assessing* the output provided by the chatbot, *Revising* the prompt and generating new output, *Synthesizing* chatbot output with original writing and outside sources, and *Editing* the completed text for clarity (PARSE; see Table 2). Embedded within this process are a series of complex iterative and recursive writing and information literacy practices.

Table 2. PARSE framework for AI-assisted writing

Prompt* – Tell the AI what to do
Assess – Evaluate the output using your own knowledge and lateral reading
Revise – Adjust the prompt and regenerate content as necessary
Synthesize - Combine multiple outputs with human-generated content
Edit – Proofread text for clarity, accuracy, and grammar
*Students may use any prompting framework

Graham (2023) refutes the notion of the linear writing process and argues that the best writing studies help students develop "more robust and recursive revision practices" (p. 166). Furthermore, he contends that "AI provides the opportunity to add multiple dimensions of recursion where prompt-engineering, output curation, fact-checking, and revision become an orthogonal dimension to traditional writing and learning processes" (Graham, 2023, p. 166). The PARSE method embodies Graham's assertion, integrating prompting (PAR) and writing (SE) steps into a streamlined yet highly iterative and recursive process. While working on a single assignment, a student may formulate a prompt, assess the output to be unsatisfactory, and revise the prompt several times before moving on to the drafting stage of the process. The drafting process itself is recursive, with the student synthesizing multiple sources and ideas and then organizing, reviewing, and editing in a cyclical process, making sure to check for clarity at each step.

Although at its simplest, AI-assisted writing involves engaging in these two recursive processes in a linear, step-by-step sequence, advanced practitioners will discover opportunities for recursion between the two cyclical processes of prompting and writing. The need for extensive rewriting could spur a new iteration of the original prompt, or even require a new prompt altogether, sending the writer back through a recursion of the prompting process, before resuming the task of writing.

Prompting

Prompt. Each step of the PARSE framework encompasses its own complex portion of the process. As previously mentioned, effective prompting is a task that requires a foundational understanding of rhetoric. To facilitate this process, students in the course will be introduced to multiple frameworks, allowing them to select the one that best suits their needs for prompting AI. Each of these frameworks encourages students to include not just an action in their prompt but also rhetorical guidelines for the chatbot. For example, the CISCO framework breaks down prompting into *Context, Intent, Style, Commands,* and *Outcome* (Fozrok, 2023). In contrast, the CREATE framework includes *Context, Role, Examples, Audience, Task,* and *Evaluate* (Yang, 2024). These frameworks share three common components: contextual cues, stylistic cues, and directive cues. Following these guidelines, students will employ rhetorical attributes to establish a context and tone and then instruct the chatbot to complete a desired task within those parameters. While this framework within a framework approach may feel cumbersome, employing best practices for both prompting and writing is essential to engage students in critical thinking. Although it is possible to prompt without a framework, doing so often results in students relying heavily on the chatbot, invariably leading to subpar outcomes. Working within a prompting framework requires students to think carefully about the purpose and desired outcomes of their prompt and primes them to participate in the recursive process of revising and refining prompts for future iterations by explicitly delineating multiple attributes within the prompt that can be altered in new versions.

Assess. Before a prompt can be revised for future iterations, the student must assess the output generated by the prompt. Given the tendency of large language models to produce hallucinations and make mistakes, this step is incredibly important, extending beyond merely reading the content to see if it "makes sense." On the contrary, conversational AI can convincingly fabricate information that seems logical and sensible. This is one of the chief dangers associated with this technology. To mitigate this risk, it is imperative to critically evaluate any output generated by AI, assessing both its appropriateness and accuracy. This validation requires the consultation of an authoritative source to corroborate information provided by the chatbot.

The authority of a source is determined by the context of the information (ACRL, 2016). As a result, authoritative sources for assessing AI output can take various forms. Depending on the subject matter of the requested content, the students themselves might possess sufficient authority to vet the content. For example, an individual using AI to draft an email should be able to tell upon reading whether the text conveys the intended meaning. In other cases, AI may provide links to sources used when generating information. These sources must be evaluated by the student to determine whether they are authoritative and accurate, and furthermore, whether the information reported by the AI is indeed corroborated by the provided source. If the AI does not provide sources, the student must engage in the information literacy practice known as lateral reading. Lateral reading refers to the act of leaving a website to conduct research about the source itself (Wineburg & McGrew, 2019). Researchers engaging in this practice look for information about the author or publisher of a source, such as sources of funding or ideological ties that may suggest hidden agendas. Lateral reading also often involves searches for similar articles that support or discredit the claims of the original source. Since chatbots are not human, and therefore cannot receive funding or have ideological ties, students will have to focus on similar sources when engaging in this information literacy behavior. Based on their findings during lateral reading, the student will be able to determine whether the AI output satisfactorily completes the intended task.

Assessment is particularly crucial in cases where chatbots have produced citations. Depending on the discipline and specificity of the topic, researchers have found that ChatGPT 3.5 has a hallucination rate as high as 54%, with GPT 4 having a rate of 43% (Buchanan et al., 2023). Hallucination rates for individual prompts can vary widely. In some cases, the cited source simply does not exist. In others, the source may exist but not contain the information attributed to it by the chatbot. Moreover, even authentic citations that properly attribute information contained in the text may not fully adhere to the correct citation style if one was specified.

Revise. Revising the prompt to generate additional text or a new iteration of the initial response is an essential part of the AI-assisted writing process. Whether the original prompt is seeking original content or suggested revisions, it is unlikely that the first response will be the best. In some cases, the answer will simply not make sense, and it will become clear that the chatbot did not understand the prompt as given. Prompt revisions may include clarification of a task or context that the AI did not understand the first time or explicit directives to include or exclude parts of a previous response. Chatbots have large context windows that allow them to "remember" previous parts of the conversation, so feedback about a prior response may assist in achieving the desired results.

In situations where the chatbot produced erroneous information (hallucinations), this can be explicitly addressed in a subsequent prompt. In most cases, the chatbot will apologize and attempt to correct its answer. However, there is no guarantee that a second or any following attempt will produce the desired response. In these cases, making the revision manually may be preferable to subsequent prompt iterations that could introduce new hallucinations.

Writing

Synthesize. A complete draft begins to take shape as the student combines multiple iterations of AI-generated content and original writing into a unified, cohesive draft. The ratio of AI-generated content to student-authored writing will vary depending on the parameters of the assignment. The synthesis process requires attention to the logical progression and transition of arguments and counterarguments throughout the text. Preliminary drafts generated by AI are likely to follow a logical order. The responsibility lies with the student to maintain that order through subsequent iterations and additions of both AI- and human-generated text.

Edit. Ultimately, the student is responsible for ensuring that the final product is cohesive, error-free, and correctly formatted. Regardless of the extent to which the draft was written by AI, the accountability for any mistakes rests solely with the human author. During this phase of the process, students must correct any formatting errors and ensure that the final draft conforms to the style indicated by their instructor. This includes final verifications of in-text citations and the works cited or references page, as citations generated by AI are prone to errors, and chatbots frequently confuse citation styles, even when these styles are specified in the prompt.

At this juncture, the student may consider further AI intervention by copying and pasting passages into a chatbot and requesting suggested revisions. As with the initial prompting, specificity is key. Students will need to instruct the chatbot to focus on style, tone, rhetorical appeals, and conciseness to receive useful feedback. Suggestions given by AI at this stage will necessitate a brief additional recursion through the prompting and writing framework to ensure that the suggestions are suitable and seamlessly integrated into the final product.

Levels of Intervention

The frameworks described above are applicable to multiple levels of AI-assisted writing intervention. Throughout the course, students will use these frameworks to engage in learning activities requiring various levels of intervention. Some levels, such as information gathering and brainstorming, will only use the prompting skills described in the framework since they do not require the student to go through the full writing process. In many cases, elements of the prompting framework may be implied rather than stated explicitly, showcasing the ability of large language models to parse complex meanings from context.

Information Gathering. Not all exchanges with chatbots begin with the goal of creating a deliverable written product. Often, users are seeking information, turning to the conversational interface of a chatbot because of how well it quickly summarizes and explains a wide variety of topics. In an academic setting, this can be a powerful tool for personalized learning, allowing students to seek explanations or additional examples of concepts introduced in class, as in the prompting assignment described in Week 2 of the course outline (Table 3). The risk of hallucination is high in this use case, so students should be prepared to corroborate information with a textbook, lecture notes, or other outside sources when necessary.

Table 3. Example of an information gathering process shown using the CREATE and PARSE frameworks.

Prompt: Act as a literature professor teaching a class about artificial intelligence in literature. Explain to me as simply as possible how creation myths from human culture compare to creation stories of intelligent machines.
      Contextual cues
      Context: teaching a class about artificial intelligence in literature
      Role: literature professor
      Stylistic cues
      Example: tone - "as simply as possible"
      Audience: me (user)
      Directive cues
      Task: Explain creation myths and stories...
Assess (*Evaluate*): Does this match what I know? Am I familiar with the narratives mentioned? If not, it may be necessary to research them to verify this information.
Revise: If answer is not clear or mistakes are found
Synthesize: N/A
Edit: N/A

Brainstorming and Ideation. The start of any project is often the most intimidating. The fear of the blank page is well-known to creatives and academics alike. In this context, the AI chatbot can take on the role of collaborator, suggesting multiple ideas to help jumpstart the writing process. This use case is likely to involve multiple recursions and prompt iterations as the user seeks a satisfactory idea. Hallucination risks are not quite so dangerous here since it is easy for the user to disregard ideas that are not helpful or appropriate. Brainstorming prompts are often short and may not always use the full prompting framework, though they likely include, at the very least, contextual and directive cues (Table 4).

Table 4. Example of a brainstorming process shown using the CREATE and PARSE frameworks.

Prompt: brainstorm research projects for a college reference and instruction librarian
 	
      Contextual cues
      Context: college
      Role: reference and instruction librarian
      Stylistic cues
      Example: N/A
      Audience: academic audience (implied by context and task)
      Directive cues
      Task: brainstorm research projects
Assess (*Evaluate*): the librarian would have the necessary expertise to assess the value of ideas given
Revise: multiple prompt iterations for additional ideas, making changes for more specific outcomes as needed
Synthesize: selected ideas may be included in future academic work
Edit: N/A

Outlining and Organizing. Chatbots are extremely good at creating structured lists, a skill that can be put to good use for creating outlines, organizing thoughts, or drafting structured lesson plans. Output for this use case must be assessed carefully. AI-generated outlines are typically created with the goal of drafting public-facing content, and therefore the human author is responsible for verifying the output and carefully synthesizing it into the completed draft (Table 5).

Table 5. Example of an outlining and organizing process shown using the CREATE and PARSE frameworks

Prompt: create a lesson plan for teaching MLA style citation to college students
    Contextual cues
    Context: college (implied by audience)
    Role: college instructor (implied by task)
    Stylistic cues
    Example: lesson plan (implies format and tone)
    Audience: college students
    Directive cues
    Task: create a lesson plan
Assess (*Evaluate*): the librarian has the necessary expertise to assess the output here
Revise: subsequent prompts might request new activities or ask the chatbot to redo the lesson plan with a shorter time frame in mind
Synthesize: the librarian will use the outline to draft instructional materials, combining the AI-generated outline with additional content
Edit: edit instructional materials for clarity and accuracy

Revising. Typically, revision prompts bear the lowest risk of hallucination since the human author will be able to tell if their original meaning and intent have been preserved in the suggested revision. Contextual and stylistic cues are important aspects of any revision prompt since they help guide the chatbot's recommendations toward a desired goal (Table 6).

Table 6. Example of a revision process shown using the CREATE and PARSE frameworks

Prompt: Act as an editor. Suggest revisions for the passage below. The passage is from an academic paper written by a professor and a librarian. The tone should be formal, informative, and confident.
    Contextual cues
    Context: academic paper written by a professor and librarian
    Role: editor
    Stylistic cues
    Example: passage provided, tone directives
    Audience: Academic (implied by context)
    Directive cues
    Task: suggest revisions
Assess (*Evaluate*): The human author is the authority in this case. Does it still say what was intended?
Revise: not necessary, the author will ignore unwanted suggestions
Synthesize: Choose sentences or words to replace
Edit: Make sure revisions are integrated correctly.

Generating Text. The highest level of AI-assisted writing intervention involves having the chatbot generate the entire written text. Using AI in this fashion requires a human author to take full responsibility for content – as if they'd written it themselves. Yet, given current concerns about AI-generated content, plagiarism, and intellectual property, human authors must also be transparent about their use of AI, lest they be accused of misrepresenting their own work. Regardless of the length of the text or the context in which it will be published, generating a complete draft with AI-assisted writing requires the author to follow the entire PARSE writing framework (Table 7).

Table 7. Example of a text generation process shown using the CREATE and PARSE frameworks

Prompt: Describe plagiarism to a college audience in 250 words or less
Contextual cues
Context: college (implied by audience)
Role:
Stylistic cues
Example: word limit
Audience: college audience
Directive cues
Task: describe
Assess: The human author will need to verify that the definition is correct, either via personal expertise or lateral reading.
Revise: Additional prompting may be needed to adjust the tone or format or correct mistakes
Synthesize: Writing may be combined with human-authored content to create a final product
Edit: Final drafts must be edited for clarity and accuracy

The Librarian's Role

Resource Curation

Course development often happens in isolation, with the instructor shouldering the primary responsibility for resource curation. Often, librarians are not brought in until the semester the course is being offered, at which point most resources have already been integrated into the course. In such cases, the librarian's primary role is to support students' research efforts, with minimal support offered to the instructor. However, in this instance, the dialogue between the instructor and librarian began early, during the ideation and conceptualization of the course. This early engagement facilitated collaborative resource curation throughout the course development process. The collaboration in the discovery process yielded a wider range of resources than either researcher would have discovered independently.

As is typical with any collaboration, the integration of multiple perspectives and strategies enhances productivity.

In response to the initial discussions about the instructor's intentions for the course, the librarian sought out both literary depictions of AI and scholarly texts discussing portrayals of AI in literature. One of the first scholarly sources encountered was Dr. Stephen Cave and Dr. Kanta Dihal's (2019) literary analysis of AI narratives, *Hopes and Fears for Intelligent Machines in Fiction and Reality*. This text sparked a conversation about organizing the course around literary themes rather than chronology, which subsequently informed the remainder of the resource curation process. Guided by the dichotomies introduced by Cave & Dihal (2019), the librarian searched for and categorized literary texts based on their primary portrayal of AI: utopian or dystopian. From there, the instructor analyzed the accumulated resources and integrated them into the course modules where appropriate.

AI tool selection and support

Both the librarian and instructor were integral to discussions that aimed to formulate an institutional policy for the acceptable use of AI. These discussions also addressed safety, privacy, and intellectual property concerns that determine the feasibility of institutional adoption of AI tools. At present, Microsoft's Copilot is available to all students, faculty, and staff, while Grammarly's AI assistant is undergoing testing. Institutionally adopted tools will be recommended to faculty and students on the basis that they meet institutional standards for privacy, cybersecurity, and accessibility.

Course assignments should be optimized for as many AI tools as possible, with special attention to the capabilities and limitations of the tools most readily available to students. For example, the context window (the amount of text the chatbot can "remember") is considerably smaller in Copilot and Grammarly than in other tools such as ChatGPT or Claude. What this means is that prompts requiring a large amount of text to be summarized, edited, or used as an example are not suitable for use with tools with smaller context windows.

To ensure that all students can complete the assignment as given, the instructor must be familiar with a broad range of AI tools and design assignments with as much flexibility as possible. The rapidly evolving nature of AI tools means that keeping up to date is a significant challenge for a single faculty member. However, as information professionals with an interest in information fluency (the intersection of information literacy and technological literacy), librarians are ideally positioned to facilitate this process through continuous professional development, research, and experimentation alongside faculty and students. Likewise, librarians can support pedagogy through literature review, either by directly reading and informing faculty or by recommending literature based on the personal and research interests of faculty. These activities fostered the relationship and collaboration between the instructor and librarian involved in the development of this course and have become the foundation of a productive professional relationship.

Direct Instruction

This course will follow an embedded librarian model already implemented in the institution's first-year writing course. The librarian will provide instruction and reference services during multiple class meetings and will be embedded in the learning management system. Library instruction will focus on the information literacy skills of source evaluation and lateral reading.

The librarian and instructor will co-teach prompting, with the English instructor focusing on rhetorical aspects and the librarian providing instruction on evaluating chatbot output for hallucinations. Deliberately interweaving writing and information literacy instruction as a back-and-forth interplay of co-teaching during a single class session is designed to underscore the interdisciplinary nature of AI-assisted writing.

Prompting and writing instruction will be accomplished using a scaffolded method of gradual release. Initially, the instructor and librarian will model the process, followed by collaborative work with students, and ultimately, the students will engage in guided practice with the support of the instructor and librarian.

Conclusion: Challenges & Opportunities

Challenges

In the endeavor to infuse AI tools into literature courses, instructors and embedded librarians may confront an array of challenges, ranging from technical hurdles to ethical considerations. While AI holds promise in revolutionizing pedagogical practices, its integration into the humanities classroom demands careful navigation of various complexities.

Technical Competence. One primary challenge instructors may encounter is the need for technical competence to effectively incorporate AI tools. Many educators may remain reticent in engaging with AI tools, resulting in a lack of the requisite skills to harness the full potential of AI applications. Professional development in AI technology usage and applications will be critical in remedying this potential challenge, not just to equip instructors with the required technical competence but to help them facilitate learning for students who may have limited experience.

Access. Accessibility to sophisticated AI platforms might pose a barrier for institutions with limited resources, potentially exacerbating inequalities in educational experiences. In addition, AI tools designed with advanced features for privacy and cybersecurity protection may not be available to faculty and students at smaller institutions. Effectively harnessing the potential of AI tools in courses requires specialized expertise and training among faculty and staff. However, institutions with limited resources may face challenges in providing comprehensive professional development opportunities for educators to develop the requisite skills in AI integration. Without adequate training, educators may feel ill-equipped to leverage AI technologies effectively, hindering their ability to provide enriching learning experiences for students.

Ethical Considerations. The ethical dimension of AI implementation in literature courses cannot be overstated. As AI algorithms shape reading lists, offer literary analysis, or recommend personalized learning paths, concerns arise regarding biases embedded within these systems. Biases, whether conscious or inadvertent, could perpetuate existing inequalities or homogenize diverse perspectives in literary interpretation. Submitting literary texts to analysis by AI could raise concerns over intellectual property and copyright. Moreover, the transparency of AI algorithms and the extent to which students are made aware of their influence on their learning experience raise ethical dilemmas.

Preservation of Human Element. Literature courses inherently emphasize critical thinking, creativity, and empathetic engagement with texts – a distinctly human endeavor. The integration of AI risks diluting this human element if not framed in such a way that students are still the primary generators of literary analysis. Maintaining a balance between AI assistance and human interpretation is essential to preserve the essence of literary study.

Scalability of Librarian Involvement. Smaller institutions often have limited staffing and resources available to support librarian involvement in course development and instruction. With fewer librarians available to collaborate with instructors across multiple departments or courses, the scalability of librarian involvement becomes a significant challenge. While this could potentially be addressed by creating and curating digital resources that may be embedded in the course in lieu of a physically embedded librarian, the act of doing so may come in conflict with the preservation of human elements and the benefits students experience from direct contact with a librarian in a course.

Adaptation and Sustainability. The rapid evolution of AI technology necessitates a proactive approach to adaptation and sustainability. Even with the assistance of an embedded librarian, instructors must continually update their knowledge and skills to harness the latest advancements in AI tools relevant to literature courses. Institutions will need to invest in ongoing professional development and infrastructure to ensure the long-term viability of AI integration in the curriculum.

Long-term Impact and Sustainability. As AI technology continues to evolve, the long-term impact on AI-enhanced courses – literature-focused or not – will hinge on the ability of educators to adapt and innovate. Sustainable integration of AI requires a holistic approach that acknowledges both the potential benefits and challenges inherent in its application. Furthermore, fostering a culture of critical inquiry and ethical reflection will be instrumental in mitigating risks and maximizing the transformative potential of AI in literature education.

Opportunities

The integration of AI tools within college literature courses holds promise for enhancing learning experiences and fostering pedagogical innovation. These advancements offer various avenues for growth and improvement, shaping the trajectory of future iterations of literature curricula.

Perhaps the most obvious opportunity to emerge from discussions posed by this chapter is the advancement of enhanced textual analysis through interdisciplinary connection. The incorporation of AI tools within an AI literature course promises to illuminate the practical relevance of literary study to students' real-world experiences. Frequently, students express skepticism regarding the utility of studying literature, questioning the significance of concepts like symbolism and theme, particularly when they perceive limited relevance to their intended career paths. However, through the interdisciplinary exploration of AI literature and the integration of AI tools, coupled with discussions encompassing ethics, philosophy, and computer science, students are afforded a unique opportunity to grasp the immediate applicability of their learning. By contextualizing literature within the emerging "Age of AI" (Gates, 2023) and elucidating the tangible impact of AI technologies, students are encouraged to develop a deeper appreciation and comprehension of literature, transcending traditional barriers that often impede engagement and understanding.

There is also opportunity in the first-time application of an old-but-new field: AI ethics. While the study of AI ethics has existed since at least the 1980s (Borenstein et al., 2021), literary authors dating into the 1920s were concerned with creation and control over intelligent machines (an observation this proposed course seeks to point out to scholars). However, though the study of AI ethics has existed in theory, that past study was the precipice and we have now collectively stepped off the edge and down the rabbit hole with the advent of and public access to AI. What was perpetuated in theory and literature is now a reality with which we must contend. Artificial intelligence, intelligent machines, the robot-filled future of the Jetsons has arrived, and we are situated in a moment akin to the opening of westward expansion in the United States: a moment of lawlessness and uncertainty, but equally a moment of opportunity to address such uncertainty and lack of regulation. As the first generation of practitioners, educators, industry leaders, and end-users, we possess the unique opportunity to be the ones who determine what AI ethics will look like in practice. In the spirit of acknowledging the hopes and fears of intelligent machines laid out in the proposed AI literature course outlined in this chapter, let us all pray we make the right decisions when defining what AI ethics represents. Of course, let us all work hard to educate ourselves, too, so that our decisions are best informed.

When prompted to conclude this chapter, the ChatGPT-generated text offered this: "By embracing these opportunities, we can foster a generation of learners who are not only adept in literary analysis but also equipped to navigate the complexities of the AI-driven world with wisdom and foresight" (OpenAI, 2024). Of course, the authors of this chapter completely agree with our AI collaborator, and we hope you do as well.

REFERENCES

Association of College and Research Libraries. (2016). *Framework for information literacy for higher education.* https://www.ala.org/acrl/standards/ilframework

Borenstein, J., Grodzinsky, F. S., Howard, A., Miller, K. W., & Wolf, M. J. (2021). AI ethics: A long history and a recent burst of attention. *Computer,* 53(1), 96–102. https://doi.ieeecomputersociety.org/10.1109/MC.2020.3034950. DOI: 10.1109/MC.2020.3034950

Buchanan, J., Hill, S., & Shapoval, O. (2024). ChatGPT hallucinates non-existent citations: Evidence from economics. *The American Economist,* 69(1), 80–87. DOI: 10.1177/05694345231218454

Caines, A. (n.d.). *Close reading the terms of service.* AI Pedagogy Project: metaLAB (at) Harvard. https://aipedagogy.org/assignment/close-reading-the-tos/

Cave, S., Craig, C., Dihal, K., Dillon, S., Montgomery, J., Singler, B., & Taylor, L. (2018). *Portrayals and perceptions of AI and why they matter.* Royal Society https://royalsociety.org/-/media/policy/projects/ai-narratives/AI-narratives-workshop-findings.pdf

Cave, S., & Dihal, K. (2019). *Hopes and fears for intelligent machines in fiction and reality.* University of Cambridge Repository. https://www.repository.cam.ac.uk/bitstream/handle/1810/288940/ACCEPTED%20VERSION%20-%20Cave%20and%20Dihal%20-%20Hopes%20and%20Fears%20v3.docx?sequence=1

Christian, B. (2020). *The alignment problem: Machine learning and human values.* W. W. Norton & Company.

College Board. (2004). *Sample activity: Analyzing the narrative from the Pre-AP workshop Pre-AP: Strategies in English – writing tactics using SOAPSTone.* College Entrance Examination Board. https://secure-media.collegeboard.org/apc/ap04_preap_11_eng_soa_35968.pdf

Cummings, L. (2024). *How to use rhetoric to repurpose content with ChatGPT.* iSophist. https://www.isophist.com/p/how-to-use-rhetoric-to-repurpose?r=2519k4&utm_campaign=post&utm_medium=web

Fozrok. (2023, August 8). *The art of ChatGPT prompts with CISCO structure.* Reddit. https://www.reddit.com/r/ChatGPTPromptGenius/comments/15lenfo/the_art_of_chatgpt_prompts_with_cisco_structure/

Gates, B. (2023, March 21). *The age of AI has begun.* GatesNotes. https://www
.gatesnotes.com/The-Age-of-AI-Has-Begun

Graham, S. S. (2023). *Post-process but not post-writing: Large Language Models
and a future for composition pedagogy* (EJ1390327). ERIC. https://files.eric.ed
.gov/fulltext/EJ1390327.pdf

Grammarly. (2024). *2024 State of business communication.*https://go.grammarly
.com/2024-state-of-business-communication-report

Mollick, E. (2023, June 18). *Detecting the secret cyborgs: The AI trap for organizations.* One Useful Thing. https://www.oneusefulthing.org/p/detecting-the-secret
-cyborgs

Nam, J. (2023, November 22). *56% of college students have used AI on assignments
or exams.* Best Colleges. https://www.bestcolleges.com/research/most-college
-students-have-used-ai-survey/

Newbold, C. (2021, January 28). SPACECAT method of rhetorical analysis: Description and worksheet. *The Visual Communcation Guy.*https://thevisualcommun
icationguy.com/2021/01/28/spacecat-method-of-rhetorical-analysis-description
-and-worksheet/

Open, A. I. (2024). *ChatGPT* (3.5 Version) [Large language model]. https://chat
.openai.com/share/977a06ca-7cb8-46b9-91e7-afe6b405152e

Welding, L. (2023, March 17). *Half of college students say using AI on schoolwork
is cheating or plagiarism.* Best Colleges. https://www.bestcolleges.com/research/
college-students-ai-tools-survey/

Wineburg, S., & McGrew, S. (2019). Lateral reading and the nature of expertise:
Reading less and learning more when evaluating digital information. *Teachers
College Record*, 121(11), 1–40. DOI: 10.1177/016146811912101102

Yang, C. [@CoraEdTech] (2024, March 4). *Excited to share the updated AI prompt
craft guide for educators* [image attached] [Tweet]. Twitter. https://twitter.com/
CoraEdTech/status/1763842120635609368

APPENDIX I

Course Readings

Antiquity

"Pandora," *Works and Days* by Hesiod
Genesis 2:4-2:25
Argonautica by Apollonius Rhodius

19th Century Literature

"The Sandman" by E.T.A. Hoffman

20th Century Literature

Selections from *I, Robot* by Isaac Asimov
"There Will Come Soft Rains" by Ray Bradbury
"The Veldt" by Ray Bradbury
"The Nine-Billion Names of God" by Arthur C. Clarke
"I Have No Mouth and I Must Scream" by Harlan Ellison

Contemporary Literature

Terminator (1984)
"The Gentle Seduction" by Marc Stiegler
WALL-E (2008)
"The Truth of Fact, the Truth of Feeling" by Ted Chiang

Chapter 10
Innovation and Skills Needed for Sustainable Knowledge Systems in the Fifth (5th) Industrial Revolution:
Implications for Libraries and the Users

Ganiyu Ojo Adigun
Ladoke Akintola University of Technology, Nigeria

Gboyega Adio
Ladoke Akintola University of Technology, Nigeria

Oluwole O. Durodolu
https://orcid.org/0000-0003-2734-8165
University of South Africa, South Africa

ABSTRACT

In the dynamic currents of the Fifth Industrial Revolution (5IR), we witness a profound transformation shaping knowledge systems and redefining the roles of both librarians and users. This epoch marks a significant departure propelled by cutting-edge technologies such as AI, IoT, and biotechnology. Fundamental principles guiding this revolution encompass sustainability, interdisciplinary expertise, ethical considerations, and adaptability. In this evolving landscape, libraries have evolved into vibrant centers offering digital resources, expert data management,

DOI: 10.4018/979-8-3693-3053-1.ch010

and tailored services. Consequently, librarians and users alike must acquire crucial skills like digital literacy, data literacy, and information curation. Embracing AI, understanding cybersecurity, and adapting to evolving responsibilities are imperative for both stakeholders. The 5IR heralds an era of democratized access to knowledge, breaking down geographical barriers and positioning libraries as pivotal hubs for data management.

INTRODUCTION AND BACKGROUND TO THE STUDY

The conception of industrial revolutions, starting from the transformation and innovation that gave birth to the First Industrial Revolution to the present digitalization of the Fourth Industrial Revolution (4IR), has reformed societies, culture, mindset, economies, and most importantly the techniques in which information is accessed and utilized. Developing on the digital improvements of its predecessors, the 5IR is pigeonholed by the combination of technologies such as artificial intelligence, robotics, nanotechnology, and biotechnology, thereby obscuring the lines between the physical, digital, and biological spheres (World Economic Forum, 2020).

In view of this, the responsibility of libraries as sources of knowledge is confronting extraordinary challenges. Traditional methods of information dissemination are being unsettled by the advent of digital platforms and evolving technologies, which requires libraries to remodel their functionalities. Additionally, the skills require to efficiently take advantage and exploit information are experiencing a paradigm shift. Hence, users must cultivate digital literacy skills, critical thinking, problem-solving abilities, and flexibility to flourish in the 5IR landscape (Association of College & Research Libraries, 2018).

Amid the tumultuous tides of the Fifth Industrial Revolution (5IR), the landscape of knowledge systems, information management, and the roles of librarians and information users is undergoing a seismic transformation (Ajani *et al.,* 2022). This epochal shift underscores the pivotal significance of innovation and the acquisition of new skills in the context of knowledge systems. Traditionally seen as quiet sanctuaries of knowledge, libraries are undergoing a remarkable transformation in the 5IR. Tella *et al.,* (2023) pointed out that libraries are now becoming dynamic hubs actively curating, organizing, and disseminating knowledge. This shift is driven by the evolving needs of users, who increasingly demand innovative technologies and new avenues for learning and research. These changes empower libraries to provide users with the necessary tools and resources to navigate the complexities of this era. As we teeter on the brink of this monumental transformation, a profound and far-reaching research inquiry emerges: *"How can the fusion of innovation and skills be strategically harnessed to not only sustain but fortify knowledge systems within the maelstrom of the 5IR, and what profound implications does this bear for the custodians of knowledge, the librarians, and the avid seekers of information?"*

This overarching research question encapsulates the core challenges and extraordinary prospects that the 5IR unfurls. It beckons us to embark on an exhaustive exploration of the intricate interplay between innovation, skill acquisition, and the enduring sustenance of knowledge systems in the face of a tumultuous and ever-evolving landscape. As Innovation stands as a linchpin for the sustainability of knowledge systems within libraries during the 5IR. Awoyemi (2023) assert that innovation encompasses a wide range of activities, from digitizing collections and offering remote access to embracing cutting-edge technologies such as data analytics and machine learning to enhance information retrieval. Libraries that foster innovation function as hubs for knowledge creation, making significant contributions to societal progress by facilitating access to the latest information and tools for problem-solving. However, as libraries evolve, users must acquire a fresh set of skills to effectively utilize the resources and opportunities at hand. Sharma *et al.,* (2023) emphasizes that information literacy, critical thinking, and digital proficiency are foundational skills necessary to navigate the vast sea of available information.

Furthermore, in a time marked by rapid technological advancement, adaptability, and the ability to learn continuously are crucial skills (Karneli, 2023). These skills empower users to harness the potential of the 5IR, allowing them to remain agile and competent in an ever-evolving landscape. Furthermore, it compels us to venture into the transformative domains of the librarians, whose roles and responsibilities are being profoundly reshaped, as well as the information users, whose expectations and needs are evolving in unprecedented ways. The pursuit of answers to this grand question takes us through a multidimensional terrain. It demands a comprehensive analysis of the imperatives of innovation, the dynamic skill sets essential for flourishing in this mercurial environment, and the cascading ramifications for the guardians of knowledge librarians and the beneficiaries of their information users. Moreover, it obliges us to confront the imminent and formidable challenges that loom on the horizon. These encompass the preservation and accessibility of knowledge, the ability to remain relevant in the face of the relentless march of technological progress, and the imperative of delivering sustainable knowledge systems for future generations.

This research attempt stands as an illuminating beacon, expertly guiding us through the intricate nexus of innovation and skills within the tumultuous 5IR. The insights unearthed possess the potential to revolutionize the foundations of our knowledge ecosystem, fostering resilience, and adaptability in harmony with the relentless spirit of innovation, all while serving the evolving needs of our information-driven society with unwavering precision and finesse. However, this study adopted an interpretive content/document analysis methodology to conduct a thorough review and analysis of literature gathered from diverse databases, including Scopus and Web of Science.

This methodological selection was made to ensure a comprehensive and well-rounded examination of the subject matter, incorporating a wide range of perspectives and insights. The interpretive content/document analysis process involves a meticulous examination and interpretation of textual materials, allowing for a nuanced understanding of the topic under investigation. The inclusion of literature from reputable databases like Scopus and Web of Science enhances the credibility and reliability of the findings. Moreover, this methodology facilitates a holistic exploration of the subject, encompassing a wide range of research papers, articles, and publications.

As libraries traverse this new territory, knowing the consequences of this advancement and skill set required for sustainable knowledge systems is vital. This study seeks to discover the changing responsibility of libraries in the 5IR, ascertaining the innovation and skills necessary to sustain knowledge systems. By scrutinizing the intersection of technology, education, and information access, therefore, this research aims to provide intellectual binocular into how libraries can acclimatize and prosper in the epoch of the Fifth Industrial Revolution, guaranteeing equitable access to information and nurturing lifelong learning for all.

Defining the 5th Industrial Revolution

The 5IR represents the contemporary and forthcoming epoch of industrial and technological transformation, building upon the legacy of its four predecessors. This era marks a monumental shift characterized by the convergence of cutting-edge technologies, including artificial intelligence, the Internet of Things, blockchain, biotechnology, and advanced robotics, among others (Alojaiman, 2023). This convergence ushers in a transformative era in human progress, fundamentally reshaping the very fabric of our existence. At its core, the 5IR heralds a profound societal and technological transition. It introduces a fundamental shift underpinned by the extensive proliferation of automation, interconnectedness, and data-driven decision-making, which permeates every facet of our lives (Callaghan, 2023). Within the backdrop of 5IR, there is a pressing demand for the cultivation of a new set of skills, integral to navigating this transformative landscape. The ability to adapt to rapidly changing technologies and environments becomes paramount. One of the defining characteristics of 5IR is its unwavering commitment to sustainability, environmental responsibility, and ethical considerations.

Diverging from its predecessors, this revolution is not solely about technological advancement; it is about harnessing these technologies to address pressing global challenges (Noble *et al.*, 2022). These challenges span from addressing climate change and healthcare disparities to mitigating resource scarcity and fostering social equity. Furthermore, 5IR is characterized by the convergence of the physical, digital, and biological realms. This fusion transcends traditional boundaries, unlocking new possibilities limited only by the bounds of human imagination (Schwab, 2020). In this context, the development of interdisciplinary skills and the capacity to bridge knowledge gaps between different fields become imperative, as this fusion of knowledge is the driving force behind innovation. The evolution of 5IR is intrinsically linked to questions of governance, ethics, and the equitable distribution of its benefits. This revolution challenges societies to rethink and adapt existing systems and structures to ensure that the benefits are inclusive and accessible (Porter & Heppelmann, 2015). Additionally, it underscores the importance of preparing a workforce with the skills and adaptability necessary to thrive in this evolving landscape. Skills such as adaptability, digital literacy, and a deep understanding of ethical considerations in technology become invaluable in this context.

The Intersection of Innovation and Skills in the 5IR

In the dynamic landscape of the Fifth Industrial Revolution (5IR), the intricate interplay between innovation and skills emerges as a central narrative, guiding our understanding of this transformative era. Within the heart of 5IR, innovation serves as the catalytic force propelling progress and change in unprecedented ways (Ross & Maynard, 2021). It encompasses the creation of groundbreaking technologies, the redefinition of traditional business models, and visionary solutions that address pressing global challenges. Consequently, the skills required to foster creativity, innovative problem-solving, and adaptability emerge as indispensable elements in this narrative. What sets 5IR apart is the perpetual evolution of skills in response to the ever-shifting technological landscape (Petrakis, 2022). The static concept of a fixed skill set is replaced by a dynamic continuum. In this context, individuals must continuously update and acquire new skills to remain relevant in a rapidly changing environment.

Within the multidisciplinary realm of 5IR, innovation frequently finds its roots at the crossroads of diverse fields and technologies, emphasizing the need for skills that facilitate interdisciplinary collaboration and the cross-fertilization of ideas (Claus & Wiese, 2019). Those possessing the ability to bridge knowledge gaps and navigate these intersections become the driving forces behind innovation. Technological literacy, another fundamental aspect, is indispensable due to the proliferation of advanced technologies. Proficiency in understanding and utilizing technologies such as artificial intelligence, the Internet of Things, and blockchain is no longer a luxury but an imperative requirement (Choithani *et al.*, 2022). The tremendous technological power in 5IR necessitates ethical guidance, placing skills related to ethical decision-making and understanding the societal implications of innovation at the forefront. Innovators must adeptly navigate complex ethical dilemmas and ensure that their creations ultimately serve the betterment of society (McIntosh *et al.*, 2021).

In 5IR, adaptability is not merely a skill but a fundamental mindset. The capacity to embrace change and engage in lifelong learning forms the bedrock of success. Individuals capable of swiftly acquiring new skills and discarding obsolete ones are those who thrive amidst the ceaseless pace of change (Choithani *et al.*, 2022). Entrepreneurial acumen also plays a pivotal role in this narrative. The ability to identify opportunities, take calculated risks, and transform innovative concepts into tangible reality becomes essential in a landscape where innovation often leads to the creation of entirely new markets (Petrakis, 2022). Collaborative competence, the capacity to work effectively with others, is equally vital. Many of the transformative innovations in 5IR are the outcomes of collaborative endeavors. Proficiencies such as effective communication, teamwork, and the ability to work across geographical and cultural boundaries serve as the foundations of groundbreaking innovation (McIntosh *et al.*, 2021). Thus, as innovation propels us into uncharted territories, the ability to develop, adapt, and leverage a diverse skill set becomes the compass guiding us through the complexities of this revolutionary age.

Innovation in Knowledge Systems

Innovation within knowledge systems stands as a paramount endeavor, especially in the dynamic landscape of the Fifth Industrial Revolution (5IR). As we navigate this transformative era, innovation takes the central stage in shaping the future of knowledge management and dissemination, with an expanding focus on the metaverse. This innovative landscape encompasses the following key facets:

Digital Transformation: The adoption of advanced digital technologies, including big data analytics, plays a pivotal role in elevating knowledge acquisition, organization, and retrieval (AbdRazak *et al.*, 2021). This digital transformation empowers more efficient knowledge management, especially in virtual and augmented reality environments.

Collaborative Metaverse Platforms: Innovation fuels the development of collaborative knowledge-sharing platforms within the metaverse. These platforms encourage users to contribute, share, and collaborate on knowledge within immersive virtual spaces, fostering a dynamic and evolving knowledge ecosystem (De Felice *et al.*, 2023).

Personalized Metaverse Experiences: Leveraging innovations in machine learning and data analytics, knowledge delivery within the metaverse becomes highly personalized. Users receive tailored content, recommendations, and experiences, enhancing their learning and information-seeking journeys (Lee *et al.*, 2023)

Metaverse Data Integration: Innovations in data integration technologies extend into the metaverse, unifying diverse knowledge sources across the virtual realm. This integration allows for a more holistic and comprehensive view of information, breaking down the boundaries between the physical and digital worlds (Lee *et al.*, 2023)

Augmented Reality (AR) and Virtual Reality (VR): AR and VR technologies continue to redefine how knowledge is experienced within the metaverse. These immersive technologies create interactive learning environments, enabling users to engage with knowledge in three-dimensional spaces, blurring the lines between the real and virtual worlds (Dwivedi *et al.*, 2022).

Blockchain for Trust and Traceability: The metaverse benefits from blockchain technology, offering transparent and immutable records of knowledge transactions. This technology plays a pivotal role in ensuring trust and traceability, particularly in virtual economies and academic research environments (Gadekallu *et al.*, 2022)

Open Access and Crowdsourcing in the Metaverse: Innovations in open access models and crowdsourcing strategies extend into the metaverse, democratizing knowledge creation and dissemination. This approach fosters inclusivity and leverages collective intelligence within virtual realms (Bousba & Arya, 2022).

Ethical AI and Bias Mitigation: Innovations focus on the development of ethical AI systems that mitigate bias in knowledge representation and recommendation within the metaverse. These advancements ensure fairness and accuracy in information delivery, promoting ethical practices within virtual environments (Varona & Suárez, 2022).

Metaverse Knowledge Graphs: Knowledge graph technology is extended into the metaverse, connecting concepts and entities within virtual spaces. This innovation allows for more effective semantic search and exploration of knowledge, creating richer connections between pieces of information in the virtual world (Ali *et al.*, 2022)

Quantum Computing in the Metaverse: While in its nascent stages, quantum computing holds the potential to revolutionize knowledge systems within the metaverse. Its immense processing power can solve complex problems and process vast datasets at unprecedented speeds, significantly impacting virtual environments (Kwon *et a.*, 2022).

In essence, innovation within knowledge systems is not only essential for adapting to the demands of 5IR but also for thriving within the immersive metaverse. It empowers knowledge organizations, such as libraries and information providers, to revolutionize their approaches, ensuring the accessibility, relevance, and efficiency of knowledge within these dynamic virtual realms. As innovation continues to drive progress, knowledge systems are well-positioned to evolve and thrive in the metaverse, a frontier of limitless possibilities.

Innovation and Skills Needed by Librarians and Users in the 5IR

In the dynamic landscape of the 5IR, both librarians and information users find themselves at a crucial juncture where innovation and skills have assumed paramount significance. This era of profound change demands a set of competencies and proficiencies to navigate the evolving knowledge systems effectively. Here, we delve into the key areas that underscore the necessity for innovation and skills in the 5IR for librarians and users.

Digital Literacy: Literacy in navigating digital platforms, databases, and electronic resources is now an essential skill. Librarians must effectively manage digital cataloguing and online research tools, while users should be adept at accessing these resources (Baro *et al.*, 2019).

Data Literacy: The proliferation of data in the 5IR requires the acquisition of data literacy skills. This includes the ability to collect, analyze, and interpret data, facilitating data-informed decision-making and understanding complex information (Oseghale, 2023).

Information Curation: In the digital age, librarians play a pivotal role in curating relevant, high-quality digital content. The ability to evaluate, organize, and maintain digital collections is critical. Users, too, should curate their information sources, filtering out irrelevant information (Khan, *et al.,* 2023).

AI and Automation: As AI technologies advance, librarians need to understand how to integrate AI tools into library services. This encompasses using chatbots for user support, implementing AI-driven recommendation systems, and automating cataloguing processes. Users should be familiar with AI-based search and recommendation features (Affum & Dwomoh, 2023).

Cybersecurity: Given the increasing digital presence of libraries and online research, a strong grasp of cybersecurity is imperative. Librarians should safeguard library data and user privacy, and users must be aware of online security best practices (Cornelius *et al.*, 2023).

Critical Thinking: The deluge of information necessitates robust critical thinking skills. Both librarians and users must be able to evaluate sources, recognize bias, and make well-informed decisions. Critical thinking is foundational to information literacy (Goodsett & Schmillen, 2022).

Interdisciplinary Collaboration: 5IR often involves interdisciplinary approaches. Librarians should collaborate with researchers and professionals across diverse fields to support cross-disciplinary projects. Users should embrace interdisciplinary learning, recognizing the value of integrating knowledge from various domains (Ajakaye, 2021).

Innovation Mindset: Encouraging an innovation mindset is essential. Librarians can foster innovation by exploring new technologies and service models. Users, too, should be open to novel methods of accessing and utilizing information (Calkins, 2019).

Continual Learning: The fast pace of 5IR necessitates a commitment to lifelong learning. Librarians should stay updated on emerging technologies, information trends, and research methods. Users, too, should embrace continuous learning to adapt to evolving information landscapes (Oseji, 2020).

Global Awareness: An understanding of global trends, geopolitics, and international dynamics is increasingly relevant. Librarians should provide global perspectives, and users should recognize the impact of international issues on information and knowledge, fostering a more comprehensive worldview (Myers & Rivero, 2020).

Ethical Information Use: Adhering to ethical standards in information use is paramount. Both librarians and users should practice proper citation, comply with copyright regulations, and responsibly handle data. Ethical considerations are vital in the digital age (Wharton, 2018).

Community Engagement: Librarians should actively engage with their communities, comprehending local information needs, and tailoring services accordingly. Users can benefit from participating in library programs, workshops, and community initiatives, creating a collaborative and enriching environment Okafor, 2020).

In essence, the 5IR underscores the critical role of innovation and skills for librarians and users. Librarians must adapt to their evolving role as digital curators and data experts, while users need to equip themselves with essential digital literacy, critical thinking, and lifelong learning skills. Both parties should embrace the changing information landscape and adapt to the challenges and opportunities presented by 5IR to foster sustainable and vibrant knowledge systems.

Impacts of 5IR on Libraries and the Users

The 5IR has instigated a profound transformation in libraries, redefining their role in the digital age and reshaping user expectations. This evolution is marked by a confluence of technological advancements and shifting user demands, prompting a reimagining of the library's mission and services. The profound effects brought about by 5IR have paved the way for a digital revolution in libraries in the advanced world, with an emphasis on accessibility, data management, and personalized services. Libraries, traditionally known for their physical book collections, have undergone a significant digital transformation. They now function as digital resource hubs, offering extensive e-book collections, e-journals, and online databases, granting users unprecedented access to knowledge (Ciarli *et al.*, 2021). This transition is a response to the increasing digitization of information, making it more widely accessible to a diverse audience, encompassing students, researchers, and the general public. The central impact of 5IR on libraries lies in the expanded accessibility of information.

The proliferation of online databases and digital collections has allowed users to access information from anywhere, effectively eradicating geographical barriers to knowledge acquisition. This democratization of information access is invaluable in the digital era, facilitating research, learning, and innovation (Suherlan, 2023). In response to the changing data landscape in 5IR, libraries in the advanced world are emerging as critical players in data management. They are now central hubs for data storage, analysis, and visualization. This adaptation is a direct response to the growing importance of big data and analytics, with libraries in the advanced world providing services to help researchers and businesses manage and make sense of extensive datasets (Signé, 2023). This expansion of roles positions libraries in the advanced world as indispensable players in the data-driven economy. Furthermore, libraries in the advanced world are embracing AI and machine learning to offer personalized services. Users receive tailored book recommendations, and libraries in the advanced world can customize their resources and services according to individual preferences. This personalization enhances the user experience, making information retrieval more efficient and engaging (Okunlaya *et al.*, 2022).

Libraries in the advanced world have also evolved into collaborative spaces, reflecting the changing nature of work in 5IR. With dedicated areas for group work, discussions, and problem-solving, libraries in the advanced world support the collaborative endeavors that define modern workplaces (Suherlan, 2023). These spaces foster innovation and teamwork. Simultaneously, libraries in the advanced world play a pivotal role in skill development by offering programs and resources for digital literacy. These initiatives empower users to thrive in the digital age by equipping them with the skills needed to navigate and harness emerging technologies (World Economic Forum, 2020). However, the transition to a digitally-driven library ecosystem is not without its challenges. Libraries in the advanced world must address concerns related to user privacy and data security, particularly as they handle vast amounts of data in a world of increasing interconnectivity (Waite, 2022). Striking a balance between open access to information and safeguarding user data becomes a critical task. Incorporating virtual reality and augmented reality, libraries in the advanced world offer immersive educational experiences, enabling users to explore historical sites, conduct virtual experiments, and access content in novel ways (Suherlan, 2023).

This engagement with emerging technologies aligns with the spirit of innovation characterizing 5IR. Furthermore, libraries in the advanced world are at the forefront of advocating for open access to information. They provide platforms for publishing research and educational materials freely, contributing to the global dissemination of knowledge (Waite, 2022). In a world driven by technological advancements and ethical considerations, libraries in the advanced world also play a significant role in educating users about the societal and ethical implications of emerging technologies such as AI, robotics, and biotechnology. They become spaces for critical reflection and ethical discourse (Waite, 2022). Additionally, libraries in the advanced world act as catalysts for global accessibility to information, promoting education and research on a worldwide scale. This is particularly valuable for regions with limited resources, as libraries in the advanced world bridge the gap by providing access to a wealth of information and knowledge (Yin *et al.*, 2018). Thus, the impact of 5IR on libraries in the advanced world and their users are extensive and multifaceted. Libraries in the advanced world have transformed into dynamic, tech-savvy institutions, adapting to the digital age by providing enhanced accessibility, personalized services, data management, and collaborative spaces. While these changes present opportunities for innovation and learning, they also entail challenges related to privacy, data security, and ethical considerations.

The Challenges Ahead of Libraries and Users toward Sustainable Knowledge Systems in the 5IR

Libraries and users encounter a multitude of complex challenges within the landscape of the Fifth Industrial Revolution (5IR). Addressing these challenges necessitates a well-considered strategy to uphold the sustainability of knowledge systems. During this transformative era, several significant challenges emerged for both libraries and their clientele:

Transition to Digital Libraries: Moving from traditional to digital libraries involves the transformation of library infrastructure and services. This includes digitizing collections, adopting digital cataloguing systems, and ensuring access to electronic resources while preserving physical materials (Singh, 2020).

Information Overload: In the digital age, users are inundated with vast amounts of data. To address this, libraries must implement effective search and content recommendation systems, as well as provide information literacy programs to help users find reliable and relevant sources (Mahdi *et al.,* 2020.

User Privacy and Data Security: Safeguarding user data is a complex challenge. This entails implementing strong cybersecurity measures, complying with data protection regulations, and ensuring that user data remains confidential while delivering personalized services (Habibzadeh *et al.*, 2023)

Evolving Librarian Roles: Librarians must adapt to new roles, including data management, digital preservation, and technology training. They need to acquire expertise in these areas to meet the evolving needs of users and effectively manage digital resources (Hickerson *et al.,* 2022).

Access to Digital Resources: Ensuring equal access to digital resources is a priority. Libraries must address the digital divide by offering training programs for users with varying digital literacy levels and providing accessible content, software, and hardware.

Digital Content Curation: Managing digital collections involves the selection, evaluation, organization, and preservation of digital resources to maintain their relevance and reliability. This also includes addressing content quality and metadata management (Khan, *et al.,* 2023).

Copyright and Intellectual Property: Navigating copyright and intellectual property regulations in the digital age is a challenge. Libraries must provide access to digital content while complying with copyright laws and developing policies that balance user access rights with legal and ethical considerations (Shrayberg & Volkova, 2021.

Ethical Technology Use: Libraries and users must consider the ethical implications of emerging technologies like AI and machine learning. This challenge involves developing guidelines for responsible and ethical technology use, addressing issues such as bias, privacy, and transparency (Nguyen *et al.,* 2023).

Lifelong Learning: Encouraging users to embrace lifelong learning and digital literacy is an ongoing challenge. Libraries must offer educational programs and resources to cater to diverse needs, including digital literacy courses, technology workshops, and skill development resources (Vodă *et al.,* 2022) .

Resource Management: Managing resources for digital acquisitions, technology upgrades, and staff training is a complex task. Efficient resource allocation requires strategic planning and decision-making to meet the demands of the digital era (Bansal *et al.,* 2023).

Community Engagement: Engaging with the community and understanding their evolving information needs is crucial. Libraries must actively involve the community in programs and decision-making processes to remain responsive to changing demands and preferences (Maspul & Almalki, 2023).

Interinstitutional Collaboration: Enhancing services through collaboration with other institutions is beneficial. This challenge involves building partnerships, sharing resources, and expanding services to create a more comprehensive and accessible information ecosystem (Mahardhani, 2023).

Addressing these challenges is essential for libraries and users to ensure that knowledge systems remain vibrant, relevant, and sustainable in the ever-evolving landscape of 5IR. It requires proactive measures, adaptability, and a commitment to creating a future that balances technological advancement with ethical, social, and environmental responsibility.

CONCLUSION

In conclusion, the onset of the Fifth Industrial Revolution (5IR) has inaugurated an era of profound transformation in the realm of knowledge systems, information management, and the roles of librarians and information users. As we navigate this tumultuous landscape, the fusion of innovation and the acquisition of new skills emerge as the cornerstone for sustaining and strengthening knowledge systems within this dynamic milieu. This intricate interplay carries profound implications for the custodians of knowledge, the librarians, and the avid seekers of information. In this epoch of relentless change, libraries have undergone a digital metamorphosis, evolving from traditional repositories of physical books into dynamic hubs of digital resources. Libraries have become central players in data management, knowledge curation, and the dissemination of digital content. They have harnessed the power of emerging technologies to offer personalized services, fostering a more engaging and efficient user experience. Concurrently, libraries have embraced an essential role in education and the exploration of ethical considerations, thus contributing to the ethical discourse of society.

To navigate this dynamic environment, librarians and information users require a comprehensive set of skills. These include digital literacy, data literacy, and the ability to critically evaluate sources in an era of information overload. Ethical considerations, interdisciplinary collaboration, and an innovation mindset are equally vital in this transformative landscape. Continuous learning and global awareness are prerequisites for understanding and adapting to a rapidly changing world. Nonetheless, substantial challenges lie ahead. The transition to digital libraries, the preservation of privacy and data security, and managing an evolving librarian's role are all formidable tasks. Striking a balance between open access to information and the ethical use of technology is a challenge. Moreover, resource management, community engagement, and inter-institutional collaboration require meticulous planning and execution. Sustainability and environmental responsibility have become paramount concerns, as libraries strive to minimize their ecological footprint while fulfilling their educational and information dissemination missions.

In this era of monumental change, libraries and users must work in tandem to confront these challenges, adapt to the evolving landscape, and shape the future of knowledge systems. Through the seamless integration of innovation and skill acquisition, librarians and users alike can embark on a transformative journey to ensure the sustainability, relevance, and vibrancy of knowledge systems in the ever-evolving landscape of the Fifth Industrial Revolution. This endeavour is a testament to the enduring spirit of human progress, innovation, and adaptability, which will serve as the guiding light through the complexities and opportunities that 5IR unfolds.

Implications for Librarians and Information Users

In the context of the Fifth Industrial Revolution (5IR), libraries are faced with the task of transitioning from their traditional roles to becoming digital hubs. This transformation involves the digitization of their collections, the adoption of digital cataloguing systems, and ensuring access to electronic resources while still preserving physical materials. For users, this implies adapting to digital platforms as the primary means of accessing knowledge and information.

The digital age has inundated users with an overwhelming amount of data. To address this, libraries must implement effective search and content recommendation systems, and they should offer information literacy programs to help users navigate and make sense of this information deluge. Users, in turn, must develop the skills to discern reliable and relevant sources from this sea of data.

Safeguarding user data has become increasingly complex. Libraries need to invest in robust cybersecurity measures, ensure compliance with data protection regulations, and maintain the confidentiality of user data while providing personalized services. Users should also be vigilant about their online privacy and data security.

Librarians must embrace new roles in this digital era, including data management, digital preservation, and technology training. Acquiring expertise in these areas is essential to meet the evolving needs of users and effectively manage digital resources. Users should recognize the changing role of librarians and leverage their expertise for their benefit.

Equal access to digital resources is a priority. Libraries must address the digital divide by offering training programs for users with varying levels of digital literacy and providing accessible content, software, and hardware. Users should be proactive in improving their digital literacy to fully benefit from these resources.

Acknowledgement:

The lead author would like to acknowledge the Tertiary Education Trust Fund (TETFund) of Nigeria, for funding my Postdoctoral Fellowship with Department of Information Science, College of Human Sciences, University of South Africa (UNISA), South Africa.

REFERENCES

Abd Razak, S. N. A., Noor, W. N. B. W. M., & Jusoh, Y. H. M. (2021). Embracing digital economy: Drivers, barriers and factors affecting digital transformation of accounting professionals. *International Journal of Advanced Research in Economics and Finance*, 3(3), 63–71.

Affum, M. Q., & Dwomoh, O. K. (2023). Investigating the Potential Impact of Artificial Intelligence in Librarianship. *Library Philosophy and Practice*, 1-12.

Ajakaye, J. E., & Ogunniyi, S. O. (2021). 21st-Century multidisciplinary collaboration in research in library. *Library Philosophy and Practice (e-journal)*. 6228. https://digitalcommons.unl.edu/libphilprac/6228

Ajani, Y. A., Adeyinka, T., Dunmade, A. O., & Adeniran, C. O. (2022). Information Professionals of the Future and their Prospects in the Era of Fourth Industrial Revolution: The Need for Transformative Potential in Nigeria. *Mousaion*, 40(3). Advance online publication. DOI: 10.25159/2663-659X/12219

Ali, M., Naeem, F., Kaddoum, G., & Hossain, E. (2022). Metaverse Communications, Networking, Security, and Applications: Research Issues, State-of-the-Art, and Future Directions. *arXiv preprint arXiv:2212.13993*.

Alojaiman, B. (2023). Technological Modernizations in the Industry 5.0 Era: A Descriptive Analysis and Future Research Directions. *Processes (Basel, Switzerland)*, 11(5), 1318. DOI: 10.3390/pr11051318

Association of College & Research Libraries. (2018). *Framework for Information Literacy for Higher Education*. American Library Association.

Awoyemi, R. R. (2023). Library Engagement With Emerging Technologies in Research and Learning. *Handbook of Research on Facilitating Collaborative Learning Through Digital Content and Learning Technologies*, 400-418.

Bansal, A., Panchal, T., Jabeen, F., Mangla, S. K., & Singh, G. (2023). A study of human resource digital transformation (HRDT): A phenomenon of innovation capability led by digital and individual factors. *Journal of Business Research*, 157, 113611. DOI: 10.1016/j.jbusres.2022.113611

Baro, E. E., Obaro, O. G., & Aduba, E. D. (2019). An assessment of digital literacy skills and knowledge-based competencies among librarians working in university libraries in Africa. *Digital Library Perspectives*, 35(3/4), 172–192. DOI: 10.1108/ DLP-04-2019-0013

Bousba, Y., & Arya, V. (2022). Let's connect in metaverse. Brand's new destination to increase consumers' affective brand engagement & their satisfaction and advocacy. *Journal of Content. Community & Communication*, 15(8), 276–293.

Callaghan, C. (2023). Revisiting how scientific research drives technological change: The Fifth Industrial Revolution. *South African Journal of Science*, 119(7/8). Advance online publication. DOI: 10.17159/sajs.2023/15556

Choithani, T., Chowdhury, A., Patel, S., Patel, P., Patel, D., & Shah, M. (2022). A comprehensive study of artificial intelligence and cybersecurity on Bitcoin, crypto currency and banking system. *Annals of Data Science*, ●●●, 1–33.

Ciarli, T., Kenney, M., Massini, S., & Piscitello, L. (2021). Digital technologies, innovation, and skills: Emerging trajectories and challenges. *Research Policy*, 50(7), 104289. DOI: 10.1016/j.respol.2021.104289

Claus, A. M., & Wiese, B. S. (2019). Development and test of a model of interdisciplinary competencies. *European Journal of Work and Organizational Psychology*, 28(2), 191–205. DOI: 10.1080/1359432X.2019.1567491

Cornelius, F. P., van Rensburg, S. K. J., & Kader, S. (2023). Cyber Security Risks in Emerging South African Smart Cities: Towards a Cyber Security Framework. *Perspectives on Global Development and Technology*, 22(1-2), 107–141. DOI: 10.1163/15691497-12341654

De Felice, F., Petrillo, A., Iovine, G., Salzano, C., & Baffo, I. (2023). How Does the Metaverse Shape Education? A Systematic Literature Review. *Applied Sciences (Basel, Switzerland)*, 13(9), 5682. DOI: 10.3390/app13095682

Dwivedi, Y. K., Hughes, L., Baabdullah, A. M., Ribeiro-Navarrete, S., Giannakis, M., Al-Debei, M. M., Dennehy, D., Metri, B., Buhalis, D., Cheung, C. M. K., Conboy, K., Doyle, R., Dubey, R., Dutot, V., Felix, R., Goyal, D. P., Gustafsson, A., Hinsch, C., Jebabli, I., & Wamba, S. F. (2022). Metaverse beyond the hype: Multidisciplinary perspectives on emerging challenges, opportunities, and agenda for research, practice and policy. *International Journal of Information Management*, 66, 102542. DOI: 10.1016/j.ijinfomgt.2022.102542

Gadekallu, T. R., Huynh-The, T., Wang, W., Yenduri, G., Ranaweera, P., Pham, Q. V., . . . Liyanage, M. (2022). Blockchain for the metaverse: A review. *arXiv preprint arXiv:2203.09738*.

Goodsett, M., & Schmillen, H. (2022). Fostering critical thinking in first-year students through information literacy instruction. *College & Research Libraries*, 83(1), 91. DOI: 10.5860/crl.83.1.91

Habibzadeh, H., Nussbaum, B. H., Anjomshoa, F., Kantarci, B., & Soyata, T. (2019). A survey on cybersecurity, data privacy, and policy issues in cyber-physical system deployments in smart cities. *Sustainable Cities and Society*, 50, 101660. DOI: 10.1016/j.scs.2019.101660

Hickerson, H. T., Brosz, J., & Crema, L. (2022). Creating new roles for libraries in academic research: Research conducted at the University of Calgary, 2015–2020. *College & Research Libraries*, 83(1), 129. DOI: 10.5860/crl.83.1.129

Karneli, O. (2023). The Role of Adhocratic Leadership in Facing the Changing Business Environment. [ADMAN]. *Journal of Contemporary Administration and Management*, 1(2), 77–83. DOI: 10.61100/adman.v1i2.26

Khan, M., Alharbi, Y., Alferaidi, A., Alharbi, T. S., & Yadav, K. (2023). Metadata for Efficient Management of Digital News Articles in Multilingual News Archives. *SAGE Open*, 13(4), 21582440231201368. DOI: 10.1177/21582440231201368

Kwon, H. J., El Azzaoui, A., & Park, J. H. (2022). MetaQ: A Quantum Approach for Secure and Optimized Metaverse Environment. *Hum.-. Cent. Comput. Inf. Sci*, 12, 42.

Lee, L. H., Braud, T., Zhou, P., Wang, L., Xu, D., Lin, Z., . . . Hui, P. (2021). All one needs to know about metaverse: A complete survey on technological singularity, virtual ecosystem, and research agenda. *arXiv preprint arXiv:2110.05352*.

Mahardhani, A. J. (2023). The Role of Public Policy in Fostering Technological Innovation and Sustainability. [ADMAN]. *Journal of Contemporary Administration and Management*, 1(2), 47–53. DOI: 10.61100/adman.v1i2.22

Mahdi, M. N., Ahmad, A. R., Ismail, R., Natiq, H., & Mohammed, M. A. (2020). Solution for information overload using faceted search–a review. *IEEE Access : Practical Innovations, Open Solutions*, 8, 119554–119585. DOI: 10.1109/AC-CESS.2020.3005536

Maspul, K. A., & Almalki, F. A. (2023). From Cafés to Collaborative Hubs: Empowering Communities and Transforming the Coffee Value Chain in Buraydah. *EKOMA: Jurnal Ekonomi, Manajemen. Akuntansi*, 3(1), 179–206.

McIntosh, T., Antes, A. L., & DuBois, J. M. (2021). Navigating complex, ethical problems in professional life: A guide to teaching SMART strategies for decision-making. *Journal of Academic Ethics*, 19(2), 139–156. DOI: 10.1007/s10805-020-09369-y PMID: 34177401

Myers, J. P., & Rivero, K. (2020). Challenging preservice teachers' understandings of globalization: Critical knowledge for global citizenship education. *Journal of Social Studies Research*, 44(4), 383–396. DOI: 10.1016/j.jssr.2020.05.004

Nguyen, A., Ngo, H. N., Hong, Y., Dang, B., & Nguyen, B. P. T. (2023). Ethical principles for artificial intelligence in education. *Education and Information Technologies*, 28(4), 4221–4241. DOI: 10.1007/s10639-022-11316-w PMID: 36254344

Noble, S. M., Mende, M., Grewal, D., & Parasuraman, A. (2022). The Fifth Industrial Revolution: How harmonious human–machine collaboration is triggering a retail and service [r] evolution. *Journal of Retailing*, 98(2), 199–208. DOI: 10.1016/j.jretai.2022.04.003

Okafor, K. (2020). Public library services in Nigeria: Challenges and strategies. *Library and Information Science Digest*, 13, 116–125.

Okunlaya, R. O., Syed Abdullah, N., & Alias, R. A. (2022). Artificial intelligence (AI) library services innovative conceptual framework for the digital transformation of university education. *Library Hi Tech*, 40(6), 1869–1892. DOI: 10.1108/LHT-07-2021-0242

Oseghale, O. (2023). Digital information literacy skills and use of electronic resources by humanities graduate students at Kenneth Dike Library, University of Ibadan, Nigeria. *Digital Library Perspectives*, 39(2), 181–204. DOI: 10.1108/DLP-09-2022-0071

Oseji, N. A. (2020). Training of Librarians for Service Delivery in the Digital Age in Federal University Libraries in North Central Nigeria. *Niger Delta Journal of Library and Information Science*, 1(1), 59–69.

Petrakis, P. E. (2022). Labor Market Analysis Based on the Knowledge, Skills, Abilities and Working Activities of Employees in the Present and Future Production Structure of 2027. In *Human Capital and Production Structure in the Greek Economy: Knowledge, Abilities, Skills* (pp. 261–301). Springer International Publishing. DOI: 10.1007/978-3-031-04938-5_10

Ross, P., & Maynard, K. (2021). Towards a 4th industrial revolution. *Intelligent Buildings International*, 13(3), 159–161. DOI: 10.1080/17508975.2021.1873625

Sharma, R. S., Mokhtar, I. A., Ghista, D. N., Nazir, A., & Khan, S. Z. (2023). Digital literacies as policy catalysts of social innovation and socio-economic transformation: Interpretive analysis from Singapore and the UAE. *Sustainable Social Development, 1*(1).

Shrayberg, Y. L., & Volkova, K. Y. (2021). Features of copyright transformation in the information environment in the age of digitalization. *Scientific and Technical Information Processing*, 48(1), 30–37. DOI: 10.3103/S014768822101007X

Signé, L. (2023). *Africa's Fourth Industrial Revolution*. Cambridge University Press. DOI: 10.1017/9781009200004

Singh, S. (2020). Digitization of library resources and the formation of digital libraries: Special reference in green stone digital library software. *IP Indian Journal of Library Science and Information Technology*, 3(1), 44–48. DOI: 10.18231/2456-9623.2018.0010

Suherlan, S. (2023). Digital Technology Transformation in Enhancing Public Participation in Democratic Processes. [TACIT]. *Technology and Society Perspectives*, 1(1), 10–17. DOI: 10.61100/tacit.v1i1.34

Tella, A., Bamidele, S. S., Olaniyi, O. T., & Ajani, Y. A. (2023). Library and Information Science Graduate Skills Needed in the Fourth Industrial Revolution: A Nigerian. *Information Services for a Sustainable Society: Current Developments in an Era of Information Disorder*, 183, 342–360. DOI: 10.1515/9783110772753-023

Varona, D., & Suárez, J. L. (2022). Discrimination, bias, fairness, and trustworthy AI. *Applied Sciences (Basel, Switzerland)*, 12(12), 5826. DOI: 10.3390/app12125826

Vodă, A. I., Cautisanu, C., Grădinaru, C., Tănăsescu, C., & de Moraes, G. H. S. M. (2022). Exploring digital literacy skills in social sciences and humanities students. *Sustainability (Basel)*, 14(5), 2483. DOI: 10.3390/su14052483

Waite, A. M. (2022). Exploring Digital Technologies and Data: A Societal Level of Analysis Approach. In *Technological Challenges: The Human Side of the Digital Age* (pp. 1–24). Springer International Publishing. DOI: 10.1007/978-3-030-98040-5_1

Wharton, L. (2018). Ethical implications of digital tools and emerging roles for academic librarians. *Applying Library Values to Emerging Technology: Decision-Making in the Age of Open Access, Maker Spaces, and the Ever-Changing Library*, 35-54.

World Economic Forum. (2020). Accelerating Digital Transformation: Shaping the Future of Production. Geneva: World Economic Forum.

Yin, Y., Stecke, K. E., & Li, D. (2018). The evolution of production systems from Industry 2.0 through Industry 4.0. *International Journal of Production Research*, 56(1-2), 848–861. DOI: 10.1080/00207543.2017.1403664

Chapter 11
Clarivate's New Generative AI Reading Engagement Platform:
A Development Partnership Led by the University Library

Tracy Ann Elliott
https://orcid.org/0000-0002-2782-6385
Florida Gulf Coast University, USA

Katelyn Ramirez Velazco
Florida Gulf Coast University, USA

Precious A. Goodson
Florida Gulf Coast University, USA

ABSTRACT

During the 2023-24 academic year, Florida Gulf Coast University piloted education start-up Pangea's reading engagement tool, Alethea, which incorporates generative AI (GPT-4). The development partnership with FGCU was a contributing factor in Clarivate's purchase of Pangea. The results of the pilot have been extraordinary. Using FGCU library as a case study, this chapter describes a development partnership with commercial products integrating AI. The case study describes how the product has been utilized, the role of librarians in implementation, findings from multiple studies, including encouraging results of a mixed methods study in which 85% of students reported Alethea helped them understand and recall important themes and main ideas from course reading material. Faculty using Alethea reported student mastery of threshold concepts as described within the ACRL Framework

DOI: 10.4018/979-8-3693-3053-1.ch011

for Information Literacy.

Those libraries that stay connected to the needs of their campus communities often lean into new technologies, not just as early adopters but as developers and partners in development with vendors (Abram, 2022). Many small and medium-sized academic libraries often do not have the expertise, such as programmers, to incorporate new technology into their systems, applications and services. According to Abram (2022) "Libraries and information vendors need to think about change and adaptation in a new way. It is not about adapting to a new normal. It is about creating the next normal for information organizations and the communities they serve" (pg. 29). The introduction of generative artificial intelligence (GenAI), which can produce information in various formats such as text, images, video, audio, and other data using generative language models, makes Abram's philosophy more important than ever. This is particularly significant due to GenAI's unprecedented growth and its impact on nearly every aspect of life (Feuerriegel et al., 2024). An even more important reason for libraries to develop GenAI applications is a perceived increase in the digital divide for those who do not have the resources or training to use them (Daeep & Counts, 2024). For Florida Gulf Coast University, the motivation to enter a development partnership with Clarivate was the potential of GenAI to improve student learning, including the most elusive threshold concepts within the information literacy framework. This chapter will explore the history of the development partnership between FGCU and Clarivate, including the library's role in leading the effort and the result of the first-year pilot.

LITERATURE REVIEW

In the rapidly growing landscape of higher education, GenAI technologies have quickly become vital components of teaching and learning strategies (Chan & Colloton, 2024). This literature review will examine existing research on the impact of technology integration on student success and self-efficacy related to student reading and comprehension. Understanding the student perspective is an essential part of our decision to integrate GenAI tools such as Clarivate's *Alethea Academic Coach* throughout the curriculum. Therefore, the first part of this literature review will focus on the current literacy challenges, including information literacy, present in higher education today, student's perceptions of using technology in their college courses, the willingness of students to try new technology for learning purposes, and the best strategies when using surveys to gather feedback from students about these technologies. The second part of this literature review will focus on current literature highlighting the role of university libraries when introducing and incorporating generative AI technologies into the learning environment. There will also be a discussion on how libraries are leveraging new technologies to collaborate with faculty and become leaders of change and innovation within their respective institutions.

Current Literacy Challenges for College Students

To demonstrate the need for new technologies in the learning environment, it is important to understand the current literacy challenges college students face today. Current literature suggests that the most prominent challenges students face with college-level reading are the financial obligation of course materials, perceived lack of importance, lack of college readiness, lack of time, and lack of motivation (Harvey & Anderson, 2020; Kerr & Frese, 2017). These challenges alone are sufficient to influence student success and perceptions of earning a college degree. In fact, a study conducted by Becker et al. (2023) at a community college in the Southwest region of the United States examined the correlation between textbook costs and student success rates. After comparing student pass rates, the chi-square test indicated a statistically significant relationship between cost and success (Becker et al., 2023). Overcoming financial obstacles is a common theme in higher education literature. Marty and Teeman (2020) conducted a mixed-method study on students' perceptions of purchasing course reading materials. Twenty-four percent of students indicated that they only buy textbooks they can afford and often go without a textbook due to high costs. The sad reality is that college students today are missing out on their full learning potential because of the costs of textbooks (Marty & Teeman, 2020). Therefore, leaders in higher education must find cost-effective solutions to fill learning gaps.

Reading Comprehension

With student comprehension at an all-time low, students are struggling with the transition from high school to college (National Center for Education Statistics, 2024). Faculty have indicated that students are entering college with low critical thinking, information literacy, and summarizing skills (Braten, et al., 2014; Fleck et al., 2017). Researchers also suggest that students are struggling to understand complex concepts, read charts and graphs, and memorize key topics, causing an academic lag and demotivating them from purchasing or reading course materials (Kerr & Frese, 2017). This lack of preparedness is a common obstacle in higher education today and contributes to the need for reform and adoption of effective teaching and learning strategies. A cross-sectional study analyzed the academic reading proficiency of 848 undergraduates to determine if there is a common issue of unpreparedness in college students today. The results determined that the average reading comprehension score was a 6 out of 10 (Gorzycki et al., 2016). This proportion signifies that undergraduates are struggling to read and interpret academic texts across the board. College readiness is an ever-evolving concept; as texts increase in depth and complexity throughout one's academic experience, the strategies and proficiency should evolve as well (Paulson & Holschuh, 2018). Therefore, the purpose of the mixed-method study included in this chapter is to identify effective ways to enhance the student learning experience when facing reading challenges.

Information Literacy Threshold Concepts

The ability to summarize and synthesize written text to develop a new idea is embedded in the threshold concept of "scholarship as conversation" within the Framework for Information Literacy filed by the Association of College & Research Libraries (ACRL) in 2015 (Association of College & Research Libraries, 2015). This is essential for students to master their field of study. According to Olaniyi (2020), understanding the text's meaning and drawing inferences must happen if the student is to achieve a course's learning objectives. In their systematic review and meta-analysis of studies published between 2010 and 2021, de la Peña and Luque-Rojas (2021) endeavored to determine the proportion of students crossing this threshold. They found that only 22% of the college students in the review were able to perform tasks requiring them to make critical inferences from the text. This was consistent across disciplines, including social sciences, engineering, humanities, health sciences, and business (de la Peña & Luque-Rojas, 2021). Several studies suggest that reading comprehension is a barrier to student learning among college students in every discipline, especially at the level of mastering threshold concepts (Mason, 2018; Gomez et al., 2020; Kotzner et al., 2021). According to Francis (2017), threshold concepts are points at which the student finds the information extremely difficult to comprehend, requiring them to move beyond their current knowledge or abilities they do not have. By crossing the threshold, they gain the essential knowledge required of the discipline. Unfortunately, many students give up, willing to accept only what they already know, and often have negative opinions or feelings about the information, discipline, and their ability to learn (Francis, 2017).

Importance of Student Engagement with Text

In a world where students face economic obstacles and enter college underprepared, it is imperative for educators to keep students engaged with course reading material and emphasize the importance of engaging with the text. Recent studies indicate that students feel professors do not stress the importance of course reading, leading them to complete their assignments by skimming the text for answers (Marty & Teeman, 2020). From the student perspective, academic reading has become busy work, and students feel demotivated to read course material when it does not specifically correlate to their interests or degree program (Mason & Warmington, 2024; Kerr & Frese, 2017). Content that is difficult to read and extensive makes reading a grudging task, and students have difficulties identifying main ideas or takeaways from the material (Mason & Warmington, 2024). Therefore, students need better reading tools and strategies to stay engaged in their courses and obtain knowledge of their degree program. This will take faculty engagement to make the text relatable and students to see the value in academic reading (Aldrige, 2019).

Student Willingness and Perceptions of Using Technology in The Classroom

The adoption and integration of new technologies in higher education institutions rely heavily on product end users, or student perceptions, as part of their learning experience (Karp & Fletcher, 2014; Office of Survey Research & Analysis, 2024). Strydom et al. (2017) advise the strategic introduction of new resources that promote innovation and efficiency in student learning, stating that it should be rooted in delivering academically engaging experiences. Many reasons contribute to the overall literacy struggles or poor performance faced by postsecondary students, including a lack of preparedness, time, motivation, and financial resources, which affect each other (Aldrige, 2019; Harvey & Anderson, 2020; Kerr & Frese, 2017; Marty & Teeman, 2020).

Student performance metrics elucidate a clear disconnect between the skill level required for postsecondary academic success and the current mitigating efforts implemented for smooth matriculation into most universities. As a result, many institutions have elected to integrate learning technologies into their program planning (Harvey & Anderson, 2020; Paulson & Holschuh, 2018). Instructional tools used to enhance student learning are indispensable as technology becomes increasingly embedded in everyday life and helps institutions address deficiencies (Henderson et al., 2017).

The Readiness for Technology Adoption Framework (RTAF) addresses an institution's capacity and best practices in implementing new technologies to the student populations as the process relates to various stakeholders (Karp & Fletcher, 2014). For successful implementation phases, both students and key stakeholders in the learning process should possess a high level of awareness of their current standing and desired outcomes for smooth adoptions. This theme of accountability is echoed in an article by Harvey and Anderson (2020), which explores educational IT standards designed to help students and staff on their journeys to technologically enhanced learning. This means that both take ownership of their experiences, seeking adequate task completion and performance reflection. Similarly, Perusall, a learning technology platform investigated by Benjamin (2023), was designed to hold students accountable for reading course materials outside of class with faculty-designed questions and tasks.

Students are more likely to use new technologies if they understand the void the intervention fills (Karp & Fletcher, 2014). The literature on this topic alludes to the advantages technology has for younger generations, who have higher levels of comfort and expertise with technology integration in other aspects of their lives (Gray et al., 2021; Jazlin et al., 2017). Students successfully adopt and incorporate technologies if the benefits, including enhancing their academic experience, are clear and specific (Jazlin et al., 2022; Karp & Fletcher, 2014). Complex and repetitive exposure to educational technology further supports student success by helping them revive and reimagine the pathways to completing tasks they felt burdened with, bored of, or ill-equipped to execute (Henderson et al., 2017; Jazlin et al., 2022; Karp & Fletcher, 2014). Studies following the experiences of medical, architecture, and digital natives in other disciplines show benefits from the use of learning technology (Gray et al., 2021; Jazlin et al., 2017). A student's willingness to interact with new educational technologies parallels their perception of the academic content assigned by faculty (Henderson et al., 2017; Jazlin et al., 2017). Strydom et al. (2017) advise that the strategic introduction of new resources that promote innovation and efficiency in student learning should be rooted in academically engaging experiences. A study on the perceptions of learning technologies by students from two universities found that 46% agreed educational technology helped them meet deadline expectations, 30% found it promoted flexibility, access, and convenience, and 26% said the course supplement made assignments easier (Henderson et al., 2017)."

Getting Student Feedback Through Surveys

Incentivized student surveys have evolved as key solutions to low response rates experienced by postsecondary education researchers (Laguilles et al., 2011; Royal & Flammer, 2017; Standish et al., 2018). Gathering student data and evaluative information on engagement, quality, and faculty performance has presented institution stakeholders with vital information needed to assess planning efforts, performance improvement, and other components relevant to campus and student experiences (Cole et al., 2015; Laguilles et al., 2011; Standish et al., 2018). Incentives serve to improve student response rates, which have undergone a steady decrease; these incentives include lotteries, pre-paid, post-paid, and participatory rewards (Cole et al., 2015). Royal and Flammer (2017) found that an impactful incentive to consider in the administration of student surveys is the effective communication of the reasons for data collection. Assuring students of the value of their participation can greatly improve their approach to providing feedback. Dedicating class time to submitting surveys lessens the burden on students, who may feel that taking surveys does not provide a valuable return for their time (Standish et al., 2018). The authors also discovered that improvements in student response rates were found with mobile device survey compatibility. The length of responses, however, heavily depended on the type of device used during surveying; the presence of a full keyboard resulted in responses over 60% longer than those retrieved from a smartphone or tablet (Standish et al., 2018).

Libraries Leading Change

In a literature review of library innovation spanning 30 years, Brundy (2015) determined that a flatter organizational structure or one that eliminated silos and promoted greater shared decision-making led to more innovation in academic libraries. In a more recent literature review of library innovation, Llewellyn (2019) identifies themes where innovative libraries aligned their efforts with the mission of the parent institution, led efforts towards digital transformation, and utilized new technologies and approaches to support teaching, learning, and research. According to Llewellyn, the literature identified innovative libraries as those demonstrating their value through measurable influence on student success, increasing impact and funding of university research, and elevating the profile of the institution through community engagement. Khalil and Khalil (2023) and Brundy (2015) suggest that innovation is a matter of survival for academic libraries, as most library budgets have not kept pace with institutional expenditures over the past two decades, indicating a decline in senior leadership's view of the return on investment in the library. Library innovation is intrinsically linked with innovations in technology and management strategies (Brundy, 2015; Khalil & Khalil, 2023). The research findings of Khalil and Khalil (2023) suggest that libraries innovating new service delivery and knowledge management techniques were significantly influenced by the library's development and use of new technologies, new management strategies, and new organizational structures. They imply that those academic libraries that operate under traditional management and organizational paradigms, or lack the ability to adopt new technologies, will not be able to effectively respond to the evolving needs of their users and, therefore, will diminish in value to their campus community (Khalil & Khalil, 2023).

Academic Libraries' Response to Generative AI

In interviews with 33 library directors, Cox et al. (2019) found that only a few academic library leaders viewed AI as having a significant impact on library service delivery and knowledge management. Four years later, Huang et al. (2023) studied the library strategic planning documents of the top 25 universities in both the UK and China and found little mention of AI utilization as a strategy. Hussain and Ahmad (2023) conducted a bibliometric review utilizing Scopus, examining publications that focused on AI in academic libraries from 2002 to 2022. They found that in 2022, corresponding with the launch of ChatGPT, there was a significant spike in publications, with 64 out of a total of 373 publications produced that year (Hussain & Ahmad, 2023). This dramatic increase may suggest that academic libraries are realizing the implications and potential of GenAI in transforming library services and resource delivery. Cox (2022) presents multiple conceptual frameworks for future research on the impact of AI on the profession of academic librarianship. Cox includes a framework in which librarianship as a profession, grounded in research, scholarship, and management, could lead to a transformation where AI enhances academic library endeavors rather than replaces them (Cox, 2022).

Library as a Development Partner with Private Industry

Cox (2022) suggests that if early adopters of artificial intelligence technologies are made visible, including those working with the commercial sector, they may position the academic library as a transformational leader on campus. This could convince campus leadership to invest in the efforts of their library (Cox, 2022). Collins et al. (2014) describe a development partnership between North Carolina State University (NCSU) and EBSCO. According to the authors, successful development partnerships have negotiated terms with clear expectations from the vendor on deliverables and timelines. They emphasize that library staff should be experimental, accepting significant trial and error and potential disruptions in workflow or system failures during the development process (Collins et al., 2014).

Piloting Alethea at FGCU

The FGCU Library has a history of development partnerships with Clarivate, including the piloting of Rialto, the company's advanced acquisition and selection companion tool to Alma. The partnership began when the library was approached by Clarivate to participate in a pilot launch. FGCU joined others under a legal agreement to pilot the application and provide feedback for improvements. Later, the library became one of the first adopters. This type of partnership, while time-consuming, provided dividends including: allowing for consensus among all members of the library staff and faculty on the decision to implement, an easy transition to the new system, and the ability to assist peer institutions with their adoption of the product.

The FGCU University Library is preparing to pilot a couple of new products from Clarivate in fall 2024.

However, the partnership with Alethea began very differently. The dean of the library was approached by a former colleague from the library technology industry who was working with an ed tech start-up company, Pangea. The dean was convinced to preview the product and invited her colleague, the director of digital learning, to the product demonstration. After previewing Alethea, they were both convinced the tool was compelling and could address some of the student success barriers many FGCU students face, including interpreting and articulating the main ideas from complex texts required as course readings.

The library dean informed the provost of the application, who agreed that students who were not successful in gateway courses in economics, chemistry, finance, and biology were likely struggling with reading comprehension. He mentioned that he had visited a class that was experiencing a 40% fail rate, almost exclusively among students required to take the course to progress in their degree program. The faculty were convinced that the students were unprepared for the math required in the course, but the provost was convinced that the problem was reading comprehension, especially the threshold concepts within the discipline of the course (M. Rieger, personal communication, March 2023).

Alethea and the Alethea Academic Coach

Eran Segal, founder of Alethea and now the director of Alethea product development at Clarivate, created Alethea to assist students struggling with comprehensive reading. As a college philosophy student, Segal found it difficult to focus while reading required course materials and was in search of a solution (E. Segal, personal communication, March 8, 2023). According to Segal, reading comprehension methodologies such as SQ3R (Survey, Question, Read, Recite, Review) and SOAR (Select, Organize, Associate, Regulate) were integrated into Alethea to engage students in a metacognitive process while reading, increasing their reading efficacy. Numerous studies suggest that metacognition is enhanced through SQ3R and SOAR in all disciplines, including science, technology, engineering, and math (STEM), leading to enhanced comprehension, including threshold concepts (Jairam, 2014; Barzililai & Ka'adan, 2016; Suherman, 2020; Davis & Ritchie, 2023). There are three steps for instructors creating reading tasks in Alethea, upload required course reading, devise questions that stimulate metacognitive processing, and highlight the sections in the text that answer the questions. Instructors have features such as scoring each question, limiting the amount of text highlighted by the students, the type of answers required, and more. The students have five recommended steps to complete the reading tasks, review the questions, scan the text for headings and organization, highlight the section of the text that contains the answer, organize each highlight as an annotation, answer the question in their own words.

The Academic Coach

While Alethea was already being piloted by several faculty at universities such as Johns Hopkins, Tel Aviv, and Yale, Segal and his development team were able to integrate GenAI with the release of GPT-4 during the initial pilot. The chatbot is referred to as the Academic Coach. Students can activate the coach when they need assistance with formulating answers in their own words (E. Segal, personal communication, March 8, 2023). The Academic Coach engages the students in a chat session. Figure 1 provides a view of the Academic Coach feature in action.

Figure 1. Screen capture of student engaging with the Alethea academic coach

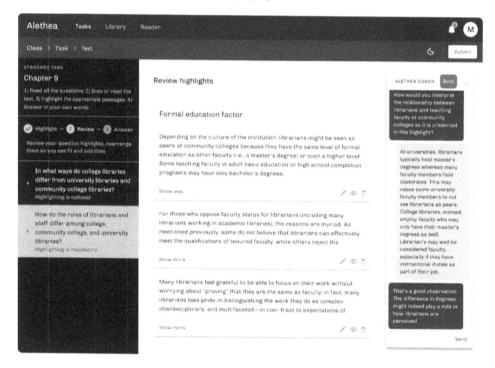

Recruiting faculty to the pilot

Convinced of the application's potential to improve student academic success, the library dean and the director of digital learning developed a plan to determine interest in Alethea. MIT's Justin Reich (2023) presents a framework for implementing innovative practices in educational settings. Reich suggests that inviting faculty to experiment with new technologies, engaging in the scholarship of teaching and learning within their disciplines using the products, and gaining experience in best practices is an effective way to implement new technologies for teaching and learning.

Therefore, with the provost's blessing, the pilot began with an open forum in which the CEO of Pangea and the founder of Alethea visited the campus and presented his product in April of 2022. To compel faculty to attend the presentation, they were emailed a digital flyer with a provocative title (see Figure 2). Lunch was served to the first 30 who registered for the in-person presentation in our faculty development center, the co-sponsor of the event, and the remaining were provided a Zoom link. Over 80 faculty attended, the highest attendance for any event sponsored by the faculty development center. During the forum, five faculty were identified to participate in the summer and fall pilot. These faculty members were teaching courses in education, biology, sociology, business, and physical therapy. Each faculty member identified one section of their course to integrate Alethea. Three of the faculty were department chairs, and one had recently been selected as the provost's faculty fellow for artificial intelligence. The final faculty member was the Dean of the University Library and a professor in the College of Education. The strategic decision to include these faculty was based on the influence they would have on their peers. These were the faculty champions.

Figure 2. Flyer emailed to faculty for introduction to Alethea

THE PILOT

The first implementation of Alethea was in Summer B classes, the second 8 weeks of the summer 2022 semester. The courses were an interdisciplinary sociology class and a business strategies capstone course. The sociology class required the library to negotiate unlimited downloading of the book used for the class which has already been added to the library's collection as part of the library's textbook affordability program. The business strategies course chose three business cases from the Sage Business Cases collection, also licensed by the library. Subject librarians worked with each faculty to secure copyright-compliant texts including library purchased, OER, or open access reading materials. Before the classes began, the faculty, librarians, instructional designers and the coordinator of the writing center met with Alethea developers to discuss strategies for implementing Alethea. During the 2-hour session, they were given access to a sandbox of courses and sample assignments called reading tasks. The Alethea team walked the attendees through the student and instructor sides of the application. The rest of the time was set aside for strategy, including a discussion of how each faculty member would implement the tool, and the efficacy research they were interested in exploring. It was incredibly helpful to have both the librarians and the instructional designers engaged in the discussion. These individuals provided insight into the potential barriers students may have using the system and allowed the group to brainstorm possible solutions. These sessions were repeated multiple times throughout the year as more faculty joined the pilot.

Expanding the Pilot

During the fall of 2023, faculty using Alethea were invited to take part in a teaching and learning with AI workshop series. During the panel presentation, faculty were once again invited to join the pilot. By spring, 18 faculty members were onboarded from 12 different disciplines. The onboarding process was made more accessible by integrating Alethea into the university's LMS, Canvas. However, not every faculty member was successful in launching Alethea in time for full integration into their spring courses. Full integration requires a significant investment in time, including selecting appropriate reading materials and developing metacognitive questions for each text. Several faculty members, therefore, only utilized Alethea for one of their assignments or had to forgo utilization until the next semester.

Many of the issues encountered were related to the reading materials. For some, the issue was potential copyright infringement, particularly with textbook publishers. FGCU librarians were unsuccessful in securing copyright permissions from any of the textbook publishers, requiring them to look for alternative reading materials, including open educational resources (OER) and library-licensed content allowing unlimited downloads. One faculty member needed more time to prepare course lecture transcripts for OCR recognition and better engagement with the GenAI feature.

All these issues were instrumental in discovering the most effective process for onboarding faculty as first-time users of Alethea. FGCU has established an onboarding process that includes having each faculty member meet with a librarian first. The digital learning instructional design team has created a Canvas course, similar to ones they have created for other products integrated into Canvas, such as Kaltura and Respondus. After a meeting between the three entities supporting Alethea: university library, digital learning, and writing center; an agreement was established for supporting faculty and students (see Figure 3)

Figure 3. Internal agreement between FGCU departments supporting Alethea course integration

---

Alethea support

Clarivate provides technical support for Alethea and FGCU support for Alethea is shared between Library, Digital Learning, and the Writing Center.

Roles and Responsibilities

- Library:
  - Content is king! Designated Library staff are the first point of contact for faculty interested in using Alethea so they can review the reading material for use in Alethea or assist in sourcing reading material.
  - Promote Alethea through information sessions, discussions, and other events. Promotion may be subject or course specific.
  - Schedule onboarding events.
  - Monitor changes to Alethea.
- Digital Learning:
  - IT Team:
    - Designated Alethea experts
    - Develop and maintain resources for faculty to add to their course, such as student tutorials and a practice assignment.
    - Assist faculty with integrating Alethea in their course.
    - First contact for issues to verify if it is a technical issue. Reassign technical issues to Clarivate/Alethea support.
    - One or more IT team members attend Alethea events when appropriate.
    - Monitor changes to Alethea.
  - ID Team:
    - Consult with faculty on adding Alethea assignment(s) to a course.
    - Assist with proper structure for questions used in Alethea.
    - One or more ID team members attend Alethea events when appropriate.
    - Monitor changes to Alethea.
- Writing Center:
  - Provide writing support to students.

Process

1. Faculty work with Library staff to identify/review reading content to use in Alethea.
2. After reading content has been identified, faculty work with DL's IT team to integrate Alethea into the course, discuss the available resources and assist with setting up the practice test using the course syllabus or preferred reading material.
3. Faculty works with ID as needed for assistance in creating assignments, question structure, etc.
4. Students work with the Writing Center if they need assistance with writing.

Note: This agreement established the Alethea support team at FGCU. While digital learning was reluctant to establish a team lead since this is not a standard practice, the library and writing center identified lead contacts for faculty interested in learning more about Alethea.

THE FACULTY EXPERIENCE USING ALETHEA

Faculty members who have utilized Alethea have all reported increased student learning. Every instructor who has used Alethea has continued to do so. One of the professors engaged in the pilot from the very beginning has embedded it in three courses. Furthermore, every faculty member is involved in at least one research project, and several are creating OER, believing that student access to course readings is essential to their success. In these cases, faculty reported that the more their students engaged with the required course readings, the more they realized that the readings initially chosen for the course, fell short of the learning objectives. This realization motivated them to create course readings that were better aligned with the course learning objectives and the financial needs of their students

Alethea Use Cases

The college of business had the most faculty members utilizing Alethea during the spring pilot, primarily to analyze business case studies. Alethea is currently being used in two courses in the business management degree program taught by six different faculty members. These faculty all agreed to deploy Alethea in the same way. All case studies and questions were standardized to eliminate the instructor as a potential confounding variable when determining efficacy.

One of the most astounding potential impacts of Alethea during that spring semester, was related to a long-running group assignment in one of the courses. Every semester, the students compete in a national business strategies game. This year, two FGCU teams tied for first place, and one tied for second place. The first FGCU team to win "overall best team" was taught by one of the first faculty members to use Alethea in the summer of 2023. The students reported that Alethea was instrumental in their preparation for the competition.

In most use cases, the faculty have utilized Alethea to create a flipped classroom. The faculty could hold class discussions knowing that their students had read the materials and engaged with the readings by answering the assigned questions. Alethea allows the faculty to show a heat map of which sections of the text students highlighted and their anonymized answers. This provides a unique opportunity to discuss which answers were correct or incorrect. There was only one instructor who utilized Alethea in a fully asynchronous online course. The instructor simulated this discussion by creating a video announcement and asking students to comment.

In all but the business courses mentioned above, each instructor utilized Alethea differently. This was the reason many of the faculty attended brainstorming sessions with Clarivate's Alethea development team: to hear about the various ways their peers were implementing the tool in their courses. At each of these meetings, subject librarians were at the table to brainstorm potential reading materials that were appropriate for the learning objectives of the courses.

Technical issues

As expected when engaging in a development partnership (Collins et al., 2014), FGCU faculty and students encountered technical issues. However, also typical of these partnerships, the vendor support teams were extremely responsive, and issues were quickly remedied. Several features were added to Alethea as a result of FGCU faculty and student feedback. In fact, technical issues encountered during the development partnership led to essential improvements in the product (Collins et al., 2014).

The Scholarship of Teaching and Learning

It was mentioned earlier in the chapter that the FGCU faculty involved with Alethea have all engaged in at least one research study on the platform's efficacy. However, many have multiple studies underway. One faculty member is leading the comparison study within the two business courses. That same faculty member, in collaboration with the director of digital learning, is also studying the anonymized transcripts of the student chat interactions with the GenAI Coach. This work has been incredibly illuminating. By studying the transcripts, they can determine whether the coach was instrumental in helping students formulate answers using their own words rather than paraphrasing or directly quoting. The researchers found that the Academic Coach provides gentle nudging to make the students question why they highlighted certain passages and asks them why they didn't think other passages were relevant. While this is incredibly helpful to many students, it helps explain why some students say the GenAI makes it too easy to formulate answers. This study, although not yet published, has challenged the Alethea development team to consider different levels of assistance based on either the instructor's or the student's choice.

The faculty members who have successfully implemented Alethea in their courses continue to provide evidence of improved learning. For example, one faculty member began tracking the academic performance of the students who took her course in which Alethea was utilized, in other more advanced courses. In every case, the students who took the Alethea-integrated course outperformed as a cohort compared to the cohort of students who had not taken the Alethea-integrated course. The Alethea faculty user group at FGCU presents at conferences, is being interviewed by the media, and is publishing their findings, including this chapter. They are steeped in the scholarship of teaching and learning and have contributed to a preliminary framework for determining the efficacy of other GenAI-integrated learning tools, which will be tested this summer by faculty and graduate student interns and published in a whitepaper that will be presented to the provost.

Alethea Student Interns

As the pilot expanded, student involvement and feedback became essential. The library dean was approached by two former master's degree students requesting an internship. One of the students had experience with Alethea in the dean's fall course, while the other had taken the same course the previous fall without the benefit of Alethea. They were recruited as the "Alethea Interns" and introduced to the Alethea development team, the FGCU Alethea support team, and several faculty members participating in the spring pilot. The interns were instrumental in capturing the student experience. They completed half of the literature review for this chapter and developed, administered, and analyzed the student survey. The original plan for the interns was to create a whitepaper regarding the efficacy of Alethea and recommendations for further integration across the curriculum. This whitepaper will now be completed by summer interns.

The Student Experience Using Alethea

Throughout the pilot, the student feedback about Alethea was captured through focus groups, class reflection exercises, conversations during class visits by Alethea's staff and the library dean, and comments included by some students on the university deployed evaluation of instruction. It was important to gather feedback on the student experiences and challenges students faced. Prior to this case study, however, there was no systematic method used to capture the student experience with new teaching and learning tools. The university needed to be able to compare the student experience across the different courses to be able to determine the extent to which the instructor, materials, or how Alethea was integrated into the course, made a difference in how students viewed the platform. This feedback was essential, allowing leaders within FGCU to make educated and calculated decisions on whether A.I. learning tools such as Alethea, should be regularly implemented into the learning environment. According to Creswell and Plano-Clark (2018), mixed methods studies can contribute to learning intervention implementation research in educational settings, by providing information about what core components were adopted and by whom, and how to implement based upon the teaching modality and the resources available to faculty and students. To complete the study, the Alethea interns and the dean of the library deployed a survey instrument.

The Research Plan

Creswell and Plano-Clark (2018) suggest that researchers trying to identify unknown variables and hoping to determine the generalizability of their sample results to the population should consider an exploratory mixed-methods research design. Since monetary incentives or extra-credit or would not be included in the survey, the researchers were unsure of the potential response rate. The population included all students enrolled in courses using Alethea for more than one reading assignment. By including open-ended questions in the survey, the qualitative component allowed the researchers to identify trends within the quantitative results, even if participation fell below the desired confidence level (Creswell & Plano-Clark, 2018). When the survey was administered, 295 students (N=295) were enrolled in the courses meeting the criteria. For a population of 295, to achieve the desired confidence level of 95% (Z = 1.96), a proportion estimate of 0.05, and a margin of error of 5%, the calculated sample size would need to be n=59. There were three factors that may have created a low participation rate: whether the students would be interested in participating in the survey without a monetary incentive or gift, whether the faculty would encourage them to participate, and the limited timeframe while waiting for IRB approval and the end of the semester looming. The survey was administered through the university learning management system (LMS) as a "blueprint course." The course included an assignment worth no points. Faculty would have to accept the blueprint course to overlay the course in which they were using Alethea. The assignment due date was set to allow the students one week to take the survey. If accepted by the faculty member, the survey would show up in their assignment task list. The survey was closed when the sample size reached n=100. The researchers believed the number of participants was achieved by stating the purpose of the survey in the informed consent. According to Royal and Flammer (2017), including how the data collected will be used, students can determine whether the return on the investment of their time is warranted. In this case, the researchers informed the students that their feedback would impact the decision to fully implement Alethea throughout the curriculum and how to do so effectively.

Creating the Survey

Creating a new survey requires several steps to ensure the validity and reliability of the data collected (Creswell & Guetterman, 2019). To improve validity, researchers engaged the faculty and Alethea support staff, the content experts, to review the questions to establish content validity (Creswell & Guetterman, 2019). The researchers measured the Cronbach's alpha (α) of the survey, which according to Creswell and Guetterman, a value of 0.7 or higher generally indicates good internal consistency. The score for this survey was α=.87, which is considered good reliability (Creswell & Guetterman, 2019).

RESULTS

Quantitative Results

Overwhelmingly, students who completed the survey indicated that Alethea and the Alethea Academic Coach (the GenAI chatbot) were instrumental in their learning. A one-way analysis of variance (ANOVA) was used to determine whether the course the student was enrolled in had any significant effect on students' answers. According to Creswell and Guetterman (2019), a one-way ANOVA is a parametric test used to compare the means of three or more independent groups to determine whether there are statistically significant differences between them. The p-value of the ANOVA was 0.43531, which is greater than 0.05, suggesting that there is no statistically significant difference in the student answers across different courses at the 5% significance level. Figures 4 through 9 chart the frequencies of student answers to each question using a 5-point Likert scale

Figure 4. Question 1 answer frequencies: course material engagement

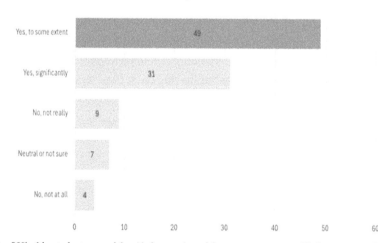

Did using Alethea motivate you to engage more with the course reading materials?

Yes, to some extent	49
Yes, significantly	31
No, not really	9
Neutral or not sure	7
No, not at all	4

Note: 80% of the students agreed that Alethea motivated them to engage more with the course reading materials.

Figure 5. Question 2 answer frequencies: reading comprehension

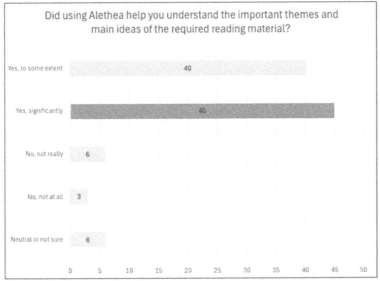

Note: 85% of students agreed that Alethea helped them understand the important themes of the required reading materials.

Figure 6. Question 3 answer frequencies: The Alethea academic coach chatbot

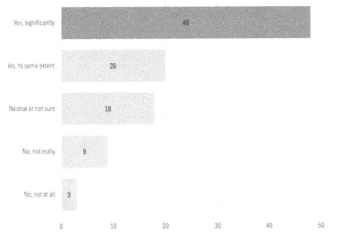

Note: 68% of students agreed that the Alethea Academic Coach GenAI feature was helpful in formulating the answers in their own words.

Figure 7. Question 4 answer frequencies: remembering the main ideas

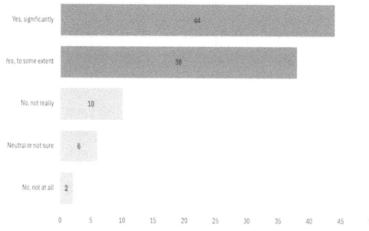

Note: 86% of the students agreed that Alethea helped them remember the main ideas within the reading materials.

Figure 8. Question 5 answer frequencies: recommending Alethea to peers

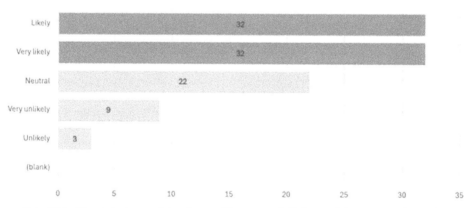

Note: 64% of the students agreed that they would recommend Alethea to their peers to enhance their text analysis skills.

Figure 9. Question 6 answer frequencies: using Alethea for research assignments

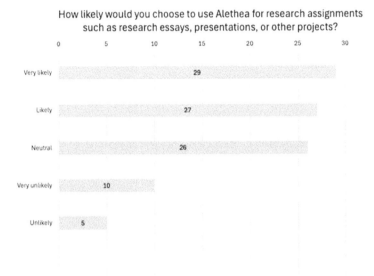

How likely would you choose to use Alethea for research assignments such as research essays, presentations, or other projects?

Very likely	29
Likely	27
Neutral	26
Very unlikely	10
Unlikely	5

Note: 56% of students envision using Alethea to complete research assignments. Alethea is currently not designed for this purpose. However, this may suggest that students were interested in using a product like Alethea, such as a GenAI research assistant, when working on research assignments.

Qualitative Survey Results

According to Morgan (2023), ChatGPT can be a viable alternative to hand-coding data as it does well at producing descriptive themes. Therefore, a combination of two GenAI platforms was enlisted including ChatGPT GPT-4 and Microsoft Bing's Copilot. Both systems were asked to "Categorize the following answers based on the question." Answers were also hand-coded to ensure nuances were not missed (Morgan, 2023).

The themes identified below helped the researchers and faculty better understand the answers students provided to the Likert-scale questions. For example, when students indicated that Alethea did not help them understand the main ideas of the text (12%), some also indicated in their open-ended responses that they found the materials easy to understand, so they did not feel they needed assistance interpreting the main ideas. Another connection was made using the GenAI Academic Coach (chatbot); several students who did not find the GenAI feature helpful (11%) also indicated that they felt the chatbot should challenge them more. A student suggested that they should have to write the answer themselves and then have the chatbot critique their answers. This insightful feedback is being incorporated into the platform, aligning with the chatbot transcript study recently completed by the faculty. The following are a few of the themes that either confirm or negate the research questions of the study.

Ease of Use and Convenience: Focus and Organization

"I liked Alethea because it was all in one place, which made it easier to see what I had to do."

"It helped me stay up to date on my studying for each chapter."

"I really like Alethea because she helped me put my ideas in order and helped me answer the questions in an easier, faster, and more effective way."

Educational Support: Threshold Concepts

"I found Alethea to be very helpful as it helped to guide me by helping me put my thoughts into my writing and also helped lead me towards the key points of the material."

"For example, in our class, dissecting pieces of literature written by Ernest Hemingway has been super helpful in the analysis process."

"For the most part, Alethia was a great experience using to better understand the readings in the class."

"Talking to the bot feature and having an actual conversation about the material is significantly helpful and should be kept."

"Out of all the external websites I used in my four years of college I believe this one helped me the most. Highlighting, asking questions and then answering was very helpful."

Differing Abilities: Suggesting Levels of Difficulty

"To improve student learning, I think students should be tasked with fully writing the response, however Alethea should be there to provide feedback and act as a devil's advocate to students."

"I really like the concept, maybe after the highlighting section the AI can give more personal responses rather than just a broad pat on the shoulder kind of response."

CONCLUSION

Based upon both the qualitative and quantitative data from the student survey, researchers were able to confirm three of the four research hypotheses: H_1 - Students engaged more with the course readings because of Alethea, H_2 - Students report that Alethea helped them learn the course content and H_3 - Students prefer using Alethea in future courses. However, results of the one-way ANOVA suggested there were no significant differences in student answers based on the course they were enrolled in, or the instructor teaching the course, which was the final hypothesis H_4 - Student responses differed based on course content, instructor, course material, or how Alethea was integrated into the course.

These results also align with the early results of faculty studies on the efficacy of Althea and the GenAI Alethea Academic Coach in student learning gains. The desire of students and faculty to continue investing in Alethea beyond the pilot was confirmed. The next steps will be to complete a whitepaper comparing the efficacy of Alethea with other GenAI learning tools, which the authors have not found, so far, as effective in engaging students in the metacognitive processing of the required course reading materials. Therefore, the recommendation to continue with Alethea in the fall of 2024 was assured. As with any case study, there is difficulty generalizing findings from this study to other settings (Hirose & Creswell, 2023). Hirose and Creswell also warn that there is a risk of bias, as the researchers' personal opinions and preferences may influence the research. They claim the best way to address these limitations is by replicating the study among other use cases (Hirose & Creswell, 2023). Therefore, along with the authors of this chapter, FGCU faculty and administrators involved with the Alethea pilot encourage other institutions to join in the development of Alethea. This will not only allow for comparison of results among multiple institutions, suggesting this FGCU case study is not an outlier, but also because the more the platform is used, the more it can be refined and meet the needs of all students, regardless of their academic preparation for college.

REFERENCES

Aldridge, D. (2019). Reading, engagement, and higher education. *Higher Education Research & Development*, 38(1), 38–50. DOI: 10.1080/07294360.2018.1534804

Association of College & Research Libraries. (2015, February 2). *Framework for information literacy*. American Library Association. https://www.ala.org/acrl/standards/ilframework

Barzilai, S., & Ka'adan, I. (2017). Learning to integrate divergent information sources: The interplay of epistemic cognition and epistemic metacognition. *Metacognition and Learning*, 12(2), 193–232. DOI: 10.1007/s11409-016-9165-7

Becker, K. L., Safa, R., & Becker, K. M. (2023). High-priced textbooks' impact on community college student success. *Community College Review*, 51(1), 128–141. DOI: 10.1177/00915521221125898

Benjamin, R. G. (2023). High-tech versus low tech: Comparing approaches to increase college student reading compliance and engagement. *Scholarship of Teaching and Learning in Psychology*. Advance online publication. DOI: 10.1037/stl0000366

Bingham, T. J., Wirjapranata, J., & Bartley, A. (2017). Building resilience and resourcefulness: The evolution of an academic and information literacy strategy for first year social work students. *Information and Learning Science*, 118(7–8), 433–446. DOI: 10.1108/ILS-05-2017-0046

Braten, I., Ferguson, L. E., Stromso, H. I., & Anmarkrud, O. (2014). Students working with multiple conflicting documents on a scientific issue: Relations between epistemic cognition while reading and sourcing and argumentation in essays. *The British Journal of Educational Psychology*, 84(1), 58–85. DOI: 10.1111/bjep.12005 PMID: 24547754

Breeding, M. (2022). Managing Technology. In Hirsh, S. (Ed.), *Information services today* (3rd ed., pp. 342–357). Rowman & Littlefield.

Brundy, C. (2015). Academic libraries and innovation: A literature review. *Journal of Library Innovation*, 6(1), 22–39.

Chan, C. K., & Colloton, T. (2024). *Generative AI in higher education*. Directory of Open Access Books. https://directory.doabooks.org/handle/20.500.12854/135718

Collins, M. D., Somerville, M. M., Pelsinsky, N., & Wood, A. (2014). Working better together: Library, publisher, and vendor perspectives. In B. R. Bernhardt, L. H. Hinds, & K. P. Strauch (Eds.), *Too much is not enough: Charleston conference proceedings, 2013* (pp. 312–318). Purdue University Press.

Cox, A. (2023). How artificial intelligence might change academic library work: Applying the competencies literature and the theory of the professions. *Journal of the Association for Information Science and Technology*, 74(3), 367–380. DOI: 10.1002/asi.24635

Cox, A. M., Pinfield, S., & Rutter, S. (2019). The intelligent library: Thought leaders' views on the likely impact of artificial intelligence on academic libraries. *Library Hi Tech*, 37(3), 418–435. DOI: 10.1108/LHT-08-2018-0105

Creswell, J. W., & Guetterman, T. C. (2019). *Educational research: Planning, conducting, and evaluating quantitative and qualitative research* (6th ed.). Pearson.

Creswell, J. W., & Plano Clark, V. L. (2018). *Designing and conducting mixed methods research* (3rd ed.). Sage.

Daeep, M. I. G., & Counts, C. (2014). *The emerging AI divide in the United States.* https://doi.org//arXiv.2404.11988DOI: 10.48550

Davis, S. R., & Ritchey, K. A. (2023). Helping college students read: An investigation of the SOAR strategy. *College Teaching*, ●●●, 1–8. DOI: 10.1080/87567555.2023.2271619

Feuerriegel, S., Hartmann, J., Janiesch, C., & Zschech, P. (2024). Generative AI. *Business & Information Systems Engineering*, 66(1), 111–126. DOI: 10.1007/s12599-023-00834-7

Fleck, B., Richmond, A. S., Rauer, H. M., Beckman, L., & Lee, A. (2017). Active reading questions as a strategy to support college students' textbook reading. *Scholarship of Teaching and Learning in Psychology*, 3(3), 220–232. DOI: 10.1037/stl0000090

Francis, M. (2017). *The fun of motivation: Crossing the threshold concepts.* Association of College and Research Libraries.

Gomez, A. L., Pecina, E. D., Villanueva, S. A., & Huber, T. (2020). The undeniable relationship between reading comprehension and mathematics performance. *Issues in Educational Research*, 30(4), 1329–1354. http://www.iier.org.au/iier30/gomez.pdf

Gorzycki, M., Howard, P., Allen, D., Desa, G., & Rosengard, E. (2016). An exploration of academic reading proficiency at the university level: A cross-sectional study of 848 undergraduates. *Literacy Research and Instruction*, 55(2), 142–162. DOI: 10.1080/19388071.2015.1133738

Gray, A. C., Steel, A., & Adams, J. (2021). Complementary medicine students' perceptions, perspectives and experiences of learning technologies. A survey conducted in the US and Australia. *European Journal of Integrative Medicine, 42*, 101304-. DOI: 10.1016/j.eujim.2021.101304

Harvey, F., & Anderson, J. (2020). *Empowering students as champions in technology enhances learning (TEL) to improve digital literacies. Handbook for Student Engagement in Higher Education: Theory into practice.* Routledge.

Henderson, M., Selwyn, N., & Aston, R. (2017). What works and why? Student perceptions of "useful" digital technology in university teaching and learning. *Studies in Higher Education (Dorchester-on-Thames), 42*(8), 1567–1579. DOI: 10.1080/03075079.2015.1007946

Hirose, M., & Creswell, J. W. (2023). Applying core quality criteria of mixed methods research to an empirical study. *Journal of Mixed Methods Research*, 17(1), 12–28. DOI: 10.1177/15586898221086346

Huang, Y., Cox, A. M., & Cox, J. (2023). Artificial intelligence in academic library strategy in the United Kingdom and the Mainland of China. *The Journal of Academic Librarianship, 49*(6), 102772-. DOI: 10.1016/j.acalib.2023.102772

Hussain, A., & Ahmad, S. (2023). Mapping the literature on artificial intelligence in academic libraries: A bibliometrics approach. *Science & Technology Libraries*, •••, 1–16. DOI: 10.1080/0194262X.2023.2238198

Jairam, D., Kiewra, K. A., Rogers-Kasson, S., Patterson-Hazley, M., & Marxhausen, K. (2014). SOAR versus SQ3R: A test of two study systems. *Instructional Science*, 42(3), 409–420. DOI: 10.1007/s11251-013-9295-0

Jazlin, E., Jirarat, S., & Na, K. S. (2022). Architecture students' conceptions, experiences, perceptions, and feelings of learning technology use: Phenomenography as an assessment tool. *Education and Information Technologies*, 27(1), 1133–1157. DOI: 10.1007/s10639-021-10654-5

Karp, M. J. M., & Fletcher, J. (2014). Adopting new technologies for student success: A readiness framework. DOI: 10.7916/D8862DMC

Kerr, M. M., & Frese, K. M. (2017). Reading to learn or learning to read? Engaging college students in course readings. *College Teaching*, 65(1), 28–3. DOI: 10.1080/87567555.2016.1222577

Khalil, O., & Khalil, H. (2023). Knowledge sharing and service innovation in academic libraries. *European Conference on Knowledge Management, 24*(1), 635–644. DOI: 10.34190/eckm.24.1.1359

Kotzer, M., Kirby, J. R., & Heggie, L. (2021). Morphological awareness predicts reading comprehension in adults. *Reading Psychology*, 42(3), 302–322. DOI: 10.1080/02702711.2021.1888362

Llewellyn, A. (2020). Innovations in learning and teaching in academic libraries: A literature review. *New Review of Academic Librarianship*, 25(2-4), 129–149. DOI: 10.1080/13614533.2019.1678494

Marty, L., & Teeman, J. (2020). College students and textbooks: Preliminary investigation of gender, international status, and major. *Southern Journal of Business and Ethics*, 12, 75–90.

Mason, W., & Warmington, M. (2024). Academic reading as a grudging act: How do higher education students experience academic reading and what can educators do about it? *Higher Education*, 88(3), 839–856. Advance online publication. DOI: 10.1007/s10734-023-01145-2

Morgan, D. L. (2023). Exploring the use of artificial intelligence for qualitative data analysis: The case of ChatGPT. *International Journal of Qualitative Methods*, 22, 16094069231211248. Advance online publication. DOI: 10.1177/16094069231211248

National Center for Education Statistics. (2024, March 21). *NAEP: National Assessment of Educational Progress*. Retrieved May 11, 2024, from https://nces.ed .gov/ Nationsreportcard

Office of Survey Research & Analysis. (2024). *How to increase response rates*. The George Washington University. https://survey.gwu.edu/how-increase-response-rates

Olaniyi, N. E. E. (2020). Threshold concepts: Designing a format for the flipped classroom as an active learning technique for crossing the threshold. *Research and Practice in Technology Enhanced Learning*, 15(2), 1–15. DOI: 10.1186/s41039-020-0122-3

Paulson, E. J., & Holschuh, J. P. (2018). College Reading. In Flippo, R. F. (Ed.), *Handbook of college reading and study strategy research* (3rd ed.). Routledge. DOI: 10.4324/9781315629810-3

Sedoti, O., Gelles-Watnick, R., Faverio, M., Atske, S., Radde, K., & Park, E. (2024, April 25). *Mobile fact sheet*. Pew Research Center. https://www.pewresearch.org/internet /fact-sheet/mobile/

Strydom, F., Kuh, G. D., & Loots, S. (Eds.). (2017). *Engaging student: Using evidence to promote student success*. UJ Press. DOI: 10.18820/9781928424093

Suherman, N., Rahmadani, A., & Vidákovich, T. (1796). Mujib, Fitria, N., Nur Islam, S. P., Rofi'uddin Addarojat, M., & Priadi, M. (2021). SQ3R method assisted by ethnomathematics-oriented student worksheet: The impact of mathematical concepts understanding. *Journal of Physics: Conference Series*, (1). Advance online publication. DOI: 10.1088/1742-6596/1796/1/012059

Compilation of References

Abayomi, O. W., Adenekan, F. N., Abayomi, A. O., Ajayi, T. A., & Aderonke, A. O. (2021). *Awareness and Perception of the Artificial Intelligence in the Management of University Libraries in Nigeria. Journal of Interlibrary Loan.* Document Delivery & Electronic Reserve., DOI: 10.1080/1072303X.2021.19186

Abbadia, J. (2023) Exploring the role of AI in academic research. Retrieved from https://mindthegraph.com/blog/ai-in-academic-research/

Abd Razak, S. N. A., Noor, W. N. B. W. M., & Jusoh, Y. H. M. (2021). Embracing digital economy: Drivers, barriers and factors affecting digital transformation of accounting professionals. *International Journal of Advanced Research in Economics and Finance*, 3(3), 63–71.

Abramovich, S., Schunn, C., & Higashi, R. M. (2013). Are badges useful in education?: It depends upon the type of badge and expertise of learner. *Educational Technology Research and Development*, 61(2), 217–232. DOI: 10.1007/s11423-013-9289-2

Acemoglu, D., & Restrepo, P. (2017). Robots and jobs: Evidence from U.S. labour markets. *The American Economic Review*, 107(5), 1608–1638. https://www.nber.org/system/files/working_papers/w23285/w23285.pdf

Adetayo, A. J. (2023a). ChatGPT and Librarians for Reference Consultations. *Internet Reference Services Quarterly*, 27(3), 131–147. Advance online publication. DOI: 10.1080/10875301.2023.2203681

Adetayo, A. J. (2023b). Conversational assistants in academic libraries: Enhancing reference services through Bing Chat. *Library Hi Tech News*. Advance online publication. DOI: 10.1108/LHTN-08-2023-0142

Adetayo, A. J., Adekunmisi, S. R., Otonekwu, F. O., & Adesina, O. F. (2023). The role of academic libraries in facilitating friendships among students. *IFLA Journal*, 49(4), 694–703. Advance online publication. DOI: 10.1177/03400352231191540

Adetayo, A. J., & Gbotoso, A. O. (2023). Outreach Programs Revitalizing the Patronage of Public Libraries in Nigeria. *Portal (Baltimore, Md.)*, 23(2), 231–247. DOI: 10.1353/pla.2023.0017

Affum, M. Q., & Dwomoh, O. K. (2023). Investigating the Potential Impact of Artificial Intelligence in Librarianship. *Library Philosophy and Practice*, 1-12.

Ahaley, S. S., Pandey, A., Juneja, S. K., Gupta, T. S., & Vijayakumar, S. (2023). ChatGPT in medical writing: A game-changer or a gimmick? *Perspectives in Clinical Research*, •••, 10–4103. DOI: 10.4103/picr.picr_167_23

AIstraight. (2023, June 20). *Will AI Replace Librarians? Uncovering the Positive Impacts of AI*. https://aistraight.com/ai-replace-librarians/

Aiyeblehin, J. A., Onyam, I. D., & Akpom, C. C. (2018). Creating Makerspaces in Nigerian Public Libraries as a Strategy for Attaining National Integration and Development. *International Journal of Knowledge Content Development & Technology*, 8(4), 19–31. DOI: 10.5865/IJKCT.2018.8.4.019

Ajakaye, J. E., & Ogunniyi, S. O. (2021). 21st-Century multidisciplinary collaboration in research in library. *Library Philosophy and Practice (e-journal)*. 6228. https://digitalcommons.unl.edu/libphilprac/6228

Ajani, Y. A., Adeyinka, T., Dunmade, A. O., & Adeniran, C. O. (2022). Information Professionals of the Future and their Prospects in the Era of Fourth Industrial Revolution: The Need for Transformative Potential in Nigeria. *Mousaion*, 40(3). Advance online publication. DOI: 10.25159/2663-659X/12219

ALA. (2019). *Privacy and Confidentiality Q&A*. https://www.ala.org/advocacy/intfreedom/privacyconfidentialityqa

Aldridge, D. (2019). Reading, engagement, and higher education. *Higher Education Research & Development*, 38(1), 38–50. DOI: 10.1080/07294360.2018.1534804

Ali, M., Naeem, F., Kaddoum, G., & Hossain, E. (2022). Metaverse Communications, Networking, Security, and Applications: Research Issues, State-of-the-Art, and Future Directions. *arXiv preprint arXiv:2212.13993*.

Alojaiman, B. (2023). Technological Modernizations in the Industry 5.0 Era: A Descriptive Analysis and Future Research Directions. *Processes (Basel, Switzerland)*, 11(5), 1318. DOI: 10.3390/pr11051318

Altay, S., Berriche, M., Heuer, H., Farkas, J., & Rathje, S. (2023). A survey of expert views on misinformation: Definitions, determinants, solutions, and future of the field. *Harvard Kennedy School (HKS). Misinformation Review*, 4(4). Advance online publication. DOI: 10.37016/mr-2020-119

American Libraries Magazine. (2011, May 25). *The Digital Revolution and the Transformation of Libraries*. https://americanlibrariesmagazine.org/2011/05/25/the-digital-revolution-and-the-transformation-of-libraries/

Anderson, J. R., Corbett, A. T., Koedinger, K. R., & Pelletier, R. (1997). K. R., & Pelletier, R. (1995). Cognitive tutors: Lessons learned. *Journal of the Learning Sciences*, 4(2), 167–207. DOI: 10.1207/s15327809jls0402_2

Ankel, S. (2023, May 17). *Professor fails half his class after ChatGPT falsely said it wrote their papers*. Business Insider. https://www.businessinsider.com/professor-fails-students-after-chatgpt-falsely-said-it-wrote-papers-2023-5

Artificial intelligence draft policies (2023). Institutional Effectiveness and Grant Development. Austin Community College. https://offices.austincc.edu/institutional-effectiveness-and-grant-development/master-syllabi/artificial-intelligence-draft-policies/

Ashikuzzaman. (2020, September 22). *Library Collection Development Process*. https://www.lisedunetwork.com/collection-development-process/

Ask.com. (2023, October 17). *Chatbot vs Human Interaction: The Pros and Cons of AI-Powered Conversations*. https://www.ask.com/news/chatbot-vs-human-interaction-pros-cons-ai-powered-conversations

Association of College & Research Libraries. (2015, February 2). *Framework for information literacy*. American Library Association. https://www.ala.org/acrl/standards/ilframework

Association of College & Research Libraries. (2018). *Framework for Information Literacy for Higher Education*. American Library Association.

Association of College and Research Libraries. (2016). *Framework for information literacy for higher education.* https://www.ala.org/acrl/standards/ilframework

Awosanya, O. D., Harris, A., Creecy, A., Qiao, X., Toepp, A. J., McCune, T., Kacena, M. A., & Ozanne, M. V. (2024). The utility of AI in writing a scientific review article on the impacts of COVID-19 on musculoskeletal health. *Current Osteoporosis Reports*. Advance online publication. DOI: 10.1007/s11914-023-00855-x PMID: 38216806

Awoyemi, R. R. (2023). Library Engagement With Emerging Technologies in Research and Learning. *Handbook of Research on Facilitating Collaborative Learning Through Digital Content and Learning Technologies*, 400-418.

Babbie, E. R. 91998). The practice of social research (8ᵗʰ ed). Belmont: Wadsworth Publishing Co., Bakare-Fatungase, O. D., Adejuwon, F. E & Idowu-Davies, T. O. (2024). Integrating artificial intelligence in education for sustainable development. In *Using Traditional Design Methods to Enhance AI-Driven Decision Making* (pp. 231-245). IGI Global.

Bahdanau, D., Cho, K., & Bengio, Y. (2014). Neural machine translation by jointly learning to align and translate. *arXiv preprint arXiv:1409.0473*.

Bakare-Fatungase, O. D. (2024). Staying ahead of the digital curve: librarians as panacea of the g-ai conundrum [Powerpoint Slides]. Institute of African Studies, Carleton University, https://carleton.ca/qes/2024/presentation-by-dr-oluwabunmi -bakare-fatungase-at-royal-military-college-kingston/

Bakare-Fatungase, O. D., Adejuwon, F. E., & Idowu-Davies, T. O. (2024). Integrating artificial intelligence in education for sustainable development. In *Using Traditional Design Methods to Enhance AI-Driven Decision Making* (pp. 231–245). IGI Global. DOI: 10.4018/979-8-3693-0639-0.ch010

Bakare, O. D., Oladokun, T., Quadri, G. O., & Idowu-Davies, T. O. (2023). ChatGPT and other generative artificial intelligence (AI) tools in teaching and learning as integrative pathways to contemporary university education. In *Creative AI Tools and Ethical Implications in Teaching and Learning* (pp. 168–180). IGI Global. DOI: 10.4018/979-8-3693-0205-7.ch009

Baker, R. S., D'Mello, S. K., Rodrigo, M. M. T., & Graesser, A. C. (2010). Better to be frustrated than bored: The incidence, persistence, and impact of learners' cognitive–affective states during interactions with three different computer-based learning environments. *International Journal of Human-Computer Studies*, 68(4), 223–241. DOI: 10.1016/j.ijhcs.2009.12.003

Balleste, R. (2002). The future of artificial intelligence in your virtual libraries. *Computers in Libraries*, 22(9), 10–15.

Ballesteros, S., Prieto, A., Mayas, J., Toril, P., Pita, C., Ponce de Leon, L., & Waterworth, J. (2014). Brain training with non-action video games enhances aspects of cognition in older adults: A randomized controlled trial. *Frontiers in Aging Neuroscience*, 6, 277. DOI: 10.3389/fnagi.2014.00277 PMID: 25352805

Bansal, A., Panchal, T., Jabeen, F., Mangla, S. K., & Singh, G. (2023). A study of human resource digital transformation (HRDT): A phenomenon of innovation capability led by digital and individual factors. *Journal of Business Research*, 157, 113611. DOI: 10.1016/j.jbusres.2022.113611

Baro, E. E., Obaro, O. G., & Aduba, E. D. (2019). An assessment of digital literacy skills and knowledge-based competencies among librarians working in university libraries in Africa. *Digital Library Perspectives*, 35(3/4), 172–192. DOI: 10.1108/ DLP-04-2019-0013

Barzilai, S., & Ka'adan, I. (2017). Learning to integrate divergent information sources: The interplay of epistemic cognition and epistemic metacognition. *Metacognition and Learning*, 12(2), 193–232. DOI: 10.1007/s11409-016-9165-7

Basak, R., Paul, P., Kar, S., Molla, I. H., & Chatterjee, P. (2024). The Future of Libraries with AI: Envisioning the Evolving Role of Libraries in the AI Era. In Senthilkumar, K. R. (Ed.), *AI-Assisted Library Reconstruction* (pp. 34–57). IGI Global., DOI: 10.4018/979-8-3693-2782-1.ch003

Batchelor, O. (2017). Getting out the truth: The role of libraries in the fight against fake news. *RSR. Reference Services Review*, 45(2), 143–148. DOI: 10.1108/RSR-03-2017-0006

Bateman, D., & Cline, J. (2019). *Special Education Leadership*. Routledge. DOI: 10.4324/9781351201353

Becker, K. L., Safa, R., & Becker, K. M. (2023). High-priced textbooks' impact on community college student success. *Community College Review*, 51(1), 128–141. DOI: 10.1177/00915521221125898

Belabbes, M. A., Ruthven, I., Moshfeghi, Y., & Rasmussen Pennington, D. (2023). Information overload: A concept analysis. *The Journal of Documentation*, 79(1), 144–159. DOI: 10.1108/JD-06-2021-0118

Bender, E. M., Gebru, T., McMillan-Major, A., & Shmitchell, S. (2021, March). On the dangers of stochastic parrots: Can language models be too big? In *Proceedings of the 2021 ACM Conference on Fairness, Accountability, and Transparency* (pp. 610-623). DOI: 10.1145/3442188.3445922

Benjamin, R. G. (2023). High-tech versus low tech: Comparing approaches to increase college student reading compliance and engagement. *Scholarship of Teaching and Learning in Psychology*. Advance online publication. DOI: 10.1037/stl0000366

Beukelman, D., & Light, J. (2020). Augmentative and alternative communication: Supporting children and adults with complex communication needs.

Bhattacharjee, A., & Liu, H. (2024). Fighting fire with fire: Can ChatGPT detect AI-generated text? *SIGKDD Explorations*, 25(2), 14–21. DOI: 10.1145/3655103.3655106

Biden, J. (2023, October 30). *Executive order on the safe, secure, and trustworthy development and use of artificial intelligence*. The White House. https://www.whitehouse.gov/ briefing-room/presidential-actions/2023/10/30/executive-order-on-the-safe-secure-and-trustworthy-development-and-use-of-artificial-intelligence/

Bieraugel, M., & Neill, S. (2017). Ascending Bloom's Pyramid: Fostering Student Creativity and Innovation in Academic Library Spaces. *College & Research Libraries*, 78(1), 35–52. DOI: 10.5860/crl.78.1.35

Bingham, T. J., Wirjapranata, J., & Bartley, A. (2017). Building resilience and resourcefulness: The evolution of an academic and information literacy strategy for first year social work students. *Information and Learning Science*, 118(7–8), 433–446. DOI: 10.1108/ILS-05-2017-0046

Blackman, R., & Ammanath, B. (2022, June 20). *Building Transparency into AI Projects*. https://hbr.org/2022/06/building-transparency-into-ai-projects

Blanco-Gonzalez, A., Cabezon, A., Seco-Gonzalez, A., Conde-Torres, D., Antelo-Riveiro, P., Pineiro, A., & Garcia-Fandino, R. (2023). The role of AI in drug discovery: Challenges, opportunities, and strategies. *Pharmaceuticals (Basel, Switzerland)*, 16(6), 891. DOI: 10.3390/ph16060891 PMID: 37375838

Bodaghi, N. B., Cheong, L. S., & Zainab, A. N. (2016). Librarians Empathy: Visually Impaired Students' Experiences Towards Inclusion and Sense of Belonging in an Academic Library. *Journal of Academic Librarianship*, 42(1), 87–96. DOI: 10.1016/j.acalib.2015.11.003

Borenstein, J., Grodzinsky, F. S., Howard, A., Miller, K. W., & Wolf, M. J. (2021). AI ethics: A long history and a recent burst of attention. *Computer*, 53(1), 96–102. https://doi.ieeecomputersociety.org/10.1109/MC.2020.3034950. DOI: 10.1109/MC.2020.3034950

Borg, J., Larsson, S., Östergren, P. O., Rahman, A. A., Bari, N., & Khan, A. N. (2012). Assistive technology use and human rights enjoyment: A cross-sectional study in Bangladesh. *BMC International Health and Human Rights*, 12(1), 1–11. DOI: 10.1186/1472-698X-12-18 PMID: 22992413

Borji, A. (2023). A categorical archive of ChatGPT failures. *arXiv preprint arXiv:2302.03494*. DOI: 10.21203/rs.3.rs-2895792/v1

Bousba, Y., & Arya, V. (2022). Let's connect in metaverse. Brand's new destination to increase consumers' affective brand engagement & their satisfaction and advocacy. *Journal of Content. Community & Communication*, 15(8), 276–293.

Braten, I., Ferguson, L. E., Stromso, H. I., & Anmarkrud, O. (2014). Students working with multiple conflicting documents on a scientific issue: Relations between epistemic cognition while reading and sourcing and argumentation in essays. *The British Journal of Educational Psychology*, 84(1), 58–85. DOI: 10.1111/bjep.12005 PMID: 24547754

Breeding, M. (2022). Managing Technology. In Hirsh, S. (Ed.), *Information services today* (3rd ed., pp. 342–357). Rowman & Littlefield.

Britannica (2024). "Definition and meaning of artificial intelligence". https://www.britannica.com/technology/artificial-intelligence

Britannica (2024). Definition and meaning of artificial intelligence. Available at https://www.britannica.com/technology/artificial-intelligence

Brophy, P. (2007). Communicating the library: Librarians and faculty in dialogue. *Library Management*, 28(8–9), 515–523. DOI: 10.1108/01435120710837792

Brown, T., Mann, B., Ryder, N., Subbiah, M., Kaplan, J. D., Dhariwal, P., & Amodei, D. (2020). Language models are few-shot learners. *Advances in Neural Information Processing Systems*, 33, 1877–1901.

Brundy, C. (2015). Academic libraries and innovation: A literature review. *Journal of Library Innovation*, 6(1), 22–39.

Buchanan, J., Hill, S., & Shapoval, O. (2024). ChatGPT hallucinates non-existent citations: Evidence from economics. *The American Economist*, 69(1), 80–87. DOI: 10.1177/05694345231218454

Buholayka, M., Zouabi, R., & Tadinada, A. (2023). The readiness of ChatGPT to write scientific case reports independently: A comparative evaluation between human and artificial intelligence. *Cureus*, 15(5). PMID: 37378091

Buolamwini, J., & Gebru, T. (2018, January). Gender shades: Intersectional accuracy disparities in commercial gender classification. In Conference on fairness, accountability and transparency (pp. 77-91). PMLR.Noble, S. U. (2018). Algorithms of oppression: How search engines reinforce racism. NYU Press.

Buraimo, O., Madukoma, E., Oduwole, A. A., & Olusanya, F. O. (2023). Collection development policy and utilization of academic library resources in Nigeria. *Library and Information Perspectives and Research*, 5(2), 28–40. DOI: 10.47524/lipr.v5i2.29

Burnette, M. (2017). Tacit knowledge sharing among library colleagues: A pilot study. *RSR. Reference Services Review*, 45(3), 382–397. DOI: 10.1108/RSR-11-2016-0082

Caines, A. (n.d.). *Close reading the terms of service*. AI Pedagogy Project: metaLAB (at) Harvard. https://aipedagogy.org/assignment/close-reading-the-tos/

Callaghan, C. (2023). Revisiting how scientific research drives technological change: The Fifth Industrial Revolution. *South African Journal of Science*, 119(7/8). Advance online publication. DOI: 10.17159/sajs.2023/15556

Cassidy, C. (2023). Australian universities to return to 'pen and paper' exams after students caught using AI to write essays. *The Guardian, 10*.

Cave, S., & Dihal, K. (2019). *Hopes and fears for intelligent machines in fiction and reality*. University of Cambridge Repository. https://www.repository.cam.ac.uk/bitstream/handle/1810/288940/ACCEPTED%20VERSION%20-%20Cave%20and%20Dihal%20-%20Hopes%20and%20Fears%20v3.docx?sequence=1

Cave, S., Craig, C., Dihal, K., Dillon, S., Montgomery, J., Singler, B., & Taylor, L. (2018). *Portrayals and perceptions of AI and why they matter*. Royal Society https://royalsociety.org/-/media/policy/projects/ai-narratives/AI-narratives-workshop-findings.pdf

Celik, I. (2023). Exploring the determinants of artificial intelligence (AI) literacy: Digital divide, computational thinking, cognitive absorption. *Telematics and Informatics*, 83, 102026. DOI: 10.1016/j.tele.2023.102026

Cesnik, B. (2001). Digital Libraries. *Yearbook of Medical Informatics*, 10(01), 147–150. DOI: 10.1055/s-0038-1638099 PMID: 27701600

Chakraborty, S., Bedi, A. S., Zhu, S., An, B., Manocha, D., & Huang, F. (2023). On the possibilities of AI-generated text detection. *arXiv preprint arXiv:2304.04736*.

Chan, C. K., & Colloton, T. (2024). *Generative AI in higher education*. Directory of Open Access Books. https://directory.doabooks.org/handle/20.500.12854/135718

Chemulwo, M. J., & Sirorei, E. C. (2019). Managing and adapting library information services for future users: Applying artificial intelligence in libraries. In Osuigwe, N. E. (Ed.), *Managing and adapting library information services for future users* (pp. 145–164). IGI Global., DOI: 10.4018/978-1-7998-1116-9.ch009

Chen, G., Davis, D., Hauff, C., & Houben, G. J. (2016, April). Learning transfer: Does it take place in MOOCs? An investigation into the uptake of functional programming in practice. In *Proceedings of the Third(2016) ACM Conference on Learning @ Scale* (pp. 409-418).

Cheng, K., & Wu, H. (2024). Policy framework for the utilization of generative AI. *Critical Care*, 28(1), 128. DOI: 10.1186/s13054-024-04917-z PMID: 38637898

Chen, Q., Allot, A., & Lu, Z. (2021). LitCovid: An open database of COVID-19 literature. *Nucleic Acids Research*, 49(D1), D1534–D1540. DOI: 10.1093/nar/gkaa952 PMID: 33166392

Chen, T. Y., Chiu, Y. C., Bi, N., & Tsai, R. T. H. (2021). Multi-Modal Chatbot in Intelligent Manufacturing. *IEEE Access : Practical Innovations, Open Solutions*, 9, 82118–82129. DOI: 10.1109/ACCESS.2021.3083518

Chen, X. (2023). ChatGPT and Its Possible Impact on Library Reference Services. *Internet Reference Services Quarterly*, 27(2), 121–129. Advance online publication. DOI: 10.1080/10875301.2023.2181262

Choice 360. (2023, May 15). *"Do We Need Librarians Now that We Have ChatGPT?"*. https://www.choice360.org/libtech-insight/do-we-need-librarians-now-that-we-have-chatgpt/

Choithani, T., Chowdhury, A., Patel, S., Patel, P., Patel, D., & Shah, M. (2022). A comprehensive study of artificial intelligence and cybersecurity on Bitcoin, crypto currency and banking system. *Annals of Data Science*, ●●●, 1–33.

Christensen, H., Cunningham, S. P., Fox, C., Green, P. D., & Hain, T. (2012, September). A comparative study of adaptive, automatic recognition of disordered speech. In *Interspeech* (pp. 1776-1779). DOI: 10.21437/Interspeech.2012-484

Christian, B. (2020). *The alignment problem: Machine learning and human values.* W. W. Norton & Company.

Chukwu, S. A. J., Emezie, N., Nwaohiri, N. M., Haco-Obasi, F. C., Obiano, D. C., & Bernard, I. I. (2021). "Information literacy: Academic librarians as Stakeholders in the learning process: with focus on federal university of technology, owerri". *Library Philosophy and Practice*https://digitalcommons.unl.edu/cgi/viewcontent.cgi?article=11762&context=libphilprac

Chukwu, S. A. J., Emezie, N., Nwaohiri, N. M., Haco-Obasi, F. C., Obiano, D. C., & Bernard, I. I. (2021). Information Literacy: Academic Librarians as Stakeholders in the Learning Process: with Focus on Federal University of Technology, Owerri". *Library Philosophy and Practice (e-journal)*. Available at https://digitalcommons.unl.edu/cgi/viewcontent.cgi?article=11762&context=libphilprac

Chung, C., & Huang, Y. (2022). The innovation of the AI and Big Data Mail Processing System. *Journal of Research & Method in Education*, 12(1), 1–8. DOI: 10.31031/COJEC.2022.02.000536

Ciarli, T., Kenney, M., Massini, S., & Piscitello, L. (2021). Digital technologies, innovation, and skills: Emerging trajectories and challenges. *Research Policy*, 50(7), 104289. DOI: 10.1016/j.respol.2021.104289

Claus, A. M., & Wiese, B. S. (2019). Development and test of a model of interdisciplinary competencies. *European Journal of Work and Organizational Psychology*, 28(2), 191–205. DOI: 10.1080/1359432X.2019.1567491

Colbjornsen, T., Brenna, B., & Edquist, S. (2022). Curating collections in LAMs. In Rasmussen, C. H., Rydbeck, K., & Larsen, H. (Eds.), *Libraries, Archives, and Museums in Transition* (pp. 87–99). Routledge., DOI: 10.4324/9781003188834-9

College Board. (2004). *Sample activity: Analyzing the narrative from the Pre-AP workshop Pre-AP: Strategies in English – writing tactics using SOAPSTone.* College Entrance Examination Board. https://secure-media.collegeboard.org/apc/ap04_preap_11_eng_soa_35968.pdf

Collins, M. D., Somerville, M. M., Pelsinsky, N., & Wood, A. (2014). Working better together: Library, publisher, and vendor perspectives. In B. R. Bernhardt, L. H. Hinds, & K. P. Strauch (Eds.), *Too much is not enough: Charleston conference proceedings, 2013* (pp. 312–318). Purdue University Press.

Communication Committee, T. A. C. R. L. S.ACRL Scholarly Communication Committee. (2003). SCHOLARLY COMMUNICATION: Principles and strategies for the reform of scholarly communication: Issues related to the formal system of scholarly communication. *College & Research Libraries News*, 64(8), 526–547. DOI: 10.5860/crln.64.8.526

Congressional Research Service. (2023, September 29). Generative artificial intelligence and copyright law. *CRS Reports.* https://crsreports.congress.gov/product/pdf/LSB/ LSB10922

Cornelius, F. P., van Rensburg, S. K. J., & Kader, S. (2023). Cyber Security Risks in Emerging South African Smart Cities: Towards a Cyber Security Framework. *Perspectives on Global Development and Technology*, 22(1-2), 107–141. DOI: 10.1163/15691497-12341654

Cotton, D. R., Cotton, P. A., & Shipway, J. R. (2024). Chatting and Cheating: Ensuring academic integrity in the era of ChatGPT. *Innovations in Education and Teaching International*, 61(2), 228–239. DOI: 10.1080/14703297.2023.2190148

Cox, A. (2022). How artificial intelligence might change academic library work: Applying the competencies literature and the theory of the professions. *Journal of the Association for Information Science and Technology*, 74(3), 367–380. DOI: 10.1002/asi.24635

Cox, A. M., & Mazumdar, S. (2022). Defining artificial intelligence for librarians. *Journal of Librarianship and Information Science*, 1–11. DOI: 10.1177/09610006221142029

Cox, A. M., Pinfield, S., & Rutter, S. (2019). The intelligent library: Thought leaders' views on the likely impact of artificial intelligence on academic libraries. *Library Hi Tech*, 37(3), 418–435. DOI: 10.1108/LHT-08-2018-0105

Cox, C., & Tzoc, E. (2023). ChatGPT: Implications for academic libraries. *College & Research Libraries News*, 84(3), 99. DOI: 10.5860/crln.84.3.99

Creswell, J. W., & Guetterman, T. C. (2019). *Educational research: Planning, conducting, and evaluating quantitative and qualitative research* (6th ed.). Pearson.

Creswell, J. W., & Plano Clark, V. L. (2018). *Designing and conducting mixed methods research* (3rd ed.). Sage.

Critical Thinking Sectets. (2024). *Critical Thinking and Artificial Intelligence*. https://criticalthinkingsecrets.com/critical-thinking-and-artificial-intelligence/

Cummings, L. (2024). *How to use rhetoric to repurpose content with ChatGPT*. iSophist. https://www.isophist.com/p/how-to-use-rhetoric-to-repurpose?r=2519k4&utm_campaign=post&utm_medium=web

D'Agostino, S. (2023, March 21). GPT-4 is here. But most faculty lack AI policies. *Inside Higher Ed*.https://www.insidehighered.com/news/2023/03/22/gpt-4-here-most-faculty-lack-ai-policies

Daeep, M. I. G., & Counts, C. (2014). *The emerging AI divide in the United States*. https://doi.org//arXiv.2404.11988DOI: 10.48550

Dalsgaard, C., & Ryberg, T. (2023). A theoretical framework for digital learning spaces: Learning in individual spaces, working groups, communities of interest, and open connections. *Research in Learning Technology*, 31, ●●●. https://www.researchgate.net/publication/374396037_A_theoretical_framework_for_digital_learning_spaces_learning_in_individual_spaces_working_groups_communities_of_interest_and_open_connections. DOI: 10.25304/rlt.v31.3084

Das, A., Malayiya, S., & Singh, M. (2023). The impact of ai-driven personalization on learners' performance. *International Journal on Computer Science and Engineering*, 11(08), 15–22. https://www.researchgate.net/publication/373424876_The _Impact_of_AI-Driven_Personalization_on_Learners'_Performance

Davenport, T. H., & Mittal, N. (2022). "How generative AI is changing creative work". *Harvard Business Review. Available at* https://hbr.org/2022/11/how-generative -ai-is-changing-creative-work

Davenport, T. H., & Mittal, N. (2022). "How generative AI is changing creative work". *Harvard Business Review.* https://hbr.org/2022/11/how-generative-ai-is -changing-creative-work

Davenport, T. H., & Ronanki, R. (2018). Artificial intelligence for the real world. *Harvard Business Review*, 96(1), 108–116.

Davis, S. R., & Ritchey, K. A. (2023). Helping college students read: An investigation of the SOAR strategy. *College Teaching*, •••, 1–8. DOI: 10.1080/87567555.2023.2271619

De Cremer, D., Morini Bianzino, N., & Falk, B. (2023). How generative AI could disrupt creative work. *Harvard Business Review*. https://hbr.org/2023/04/how -generative-ai-could-disrupt-creative-work

De Felice, F., Petrillo, A., Iovine, G., Salzano, C., & Baffo, I. (2023). How Does the Metaverse Shape Education? A Systematic Literature Review. *Applied Sciences (Basel, Switzerland)*, 13(9), 5682. DOI: 10.3390/app13095682

De Paor, S., & Heravi, B. (2020). Information literacy and fake news: How the field of librarianship can help combat the epidemic of fake news. *Journal of Academic Librarianship*, 46(5), 102218. DOI: 10.1016/j.acalib.2020.102218

Dia, C. P., & Ke, F. (2022). "Educational applications of artificial intelligence in simulation-based learning: A systematic mapping review". *Computer and Education: Artificial Intelligence*, 3:100087.https://www.sciencedirect.com/science/article/pii/ S2666920X2200042X?via%3Dihub

Dias, R., & Torkamani, A. (2019). Artificial intelligence in clinical and genomic diagnostics. *Genome Medicine*, 11(1), 70. Advance online publication. DOI: 10.1186/ s13073-019-0689-8 PMID: 31744524

Dobrev, D. (2018). The IQ of artificial intelligence. *arXiv preprint arXiv:1806.04915*.

Doyal, A. S., Sender, D., Nanda, M., & Serrano, R. A. (2023). ChatGPT and artificial intelligence in medical writing: Concerns and ethical considerations. *Cureus*, 15(8). PMID: 37692694

Dudden, R. F., & Protzko, S. L. (2011). The Systematic Review Team: Contributions of the Health Sciences Librarian. *Medical Reference Services Quarterly*, 30(3), 301–315. DOI: 10.1080/02763869.2011.590425 PMID: 21800987

Dusseault, B. (2024, March). *New state AI policies released: Signs point to inconsistency and fragmentation – Center on Reinventing Public Education*. Center on Reinventing Public Education. https://crpe.org/new-state-ai-policies-released-inconsistency-and-fragmentation/

Dwivedi, Y. K., Hughes, L., Baabdullah, A. M., Ribeiro-Navarrete, S., Giannakis, M., Al-Debei, M. M., Dennehy, D., Metri, B., Buhalis, D., Cheung, C. M. K., Conboy, K., Doyle, R., Dubey, R., Dutot, V., Felix, R., Goyal, D. P., Gustafsson, A., Hinsch, C., Jebabli, I., & Wamba, S. F. (2022). Metaverse beyond the hype: Multidisciplinary perspectives on emerging challenges, opportunities, and agenda for research, practice and policy. *International Journal of Information Management*, 66, 102542. DOI: 10.1016/j.ijinfomgt.2022.102542

Dwivedi, Y. K., Kshetri, N., Hughes, L., Slade, E. L., Jeyaraj, A., Kar, A. K., Baabdullah, A. M., Koohang, A., Raghavan, V., Ahuja, M., Albanna, H., Albashrawi, M. A., Al-Busaidi, A. S., Balakrishnan, J., Barlette, Y., Basu, S., Bose, I., Brooks, L., Buhalis, D., & Wright, R. (2023). Opinion Paper: So what if ChatGPT wrote it? Multidisciplinary perspectives on opportunities, challenges and implications of generative conversational AI for research, practice and policy. *International Journal of Information Management*, 71, 102642. Advance online publication. DOI: 10.1016/j.ijinfomgt.2023.102642

Ecarnot, F., Seronde, M. F., Chopard, R., Schiele, F., & Meneveau, N. J. E. G. M. (2015). Writing a scientific article: A step-by-step guide for beginners. *European Geriatric Medicine*, 6(6), 573–579. DOI: 10.1016/j.eurger.2015.08.005

Egelhofer, J. L., & Lecheler, S. (2019). Fake news as a two-dimensional phenomenon: A Frame work and research agenda. *Annals of the International Communication Association*, 43(2), 97–116. DOI: 10.1080/23808985.2019.1602782

El-Abbadi, M. (n.d.). *Library of Alexandria*. Retrieved February 10, 2024, from https://www.britannica.com/topic/Library-of-Alexandria

Elsahar, Y., Hu, S., Bouazza-Marouf, K., Kerr, D., & Mansor, A. (2019). Augmentative and Alternative Communication (AAC) Advances: A Review of Configurations for Speech Disabled Individuals.

Fair Use Index. (2023, November). *U.S. Copyright Office*. https://www.copyright.gov/fair-use/

Fallis, D. (2007). Information ethics for twenty-first century library professionals. *Library Hi Tech*, 25(1), 23–36. DOI: 10.1108/07378830710735830

Ferrara, E. (2024). Fairness and bias in artificial intelligence: A brief survey of sources, impacts, and mitigation strategies. *Sci*, 6(1), 3. DOI: 10.3390/sci6010003

Feuerriegel, S., Hartmann, J., Janiesch, C., & Zschech, P. (2024). Generative ai. *Business & Information Systems Engineering*, 66(1), 111–126. DOI: 10.1007/s12599-023-00834-7

Figueroa, M., & Shawgo, K. (2022). "You can't read your way out of racism": Creating anti-racist action out of education in an academic library. *RSR. Reference Services Review*, 50(1), 25–39. DOI: 10.1108/RSR-06-2021-0025

Fitria, T. N. (2021). Grammarly as AI-powered English writing assistant: Students' alternative for writing English. *Metathesis: Journal of English Language, Literature, and Teaching*, 5(1), 65–78. DOI: 10.31002/metathesis.v5i1.3519

Flanagin, A., Kendall-Taylor, J., & Bibbins-Domingo, K. (2023). Guidance for authors, peer reviewers, and editors on use of AI, language models, and chatbots. *Journal of the American Medical Association*, 330(8), 702. DOI: 10.1001/jama.2023.12500 PMID: 37498593

Fleck, B., Richmond, A. S., Rauer, H. M., Beckman, L., & Lee, A. (2017). Active reading questions as a strategy to support college students' textbook reading. *Scholarship of Teaching and Learning in Psychology*, 3(3), 220–232. DOI: 10.1037/stl0000090

Fleetwood, D. (2023). What is Research? Definition, methods, types & examples. Retrieved From https://www.questionpro.com/blog/what-is-research/

Fokina, M. (2024, January 23). The Future of Chatbots: 80+ Chatbot. *Stat*, 2024, •••. https://www.tidio.com/blog/chatbot-statistics/

Fozrok. (2023, August 8). *The art of ChatGPT prompts with CISCO structure*. Reddit. https://www.reddit.com/r/ChatGPTPromptGenius/comments/15lenfo/the_art_of_chatgpt_prompts_with_cisco_structure/

Francis, M. (2017). *The fun of motivation: Crossing the threshold concepts*. Association of College and Research Libraries.

Fricke, S. (2018). Semantic Scholar. *Journal of the Medical Library Association: JMLA*, 106(1), 145. DOI: 10.5195/jmla.2018.280

Gabriel, A. (2019). Artificial intelligence in scholarly communications: An elsevier case study. *Information Services & Use*, 39(4), 319–333. DOI: 10.3233/ISU-190063

Gadekallu, T. R., Huynh-The, T., Wang, W., Yenduri, G., Ranaweera, P., Pham, Q. V., . . . Liyanage, M. (2022). Blockchain for the metaverse: A review. *arXiv preprint arXiv:2203.09738*.

Gannon, K. (2024). *Guidance for syllabus statements on the sse of AI tools*. Chicago Center for Teaching and Learning. https://teaching.uchicago.edu/sites/default/files/2023-09/CCTL_AI%20Syllabus%20Statements.pdf

Gao, C. A., Howard, F. M., Markov, N. S., Dyer, E. C., Ramesh, S., Luo, Y., & Pearson, A. T. (2022). Comparing scientific abstracts generated by ChatGPT to original abstracts using an artificial intelligence output detector, plagiarism detector, and blinded human reviewers. BioRxiv, *2022-12* DOI: 10.1101/2022.12.23.521610

Gao, Z., Cheah, J. H., Lim, X. J., & Luo, X. (2024). Enhancing academic performance of business students using generative AI: An interactive-constructive-active-passive self-determination perspective. *International Journal of Management Education*, 22(2), 100958. https://www.sciencedirect.com/science/article/abs/pii/S1472811724000296. DOI: 10.1016/j.ijme.2024.100958

Garoogian, R. (1991). Librarian/patron confidentiality: An ethical challenge. *Library Trends*, 4(2), 216–233. https://www.ideals.illinois.edu/bitstream/handle/2142/7774/librarytrendsv40i2d_opt.pdf?sequ

Gates, B. (2023, March 21). *The age of AI has begun*. GatesNotes. https://www.gatesnotes.com/The-Age-of-AI-Has-Begun

Gecko. (2023). *Human versus Chatbot - what works best?* https://www.geckoengage.com/articles/human-versus-chatbot-what-works-best/

Getahun, H. (2022). After an AI Bot Wrote a Scientific Paper on Itself, the Researcher behind the Experiment Says She Hopes She Didn't Open a "Pandora's Box". *Business Insider Nederland, 9*.

Ghosal, T., Verma, R., Ekbal, A., Saha, S., & Bhattacharyya, P. (2018). An AI aid to the editors. Exploring the possibility of an AI assisted article classification system. *arXiv preprint arXiv:1802.01403*.

Giffen, B. V., Herhausen, D., & Fahse, T. (2022). Overcoming the pitfalls and perils of algorithms: A classification of machine learning biases and mitigation methods. *Journal of Business Research*, 144, 93–106. DOI: 10.1016/j.jbusres.2022.01.076

Giri, R., Sen, B. K., & Mahesh, G. (2015). Collection development in Indian academic libraries: An empirical approach to determine the number of copies for acquisition. *DESIDOC Journal of Library and Information Technology*, 35(3), 184–192. DOI: 10.14429/djlit.35.3.7806

Gomez, A. L., Pecina, E. D., Villanueva, S. A., & Huber, T. (2020). The undeniable relationship between reading comprehension and mathematics performance. *Issues in Educational Research*, 30(4), 1329–1354. http://www.iier.org.au/iier30/gomez.pdf

Goodsett, M., & Schmillen, H. (2022). Fostering critical thinking in first-year students through information literacy instruction. *College & Research Libraries*, 83(1), 91. DOI: 10.5860/crl.83.1.91

Gorzycki, M., Howard, P., Allen, D., Desa, G., & Rosengard, E. (2016). An exploration of academic reading proficiency at the university level: A cross-sectional study of 848 undergraduates. *Literacy Research and Instruction*, 55(2), 142–162. DOI: 10.1080/19388071.2015.1133738

Goulding, A. (2009). Engaging with community engagement: Public libraries and citizen involvement. *New Library World*, 110(1–2), 37–51. DOI: 10.1108/03074800910928577

Graham, S. S. (2023). *Post-process but not post-writing: Large Language Models and a future for composition pedagogy* (EJ1390327). ERIC. https://files.eric.ed.gov/fulltext/EJ1390327.pdf

Grammarly. (2024). *2024 State of business communication.* https://go.grammarly.com/2024-state-of-business-communication-report

Gray, A. C., Steel, A., & Adams, J. (2021). Complementary medicine students' perceptions, perspectives and experiences of learning technologies. A survey conducted in the US and Australia. *European Journal of Integrative Medicine, 42*, 101304-. DOI: 10.1016/j.eujim.2021.101304

Greenstein, B. (2022, April, 20) AiThority: Interview with Bret Greenstein, Partner, Cloud & Digital – Analytics Insights at PwC. Available at https://aithority.com/technology/analytics/aithority-interview-with-bret-greenstein-partner-cloud-digital-analytics-insights-at-pwc/#

Guo, L., Wang, D., Gu, F., Li, Y., Wang, Y., & Zhou, R. (2021). Evolution and trends in intelligent tutoring systems research: A multidisciplinary and scientometric view. *Asia Pacific Education Review*, 22(3), 441–461. DOI: 10.1007/s12564-021-09697-7

Gupta, A. (2018). The Evolution of Fraud: Ethical Implications in the Age of Large-Scale Data Breaches and Widespread Artificial Intelligence Solutions Deployment. Available at from https://www.researchgate.net/publication/323857997_The_Evolution_of_Fraud_Ethical_Implications_in_the_Age_of_Large-Scale_Data_Breaches_and_Widespread_Artificial_Intelligence_Solutions_Deployment

Habibzadeh, H., Nussbaum, B. H., Anjomshoa, F., Kantarci, B., & Soyata, T. (2019). A survey on cybersecurity, data privacy, and policy issues in cyber-physical system deployments in smart cities. *Sustainable Cities and Society*, 50, 101660. DOI: 10.1016/j.scs.2019.101660

Haleem, A., Javaid, M., Quadi, M. A., & Suman, R. (2022). "Understanding the role of digital technologies in education: A review". *Science Direct*, 3, 275 – 285. https://www.sciencedirect.com/science/article/pii/S2666412722000137

Haleem, A., Javaid, M., Quadi, M. A., & Suman, R. (2022). Understanding the role of digital technologies in education: A Review. Science Direct, 3, 275 – 285. Available at https://www.sciencedirect.com/science/article/pii/S2666412722000137

Haman, M., & Školník, M. (2023). Using ChatGPT to conduct a literature review. *Accountability in Research*, ●●●, 1–3. DOI: 10.1080/08989621.2023.2185514 PMID: 36879536

Han, K. (2021). Research and exploration of metadata in artificial intelligence digital library. *Journal of Physics: Conference Series*, 1915(2), 022061. DOI: 10.1088/1742-6596/1915/2/022061

Han, S., Liu, M., Pan, Z., Cai, Y., & Shao, P. (2023). Making FAQ Chatbots More Inclusive: An Examination of Non-Native English Users' Interactions with New Technology in Massive Open Online Courses. *International Journal of Artificial Intelligence in Education*, 33(3), 752–780. DOI: 10.1007/s40593-022-00311-4

Hardy, J. L., Drescher, D., Sarkar, K., Kellett, G., & Scanlon, M. (2011). Enhancing visual attention and working memory with a web-based cognitive training program. *Mensa Research Journal*, 42(2), 13–20.

Harrison, H., Griffin, S. J., Kuhn, I., & Usher-Smith, J. A. (2020). Software tools to support title and abstract screening for systematic reviews in healthcare: An evaluation. *BMC Medical Research Methodology*, 20(1), 1–12. DOI: 10.1186/s12874-020-0897-3 PMID: 31931747

Harvey, F., & Anderson, J. (2020). *Empowering students as champions in technology enhances learning (TEL) to improve digital literacies. Handbook for Student Engagement in Higher Education: Theory into practice.* Routledge.

Heaven, W. D. (2023, March 9). AI is dreaming up drugs that no one has ever seen. Now we've got to see if they work. MIT Technology Review. Retrieved from https://www.technologyreview.com/2023/02/15/1067904/ai-automation-drug -development/

Henderson, M., Selwyn, N., & Aston, R. (2017). What works and why? Student perceptions of "useful" digital technology in university teaching and learning. *Studies in Higher Education (Dorchester-on-Thames), 42*(8), 1567–1579. DOI: 10.1080/03075079.2015.1007946

Hickerson, H. T., Brosz, J., & Crema, L. (2022). Creating new roles for libraries in academic research: Research conducted at the University of Calgary, 2015–2020. *College & Research Libraries*, 83(1), 129. DOI: 10.5860/crl.83.1.129

Hirose, M., & Creswell, J. W. (2023). Applying core quality criteria of mixed methods research to an empirical study. *Journal of Mixed Methods Research*, 17(1), 12–28. DOI: 10.1177/15586898221086346

Hoofnagle, C. J., Sloot, B. V., & Borgesius, F. Z. (2019). The European union general data protection regulation: What it is and what it means. *Information & Communications Technology Law*, 28(1), 1–34. DOI: 10.1080/13600834.2019.1573501

Hoppenfeld, J., & Malaf, E. (2015). Engaging with entrepreneurs in academic and public libraries. *RSR. Reference Services Review*, 43(3), 379–399. DOI: 10.1108/ RSR-02-2015-0011

Hornsby, A. S. (2015). Research. Oxford Advanced Learner's Dictionary of Current English, Oxford University Press Johnson, B. (2020). Automation and its implications for social inequality. *Journal of Technology and Society*, 22(2), 59–63.

Horwood, L., Sullivan, S., Young, E., & Garner, J. (2004). OAI compliant institutional repositories and the role of library staff. *Library Management*, 25(4/5), 170–176. DOI: 10.1108/01435120410533756

Hosseini, M., & Horbach, S. P. J. M. (2023). Fighting reviewer fatigue or amplifying bias? considerations and recommendations for use of ChatGPT and other large language models in scholarly peer review. *Research Integrity and Peer Review*, 8(1), 4. DOI: 10.1186/s41073-023-00133-5 PMID: 37198671

Huang, Y., Cox, A. M., & Cox, J. (2023). Artificial intelligence in academic library strategy in the United Kingdom and the Mainland of China. *The Journal of Academic Librarianship, 49*(6), 102772-. DOI: 10.1016/j.acalib.2023.102772

Huang, J., & Tan, M. (2023). The role of ChatGPT in scientific communication: Writing better scientific review articles. *American Journal of Cancer Research*, 13(4), 1148. PMID: 37168339

Huang, W., Billinghurst, M., Alem, L., Xiao, C., & Rasmussen, T. (2024). *Computer-Supported Collaboration: Theory and Practice*. John Wiley & Sons. DOI: 10.1002/9781119719830

Humphreys, D., Koay, A., Desmond, D., & Mealy, E. (2024). AI hype as a cyber security risk: The moral responsibility of implementing generative ai in business. *AI and Ethics*, 4(3), 791–804. Advance online publication. DOI: 10.1007/s43681-024-00443-4

Hussain, A., & Ahmad, S. (2023). Mapping the literature on artificial intelligence in academic libraries: A bibliometrics approach. *Science & Technology Libraries*, •••, 1–16. DOI: 10.1080/0194262X.2023.2238198

IFLA. (2020, May 20). *Gateways to Cultural Diversity: Libraries as multicultural hubs*. https://blogs.ifla.org/lpa/2020/05/20/gateways-to-cultural-diversity-libraries-as-multicultural-hubs/

IFLA. (2022, January 7). *Libraries as Cultural Rights Defenders: Looking ahead to Culture, Heritage, and Development in 2022*. https://www.ifla.org/news/libraries-as-cultural-rights-defenders-looking-ahead-to-culture-heritage-and-development-in-2022/

IFLA. (2023, May 14). *ChatGPT in Libraries? A Discussion*. https://blogs.ifla.org/cpdwl/2023/05/14/chatgpt-in-libraries-a-discussion/

Iuculano, T., Rosenberg-Lee, M., Richardson, J., Tenison, C., Fuchs, L., Supekar, K., & Menon, V. (2015). Cognitive tutoring induces widespread neuroplasticity and remediates brain function in children with mathematical learning disabilities. *Nature Communications*, 6(1), 8453. DOI: 10.1038/ncomms9453 PMID: 26419418

Jairam, D., Kiewra, K. A., Rogers-Kasson, S., Patterson-Hazley, M., & Marxhausen, K. (2014). SOAR versus SQ3R: A test of two study systems. *Instructional Science*, 42(3), 409–420. DOI: 10.1007/s11251-013-9295-0

Jarrah, A. M., Wardat, Y., & Fidalgo, P. (2023). Using ChatGPT in academic writing is (not) a form of plagiarism: What does the literature say. *Online Journal of Communication and Media Technologies*, 13(4), e202346. DOI: 10.30935/ojcmt/13572

Jazlin, E., Jirarat, S., & Na, K. S. (2022). Architecture students' conceptions, experiences, perceptions, and feelings of learning technology use: Phenomenography as an assessment tool. *Education and Information Technologies*, 27(1), 1133–1157. DOI: 10.1007/s10639-021-10654-5

Jimenez, K. (2023, April 12). How AI detection tool spawned a false cheating case at UC Davis. *USA Today*.https://www.usatoday.com/story/news/education/2023/04/12/how-ai-detection-tool-spawned-false-cheating-case-uc-davis/11600777002/

Johnson, A. (2020). The role of automation in society: Implications for the future. *Journal of Automation Studies*, 5(2), 23–30.

Johnson, B. (2020). Automation and Its Implications for Social Inequality. *Journal of Technology and Society*, 22(2), 59–63.

Kacena, M. A., Plotkin, L. I., & Fehrenbacher, J. C. (2024). The use of artificial intelligence in writing scientific review articles. *Current Osteoporosis Reports*, 22(1), 1–7. DOI: 10.1007/s11914-023-00852-0 PMID: 38227177

Kamalov, F., Santandreu Calonge, D., & Gurrib, I. (2023). New era of artificial intelligence in education: Towards a sustainable multifaceted revolution. *Sustainability (Basel)*, 15(16), 12451. DOI: 10.3390/su151612451

Kamau, G. W., & Elegwa, A. L. (2022). Factors influencing collection development process at the University of Nairobi Library. *Library Management*, 43(3/4), 207–217. DOI: 10.1108/LM-09-2020-0127

Karneli, O. (2023). The Role of Adhocratic Leadership in Facing the Changing Business Environment. [ADMAN]. *Journal of Contemporary Administration and Management*, 1(2), 77–83. DOI: 10.61100/adman.v1i2.26

Karp, M. J. M., & Fletcher, J. (2014). Adopting new technologies for student success: A readiness framework. DOI: 10.7916/D8862DMC

Kenton, J., & Blummer, B. (2010). Promoting Digital Literacy Skills: Examples from the Literature and Implications for Academic Librarians. *Community & Junior College Libraries*, 16(2), 84–99. DOI: 10.1080/02763911003688737

Kerr, M. M., & Frese, K. M. (2017). Reading to learn or learning to read? Engaging college students in course readings. *College Teaching*, 65(1), 28–3. DOI: 10.1080/87567555.2016.1222577

Khalifa, A. A., & Ibrahim, M. A. (2024). Artificial intelligence (AI) and ChatGPT involvement in scientific and medical writing, a new concern for researchers. A scoping review. *Arab Gulf Journal of Scientific Research*. Advance online publication. DOI: 10.1108/AGJSR-09-2023-0423

Khalil, O., & Khalil, H. (2023). Knowledge sharing and service innovation in academic libraries. *European Conference on Knowledge Management, 24*(1), 635–644. DOI: 10.34190/eckm.24.1.1359

Khan, M., Alharbi, Y., Alferaidi, A., Alharbi, T. S., & Yadav, K. (2023). Metadata for Efficient Management of Digital News Articles in Multilingual News Archives. *SAGE Open*, 13(4), 21582440231201368. DOI: 10.1177/21582440231201368

Kirchenbauer, J., Geiping, J., Wen, Y., Katz, J., Miers, I., & Goldstein, T. (2023, July). A watermark for large language models. In *International Conference on Machine Learning(pp.* 17061-17084*). PMLR.*

Kirkwood, H., & Evans, K. (2012). Embedded Librarianship and Virtual Environments in Entrepreneurship Information Literacy: A Case Study. *Journal of Business & Finance Librarianship*, 17(1), 106–116. DOI: 10.1080/08963568.2011.630583

Klee, M. (2023, May 17). Texas A&M professor wrongly accuses class of cheating with ChatGPT. *Rolling Stone.* https://www.rollingstone.com/culture/culture-features/texas-am-chatgpt-ai-professor-flunks-students-false-claims-1234736601/

Kocoń, J., Cichecki, I., Kaszyca, O., Kochanek, M., Szydło, D., Baran, J., Bielaniewicz, J., Gruza, M., Janz, A., Kanclerz, K., Kocoń, A., Koptyra, B., Mieleszczenko-Kowszewicz, W., Miłkowski, P., Oleksy, M., Piasecki, M., Radliński, Ł., Wojtasik, K., Woźniak, S., & Kazienko, P. (2023). ChatGPT: Jack of all trades, master of none. *Information Fusion*, 99, 101861. DOI: 10.1016/j.inffus.2023.101861

Koedinger, K. R., Anderson, J. R., Hadley, W. H., & Mark, M. A. (1997). Intelligent tutoring goes to school in the big city. *International Journal of Artificial Intelligence in Education*, 8, 30–43.

Kotzer, M., Kirby, J. R., & Heggie, L. (2021). Morphological awareness predicts reading comprehension in adults. *Reading Psychology*, 42(3), 302–322. DOI: 10.1080/02702711.2021.1888362

Krivosheev, E., Casati, F., & Benatallah, B. (2018). Crowd-based multi-predicate screening of papers in literature reviews. In *Proceedings of the 2018 World Wide Web Conference, pp.* 55-64*. 2018.* DOI: 10.1145/3178876.3186036

Kryloval-Greg, Y. (2020). Advanced information technology tools for media and information literacy training. *The State University of Telecommunications, Solomenska Street.*https://ceur-ws.org/Vol-2393/paper_234.pdf

Kwon, H. J., El Azzaoui, A., & Park, J. H. (2022). MetaQ: A Quantum Approach for Secure and Optimized Metaverse Environment. *Hum.-. Cent. Comput. Inf. Sci*, 12, 42.

Labuz, M. (2023). "Regulating deep fakes in the artificial intelligence act." applied cybersecurity and internet governance. https://www.acigjournal.com/Regulating -Deep-Fakes-in-the-ArtificialIntelligence-Act,184302,0,2.html

Lacy, L. (2024, April 1). *Hallucinations: why ai makes stuff up, and what's being done about it.* CNET. https://www.cnet.com/tech/hallucinations-why-ai-makes-stuff -up-and-whats-being-done-about-it/

Landy, K. (2024, February 28). The next step in higher ed's approach to AI (opinion). *Inside Higher Ed.*https://www.insidehighered.com/opinion/views/2024/02/28/next -step-higher-eds-approach-ai-opinion

Langreo, L., & Frajtova, A. (2024, March 25). Teachers desperately need AI training. How many are getting it? *Education Week.*https://www.edweek.org/leadership/ teachers-desperately-need-ai-training-how-many-are-getting-it/2024/03

Laskowski, N., & Tucci, L. (2024). What is artificial intelligence (AI)? Retrieved from http://www.techtarget.com/what-is-artificial intelligence/

Lawton, G. (2023).What is Generative AI? Everything you need to know. Tech Accelerator, available at https://www.techtarget.com/searchenterpriseai/definition/ generative-AI

Lawton, G. (2023).What is generative AI? Everything you need to know. *Tech Accelerator,* https://www.techtarget.com/searchenterpriseai/definition/generative-AI

Lee, L. H., Braud, T., Zhou, P., Wang, L., Xu, D., Lin, Z., . . . Hui, P. (2021). All one needs to know about metaverse: A complete survey on technological singularity, virtual ecosystem, and research agenda. *arXiv preprint arXiv:2110.05352.*

Lenca, M. (2023). On artificial intelligence and manipulation. *Topoi*, 42(3), 833–842. DOI: 10.1007/s11245-023-09940-3

Liechti, R., George, N., Götz, L., El-Gebali, S., Chasapi, A., Crespo, I., Xenarios, I., & Lemberger, T. (2017). SourceData: A semantic platform for curating and searching figures. *Nature Methods*, 14(11), 1021–1022. DOI: 10.1038/nmeth.4471 PMID: 29088127

Li, J., & Chang, X. (2023). Combating Misinformation by Sharing the Truth: A Study on the Spread of Fact-Checks on Social Media. *Information Systems Frontiers*, 25(4), 1479–1493. DOI: 10.1007/s10796-022-10296-z PMID: 35729965

Lim, W. M., Gunasekara, A., Pallant, J. L., Pallant, J. I., & Pechenkina, E. (2023). Generative ai and the future of education: Ragnarök or reformation? a paradoxical perspective from management educators. *International Journal of Management Education*, 21(2), 100790. https://www.sciencedirect.com/science/article/pii/S1472811723000289. DOI: 10.1016/j.ijme.2023.100790

Lin, C. H., Chiu, D. K., & Lam, K. T. (2022, September). Hong Kong academic librarians' attitudes toward robotic process automation. *Library Hi Tech*, 7. Advance online publication. DOI: 10.1108/LHT-03-2022-0141

Lin, X., Sun, Y., & Zhang, Y., & R, K. M. (2023). Application of AI in Library Digital Reading Promotion Service. *2023 IEEE International Conference on Integrated Circuits and Communication Systems (ICICACS)*, 1–6. DOI: 10.1109/ICICACS57338.2023.10100096

Liu, M., Ren, Y., Nyagoga, L. M., Stonier, F., Wu, Z., & Yu, L. (2023). Future of education in the era of generative artificial intelligence: Consensus among Chinese scholars on applications of ChatGPT in schools. *Future in Educational Research*, 1(1), 72–101. DOI: 10.1002/fer3.10

Llewellyn, A. (2020). Innovations in learning and teaching in academic libraries: A literature review. *New Review of Academic Librarianship*, 25(2-4), 129–149. DOI: 10.1080/13614533.2019.1678494

Lo, C. K. (2023). What is the impact of ChatGPT on education? A rapid review of the literature. *Education Sciences*, 13(4), 410. DOI: 10.3390/educsci13040410

Long, D., & Magerko, B. (2020, April). What is AI literacy? Competencies and design considerations. In *Proceedings of the 2020 CHI Conference on Human Factors in Computing Systems(pp.* 1-16*).* DOI: 10.1145/3313831.3376727

Lozić, E., & Štular, B. (2023). Fluent but not factual: A comparative analysis of ChatGPT and other AI chatbots' proficiency and originality in scientific writing for humanities. *Future Internet*, 15(10), 336. DOI: 10.3390/fi15100336

Luitse, D., & Denkena, W. (2021). The great transformer: Examining the role of large language models in the political economy of AI. *Big Data & Society*, 8(2), 20539517211047734. DOI: 10.1177/20539517211047734

Lund, B. (2023). The prompt engineering librarian. *Library Hi Tech News*, 40(8), 6–8. DOI: 10.1108/LHTN-10-2023-0189

Lund, B. D., Wang, T., Mannuru, N. R., Nie, B., Shimray, S., & Wang, Z. (2023). ChatGPT and a new academic reality: Artificial Intelligence-written research papers and the ethics of the large language models in scholarly publishing. *Journal of the Association for Information Science and Technology*, 74(5), 570–581. DOI: 10.1002/asi.24750

Luo, H., Cai, M., & Cui, Y. (2021, December 16). **Cai**, M., & Cui, Y. (2021). Spread of misinformation in social networks: Analysis based on weibo tweets. *Security and Communication Networks*, 2021, 1–23. Advance online publication. DOI: 10.1155/2021/7999760

Mahardhani, A. J. (2023). The Role of Public Policy in Fostering Technological Innovation and Sustainability. [ADMAN]. *Journal of Contemporary Administration and Management*, 1(2), 47–53. DOI: 10.61100/adman.v1i2.22

Mahdi, M. N., Ahmad, A. R., Ismail, R., Natiq, H., & Mohammed, M. A. (2020). Solution for information overload using faceted search–a review. *IEEE Access : Practical Innovations, Open Solutions*, 8, 119554–119585. DOI: 10.1109/ACCESS.2020.3005536

Marty, L., & Teeman, J. (2020). College students and textbooks: Preliminary investigation of gender, international status, and major. *Southern Journal of Business and Ethics*, 12, 75–90.

Mason, W., & Warmington, M. (2024). Academic reading as a grudging act: How do higher education students experience academic reading and what can educators do about it? *Higher Education*, 88(3), 839–856. Advance online publication. DOI: 10.1007/s10734-023-01145-2

Maspul, K. A., & Almalki, F. A. (2023). From Cafés to Collaborative Hubs: Empowering Communities and Transforming the Coffee Value Chain in Buraydah. *EKOMA: Jurnal Ekonomi, Manajemen. Akuntansi*, 3(1), 179–206.

Mayer-Schönberger, V., & Cukier, K. (2013). *Big data: A revolution that will transform how we live, work, and think*. Houghton Mifflin Harcourt.

McIntosh, T., Antes, A. L., & DuBois, J. M. (2021). Navigating complex, ethical problems in professional life: A guide to teaching SMART strategies for decision-making. *Journal of Academic Ethics*, 19(2), 139–156. DOI: 10.1007/s10805-020-09369-y PMID: 34177401

Mehta, V., Mathur, A., Anjali, A. K., & Fiorillo, L. (2024). A. K. Anjali, and Luca Fiorillo. The application of ChatGPT in the peer-reviewing process. *Oral Oncology Reports*, 9, 100227. DOI: 10.1016/j.oor.2024.100227

Merga, M. K. (2020). School Librarians as Literacy Educators Within a Complex Role. *Journal of Library Administration*, 60(8), 889–908. DOI: 10.1080/01930826.2020.1820278

Mestre, L. S. (2010). Librarians working with diverse populations: What impact does cultural competency training have on their efforts? *Journal of Academic Librarianship*, 36(6), 479–488. DOI: 10.1016/j.acalib.2010.08.003

Miesenberger, K., Kouroupetroglou, G., Mavrou, K., Manduchi, R., Rodriguez, M. C., & Penáz, P. (Eds.). (2022). Computers Helping People with Special Needs: 18th International Conference, ICCHP-AAATE 2022, Lecco, Italy, July 11–15, 2022, Proceedings, Part I (Vol. 13341). Springer Nature.

Miesenberger, K., & Kouroupetroglou, G. (Eds.). (2018). Computers Helping People with Special Needs:*16th International Conference, ICCHP 2018,* Linz, Austria, July 11-13, 2018, *Proceedings, Part I* (Vol. 10896). Springer.

Miller, A., & Salinas, C.Jr. (2019). A document analysis of student conduct in Florida's community colleges. *Community College Journal of Research and Practice*, 43(10-11), 796–802. DOI: 10.1080/10668926.2019.1600606

Mindner, L., Schlippe, T., & Schaaff, K. (2023, June). Classification of human-and ai-generated texts: Investigating features for chatgpt. In *International Conference on Artificial Intelligence in Education Technology(pp.152-170).* Singapore: Springer Nature Singapore. DOI: 10.1007/978-981-99-7947-9_12

Mitrovic, S., Andreoletti, D., & Ayoub, O. (2023). ChatGPT or human? detect and explain. *Explaining Decisions of Machine Learning Model for detecting short ChatGPT Generated Text.*

Mollick, E. (2023, June 18). *Detecting the secret cyborgs: The AI trap for organizations.* One Useful Thing. https://www.oneusefulthing.org/p/detecting-the-secret-cyborgs

Mondal, H. (2021). Application of Artificial Intelligence in library of 21st century. *Library and Information Science Modern Scenario.* Available at: https://www.researchgate.net/publication/353211129

Moran, M. (2021). Public librarians and community engagement: The way forward. *Advances in Librarianship*, 48, 139–146. DOI: 10.1108/S0065-283020210000048015

Moreno, F. R. (2024). Generative ai and deepfakes: A human rights approach to tackling harmful content. *International Review of Law Computers & Technology*, 1–30. Advance online publication. DOI: 10.1080/13600869.2024.2324540

Morgan, D. L. (2023). Exploring the use of artificial intelligence for qualitative data analysis: The case of ChatGPT. *International Journal of Qualitative Methods*, 22, 16094069231211248. Advance online publication. DOI: 10.1177/16094069231211248

Mukhtarkyzy, K., Abildinova, G., & Sayakov, O. (2022). The use of augmented reality for teaching Kazakhstani students physics lessons. [iJET]. *International Journal of Emerging Technologies in Learning*, 17(12), 215–235. DOI: 10.3991/ijet.v17i12.29501

Munna, A. S., & Kalam, M. A. (2021). "Impact of active learning strategy on the student engagement". An Open Access Article Distributed Under the Creative Commons Attribution License. Available at https://creativecommons.org/licenses/by-nc/4.0/

Mupaikwa, E. (2024). The Application of artificial intelligence and machine learning in academic libraries. In Khosrow-Pour, M. (Ed.), *Encyclopedia of Information Science and Technology* (6th ed.). IGI Global., DOI: 10.4018/978-1-6684-7366-5.ch041

Murray, A., & Meyer, D. (2022, December 12). The advent of OpenAI's ChatGPT may be the most important news event of 2022. *Fortune.*https://fortune.com/2022/12/12/openai-chatgpt-biggest-news-event-of-2022/

Myers, J. P., & Rivero, K. (2020). Challenging preservice teachers' understandings of globalization: Critical knowledge for global citizenship education. *Journal of Social Studies Research*, 44(4), 383–396. DOI: 10.1016/j.jssr.2020.05.004

Nah, F. F.-H., Zheng, R., Cai, J., Siau, K., & Chen, L. (2023). Generative AI and ChatGPT: Applications, challenges and AI-human collaboration. *Journal of Information Technology Case and Application Research*, 25(3), 277–304. DOI: 10.1080/15228053.2023.2233814

Nam, J. (2023, November 22). *56% of college students have used AI on assignments or exams.* Best Colleges. https://www.bestcolleges.com/research/most-college-students-have-used-ai-survey/

National Center for Education Statistics. (2024, March 21). *NAEP: National Assessment of Educational Progress.* Retrieved May 11, 2024, from https://nces.ed.gov/ Nationsreportcard

Nebbiai, D. (2020). Scriptoria and Libraries: An overview. In *The Oxford Handbook of Latin Palaeography* (pp. 737–768). Oxford University Press. DOI: 10.1093/oxfordhb/9780195336948.013.99

Neely-Sardon, A., & Tignor, M. (2018). Focus on the facts: A news and information literacy instructional program. *The Reference Librarian*, 59(3), 108–121. DOI: 10.1080/02763877.2018.1468849

Newbold, C. (2021, January 28). SPACECAT method of rhetorical analysis: Description and worksheet. *The Visual Communcation Guy*.https://thevisualcommun icationguy.com/2021/01/28/spacecat-method-of-rhetorical-analysis-description -and-worksheet/

Ng, D. T. K., Leung, J. K. L., Chu, S. K. W., & Qiao, M. S. (2021). Conceptualizing AI literacy: An exploratory review. *Computers and Education: Artificial Intelligence*, 2, 100041.

Nguyen, A., Ngo, H. N., Hong, Y., Dang, B., & Nguyen, B. P. T. (2023). Ethical principles for artificial intelligence in education. *Education and Information Technologies*, 28(4), 4221–4241. DOI: 10.1007/s10639-022-11316-w PMID: 36254344

Noble, S. M., Mende, M., Grewal, D., & Parasuraman, A. (2022). The Fifth Industrial Revolution: How harmonious human–machine collaboration is triggering a retail and service [r] evolution. *Journal of Retailing*, 98(2), 199–208. DOI: 10.1016/j. jretai.2022.04.003

Ntoutsi, E., Fafalios, P., Gadiraju, U., Iosifidis, V., Nejdl, W., Vidal, M. E., Ruggieri, S., Turini, F., Papadopoulos, S., Krasanakis, E., Kompatsiaris, I., Kinder-Kurlanda, K., Wagner, C., Karimi, F., Fernandez, M., Alani, H., Berendt, B., Kruegel, T., Heinze, C., & Staab, S. (2020). Bias in data-driven artificial intelligence systems—An introductory survey. *Wiley Interdisciplinary Reviews. Data Mining and Knowledge Discovery*, 10(3), e1356. DOI: 10.1002/widm.1356

Nworgu, B. C. (2015). Educational Research Basic Issues and Methodology. Nsukka: University Trust Publishers Olayinka, I.A. (2023). Application and use of artificial intelligence (AI) for library services delivery in academic libraries in Kwara State, Nigeria. Library Philosophy and Practice (e-journal)-7998. https://digitalcommons .unl.edu/libphilprac/7998

Office of Survey Research & Analysis. (2024). *How to increase response rates*. The George Washington University. https://survey.gwu.edu/how-increase-response-rates

Okafor, K. (2020). Public library services in Nigeria: Challenges and strategies. *Library and Information Science Digest*, 13, 116–125.

Okunlaya, R. O., Syed Abdullah, N., & Alias, R. A. (2022). Artificial intelligence (AI) library services innovative conceptual framework for the digital transformation of university education. *Library Hi Tech*, 40(6), 1869–1892. DOI: 10.1108/ LHT-07-2021-0242

Olaniyi, N. E. E. (2020). Threshold concepts: Designing a format for the flipped classroom as an active learning technique for crossing the threshold. *Research and Practice in Technology Enhanced Learning*, 15(2), 1–15. DOI: 10.1186/s41039-020-0122-3

Oltmann, S. M. (2016). Public Librarians' Views on Collection Development and Censorship. *Collection Management*, 41(1), 23–44. DOI: 10.1080/01462679.2015.1117998

Olubiyo, P. O. (2023). Collection development in academic libraries: Challenges and way forward. *International Journal of Library and Information Science Studies*, 9(3), 1–9. DOI: 10.37745/ijliss.15/vol9n319

Omame, I. M., & Alex-Nmecha, J. C. **(2020).** Artificial Intelligence in Libraries. Available at: https://www.researchgate.net/publication/338337072

Onuoha, J., & Obiano, D. C. (2019). The impact of information technology on modern librarianship: A reflective study. *Information and Knowledge Management*, 5(11), 52–58.

Onwubiko, E. C. (2023). Analysis of serials citations in postgraduate theses in library and information science in public universities in Southeast, Nigeria. An unpublished PhD Dissertation of Nnamdi Azikiwe University, Awka, Nigeria

Onwubiko, E. C. (2020). *Library Plus*. Lambert Academic Publishing.

Onwubiko, E. C. (2021). *Modern Approaches in Librarianship*. Lambert Academic Publishing.

Open, A. I. (2024). *ChatGPT* (3.5 Version) [Large language model]. https://chat .openai.com/share/977a06ca-7cb8-46b9-91e7-afe6b405152e

Oseghale, O. (2023). Digital information literacy skills and use of electronic resources by humanities graduate students at Kenneth Dike Library, University of Ibadan, Nigeria. *Digital Library Perspectives*, 39(2), 181–204. DOI: 10.1108/ DLP-09-2022-0071

Oseji, N. A., & Sani, J. O. (2022). Utilizing the potentials of big data in library environments in Nigeria for recommender services. *Library Philosophy and Practice (e-journal)*. 7467. https://digitalcommons.unl.edu/libphilprac/7467

Oseji, N. A. (2020). Training of Librarians for Service Delivery in the Digital Age in Federal University Libraries in North Central Nigeria. *Niger Delta Journal of Library and Information Science*, 1(1), 59–69.

Otoide, G. P., & Idahosa, M. E. (2018). Faculty-librarian collaborations and improved information literacy: A model for academic achievement and curriculum development. [CJLIS]. *Covenant Journal of Library and Information Science*, 1(1), 63–73.

Oyetola, S. O., Oladokun, B. D., Maxwell, C. E., & Akor, S. O. (n.d). Artificial intelligence in the library: Potential implications to library and information services in the 21st Century Nigeria. Available at: https://ssrn.com/abstract=4396138

Parsons, S., & Mitchell, P. (2002). The potential of virtual reality in social skills training for people with autistic spectrum disorders. *Journal of Intellectual Disability Research*, 46(5), 430–443. DOI: 10.1046/j.1365-2788.2002.00425.x PMID: 12031025

Patron, M. (2023). Bias in the training data. Retrieved from https://www.mariecuriealumni.eu/newsletters/35th-mcaa-newsletter/special-issue-proceed-caution-potential-negative-impact-ai

Paullada, A., Raji, I. D., Bender, E. M., Denton, E., & Hanna, A. (2021). Data and its (dis)contents: A survey of dataset development and use in machine learning research. *Patterns (New York, N.Y.)*, 2(11), 100336. https://www.sciencedirect.com/science/article/pii/S2666389921001847. DOI: 10.1016/j.patter.2021.100336 PMID: 34820643

Paulson, O. (2024). *Is There A Risk ChatBots And AI Will Steal My Librarian Job?* https://aiwhim.com/is-there-a-risk-chatbots-and-ai-will-steal-my-librarian-job/

Paulson, E. J., & Holschuh, J. P. (2018). College Reading. In Flippo, R. F. (Ed.), *Handbook of college reading and study strategy research* (3rd ed.). Routledge. DOI: 10.4324/9781315629810-3

Peterson-Karlan, G. R. (2015). Assistive technology instruction within a continuously evolving technology environment. *Quarterly Review of Distance Education*, 16(2), 61.

Petrakis, P. E. (2022). Labor Market Analysis Based on the Knowledge, Skills, Abilities and Working Activities of Employees in the Present and Future Production Structure of 2027. In *Human Capital and Production Structure in the Greek Economy: Knowledge, Abilities, Skills* (pp. 261–301). Springer International Publishing. DOI: 10.1007/978-3-031-04938-5_10

Picard, R. W. (2000). *Affective computing*. MIT press. DOI: 10.7551/mitpress/1140.003.0008

Pullen, P. C., & Kennedy, M. J. (Eds.). (2019). *Handbook of response to intervention and multi-tiered systems of support*. Routledge.

Rahaman, T. (2023). Open Data and the 2023 NIH Data Management and Sharing Policy. *Medical Reference Services Quarterly*, 42(1), 71–78. DOI: 10.1080/02763869.2023.2168103 PMID: 36862609

Raimundo, R., & Rosário, A. T. (2021). The Impact of Artificial Intelligence on Data System Security: A Literature Review. *Sensors (Basel)*, 21(21), 7029. DOI: 10.3390/s21217029 PMID: 34770336

Rello, L., & Ballesteros, M. (2015, May). Detecting readers with dyslexia using machine learning with eye tracking measures. In *Proceedings of the 12th international web for all conference* (pp. 1-8). DOI: 10.1145/2745555.2746644

Rempel, H. G., & McMillen, P. S. (2008). Using Courseware Discussion Boards to Engage Graduate Students in Online Library Workshops. *Internet Reference Services Quarterly*, 13(4), 363–380. DOI: 10.1080/10875300802326350

Rice, S., Crouse, S. R., Winter, S. R., & Rice, C. (2024). The advantages and limitations of using ChatGPT to enhance technological research. *Technology in Society*, 76, 102426. DOI: 10.1016/j.techsoc.2023.102426

Ridley, M., & Pawlick-Potts, D. (2021). Algorithmic literacy and the role for libraries. *Information Technology and Libraries*, 40(2). Advance online publication. DOI: 10.6017/ital.v40i2.12963

Roose, K. (2022, December 5). The brilliance and weirdness of ChatGPT. *The New York Times*. https://www.nytimes.com/2022/12/05/technology/chatgpt-ai-twitter.html

Rose, D. H., & Meyer, A. (2002). Teaching every student in the digital age: Universal design for learning. Association for Supervision and Curriculum Development, 1703 N. Beauregard St., Alexandria, VA 22311-1714 (Product no. 101042: $22.95 ASCD members; $26.95 nonmembers).

Rosowsky, D. (2022). The role of research at universities: Why it matters – Forbes. Retrieved from https://www.forbes.com-davidrosowsky

Ross, P., & Maynard, K. (2021). Towards a 4th industrial revolution. *Intelligent Buildings International*, 13(3), 159–161. DOI: 10.1080/17508975.2021.1873625

Russell, S. J., & Norvig, P. (2016). *Artificial intelligence: a modern approach*. Pearson.

Saad, A., Jenko, N., Ariyaratne, S., Birch, N., Iyengar, K. P., Davies, A. M., Vaishya, R., & Botchu, R. (2024). Exploring the potential of ChatGPT in the peer review process: An observational study. *Diabetes & Metabolic Syndrome*, 18(2), 102946. DOI: 10.1016/j.dsx.2024.102946 PMID: 38330745

Saeidnia, H. R. (2023). Ethical artificial intelligence (AI): Confronting bias and discrimination in the library and information industry. *Library Hi Tech News*. Advance online publication. DOI: 10.1108/LHTN-10-2023-0182

Sani, J. O., & Oseji, N. A. (2022). Utilizing the potentials of big data in library environments in Nigeria for recommender services. *Library Philosophy and Practice (e-journal)*. 7467. https://digitalcommons.unl.edu/libphilprac/7467

Sankar Sadasivan, V., Kumar, A., Balasubramanian, S., Wang, W., & Feizi, S. (2023). Can AI-Generated Text be Reliably Detected? *arXiv e-prints, arXiv-2303*.

Scassellati, B., Admoni, H., & Matarić, M. (2012). Robots for use in autism research. *Annual Review of Biomedical Engineering*, 14(1), 275–294. DOI: 10.1146/annurev-bioeng-071811-150036 PMID: 22577778

Sedoti, O., Gelles-Watnick, R., Faverio, M., Atske, S., Radde, K., & Park, E. (2024, April 25). *Mobile fact sheet*. Pew Research Center. https://www.pewresearch.org/internet /fact-sheet/mobile/

Semeler, A. R., Pinto, A. L., Koltay, T., & Rozados, H. (2024). "Algorithmic literacy: Generative artificial intelligence technologies for data librarians". https://www.researchgate.net/publication/377336874_ALGORITHMIC_LITERACY _Generative_Artificial_Intelligence_Technologies_for_Data_Librarians/citations

Shahzad, K., & Khan, S. A. (2023). Effects of e-learning technologies on university librarians and libraries: A systematic literature review. *The Electronic Library*, 41(4), 528–554. DOI: 10.1108/EL-04-2023-0076

Shaikh, S. A. (2020). Use of AI for Manuscript Writing–A Study Based on Patent Literature. *Allana Management Journal of Research, Pune*, 10, 1–8.

Sharma, R. S., Mokhtar, I. A., Ghista, D. N., Nazir, A., & Khan, S. Z. (2023). Digital literacies as policy catalysts of social innovation and socio-economic transformation: Interpretive analysis from Singapore and the UAE. *Sustainable Social Development, 1*(1).

Sheridan Library. **(2023). What is Academic Research? Retrieved from** https://sheridancollege.libguides.com/academic-research

Shortliffe, E. H., & Buchanan, B. G. (1975). A model of inexact reasoning in medicine. *Mathematical Biosciences*, 23(3-4), 351–379. DOI: 10.1016/0025-5564(75)90047-4

Shrayberg, Y. L., & Volkova, K. Y. (2021). Features of copyright transformation in the information environment in the age of digitalization. *Scientific and Technical Information Processing*, 48(1), 30–37. DOI: 10.3103/S014768822101007X

Shumakova, N., Lloyd, J. J., & Titova, E. V. (2023). Towards legal regulations of generative ai in the creative industry. *Journal of Digital Technologies and Law*, 1(4), 880–908. DOI: 10.21202/jdtl.2023.38

Signé, L. (2023). *Africa's Fourth Industrial Revolution*. Cambridge University Press. DOI: 10.1017/9781009200004

Singh, S. (2020). Digitization of library resources and the formation of digital libraries: Special reference in green stone digital library software. *IP Indian Journal of Library Science and Information Technology*, 3(1), 44–48. DOI: 10.18231/2456-9623.2018.0010

SITNFlash. (2020, October 26). Racial discrimination in face recognition technology –science in the News. Science in the News. Retrieved from https://sitn.hms.harvard.edu/flash/2020/racial-discrimination-in-face-recognition-technology/

Smith, N. M., & Fitt, S. D. (1982). *Active Listening at the Reference Desk. 21*(3), 247–249. https://www.jstor.org/stable/25826744

Stanford. (2023, February 28). *Collecting in support of Stanford's teaching and research*. https://news.stanford.edu/report/2023/02/28/building-stanfords-collections/

Stokel-Walker, C. (2023). ChatGPT listed as author on research papers: Many scientists disapprove. *Nature*, 613(7945), 620–621. DOI: 10.1038/d41586-023-00107-z PMID: 36653617

Strydom, F., Kuh, G. D., & Loots, S. (Eds.). (2017). *Engaging student: Using evidence to promote student success*. UJ Press. DOI: 10.18820/9781928424093

Student Code of Conduct. (2023, May 2). Macomb Community College. https://www.macomb.edu/about-macomb/college-policies/administrative/student-code-of-conduct.html

Subaveerapandiyan, A., & Gozali, A. A. (2024). AI in Indian libraries: Prospects and perceptions from library professionals. *Open Information Science*, 8(1), 1–13. DOI: 10.1515/opis-2022-0164

Suherlan, S. (2023). Digital Technology Transformation in Enhancing Public Participation in Democratic Processes. [TACIT]. *Technology and Society Perspectives*, 1(1), 10–17. DOI: 10.61100/tacit.v1i1.34

Suherman, N., Rahmadani, A., & Vidákovich, T. (1796). Mujib, Fitria, N., Nur Islam, S. P., Rofi'uddin Addarojat, M., & Priadi, M. (2021). SQ3R method assisted by ethnomathematics-oriented student worksheet: The impact of mathematical concepts understanding. *Journal of Physics: Conference Series*, (1). Advance online publication. DOI: 10.1088/1742-6596/1796/1/012059

Summary artificial intelligence 2023 legislation. (2024, January 12). National Conference of State Legislatures. https://www.ncsl.org/technology-and-communication/artificial-intelligence-2023-legislation

Tapscott, D., & Tapscott, A. (2016). *Blockchain revolution: how the technology behind bitcoin is changing money, business, and the world*. Penguin.

Tech Target. (2024). How does AI works? Retrieved from https://www.techtarget.com/serachenterpriseai/definition/ai

Tella, A., Bamidele, S. S., Olaniyi, O. T., & Ajani, Y. A. (2023). Library and Information Science Graduate Skills Needed in the Fourth Industrial Revolution: A Nigerian. *Information Services for a Sustainable Society: Current Developments in an Era of Information Disorder*, 183, 342–360. DOI: 10.1515/9783110772753-023

The Biden administration launches the National Artificial Intelligence Research Resource Task Force. (2021, June 10). The White House. https://www.whitehouse.gov/ostp/news-updates/2021/06/10/the-biden-administration-launches-the-national-artificial-intelligence-research-resource-task-force/

Thorp, H. H. (2023). ChatGPT is fun, but not an author. *Science*, 379(6630), 313–313. DOI: 10.1126/science.adg7879 PMID: 36701446

Tian, Z. (2021). Application of artificial intelligence system in libraries through data mining and content filtering methods. *Journal of Physics: Conference Series*, 1952(4), 042091. DOI: 10.1088/1742-6596/1952/4/042091

Tomiuk, D., Zuccaro, C., Plaisent, M., Öncel, A. G., Benslimane, Y., & Bernard, P. (2024). Investigating factors affecting artificial intelligence (AI) adoption by libraries at top-rated universities worldwide. In Holland, B., & Sinha, K. (Eds.), *Handbook of Research on Innovative Approaches to Information Technology in Library and Information Science* (pp. 103–125). IGI Global., DOI: 10.4018/979-8-3693-0807-3.ch006

Transformer, G. G. P., Thunström, A. O., & Steingrimsson, S. (2022). *Can GPT-3 write an academic paper on itself, with minimal human input? 2022. hal-03701250*

Turnitin. (2023, January 13). *Sneak preview of Turnitin's AI writing and ChatGPT detection capability*. Turnitin. https://www.turnitin.com/blog/sneak-preview-of-turnitins-ai-writing-and-chatgpt-detection-capability

Turnitin. (2023, July 25). *Turnitin AI detection feature reviews more than 65 million papers*. Turnitin. https://www.turnitin.com/press/turnitin-ai-detection-feature-reviews-more-than-65-million-papers

U.S. Copyright Office. (1998, December). *The Digital Millennium Copyright Act of 1998*. U.S. Copyright Office. https://www.copyright.gov/legislation/dmca.pdf

U.S. Department of Education, Office of Educational Technology. (2024). *AI in Education*. https://tech.ed.gov/ai/

U.S. Department of Education. (2021, August 25). *Family Educational Rights and Privacy Act (FERPA)*. https://www2.ed.gov/policy/gen/guid/fpco/ferpa/index.html

Vanderbilt to host first AI Training Day on March 5. (2024, February 28). Vanderbilt University. https://news.vanderbilt.edu/2024/02/28/vanderbilt-to-host-first-ai-training-day-on-march-5/

VanLehn, K. (2011). The relative effectiveness of human tutoring, intelligent tutoring systems, and other tutoring systems. *Educational Psychologist*, 46(4), 197–221. DOI: 10.1080/00461520.2011.611369

Varona, D., & Suárez, J. L. (2022). Discrimination, bias, fairness, and trustworthy AI. *Applied Sciences (Basel, Switzerland)*, 12(12), 5826. DOI: 10.3390/app12125826

Veros, V. (2019). Metatextual Conversations: The Exclusion/Inclusion of Genre Fiction in Public Libraries and Social Media Book Groups. *Journal of the Australian Library and Information Association*, 68(3), 254–267. DOI: 10.1080/24750158.2019.1654741

Vijayakumar, S., & Sheshadri, K. N. (2019). Applications of artificial intelligence in academic libraries. *International Journal on Computer Science and Engineering*, 7(18), 136–140. DOI: 10.26438/ijcse/v7si16.136140

Vodă, A. I., Cautisanu, C., Grădinaru, C., Tănăsescu, C., & de Moraes, G. H. S. M. (2022). Exploring digital literacy skills in social sciences and humanities students. *Sustainability (Basel)*, 14(5), 2483. DOI: 10.3390/su14052483

Wagner, G., Lukyanenko, R., & Paré, G. (2022). Artificial intelligence and the conduct of literature reviews. *Journal of Information Technology*, 37(2), 209–226. DOI: 10.1177/02683962211048201

Waite, A. M. (2022). Exploring Digital Technologies and Data: A Societal Level of Analysis Approach. In *Technological Challenges: The Human Side of the Digital Age* (pp. 1–24). Springer International Publishing. DOI: 10.1007/978-3-030-98040-5_1

Walkington, C. A. (2013). Using adaptive learning technologies to personalize instruction to student interests: The impact of relevant contexts on performance and learning outcomes. *Journal of Educational Psychology*, 105(4), 932–945. DOI: 10.1037/a0031882

Wang, Y., Skerry-Ryan, R. J., Stanton, D., Wu, Y., Weiss, R. J., Jaitly, N., . . . Saurous, R. A. (2017). Tacotron: Towards end-to-end speech synthesis. *arXiv preprint arXiv:1703.10135*. DOI: 10.21437/Interspeech.2017-1452

Wang, B., Rau, P. L. P., & Yuan, T. (2023). Measuring user competence in using artificial intelligence: Validity and reliability of artificial intelligence literacy scale. *Behaviour & Information Technology*, 42(9), 1324–1337. DOI: 10.1080/0144929X.2022.2072768

Wardat, Y., Tashtoush, M. A., AlAli, R., & Jarrah, A. M. (2023). ChatGPT: A revolutionary tool for teaching and learning mathematics. *Eurasia Journal of Mathematics, Science and Technology Education*, 19(7), em2286. DOI: 10.29333/ejmste/13272

Welding, L. (2023, March 17). *Half of college students say using AI on schoolwork is cheating or plagiarism.* Best Colleges. https://www.bestcolleges.com/research/college-students-ai-tools-survey/

Wenborn, C. (2018, April 11). *How Technology Is Changing the Future of Libraries.* https://www.wiley.com/en-us/network/research-libraries/libraries-archives -databases/library-impact/how-technology-is-changing-the-future-of-libraries

Wharton, L. (2018). Ethical implications of digital tools and emerging roles for academic librarians. *Applying Library Values to Emerging Technology: Decision-Making in the Age of Open Access, Maker Spaces, and the Ever-Changing Library*, 35-54.

Wineburg, S., & McGrew, S. (2019). Lateral reading and the nature of expertise: Reading less and learning more when evaluating digital information. *Teachers College Record*, 121(11), 1–40. DOI: 10.1177/016146811912101102

Winston, M. D., & Li, H. (2000). Managing Diversity in Liberal Arts College Libraries. *College & Research Libraries*, 61(3), 205–215. DOI: 10.5860/crl.61.3.205

Wojciechowska, M. (2020). Social capital, trust and social activity among librarians: Results of research conducted in 20 countries across the world. *Library & Information Science Research*, 42(4), 101049. DOI: 10.1016/j.lisr.2020.101049

World Economic Forum. (2020). Accelerating Digital Transformation: Shaping the Future of Production. Geneva: World Economic Forum.

Wozniak, M., Krishnaswamy, D., Callegari, C., Takagi, H., Prasad, N. R., Que, X., & Sandhu, R. (2015). *Advances in Computing, Communications and Informatics.* ICACCI.

Wright, R. (2023, December 6). *Artificial intelligence in the states: emerging legislation.* The Council of State Governments. https://www.csg.org/2023/12/06/artificial-intelligence-in-the-states-emerging-legislation/

Wu, J., Kim, K., & Giles, C. L. (2019, May). CiteSeerX: 20 years of service to scholarly big data. In *Proceedings of the Conference on Artificial Intelligence for Data Discovery and Reuse* (pp. 1-4). DOI: 10.1145/3359115.3359119

Xue, J., Wang, Y.-C., Wei, C., Liu, X., Woo, J., & Kuo, C.-C. J. (2023). Bias and Fairness in Chatbots: An Overview. *ArXiv.* https://arxiv.org/abs/2309.08836v2

Yang, C. [@CoraEdTech] (2024, March 4). *Excited to share the updated AI prompt craft guide for educators* [image attached] [Tweet]. Twitter. https://twitter.com/CoraEdTech/status/1763842120635609368

Yang, L., Driscol, J., Sarigai, S., Wu, Q., Chen, H., & Lippitt, C. D. (2022). Google Earth Engine and artificial intelligence (AI): A comprehensive review. *Remote Sensing (Basel)*, 14(14), 3253. DOI: 10.3390/rs14143253

Yang, Z., Dai, Z., Yang, Y., Carbonell, J., Salakhutdinov, R. R., & Le, Q. V. (2019). Xlnet: Generalized autoregressive pretraining for language understanding. *Advances in Neural Information Processing Systems*, ●●●, 32.

Yin, Y., Stecke, K. E., & Li, D. (2018). The evolution of production systems from Industry 2.0 through Industry 4.0. *International Journal of Production Research*, 56(1-2), 848–861. DOI: 10.1080/00207543.2017.1403664

Yu, K., & Gong, R. Sun, L. & Jiang, C (2019). The Application of Artificial Intelligence in Smart Library. *Advances in Economics, Business and Management Research*, 100, pp. 708-712. Available at: https://creativecommons.org/licenses/by-nc/4.0/

Yusuf, T. I., Adebayo, O. A., Bello, O. A., & Kayode, J. O. (2022). Adoption of artificial intelligence for effective library service delivery in academic libraries in Nigeria. *Library philosophy and practice (e-journal).* Available at:https://digitalcommons.unl.edu/libphilprac/6804

Zielinski, C.. (2023). *(May 2023) Chatbots, generative AI, and scholarly manuscripts WAME recommendations on chatbots and generative artificial intelligence in relation to scholarly publications.* WAME. DOI: 10.32412/pjohns.v38i1.2135

Zielinski, C., Winker, M., Aggarwal, R., Ferris, L., Heinemann, M., Lapeña, J. F., & Citrome, L. (2023). Chatbots, ChatGPT, and scholarly manuscripts-WAME recommendations on ChatGPT and chatbots in relation to scholarly publications. *Afro-Egyptian Journal of Infectious and Endemic Diseases*, 13(1), 75–79.

Zoldi, S. (2024, May 9). Navigating the wild AI with Dr. Scott Zoldi. Available at https://www.fico.com>blogs>navigating-wild-ai-dr-scott-zoldi/

About the Contributors

Kathleen Sacco is the Dean of Library and Learning Services at Lake-Sumter State College. Her previous affiliations were with the State University of New York at Fredonia as Systems Librarian and also Assistant Director. She is the winner of the 2010 Chancellor's Award for Excellence in Librarianship from the State University of New York.

Alison Norton is a Professor in the Classics department at Lake-Sumter State College.

Kevin Arms, with over 10 years of experience in library and learning services, is a leader, educator, and creator who specializes in collaboration and partnerships. As the Associate Dean of Library and Learning Services at Lake-Sumter State College, Kevin Arms oversees a joint-use public library that serves a diverse community of students, faculty, and patrons in one of the fastest-growing areas of Florida. The editor has a Master of Library and Information Science (MLIS) with a focus on special collections and archival sciences, a Master of Arts (MA) in English and Creative Writing, and a certificate from the Leadership Institute for Academic Librarians at Harvard Graduate School of Education. Kevin Arms is passionate about information literacy, digital content creation, and history. Kevin teaches English as an adjunct professor and engage my students in lively discussions of literature. The editor is also the unofficial college archivist and have spearheaded and advocated for the college archives as a place of engagement and access. Kevin has published articles on fantasy fiction and historical fantasy in Public Libraries Online, and has been recognized as a writer by the BlueCat Screenplay Competition, where Kevin's short screenplay "We Were Never Right" reached the quarter finals in 2021. Kevin enjoys theater, podcasting, and video production as creative outlets, and have earned awards for my work as a playwright.

* * *

Adebowale Adetayo is an academic staff of Adeleke University. His research interest is Library Science, Social media, Knowledge Management, and Business Information Management. He has published many articles in reputable journals and currently working on projects relating to pandemics, vaccines and virtual learning. He is a graduate of Babcock University.

Ganiyu Adigun is a lecturer at the Ladoke Akintola University.

Gboyega Adio is a lecturer at the Ladoke Akintola University of Technology.

Jesubukade Ajakaye is a dedicated academic librarian currently serving at the Federal Polytechnic Ayede in Oyo State, Nigeria. He actively contributes to the accessibility of information resources for students and researchers. Using advanced IT tools, he strives to break barriers and provide inclusive access to scholarly content, especially for underserved populations irrespective of age or socioeconomic status. His commitment extends beyond the academic sphere as he endeavours to make scholarly research widely available to the public through various mediums. Jesubukade stands at the intersection of technology, information access, and social impact, embodying a passion for knowledge dissemination and community empowerment.

Oluwabunmi Bakare-Fatungase is an Information Professional/Researcher in the Dept of Information Management, Faculty of Communication & Information Sciences, Lead City University. She is a fellow of the Council for the Development of Social Science Research in Africa & a Queen Elizabeth Scholar in the Advanced Scholars West Africa (QES-AS-WA).

Basirat Olubukola Diyaolu, an Assistant Librarian at Nimbe Adedipe Library, Federal University of Agriculture Abeokuta, is a renowned scholar and educator. Born in Lagos, Nigeria, she began her academic journey at Ireti Primary School and later attended Araromi Secondary School. She pursued distance learning at the University of Ibadan, graduating with a second-class upper division. She later earned her Master's degree in Librarianship at FUNAAB. Basirat works in various library departments and has published in various journals. Her research highlights the importance of information and communication technology in library and information science.

Oluwole O. Durodolu is a researcher in University of South Africa.

Tracy Elliott has been a librarian for nearly 30 years, most of that time as a director and dean. She is currently the Dean of the Wilson G. Bradshaw Library at Florida Gulf Coast University after serving as the Dean of the University Library at San Jose State University. Prior to San Jose, she served as the Director of Libraries at the State College of Florida, Head Librarian at St. Petersburg College, and Dean of Learning Resources at Rappahannock Community College. She also served as Patent Librarian at the U.S, Patent and Trademark Office and Information Services Librarian at Columbus State University. Dr. Elliott holds a PhD from Barry University and teaches in the SJSU School of Information at SJSU and the FGCU College of Education. She received her MLIS from Florida State University. Her research areas include academic library innovation, organizational learning, and leadership.

Sanchita Ghosh is a highly driven worker who holds a Master of Computer Applications degree. Her current position as a Technical Assistant at Brainware University allows her to specialize on IoT,NLP, AI, networking, cybersecurity, and cloud computing. Sanchita is passionate about using technology to solve complicated challenges, and she actively participates in projects and activities that promote innovation and progress the digital transformation. Her diversified skill set and dedication to continual learning make her an invaluable asset in the ever-changing field of information technology.

Beverly Gibson began her career as a high school librarian in 2011 after graduating from the University of Florida with a Bachelor of Arts in English. In 2014, she received her MS in Library and Information Studies from Florida State University. While working for Lake County Schools, her school was designated a Florida Power Library School in recognition of outstanding school library programs. In 2023, she was hired as a Reference and Instruction Librarian at Lake-Sumter State College. An avid AI practitioner, she serves on institutional and statewide committees addressing AI literacy and governance. Her research interests include information literacy, writing pedagogy, and generative artificial intelligence.

Precious Goodson is a recent Educational Leadership graduate of Florida Gulf Coast University. A current employee of the University of South Florida, her current professional endeavors include scholarship management, donor stewardship, and spearheading fund-raising campaigns with the hopes of serving the institution in a learning and development capacity. Her research interests include education technology, implementation processes, and learning strategies.

Courtney Green received her Master of Arts in English with a Composition and Rhetoric Concentration from the University of North Florida in 2021. In 2023, she was hired as an English Instructor by Lake-Sumter State College and currently teaches first-year English. In addition to teaching, she is the assistant editor of Transportation Journal. Finally, she also serves on an institutional committee addressing AI literacy and governance. Her research interests include artificial intelligence in academia, information literacy instruction, literature, and open pedagogy.

Peter Olubiyo is the Head of Cataloguing and Classification Section in Adeyemi Federal University of Education Library, Ondo.

Emmanuel Onwubiko holds a B.Sc (Hons) degree (1st class upper division) in Education/Library Science and Master degree in Library Science (MLS) from Abia State University, Uturu, Nigeria and PhD in Library and Information Science from Nnamdi Azikiwe University, Awka, Nigeria. He holds a PGD in Journalism as well as a Professional Certificate as Occupational Safety and Health Manger from OSH Academy, USA with distinction. A fellow of the Institute of Corporate Administration (FCAI) and Scholars Academic and Scientific Society (FSASS), written and published eight books with five published overseas, over fifty international peer reviewed journal articles, eight international book chapters and Editorial Board member of American Journal of Information Science and Technology and Journal of Humanities and Social Sciences, UK as well as one time elected member of European Centre of Research Training and Development (ECRTD), London. He has won over sixty certificates of excellence in peer review and SASS 2022 Best Researcher Award in Library Science. Apart from being a member of Nigerian Library Association (NLA), he is also a Google, Research gate and Academia scholar.

Katelyn Ramirez Velazco, a Senior Admissions Counselor at Keiser University, emerges as a leading voice in leveraging AI technologies to revolutionize the college learning experience. Armed with a Masters of Arts in Educational Leadership with a concentration in Higher Education, Katelyn brings a wealth of knowledge and hands-on experience to the table. Driven by a profound passion for empowering students to achieve their educational aspirations, Katelyn embarked on a transformative journey to explore the intersection of AI and student learning. Recognizing the immense potential of AI tools in higher education, Katelyn spearheaded a groundbreaking survey aimed at understanding students' perspectives on the integration of AI learning tools within college courses.

Bitan Roy is working as a Technical Assistant in Computational Science Department at Brainware University.

Piyal Roy is working as an Assistant Professor at Computer Science & Engineering Department at Brainware University, Kolkata, India.

Saptarshi Kumar Sarkar is an Assistant Professor of Computer Science and Engineering (CSE) with a Master's degree (M.Tech) in Computer Science and Engineering. With a passion for technology and education, Saptarshi brings expertise in areas such as Networking, AI and Social Networking. As an educator, he is dedicated to fostering a vibrant learning environment where students can explore cutting-edge technologies and develop practical skills for the digital era. Through teaching and research, he aims to contribute to the advancement of knowledge and inspire the next generation of computer scientists.

Stefka Tzanova is an associate professor and science librarian at York College, CUNY Her research interests include: academic librarianship, science literacy, science education, history of science and technology, STEM, open educational resources (OER), scholarly communications, and patents. Professor Tzanova has a strong background in the hard sciences and holds Master's degrees in engineering and in library science.

Index